W9-AWH-241

eBay
THE MISSING MANUAL

Nancy Conner

POGUE PRESS™
O'REILLY®

Beijing · Cambridge · Farnham · Köln · Paris · Sebastopol · Taipei · Tokyo

eBay: The Missing Manual

by Nancy Conner

Published by O'Reilly Media, Inc., 1005 Gravenstein Highway North, Sebastopol, CA 95472.

O'Reilly books may be purchased for educational, business, or sales promotional use. Online editions are also available for most titles (*safari.oreilly.com*). For more information, contact our corporate/institutional sales department: (800) 998-9938 or *corporate@oreilly.com*.

Printing History:

August 2005:   First Edition.

RepKover. This book uses RepKover,™ a durable and flexible lay-flat binding.

ISBN: 0-596-00644-6
[M]

Table of Contents

eBay: The Missing Manual

The Missing Credits

About the Author

 Nancy Conner edits tech books from her home in upstate New York. She's also worked as a medievalist, an English teacher, and a corporate trainer. When she's not writing or messing around with someone else's prose, she likes to read mysteries, visit local wineries, and listen obsessively to opera. Nancy got hooked on eBay in 1998, when her daughter said, "Look, Mom—you can buy me a Beanie Baby on this cool Web site." Email: *nancy_conner@hotmail.com*.

About the Creative Team

Sarah Milstein (editor) is O'Reilly's senior editor for Missing Manuals. Her favorite curtains are from eBay. Email: *milstein@oreilly.com*.

Emily Moore (editor) Emily Moore has authored or edited 13 books to date (including this fine tome). She lives in the Twin Cities with her husband and daughter. Email: *eamoore_mm@comcast.net*.

Michele Filshie (editor) is O'Reilly's assistant editor for Missing Manuals and editor of four Personal Trainers (another O'Reilly series). Before turning to the world of computer-related books, Michele was all literature, all the time, and spent many happy years at Black Sparrow Press. She lives in Sebastopol and loves to get involved in local politics. Email: *mfilshie@oreilly.com*.

Drue Miller (tech reviewer) is a writer, designer, and avid collector of mid-century glassware, vintage clothing, and really bad clown art. Since 1998 Drue has bought and sold many items on eBay, both for herself and for others as an eBay Trading

Assistant. Drue was also the Director of Research at AuctionDrop, the first nation-wide eBay drop-off service. She is also the co-creator of WhoWouldBuyThat.com, a Weblog of weird eBay auctions. Drue lives in Silicon Valley with her husband. Email: *drue@drue.com*.

Shauna Wright (tech reviewer) is an aspiring law student, a regular contributor to eBay's Answer Center boards, and the co-creator of WhoWouldBuyThat.com. She lives on the beach near San Francisco with her four cats, none of whom appreciate the scenery as much as she does. Email: *srw@flaunt.net*.

Andy Carciere (tech reviewer) served for 25 years as a school administrator. During those years, he championed the use of technology as a tool to enhance learning. Andy currently consults with districts and schools on the administrative and instructional use of technology to improve the teaching and learning process. He also is working on a project to use achievement data to monitor student progress and guide instruction. Email: *andyc@sonic.net*.

Rose Cassano (cover illustration) has worked as an independent designer and illustrator for 20 years. Her assignments have ranged from the nonprofit sector to corporate clientele. She lives in beautiful Southern Oregon, grateful for the miracles of modern technology that make working there a reality. Email: *cassano@highstream.net*. Web: *www.rosecassano.com*.

Acknowledgements

The book you're holding is the result of many people's hard work. Thanks to everyone at O'Reilly, especially Sarah Milstein for her patience and encouragement and for helping me to organize a jumble of ideas into the chapters of a book; Michele Filshie for organizing the technical reviews; and Emily Moore for many good suggestions. I'm particularly grateful to the book's technical reviewers, Drue Miller, Shauna Wright, and Andy Carciere, for their comments, questions, and pointers—all of which helped to make this a better book.

I could never have written this book without the assistance of dozens of eBayers. Thanks for sharing your time, tips, and expertise so generously.

David Fugate started the whole thing with a single email—thanks, David, for suggesting I look into the Missing Manual series. Thanks to Michelle Brandwein and Rebecca Hanley for long-distance listening and back-patting. To my daughter, Tamsen, thanks for your loving support and letting me bounce ideas off you. And to my parents, Harold and Lois Brown, thanks for telling me to hurry up and finish so you could learn how to use eBay yourselves.

Finally, extra special thanks to Steven Holzner for all your support, advice, encouragement, and love. I couldn't have done it—or much of anything—without you.

The Missing Manual Series

Missing Manuals are witty, superbly written guides to computer products that don't come with printed manuals (which is just about all of them). Each book features a handcrafted index; cross-references to specific page numbers (not just "see Chapter 14"); and RepKover, a detached-spine binding that lets the book lie perfectly flat without the assistance of weights or cinder blocks.

Recent and upcoming titles include:

Mac OS X: The Missing Manual, Tiger Edition by David Pogue

Excel: The Missing Manual by Matthew MacDonald

iPhoto 5: The Missing Manual by David Pogue

iLife '05: The Missing Manual by David Pogue

GarageBand 2: The Missing Manual by David Pogue

iMovie 5 & iDVD: The Missing Manual by David Pogue

iPod & iTunes: The Missing Manual, Third Edition by J.D. Biersdorfer

Google: The Missing Manual, Second Edition by Sarah Milstein and Rael Dornfest

Switching to the Mac: The Missing Manual by David Pogue

Mac OS X Power Hound, Panther Edition by Rob Griffiths

Dreamweaver MX 2004: The Missing Manual by David Sawyer McFarland

Office 2004 for Macintosh: The Missing Manual by Mark H. Walker and Franklin Tessler

AppleWorks 6: The Missing Manual by Jim Elferdink and David Reynolds

iWork: The Missing Manual by Jim Elferdink

Windows XP Home Edition: The Missing Manual, Second Edition by David Pogue

Windows XP Pro: The Missing Manual, Second Edition by David Pogue, Craig Zacker, and Linda Zacker

AppleScript: The Missing Manual by Adam Goldstein

Photoshop Elements: The Missing Manual by Barbara Brundage

QuickBooks: The Missing Manual by Bonnie Biafore

FrontPage 2003: The Missing Manual by Jessica Mantaro

Creating Web Sites: The Missing Manual by Matthew MacDonald

Filemaker Pro: The Missing Manual by Geoff Coffey and Susan Prosser

Introduction

Even if you've never browsed the merchandise or placed a bid, you've probably heard about eBay, the Web's largest online auction site. From analyses of the fastest-growing company in history to stories about oddball items for sale—like the infamous Virgin Mary grilled cheese sandwich or the guy who rented out his forehead as a billboard—eBay makes headlines.

But behind the hype, there are many good reasons to actually *use* eBay. It lets you:

- Shop around the clock at an immense, worldwide marketplace.
- Name the price you're willing to pay. If you don't win one auction, there's always another.
- Buy collectibles and other items you'd never find at the local mall.
- Be your own boss—run a retail business out of your home.
- Reach millions of potential customers.
- Chat with other eBayers and watch zany auctions.

In addition, eBay's sheer size makes it an attractive place to buy and sell. Worldwide, 135 million active eBayers are looking to do business with you—to the tune of $32 billion worth of merchandise bought and sold on the site each year. And those figures are growing.

Whether you're hunting for bargains or hoping to make some cash, eBay gives you access to the biggest—and most entertaining—marketplace the world has ever seen.

On the other hand, eBay's size can make it hard to find the things or customers you want. And, once you do find them, how do you know that the person on the other end of the transaction is trustworthy? eBay is a great resource, and great fun, but it does present challenges for even the most intrepid shoppers and sellers.

A Little eBay History

You might have heard the story that eBay began as an act of love, invented by Pierre Omidyar as a way for his fiancée, Pam (now his wife), to trade Pez dispensers with other collectors. It's a nice story, and there's some truth to it, but things didn't happen in quite that way.

In 1995, Tufts University graduate Omidyar was working as a software engineer at General Magic, a Silicon Valley mobile-communications company. In his spare time, Omidyar developed Auction Web, an online auction platform. He was interested in the potential for an auction format to create a fair and open marketplace, where the market truly sets an item's value. In an auction, anyone can bid until the price reaches the highest amount someone's willing to pay. The market price changes from day to day, depending on demand and who's bidding.

While Omidyar was experimenting with Auction Web, he did consulting work under the name Echo Bay Technology Group. When he wanted to register a Web site for his company, Echo Bay was the name he planned to use. But when he filled out the paperwork, he learned that echobay.com was already taken. Faced with the need for a unique name, he decided to abbreviate—and eBay was the result.

Why It Works

When Omidyar developed Auction Web (soon to become eBay), he had a full-time job, and he wanted to enjoy life on the weekends. He didn't want his hobby—Auction Web—to steal every waking minute outside work. And he wasn't trying to build a system that could handle traffic from 40 million buyers and sellers every day. He simply designed the site to keep itself going when he couldn't be there tinkering with it. And he deliberately kept Auction Web simple so that it could handle unexpected challenges as it grew.

Beyond the technology, Omidyar envisioned the site as a community, based on five main values:

- People are basically good.

- Everyone has something to contribute.

- An honest, open environment can bring out the best in people.

- Everyone deserves recognition and respect as a unique individual.

- You should treat others the way you want to be treated.

These "community values" remain key to the site. They're why eBayers are willing to send money to a stranger across the country, trusting that the item they bought will arrive in next week's mail. The values are the underpinning of *feedback* (page 40), which eBayers use to rate a completed transaction; feedback works because it's open and (usually) honest. You can learn a little about a trading partner before you decide to do business, and your own reputation, good or bad, is out there for anyone to see.

Note: The Feedback Forum began in February, 1996. Originally, Omidyar handled disputes between buyers and sellers via email; when someone sent him a complaint, he'd put the disputing parties in touch with each other and ask them to work it out themselves. Eventually, he realized that one way to get people to trust each other was to bring their opinions about each other—not just the complaints but also the praise—into the open.

The combination of adaptable technology and a strong sense of community has probably contributed more than anything else to eBay's success.

Note: eBay faced some growing pains—in the early years, its business rocketed skyward faster than its servers could handle, causing frequent crashes. In the summer of 1999, eBay was offline for 22 hours—an eternity in the world of online auctions. After that crash, eBay staffers called eBayers to apologize. It was the kind of gesture that gains customer loyalty. And, despite the inevitable complaints, eBayers are loyal.

eBay Now

What began as a small site for individuals to trade collectibles has exploded into an international marketplace where everyone, from the lady down the street to large corporations, sells millions of items in thousands of categories. Two of eBay's fastest-growing categories are cars (eBay Motors, page 127) and real estate (page 130). eBay has spawned hundreds of imitators, but not one even comes close to being a true competitor.

eBay continues to grow; it's expanded to more than 25 countries, including Argentina, Australia, Brazil, Canada, China, Germany, India, Korea, the Netherlands, Poland, Singapore, Taiwan, and the United Kingdom, to name just a sampling. It's bought or invested in a variety of other Web sites: Half.com, a fixed-price media marketplace; Craigslist.com, a network of online communities featuring classified ads and discussion forums; Rent.com, a site to post and search listings for rental property; and Shopping.com, a price-comparison site. As this book was going to press, eBay announced the creation of *www.ebaybusiness.com,* a new marketplace where businesses can buy and sell products.

As eBay grows, it changes. Sometimes you'll notice that the home page looks a little different or a procedure you've done a hundred times has suddenly gained or lost a step. eBay tweaks the site constantly, adding new categories, upgrading sellers' tools, changing the look and feel of its pages. For this reason, some of the figures in this book might look a little different from what you see on your computer screen. Don't panic. You can always find your way from the navigation bar at the top of every page, shown in Figure I-1.

Figure I-1:
The eBay navigation bar gets you where you want to go, quickly. Buy takes you to the Search page to shop for items. Click Sell to register as a seller or, if you've already registered, list an item and get selling tips. My eBay keeps track of all your eBay activity. Community takes you to discussion forums, and Help lets you get answers to your questions.

About This Book

If you'd like to get started with eBay but you don't know an FVF (page 153) from a UPI (page 184), this book will help you get to the site, get registered, and get going. Soon you'll be using eBay like an old pro. If, on the other hand, you've been trading Pez dispensers since eBay was Auction Works, this book can help you ramp up your eBay experience—find more bargains, build better auctions, and close more sales. It's loaded with advice and info like this:

- Most new eBayers assume that a 90 percent positive-feedback rating is a good thing, but those with experience on the site rarely trade with someone whose positive-feedback score ranks below 98 percent (page 42).

- You can find bargains using sellers' spelling mistakes (page 84), even if your own spelling is lousy.

- Despite its philosophy that people are basically good, eBay's popularity has made it prime hunting ground for scammers. Don't be a victim—recognize and avoid common scams directed at buyers (page 132) and at sellers (page 232).

- More than half of eBay auctions finish with just one bid or no bids at all. Get your listings noticed with the marketing strategies in Chapter 7.

- Tools for buyers (page 117) and sellers (Chapter 9) can save you tons of time by automating searching, bidding, listing, market analysis, email, and feedback.

- Despite many requests, eBay has been reluctant to allow a feedback search that returns only the negative and neutral comments. But just because you can't do it on eBay doesn't mean you can't do it. There are a couple of ways to check out another eBayer's dirty laundry (page 120).

- Some of eBay's most explosive growth has been in its specialty auctions. Chapter 8 tells you how to get in on the action.

FREQUENTLY ASKED QUESTION

Seriously Weird Stuff

What's the strangest item ever sold on eBay?

Strangeness is in the eye of the beholder. An auction item that makes one person scratch her head makes another open his checkbook. Here are some of the weird and wonderful auctions that have added to eBay's amusement value:

- **The Virgin Mary grilled cheese sandwich.** Ten years before this auction, a Florida woman sat down to eat a grilled cheese sandwich and noticed an image that she thought looked like the Virgin Mary. The woman saved the sandwich in a clear plastic box and kept it on her nightstand—until the day she decided to sell it on eBay. After a ton of media attention and a bidding frenzy, the winning bid was $28,000.

- **The haunted cane.** The seller of this item claimed her son believed it was haunted by the ghost of his recently deceased grandfather and that she was selling it to allay his fears. The cane sold for $65,000.

- **Name that baby.** A number of parents have auctioned the right to name their newborn. And adults have auctioned off their own names, too. These auctions have been popular with Golden Palace Casino, an online casino whose advertising campaign has centered around buying far-out items on eBay. GoldenPalaceDotCom Smith, meet GoldenPalaceDotCom Jones.

- **Walking billboards.** When one enterprising young man sold a month's worth of advertising space on his forehead for more than $37,000, he started a fad. Auctions appeared for advertising space on pregnant bellies, cleavage, fingernails, an arm and a leg....

- **Elvis water.** A man received $455 for three tablespoons of water he said he'd retrieved from a styrofoam cup used by Elvis Presley in a 1977 concert and stored since then in a sealed glass vial. Later, he auctioned the right to display the styrofoam cup itself.

- **Mystery auctions.** You might wonder why on earth people would bid on something when they have no idea what they're getting, but mystery auctions have become such a craze that they have their own category. These auctions have included a mystery paycheck, mystery house contents, mystery mailbox, mystery baby-food jar—just about anything you can imagine. (According to eBay rules, the auction is for the container only; the "mystery" contents are a gift.)

- **Weirdness loves company.** If you can imagine it (and in some cases even if you can't), someone's probably tried to sell it on eBay. Real listings include a kite flown during a Florida hurricane; dryer lint; a deflated red balloon; a "time travel" machine; snow; a jar of air; a "mind-reading" helmet; a reproduction of Van Gogh's Starry Night made of Legos; a three-legged chicken preserved in a jar; an empty gum wrapper; even an auction for "absolutely nothing."

To see the weird and wacky things up for auction on eBay this month, check out *www.bizarrebids.com* or *www.whowouldbuythat.com*—two Web sites that track the strangest auctions they can find.

About the Outline

eBay: The Missing Manual is divided into four parts, each containing several chapters:

- **Part 1, Buying on eBay,** has everything you need to get started. Most new eBayers begin by buying something to learn how auctions work and to start building feedback. (And if you're here to sell, it's worth taking the time to learn how to think like a buyer.) These chapters help you register, learn the basics of searching and bidding, avoid getting scammed, and rev up your buying power with advanced techniques for bargain hunters and collectors.

- **Part 2, Selling on eBay,** is all about one of eBay's biggest attractions: the promise of making money in your spare time by selling off the stuff you no longer want or need. For some sellers, that promise evolves from part-time hobby to full-time business. Part 2 starts with the things you need to know before you sell on eBay—how to register as a seller, list an item, and close the deal. The chapters that follow guide you as your experience and your feedback score grow—how to get your auctions noticed, build customer loyalty, deal with deadbeat bidders, and handle the business side of things. You'll also find chapters on specialty auctions and tools to make selling faster and easier—no PowerSeller would be without them.

- **Part 3, Finding Other eBayers and Getting Help,** contains info that's useful to buyers and sellers alike, from networking and socializing with other eBayers to getting quick answers when you have a midnight payment crisis.

- **Part 4, Appendixes,** tells you where to learn more, covers the basics of HTML for enhancing your eBay listings, and suggests some other auction sites to explore.

The Very Basics

You'll find very little jargon or nerd terminology in this book. You will, however, encounter a few terms and concepts that you'll come across frequently in your computing life:

- **Clicking.** This book gives you three kinds of instructions that require you to use your computer's mouse or trackpad. To *click* means to point the arrow cursor at something on the screen and then—without moving the cursor at all—to press and release the clicker button on the left side of the mouse (or laptop trackpad). To *right-click* means to point the cursor and click the button on the right side of the mouse (or trackpad). And to *drag* means to move the cursor while pressing the button continuously.

- **Menus.** The menus are the words at the top of your browser: File, Edit, and so on. Click one to make a list of commands appear as though they're written on a window shade you've just pulled down.

Some people click and release the mouse button to open a menu and then, after reading the menu command choices, click again on the one they want. Other people like to hold down the mouse button continuously after the initial click on the menu title, drag down the list to the desired command, and only then release the mouse button. Either method works fine.

About → These → Arrows

Throughout this book, and throughout the Missing Manual series, you'll find sentences like this one: "Select View → Show/Hide → Personal Toolbar." That's shorthand for a much longer instruction that directs you to open three nested commands in sequence, like this: "In your browser, you'll find a menu item called View. Select that. On the View menu is an option called Show/Hide; click it to open it. On *that* menu is yet another option called Personal Toolbar. Click it to open that, too."

Similarly, this kind of arrow shorthand helps to simplify the business of choosing commands in menus, as shown in Figure I-2.

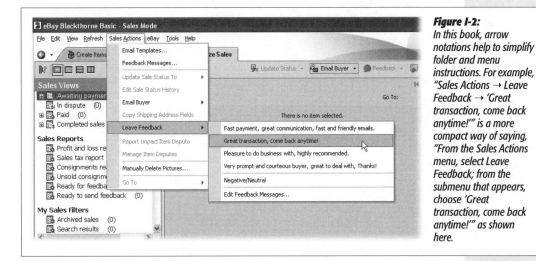

Figure I-2:
In this book, arrow notations help to simplify folder and menu instructions. For example, "Sales Actions → Leave Feedback → 'Great transaction, come back anytime!'" is a more compact way of saying, "From the Sales Actions menu, select Leave Feedback; from the submenu that appears, choose 'Great transaction, come back anytime!'" as shown here.

About MissingManuals.com

At *www.missingmanuals.com*, you'll find articles, tips, and updates to the book. In fact, you're invited and encouraged to submit such corrections and updates yourself. In an effort to keep the book as up to date and accurate as possible, each time we print more copies of this book, we'll make any confirmed corrections you've suggested. We'll also note such changes on the Web site, so that you can mark important corrections into your own copy of the book, if you like. (Click the book's name, and then click the Errata link, to see the changes.)

In the meantime, we'd love to hear your own suggestions for new books in the Missing Manual line. There's a place for that on the Web site, too, as well as a place to sign up for free email notification of new titles in the series.

Safari® Enabled

 When you see a Safari® Enabled icon on the cover of your favorite technology book, that means it's available online through the O'Reilly Network Safari Bookshelf.

Safari offers a solution that's better than e-books: it's a virtual library that lets you easily search thousands of top tech books, cut and paste code samples, download chapters, and find quick answers when you need the most accurate, current information. Try it for free at *http://safari.oreilly.com*.

Part One: Buying on eBay

1

Ready, Set, Shop!

eBay isn't like traditional online stores, where you pile up purchases in a virtual shopping cart and then check out. On eBay, the main attraction is its *auction* format; would-be buyers compete with each other by bidding on an item until everyone's made his top offer, or until the always-ticking eBay clock brings down the final hammer.

This arrangement may sound about as relaxing as rush-hour traffic when you're late for your own wedding. But once you get used to it—which isn't hard—it's straightforward and amazingly fun.

Note: In addition to auctions, eBay also has fixed-price sales, labeled Buy It Now. Page 26 tells you all about them.

Whether you want to buy, sell, or both, the best way to get started on eBay is to register and explore the site as a buyer. Learning how to buy smart helps you discover how to use eBay's search engine efficiently and familiarizes you with auction pages, where you can check out sellers' wares. Later, when you're ready to sell (Chapter 5), the skills you learn in this chapter will help you think like a buyer, attracting bidders to your auctions and getting top dollar for your merchandise.

This chapter shows you everything you need to get going on eBay:

- How to register.
- How to search eBay to find the stuff you want.

- How to decipher auction pages to score the best deal.

- How to tell the difference between the various types of eBay auctions.

- How to shop smarter using your My eBay page.

To get started, simply type *www.ebay.com* into your Web browser's address box, and then hit Enter. eBay's home page appears, as shown in Figure 1-1. You can sign up, as described below, and start shopping in mere minutes.

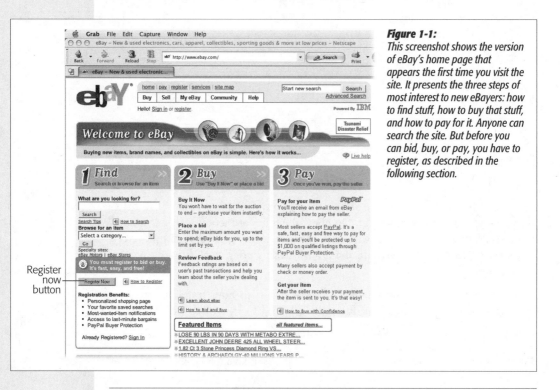

Register
now
button

Figure 1-1:
This screenshot shows the version of eBay's home page that appears the first time you visit the site. It presents the three steps of most interest to new eBayers: how to find stuff, how to buy that stuff, and how to pay for it. Anyone can search the site. But before you can bid, buy, or pay, you have to register, as described in the following section.

Note: eBay likes to rearrange things and try out new looks, so its home page design changes frequently. But you can always find prominent links letting you register, search, pay, sell, or find help.

Get Registered and Get Going

Because you can't bid if you're not registered, it's a good idea to register even before you explore the site. That way, the minute you find that pair of 1970s silver platform shoes or Holley four-barrel carburetor you've been searching for, you can place your bid. If the auction is about to end in a couple of minutes, you'll be glad you registered first.

To start the registration process, click the Register Now button you find on eBay's home page (Figure 1-1). As soon as you click it, the registration form shown in Figure 1-2 pops up.

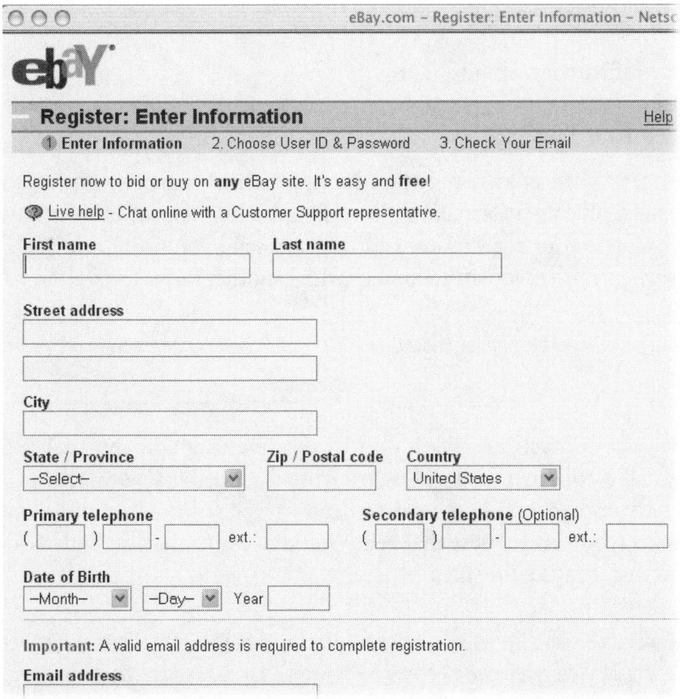

○ ○ ○   eBay.com – Register: Enter Information – Netsc

ebaY

Register: Enter Information   Help

① Enter Information   2. Choose User ID & Password   3. Check Your Email

Register now to bid or buy on **any** eBay site. It's easy and **free**!

👁 Live help - Chat online with a Customer Support representative.

First name   **Last name**

Street address

City

State / Province   **Zip / Postal code**   **Country**
–Select–   United States

Primary telephone   **Secondary telephone** (Optional)
(   )   -   ext.:   (   )   -   ext.:

Date of Birth
–Month–   –Day–   Year

Important: A valid email address is required to complete registration.

Email address

Figure 1-2:
eBay's registration form requests your name, address, date of birth—all the usual information. You have to fill in all the fields, except for a second phone number. Your email address is especially important, because that's the contact for most of the business you'll do on eBay. If you've got a question at any point, click the Live Help link to chat with an eBay staffer.

FREQUENTLY ASKED QUESTION

Look Before You Leap

Do I have to register to look around eBay?

You don't have to register to browse categories or search current auctions. You can even watch (page 34) up to 10 items as a guest—no registration required. (*Watching* means keeping track of a particular auction on a special page, so you can easily find it again among eBay's millions and millions of listings.)

To watch an item without registering, look in the upper-right part of any item page for the "Watch this item" link. Click the link to keep track of the auction. To find the item

you're watching, click the navigation bar's My eBay button. This opens My eBay for Guests, a page where you can register, track up to 10 auctions, and sign up to receive an email alert when one of the auctions you're watching is about to end.

If you're window shopping and you find an item you want to buy, just click the "register" link, which appears at the top of nearly every page on the whole site. You can see the link in Figure 1-1, to the right of the eBay logo, on eBay's navigation bar.

Just three steps, explained in detail in the sections that follow, get you registered:

- Type in your personal information and OK the User Agreement and Privacy Policy.

- Select the name by which the eBay world will know you and create a password to protect your account.

- Respond to a confirmation email.

Step One: Who Are You?

Figure 1-2 shows part of the eBay registration form, which is pretty self-explanatory. Why does eBay need all this information? Your email address gives eBay a way to contact you to complete your registration and, later, to send you notifications about auctions, such as when you've won an auction or when another buyer has outbid you.

Note: You can hear from eBay a little or a lot, whichever you prefer. Page 37 shows how to set your notification preferences.

Plus, eBay keeps your contact information in its massive database and makes this information available to other eBayers when you do business with them. For example, if the person who sold you a pirate head carved from a coconut doesn't answer your emails, you can request that seller's contact information and pick up the phone to find out what's going on.

Note: If your email address is with a free Web-based email provider (like Yahoo! or Hotmail), eBay wants confirmation of your identity. You can prove who you are by providing eBay with a credit card number that confirms your name and mailing address. eBay keeps this number on file but won't use it for any purpose other than to check that you're who you say you are. If you don't want to submit a credit card number, you can enter a second email address if you've got one. This address must be through an Internet service provider (such as AOL or EarthLink), business, school, or other organization. In other words, eBay is looking for an address that's hard to fake. This second address is where eBay sends the confirmation email, described in "Step Two: Who Do You Want to Be (on eBay, Anyway)?"

Your date of birth lets eBay know you're eligible to use the site. Each eBay transaction is a binding contract, so all eBayers must be of legal age—18 or older—to bid, buy, or sell.

After you've filled in the required text boxes, you must agree to eBay's terms before you can proceed. The bottom of the registration form (Figure 1-3) shows eBay's User Agreement and Privacy Policy, described below. You have to turn on the checkbox to tell eBay that you agree to these policies and that you give them permission to send you email; only then can you click Continue and get to step 2. (The box on page 10 explains what eBay considers private.)

So what's in the User Agreement and Privacy Policy? It's a lot to read when you're hot to shop, but you should know what you're agreeing to. The following list doesn't include everything, but it does hit the highlights:

- **Free to buy, fee to sell.** Joining eBay and bidding on items is free—there are no fees to register or to bid. If you want to sell items on eBay, you agree to pay eBay's fees (page 152), which are, of course, subject to change.

- **Transactions are between you and the seller.** eBay doesn't participate in auctions; it provides a *venue* for auctions. That distinction means that sellers and bidders—not eBay—are responsible for their own actions on the site.

  Although eBay has some safeguards in place to check information, it can't verify all the information submitted by every single eBayer. (Remember, there are millions and millions of people registered with eBay, and more sign up every day.) This means it's up to you to know who you're dealing with, and the best way to do that is through the *Feedback Forum* (page 40), where other eBayers sound off on who's good to trade with—and who's not.

- **Making a bid is a binding agreement.** If you win an auction, you agree to buy what you bid on.

Note: eBay insists that bids can only be retracted under "exceptional circumstances." It is possible to take back a bid, but there are good reasons not to overuse the privilege. For more on retracting a bid, see page 68.

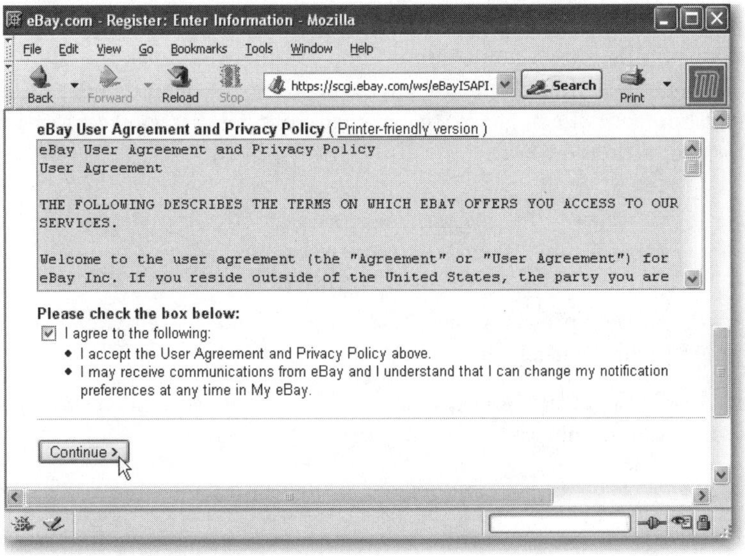

Figure 1-3:
Don't be fooled by the tiny box in which eBay presents its User Agreement and Privacy Policy. There's a lot to both these documents—and you should know what they say. If you start to get teary-eyed trying to read the agreement as it appears on the registration form, click the link just above the text box that says "Printer-friendly version." A new window opens—one with room to read and a more legible font.

- **If you're a seller, you must be legally able to sell all the items you list.** For example, you can't sell a DVD you recorded of a television program, because you don't own the rights to that program. You must also agree to sell when you receive an acceptable bid—that means a bid at or above the minimum or the *reserve* price, if you've set one. (For more on reserve prices, flip to page 25.)

- **You agree to play fair.** You won't bid on an item you don't intend to buy or otherwise interfere in auctions. For example, you'll violate eBay rules if you email bidders in an ongoing auction and you're not the seller.

- **Fraud will get you kicked off the site.** Fraud can include, but isn't limited to, listing items you don't actually have, selling designer fakes, lying in an item description (such as calling a frayed, stained shirt "like new"), and refusing to pay for an item you won. eBayers call this suspension from eBay being *NARU'd* (for *no longer a registered user*).

- **You can't sell anything illegal or anything eBay has designated a no-go.** To find out which items eBay prohibits, which is worth doing if you're thinking of selling, go to *http://pages.ebay.com/help/policies/items-ov.html*. You might not realize that some authentic WWII memorabilia or a mousepad featuring a picture of Winona Ryder is taboo, but if eBay finds such auctions, it removes them. For more on prohibited items, see page 152.

- **You're who you say you are.** The information you give eBay for registration, bidding, and selling is accurate and up to date.

- **Nobody gets to sue eBay.** You agree to release eBay from any liability relating to transactions on the site. If you commit fraud or otherwise break the law using eBay (already a violation of the User Agreement), you indemnify eBay against any claims someone else might make. Another reminder that you take responsibility for your actions on eBay.

Note: eBay does offer a Buyer Protection Program (page 72) of up to $200 on purchases you make on the site. If you pay with PayPal (page 52), you get extra buyer protection.

- **You agree to eBay's privacy policy.** eBay promises not to sell your personal information to third parties without your consent.

If you agree to eBay's policies (and you have to agree if you want to register), click the Continue button to move on to the next registration step.

Step Two: Who Do You Want to Be (on eBay, Anyway)?

After you click Continue, a page appears that lets you choose an eBay ID and password (Figure 1-4). eBay suggests some possibilities, based on your first name, that nobody has taken yet. If you don't like any of these options, select "Create your own ID" and type your preferred moniker into the box. Base your ID on your name, your hobby, your hometown, your personality, what you plan to buy or sell—whatever puts the *you* in unique.

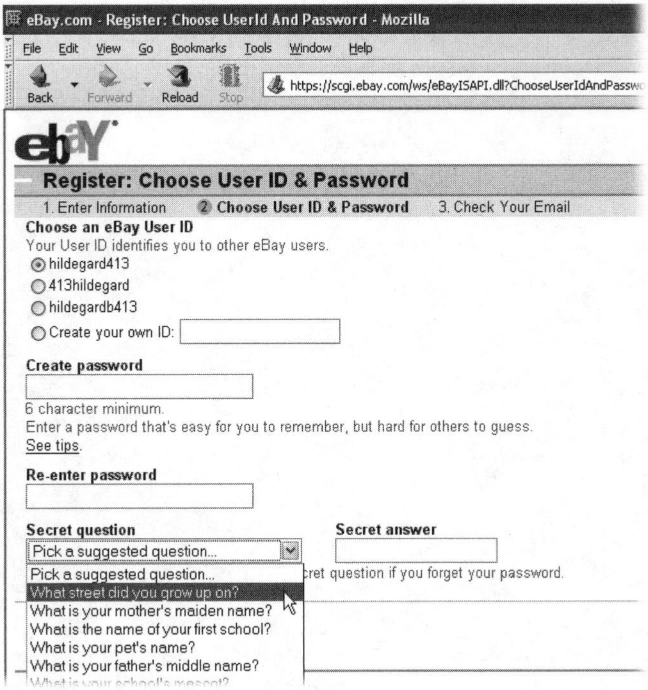

Figure 1-4:
For your eBay ID, you can accept one of eBay's suggestions or make up an ID of your own. This page is also where you create a password to protect your account and answer a secret question that goes on file in case you forget your password. The secret answer you give is sort of like a password to your password.

There are a few things eBay won't let you use in your ID. It can't contain the word *eBay*. (eBay created this policy to avoid confusion about who officially works for the company and who doesn't.) It can't contain a Web address (like *buy_from_me.com*) or a registered trademark. Also, your ID can't contain a space or any of the following characters:

- Ampersand: @ (Which means you can't use your email address as your eBay ID.)

- Parentheses: ( )

- Angle brackets: <>

If you submit an ID containing any of the above illegal characters, a page appears explaining the error and asking you to try again.

Have fun choosing an ID. But keep in mind your eBay ID is the face you present to the entire eBay community. A name like *wont_pay_up* or *spamlover* isn't going to endear you to the people you're hoping to do business with.

FREQUENTLY ASKED QUESTION

Your Privacy and eBay

How private is "private" on eBay?

eBay's privacy policy (linked at the bottom of almost every page on the site) is a fantastically long document written in dense language, and most new eBayers don't read it before signing up. It's worth knowing, however, when eBay shares your information with others.

eBay records everything: not only your registration information but every transaction you participate in, every item you put on your Watch list (page 34), every piece of feedback you leave or get (page 40)—even the comments you post in eBay's online forums (page 362).

The good news is that eBay promises not to sell or rent your personal information to other companies for their marketing. And eBay doesn't share your information with third parties unless you give your explicit consent. To see what you've authorized or to change it, go to My eBay → eBay Preferences → Authorization Settings.

On the other hand, when you turn on the I Agree checkbox during the registration process, you give your consent to these practices:

- eBay provides information about its members to advertisers and other third parties for marketing purposes, but only in a way that does not identify individuals. That means your shopping habits are fair game, but your name, address, credit card number, and password aren't. Nobody can associate those shopping habits with you personally.

- eBay provides your contact information to other eBayers involved in a transaction with you. Moreover, any eBayer can look up your home state, how long you've been on eBay, items you're selling, and any sales or purchases you've made in the last 30 days.

- eBay uses what it calls *internal service providers*: third-party companies that help provide eBay's own services, like discussion boards, bill collection, and reward and credit card programs. These internal service providers have confidentiality agreements with eBay and need your consent to use any information about you beyond their work on eBay. But if you give information about yourself to one of these providers—say you want to sign up for a credit card with the eBay logo on it—that information is ruled by the provider's own privacy policy, not eBay's.

- Any of eBay's subsidiaries, any companies eBay has a joint venture with, and any company that eBay acquires or merges with has access to your personal information.

- Here's a part of the privacy policy that's caused some controversy: *without a subpoena*, eBay hands over your personal information—including your name; city and state of residence; email address; phone number; fraud complaints; and ID, bidding, and listing history—to any law enforcement or government official who's investigating alleged illegal activity.

- eBay reserves the right to change its policy: "Due to the existing regulatory environment, we cannot ensure that all of your private communications and other personal information will never be disclosed in ways not otherwise described in this Privacy Policy." In other words, the policy you agree to now could change.

Warning: Don't use the first part of your email address as your eBay ID. eBay protects your email address: only other registered eBayers involved in an active transaction with you have access to it. You should do what you can to protect it, too.

Recently, some clever scammers who weren't even registered with eBay looked at the non-winning bidders in high-end auctions for items like computers and cars. They guessed the bidders' email addresses by putting the eBay ID in front of common email providers, like @yahoo.com, @hotmail.com, @aol.com, and so on, then sent fake emails from the "seller," saying that the auction had fallen through and offering to sell them the item. Of course, these scammers didn't have the item to sell–they just planned to take people's money and disappear.

With millions of registered buyers and sellers on eBay, it might take you a few tries to zero in on an ID nobody's using. If your chosen ID already belongs to someone else, the page shown in Figure 1-5 opens.

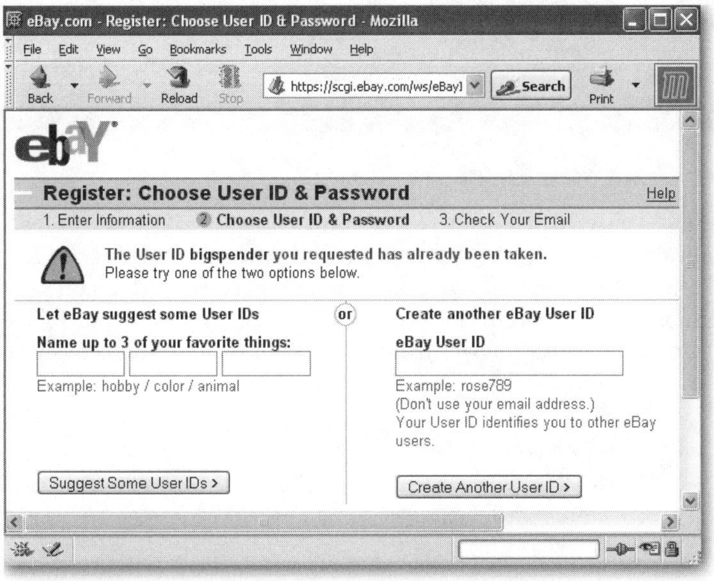

Figure 1-5:
If the ID you want already belongs to someone else, eBay offers help. You don't have to list a hobby, a color, and an animal–choose whatever words you like. eBay combines them in various ways to offer unique suggestions for your ID. Or you can try again to craft one of your own. Combining words and numbers is a good strategy.

When you've settled on an ID, create a password, select and answer your password reminder question, and then click Continue to move on to step 3.

Note: Don't share your eBay password with anyone else. You're responsible for your account, so you don't want anyone making bids or listing items without your knowledge.

Tip: Change your password periodically. Stay a step ahead by keeping 'em guessing!

Make Your Password a Tough Nut to Crack

You've probably already got a password or two for things like email accounts and online shopping. Whether you're an old password pro or a newbie, it's worth putting some thought into a good password for your eBay account.

Unfortunately, scammers who'd like to steal the identity of someone with lots of positive feedback (page 40) may someday cast their eyes at your account. Account thieves are on the lookout for reputable eBay IDs they can use to set up phony auctions. So make your password hard to guess. For example, don't make your eBay ID do double duty as your password, and don't recycle passwords you use for other accounts.

Similarly, don't use any standalone word that appears in any dictionary (of any language). Try combining letters, numbers, and special characters in a way that's easy for you to remember but hard for anyone else to guess. For example, if you have a Picasso print hanging over your desk, *picasso* would be an easy password for you to remember. To make it hard for someone else to guess, try replacing some of the letters with similar characters, such as the numerals *1* and *0* for the letters *i* and *o*. You might end up with something along these lines: *p1c@ss0*. (Even though you can't use a character like @ in your eBay ID, it's fine to use in your password.) That's not a password anyone's likely to guess anytime soon.

Step Three: Check Your Email

You're not quite registered yet. After you've chosen a unique ID and a password, eBay automatically sends you an email to confirm that you've visited the page and filled in the registration form. The automatic email also assures eBay that the email address you submitted is valid. In most cases, the email arrives in your inbox in just a few seconds. You must follow the instructions in the email to activate your account.

Note: In case you can't see the activation link—perhaps your email settings are for plain text only—eBay also gives you a confirmation code. In that case, type *http://pages.ebay.com/register* into your Web browser's address bar. In the Web page that comes up, type in your email address and the confirmation code, then click Continue.

The confirmation email contains a link you must click to activate your eBay account. Click it, and eBay congratulates you for completing the registration process. You're now ready to shop up a storm.

Tip: If you don't get a confirmation email from eBay within 24 hours, check your spam filter. Sometimes an overzealous filter catches an email from eBay and files it away as spam. If that doesn't solve the problem, odds are you made an error entering your email address. Go back to the registration page and start the process over. You can also get help registering by clicking the Live Help button (page 385) on eBay's home page. (And no, you don't have to be registered to use Live Help.)

How to Find What You're Looking For

When you head for the mall, you might be in the mood to window-shop or you might be on a search-and-purchase mission for a specific item. Similarly, you have two options for finding things to buy on eBay: you can browse, or you can use eBay's search engine to home in on what you want with laser-guided precision.

To start shopping, click the Buy link at the top of any eBay page, as shown in Figure 1-6. That link takes you to the eBay Buy page shown in Figure 1-7. The Buy page is the home of eBay's search engine.

Figure 1-6:
The eBay logo and these links appear at the top of nearly every page on eBay and are a great navigation aid. Wherever you wander on the site, Help is only a click away. To begin shopping, click the Buy link.

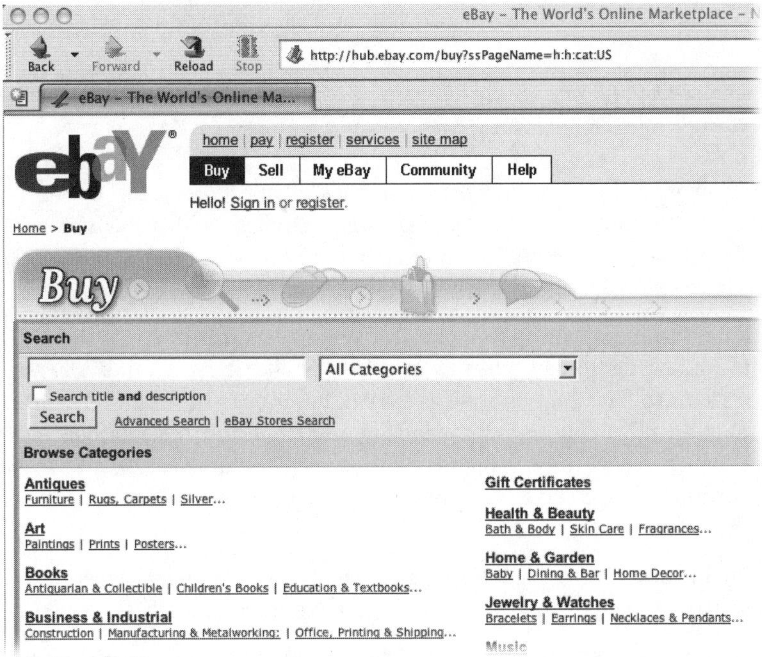

Figure 1-7:
The eBay Buy page lets you search for specific items or browse using categories or themes. Browse Categories lists eBay's main categories and gives you a peek at some of the subcategories.

Tip: You don't have to start on the Buy page when you want to search current auctions. Use the Search box in the upper-right corner of all eBay pages. Where it says "Start new search," type in your keywords, then click the Search button—and you're off.

Whether you choose to browse or to search for a particular item, you'll wind up on a results page with a list of current auctions for your topic. To look at any item in more detail, click the item title to go to its *auction page*. The auction page is where you can read a description of the specific item, check out other bidders, and, if you want, place your own bid. You can read about the ins and outs of auction pages on page 19.

Just Browsing, Thanks

If you don't have a specific item in mind, you can browse through eBay's 30-plus main categories and seemingly infinite subcategories. eBay tweaks its categories frequently, letting you drill down to what you want with ever-more precision.

From the Buy page, eBay gives you several options for browsing:

- **Browse Categories.** Under Browse Categories, if you click any of the links, eBay takes you to the main page for that category. From the category page, you can type in a *search term* (a keyword that describes the item you're looking for, like *iPod* or *nutcracker*), select a subcategory, or see what others have been searching for. To piggyback on the searches other people have conducted, simply scroll down to Popular Searches (on the left side) and click any of the listed links.

Note: Just because a search term is popular doesn't mean it's useful. Often, common but meaningless words like *of*, *the*, or *to* top the list of popular searches.

- **eBay Keywords.** If your mind works best in alphabetical order, this option is for you. eBay's computers keep track of popular searches and list them alphabetically. If you click a letter, eBay shows you terms starting with that letter that others have searched for recently.

- **Common Searches.** This option also uses keywords, organized in a slightly different—and harder to navigate—format. It's still alphabetical, but it's less selective; it seems to have every phrase anyone has ever used to search eBay, from *a 100* (auction titles containing a standalone letter *a* and the number *100*) to *zzzzzz* (which seems to be a popular, if not very descriptive, keyword in bedding auctions). Huge and cumbersome, Common Searches is not a helpful way to browse.

- **Popular Products.** This page shows popular items in popular categories. The hottest items related to entertainment and electronics frequently show up here.

- **eBay Stores.** These stores feature fixed-price items that don't always appear in regular auction searches. Listings in eBay Stores last longer than regular auctions: from 30 days to indefinite (or, of course, until sold). For more on eBay Stores, see page 259.

- **eBay Pulse.** To see what's hot on eBay, check out eBay Pulse. (You can get there directly by typing *pulse.ebay.com* into your Web browser's address bar.) eBay Pulse displays the top searches, the largest stores, and the most-watched auctions.

Searching

Searching is one of the primary things people do on eBay: buyers search for items they want to bid on; sellers search to compare prices or check the market for an item they'd like to sell. But searching on eBay is tricky business. Because there are millions of auctions running at any given moment, sifting through all that information to find that one specific item you're looking for can be trickier than finding an enthusiastic sales clerk at Wal-Mart. This section shows you the basics of searching so you can get up to speed quickly. (Chapter 3 has more info on power searching.)

You can start a search from just about any eBay page by using the Search box in the upper-right corner. Inside the box are the words "Start new search"; click this phrase to clear the text box, then type in what you're looking for—say, *DVD recorder*. Click the Search button or press Enter, and you're off and shopping.

Reading your search results

Figure 1-8 shows you a typical Search Results page. The first thing you want to do is scan the item titles listed in the middle of the page. When you see something you're interested in—say, the Sony DVD Recorder shown in Figure 1-8—slide your eyes to the right to see whether this auction lets you use *PayPal*, a service for transferring funds from your credit card or bank account directly to the seller. The PayPal icon, a small, blue double P, tells you that a seller will let you pay through this system.

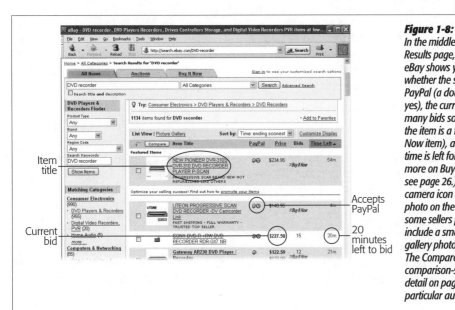

Figure 1-8:
In the middle of the Search Results page, under List View, eBay shows you the item title, whether the seller accepts PayPal (a double P icon means yes), the current price, how many bids so far (or whether the item is a fixed-price Buy It Now item), and how much time is left for bidding. (For more on Buy It Now auctions, see page 26.) The small camera icon means there's a photo on the auction page; some sellers pay a little extra to include a small photo, called a gallery photo, in the results list. The Compare button lets you comparison-shop, described in detail on page 99. To view a particular auction, click its title.

Note: PayPal is usually the easiest way to pay for things, and a lot of buyers bid only in auctions that accept PayPal. You can find out more about PayPal and other popular payment methods on page 51.

Keep sliding your eyes right to see the current bid (the price you need to beat), how many bids have been placed on the item so far (which tells you how hot an item is), and how much time's left for you to jump into the fray (*d* means days; *m* means minutes; *s* means you're out of luck unless you're a really, really fast typist).

If all systems are go and you want to learn more about an item or place a bid, just click the item description to jump to an auction page with details and bidding choices. (For the skinny on auction pages, flip to page 19.)

Tip: eBay lets you customize your search results, which can be a good way to home in on an item within a price-range, sold near your home, closing within a day, or many other factors. On the right side above the results list, click Customize Display. On the page that opens, select the options you want (such as shipping cost or distance) and click Save.

Better Searching

Often, a basic search gives you *too many* results, including a ton of items you're not even interested in. For example, if you're looking for a printer, you might get a bunch of listings for *related* results, like ink cartridges and printer cables. Save your eyes and let eBay winnow out some of those results from you. The following sections show you how.

Matching Categories

One way to narrow your search is to click one of the Matching Categories on the left-hand side of the results page. For example, in Figure 1-8, if personal video recorders are what you're really looking for, you could whittle down the 1,134 matches to only those listed under the category Digital Video Recorders PVR, which has just 20 items.

Finder

Some popular items display a Finder on the left-hand side of the results page (shown in Figure 1-8) that lets you specify product type, brand, and other parameters, like size, style, or color. Taking advantage of the Finder is another way to narrow down overwhelming search results.

Picture Gallery

eBay believes the old saying that a picture is worth a thousand words. If you're looking for something specific—for example, you've got a vision dancing in your head of a little black dress with spaghetti straps and a ruffled hem—use *gallery view* to help you weed out the wrong auctions and zero in on the right ones. Gallery view filters out auctions without a gallery picture, so you won't wear out your clicking finger (or your patience) clicking those little green cameras to see if maybe, just maybe, an auction has what you're looking for.

To switch to gallery view, look above the items listed on the Search Results page for a link called Picture Gallery (Figure 1-8). If you click this link, eBay leaves out non-picture-gallery items and reformats your search results to look like a catalog (Figure 1-9).

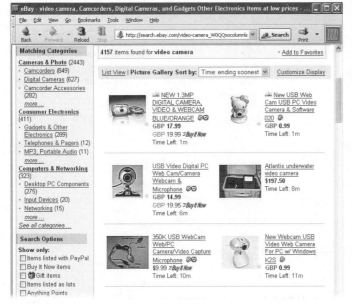

Figure 1-9:
Gallery view is a little easier on the eyes than list view. The photos are larger, and the results are less squeezed in. On the other hand, you see fewer items on a page (24 in gallery view as opposed to 50 in list view), and items without a gallery photo don't show up at all—so you might miss a good deal if you view your search results using only Picture Gallery.

Searching within a category

Searching within a category can save you a lot of time. For example, if you search for the word *matrix* without selecting a category, eBay shows you thousands and thousands of items, from shampoo to video games to snowboard boots to cars. If you're looking for memorabilia from the film trilogy, you'll go nuts sorting through all those irrelevant auctions.

To narrow down your searches to a specific category, such as *Entertainment Memorabilia*, go to eBay's navigation bar and click the Buy link. On the Buy page that appears, choose a category as shown in Figure 1-10, click the Search button, and let eBay zero in on what you want.

Tip: On the left-hand side of the Search Results page is a list of Matching Categories. Use these categories to narrow your search further. If you click a category, eBay discards all the results that don't match that category.

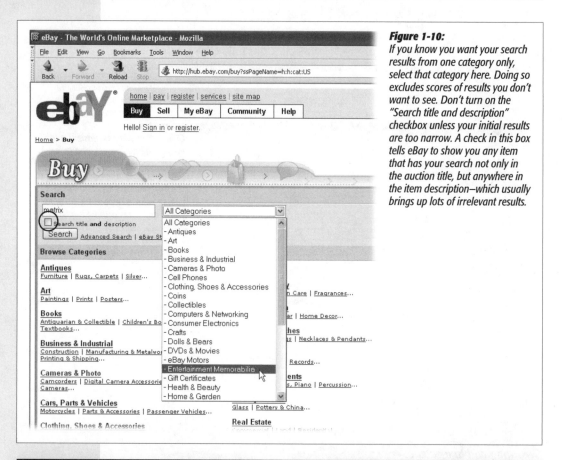

Figure 1-10:
If you know you want your search results from one category only, select that category here. Doing so excludes scores of results you don't want to see. Don't turn on the "Search title and description" checkbox unless your initial results are too narrow. A check in this box tells eBay to show you any item that has your search not only in the auction title, but anywhere in the item description—which usually brings up lots of irrelevant results.

GEM IN THE ROUGH

Just Say No

Excluding words from a search can really target your results. For example, if you're looking for a digital camera and you know you don't want a camera phone, Webcam, or camera pen, go to the Advanced Search page's "Exclude these words" box and type in *phone webcam pen* to get rid of hundreds of results you don't want to see.

And you can refine your search as you go. If you see other results you don't want, such as tripods and cases, look at the top of the Search Results page for the Search box and add these terms to the list of words you want to exclude: *-tripod -case*. (When you use the Search box instead of the Advanced Search page, the minus sign means you want to exclude that word from your search. Page 78 tells you more about the language of searching.)

Advanced Search

Advanced Search gives you even more options for targeting your search. You can search by item number, bidder, or seller; find eBay Stores (page 259) or search their inventory; and find other eBayers. Figure 1-11 shows you how it works.

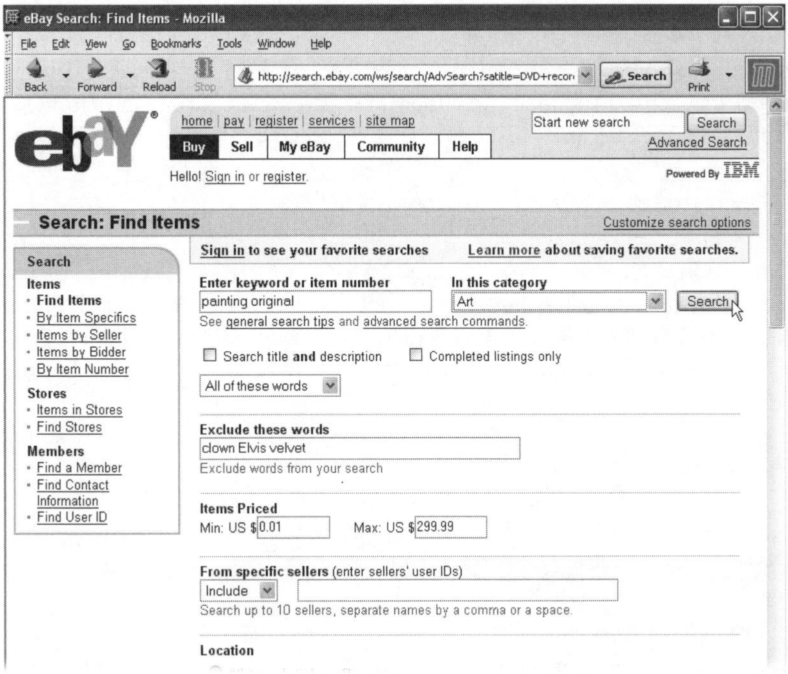

Figure 1-11:
At the top right of any page, just under the Search box, click the Advanced Search link. The Search menu on the left-hand side of the page shows you your choices. If you know what you don't want, list words to exclude from your search. You can limit results to a favorite seller (or ten), and you can sort results by time, price, distance from your registered address, or whether the seller accepts PayPal, a popular payment method explained on page 52. If you want to speed-shop, you can have eBay display as many as 200 results per page; if you'd rather take your time, display only 25 per page.

Deciphering Auction Pages

An auction page (Figure 1-12) is the place where you can read a description of an item, see extra photos, find out a seller's feedback score, find out the nitty-gritty shipping points, and more. You can also place your bid on the auction page.

At the top of the page is the auction title, written by the seller, and the item number, assigned by eBay. Just below the title and item number are details about the auction, seller information, and usually a picture of the item up for grabs. Here's a breakdown of the information:

• **Current bid.** Shows the current price of the item—in other words, the price you have to beat if you want to get in the game. In Figure 1-12, there are no bids yet, so the current bid is the same as the *starting bid,* the price (set by the seller) that the first bidder must meet to participate in the auction.

- **Place Bid button.** Click this button to submit a bid—*after* you've got all the info you need to bid with confidence.

- **Time left.** Shows how much time remains before the auction ends. Although the clock is always ticking, you need to hit the Reload or Refresh button on your browser to update the time left. The situation can change fast in an auction's final minutes, as more bids come in and the price rises, so you need to reload the auction page frequently when an auction is nearing its end.

- **Start time.** Shows when the auction started, right down to the second the listing became active. Auctions end either three, five, seven, or ten days to the very second after they began.

Note: eBay runs on Pacific time, and it lists all times in Pacific.

- **History.** On the auction page, History shows you the number of bids so far (if any) and at what price the bidding started. Click the link to check out the competition—see who bid how much and when. You might be able to find a good deal on a similar item by seeing what else these other bidders are bidding on (page 79).

Note: In private auctions (page 28), the Bid History page shows the high bids and when they were made but doesn't reveal bidders' IDs.

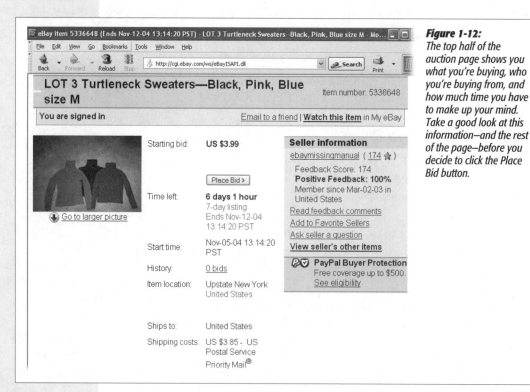

Figure 1-12:
The top half of the auction page shows you what you're buying, who you're buying from, and how much time you have to make up your mind. Take a good look at this information—and the rest of the page—before you decide to click the Place Bid button.

- **High bidder.** Shows the ID and feedback score of the current high bidder. Clicking either the ID or the number takes you to the Member Profile page for that eBayer. See page 41 for more about member profiles and how to read them.

- **Item location.** Shows the city and state or country from which the seller does business. Knowing an item's location can give you an idea of how long it will take for that item to make its way to your doorstep and what the shipping cost might be (if the seller hasn't specified one). Sometimes sellers describe the location as a region, such as Northeast or Midwest, or a bit of useless information, like My Garage. If you want more information about where the item ships from (and you probably do, if the item is large or heavy), email the seller to ask.

Tip: To email the seller a question about the item, head to the right-hand side of the auction page, and then click "Ask seller a question." The speed and professionalism with which the seller replies can tell you a lot about the person you're about to do business with. Keep in mind that eBay is a worldwide marketplace, and make allowances for time zones (also weekends and holidays) when awaiting the seller's response. Be sure that your question is courteous, professional, and not asking about something you can read for yourself in the item description. If a seller is rude, evades your question, or doesn't answer at all, you'll save yourself a lot of headaches by finding another auction.

- **Ships to.** Indicates regions to which the seller can ship the item. Many auctions ship worldwide; others restrict their auctions to certain areas or countries. For large or bulky items, like sofas or grand pianos, some sellers specify the item must be picked up locally. If you live in Oregon and you want to bid on a 125-gallon aquarium located in Florida, make sure you know in advance if you'll have to drive across the country to pick it up.

- **Shipping costs.** On eBay, the buyer almost always pays the cost of shipping the item. If the seller doesn't specify charges for shipping and handling here, check the item description and the "shipping, payment details, and return policy" at the bottom of the auction page, shown in Figure 1-13. It's also worth knowing what shipping method the seller plans to use. An item shipped by priority mail or UPS, for example, will get to you a lot faster than something coming by media mail or parcel post.

Tip: Always check the shipping cost before you bid, and factor it into the amount you're willing to pay. You don't want to end up paying $20 for the shipping and handling of a stunt kite that you won with a $1.50 bid.

The upper-right corner of the auction page shows a box with information about the seller: eBay ID, feedback score, how much of that feedback is positive, how long the seller has been an eBayer, and where the seller is registered. You might want to ask the seller a question (click that link to send an email) or view other items this person is selling. You definitely want to check out the seller's feedback, especially if the seller is someone you've never bought from before. For example, run the other way if you see a lot of negative comments—like "This thief took my

---

money and never sent my Beanie Baby!"—which probably means the seller has a history of ripping people off. For more on understanding feedback, see page 40.

The rest of the auction page has this important information (scroll down to see it all):

- **A written description of the item.** The amount of information here is up to the seller. Some give just the bare bones: size, color, model, condition. Others give an epic-length written description telling you everything the seller can think of about the item. Occasionally, you'll find the seller's personal history of the item; a guy who's selling an old gift from his ex-wife might vent about what went wrong with the marriage, or a grandchild might talk about the history of a family heirloom that's now on the auction block. Some of these are fun to read, even worthy of a Pulitzer.

Tip: If you encounter a listing that looks more like alphabet soup than plain English–NIB, MWMT, OOP, NR–decipher those strange codes with eBay's acronym guide. Go to Help → eBay Acronyms.

- **More photos.** Additional photographs are optional, but smart sellers include several photos of the item in different sizes or from various angles. Click a thumbnail photo to see a larger version of it.

- **Shipping, payment details, and return policy.** Study this section carefully to find hidden costs and limitations, like a no-return policy (common with used items) or shipping restrictions. And check to see whether insurance is optional, required, or not available. (Insurance is a good idea in case your item gets lost or damaged on its way to you. If insurance is available, the buyer pays for it, so don't forget to add it to your final cost.) Finally, this section often lets you know how soon after the auction the seller expects you to pay. See Figure 1-13.

Tip: If shipping costs aren't mentioned anywhere on the auction page, use the "Ask seller a question" link to find out how much it will cost to ship the item to you. (And save the seller's response email in case you're quoted a different shipping price after you've won the auction.) *Never* bid without knowing the shipping cost–or else you have no recourse for complaining if the seller charges excessively high shipping and handling fees.

- **Payment methods accepted.** Shows what it says. Most eBay sellers accept Pay-Pal (page 52). Many sellers accept a cashier's check or money order. (Some specify that money orders must be bought at the post office.) Personal checks are iffy—some sellers accept them, some won't. If a seller accepts personal checks and that's how you want to pay, be prepared to wait until your check has made it through the mail and cleared at the seller's bank. Only then will most sellers ship the item. For more on payment methods, see page 51.

Warning: eBay advises against using certain payment methods because they're wide open to fraud or misuse. If the seller insists that you pay with cash or via a wire transfer service like Western Union or Money-Gram, for example, something's probably fishy. For more on steering clear of scam artists, see page 132.

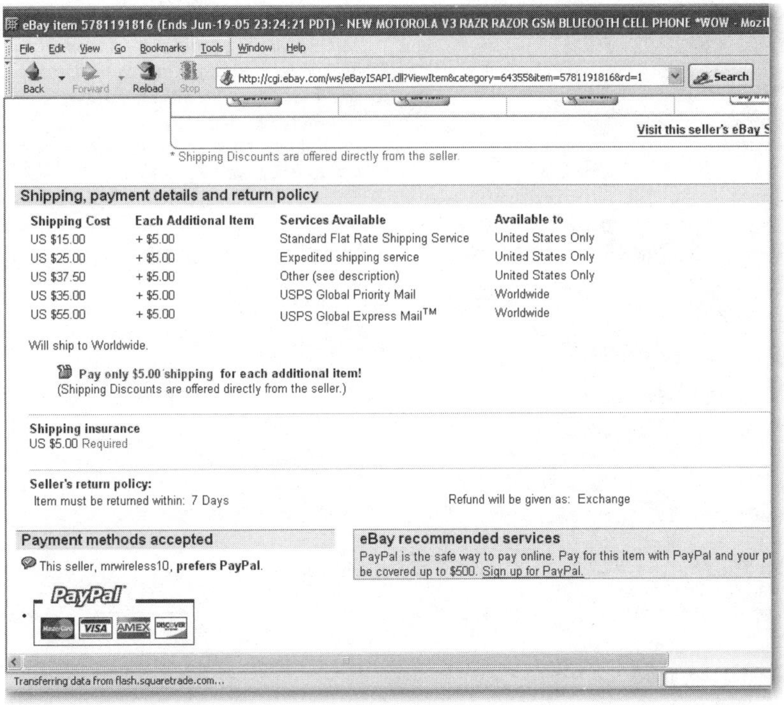

Figure 1-13:
The bottom of the auction page tells you how much shipping costs are, which payment methods the seller accepts, and specific payment instructions. Some sellers offer reduced shipping costs if you win more than one auction and have the items shipped together. The buyer pays shipping, so always know the shipping charge before you bid and add it to the amount of your bid to come up with your total cost.

- **Ready to bid?** Use this section, at the bottom on any auction page, to place a bid on the item. eBay uses *proxy bidding*, which means the system places bids for you, up to an amount you specify (see page 47 for the gory details on proxy bidding). Figure 1-14 shows you how to place a bid quickly, and Chapter 2 breaks it down for you step by step. (You can also click the Place Bid button at the top of the page under "Starting bid," as shown in Figure 1-12.)

  But don't bid until you read up on feedback on page 40, which can help you distinguish between reputable sellers and fly-by-night scam artists.

The auction page contains a lot of information, but always take the time to read it carefully before you bid. Sometimes, what looks like a great deal on a plasma TV is really an auction for a list of wholesale suppliers or the address of a Web page that sells televisions—you'll find that little tidbit of information buried somewhere in a long description. (Such deceptive listings are against eBay policy, but they do appear.) Know *exactly* what you're bidding on before you place your bid. If you're not sure, click "Ask seller a question" and ask. If the seller is evasive or doesn't respond, find another auction.

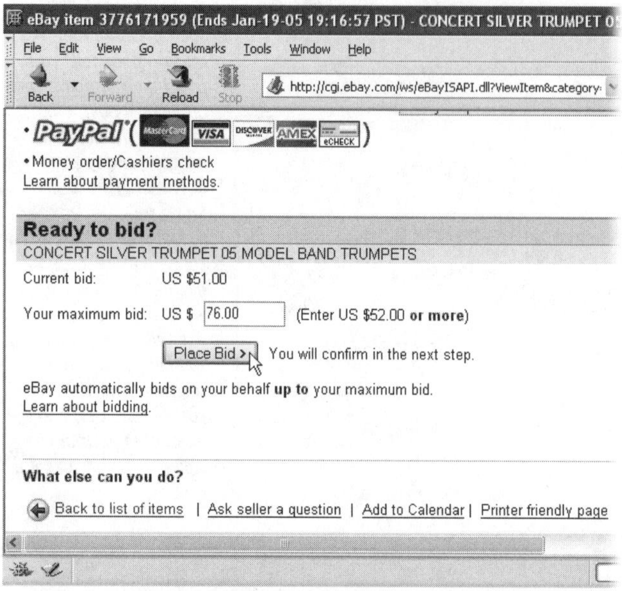

Figure 1-14:
You can place your bid at the bottom of any auction page. Type the maximum amount you're willing to pay into the text box, then click Place Bid. eBay takes you to a confirmation page, so you can check your figures before you finalize your bid.

Auction Types

eBay has several different kinds of auctions, each with different rules, so it's important to know which type you're dealing with before you bid. This section explains the different types of auctions on eBay and how to spot them.

Timed Auctions

Most eBay auctions are *timed auctions*. Not only do you have to outbid other bidders, you also have to beat the clock. With timed auctions, one second after an auction closes is no different from a whole year—both are too late. The ticking clock adds to the excitement, because in many auctions, the real action begins in the closing minutes, as bidders vie with each other to make their best bid as near as they can to the auction's close. This practice of last-moment bidding is called *sniping*; you can learn about sniping in detail on page 104.

Most eBay auctions last from three to seven days, although they may be as short as one day or as long as ten. (The seller determines the length of the auction at listing time.) eBay sets the end of the auction, right down to the second, based on the time the auction begins.

You can see how much time is left on an auction on either a search results list (check the rightmost column) or near the top of an auction page (Time Left is near the top of every page).

Note: eBay itself is in California, and all auctions run on Pacific Time. To see what the official time is according to eBay, click the eBay Official Time link at the bottom of any page.

Reserve Auctions

Sometimes a seller wants to start with a low opening bid to get buyers' attention, but doesn't want to sell at a loss. To help sellers meet these dual desires, eBay lets them set a *reserve price* on any auction, a secret price that represents the minimum the seller will accept for the item. In other words, in a reserve auction, the seller doesn't have to sell the item if bidding doesn't reach the reserve price.

For example, an auction that starts with an opening bid of a penny could have a reserve price of $100 or more—you don't know what the true selling price is until someone's bid hits the reserve. If the seller has set a reserve price, the words "Reserve not met" or "Reserve met" appear in the listing, next to the "Current bid," as shown in Figure 1-15.

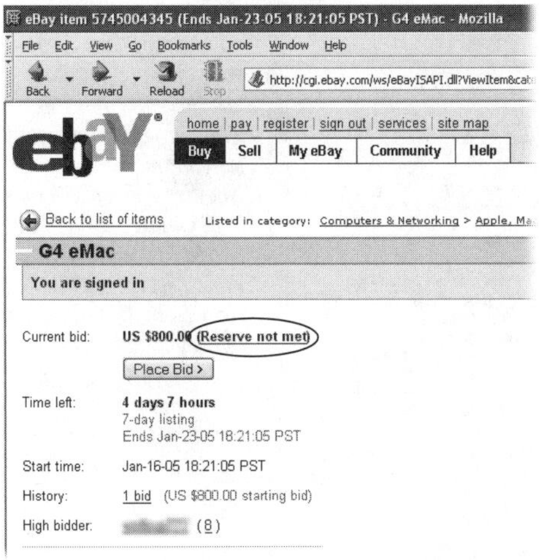

Figure 1-15:
This desktop machine started with an opening bid of $800. One bidder opened bidding with that price, but "Reserve not met" indicates that the seller isn't willing to let the computer go for such a low price. If the auction ends without meeting the reserve, the seller has no obligation to sell to the high bidder. Sellers can lower a reserve during an auction to stimulate bidding; a seller who does this usually adds a note saying they've lowered the reserve.

So if you're bidding on a CD player for your car and think you're getting a great deal because you're the high bidder at $25.00, check to see whether there's a reserve. Even if you have the winning bid of $25.00 when the auction closes, you may not get the CD player because of those three little words: "Reserve not met."

Note: The letters *NR* appear in many auction titles and stand for *no reserve*. In other words, the item sells for the highest bid when the auction closes—even if that bid is just one cent. In some NR auctions, the seller sets the opening bid at the desired selling price. In others, though, the seller takes a chance by starting with a very low opening bid, then stands back and watches the fur fly as competing bidders decide what the item is worth.

Reserve auctions make some bidders nervous: why bother trying to buy something if you don't know the seller's real asking price? You can bid and bid on an item and still not win it because your bids never get as high as the reserve. It can be frustrating, and many bidders prefer not to have to second-guess the seller on the mystery price.

But before you surf to the next auction, read the description. Some sellers will tell you right there what the reserve price is. These sellers want to protect their investment but realize that a secret reserve will turn off many bidders, so they let you know what they think is a reasonable selling price. (You can agree—by bidding—or disagree and look for another auction.)

Tip: Other sellers might clue you in on the reserve if you ask in an email. While you're on an auction page, click "Ask seller a question" (Figure 1-16) and ask away. You may not get your answer, but it's worth a try.

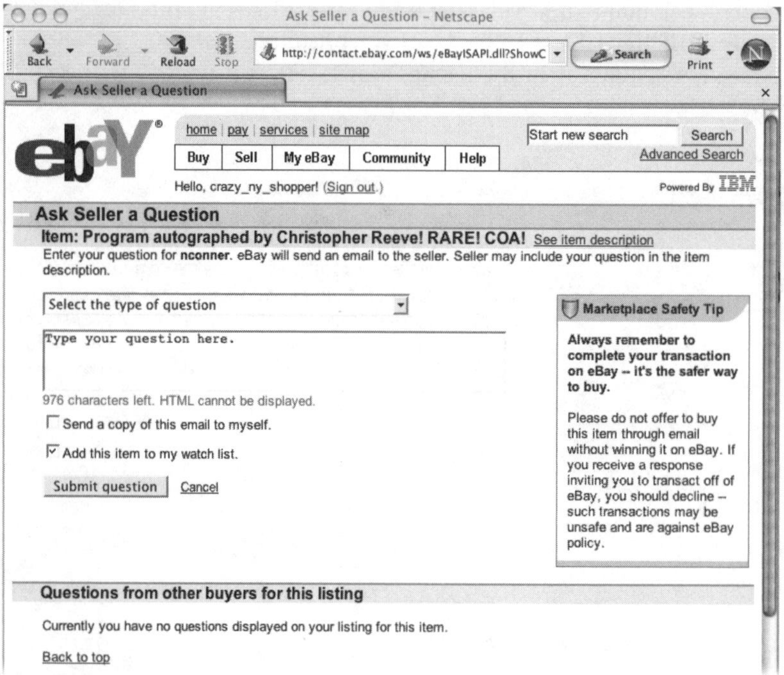

Figure 1-16:
When you click the "Ask seller a question" link on any auction page and fill in this form, eBay sends an email directly to the seller. You can ask about the item, shipping, or payment options. Type your question into the text box, and indicate whether you want a copy for your files and whether you'd like the item you're asking about added to your My eBay Watch list (page 34). Any reply from the seller goes directly to the email address you listed with eBay when you registered.

Buy It Now

A *Buy It Now* auction (*BIN* in eBay discussion-group lingo) is the opposite of an auction with a hidden reserve price. Right there, for anyone to see, is the seller's preferred price—the Buy It Now price. This price can be a little higher than the starting bid, or significantly so.

In many BIN auctions, you have the option of bidding, or you can cut out the competition and buy the item straight out. If you bid, the Buy It Now price disappears and the auction converts to a regular timed auction. If you click the Buy It Now button (Figure 1-17), the auction ends early and you're the winner. Other BIN auctions are straight, fixed-price sales without the option to bid.

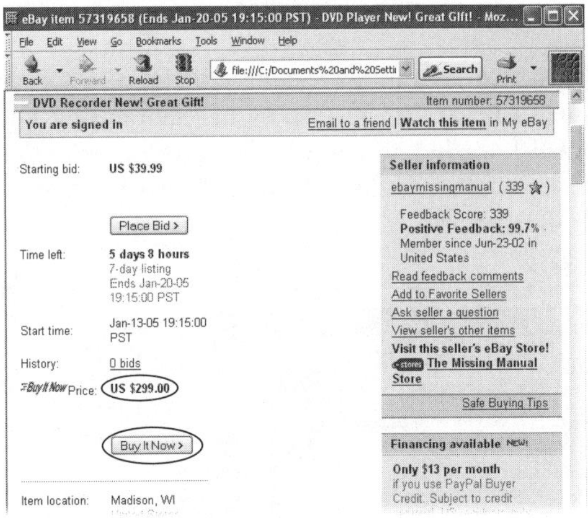

Figure 1-17:
When you click the Buy It Now button, you commit to buy an item for its BIN price. In an auction like this one, the opening bid is significantly lower than the BIN price, so if you're hoping for a bargain, put in a bid and let the auction run its course. Just remember that other eBayers are looking for a bargain, too, and will soon jump in with bids of their own.

Note: If a BIN auction also has a reserve price, the BIN button stays active until the reserve price is met; it doesn't disappear after the first bid.

Buy It Now really means "buy it, now." Some eBay newbies mistakenly think that clicking the Buy It Now button is like putting an item in your online shopping cart and that you can remove it if you change your mind. But eBay doesn't have shopping carts, and you can't change your mind with Buy It Now. If you click that Buy It Now button and confirm on the next page, you're commiting to purchase the item.

FREQUENTLY ASKED QUESTION

Bidding vs. BIN

Should I bid or buy it now?

When you have the choice of bidding in a timed auction or using Buy It Now, it can be tough to know which strategy will work better for you. Here are some tips to help you decide.

If a timed auction with no bids is nearing its end and the current price looks good, you might be able to get a bargain if you bid. Place your bid as late in the auction as possible, and bid the starting price or a little more. It's possible that someone else is watching the auction and waiting to snipe it (page 104), so you could lose out by a few cents in the closing seconds. But it's just as likely that you'll be the high bidder in an auction other eBayers overlooked—only about 15 percent of all eBay auctions are won by snipers.

The best time to click that Buy It Now button in a BIN auction is soon after the item has been listed, before other eBayers have had a chance to find it. If you see something you want at a good price (be sure to factor shipping charges into the final cost), BIN makes sense. You don't have to wait or compete against other would-be buyers to find out whether the item is yours.

For more on bidding strategies, see page 102.

Tip: If you think you might like to buy a BIN item but you want to give it some thought and come back later, add the item to your Watch list (page 34) in My eBay. Someone else might beat you to it, but at least you won't commit to purchasing something before you're sure.

Best Offer

In some BIN auctions, the seller is open to a little haggling, inviting you to make your best offer. You can recognize a Best Offer auction by the Submit Best Offer link just below the BIN button. Click the link to name your top price—and to try to convince the seller to sell you those hundred-dollar baseball tickets for 75 bucks. Figure 1-18 shows you the Best Offer form.

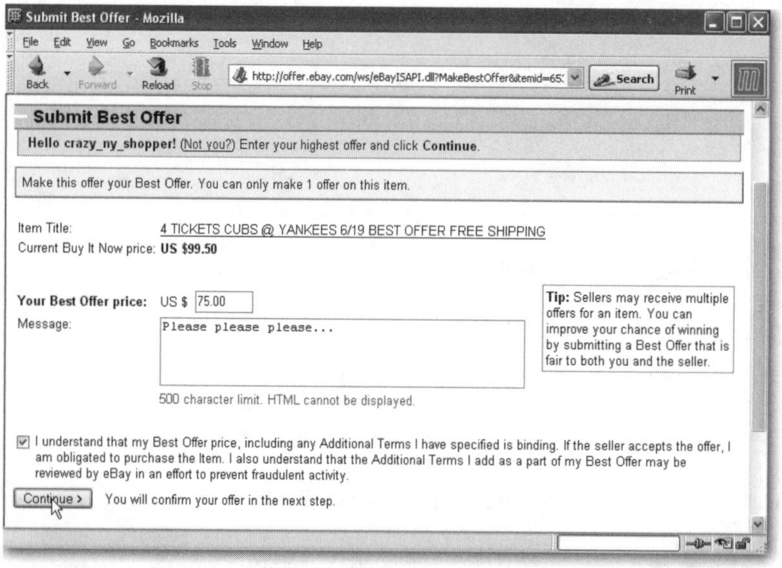

Figure 1-18:
When a seller invites offers, type the highest price you're willing to pay into the "Your Best Offer price" box. If you have a great argument that might convince the seller to take your price, type it into the Message box. The seller has 48 hours to accept or reject your offer. Submitting a Best Offer means that you agree to pay the amount offered (plus shipping) if the seller accepts.

Best offers are binding, just like a bid, so if the seller accepts your offer, you've made a purchase. And there are limits to the number of best offers you can make—these vary by category, but you get a notification from eBay when you're about to hit the limit.

Private Auctions

A seller can keep bidders' identities a secret in an auction. Sellers might do this for a couple of reasons. Some items, like certain adults-only products, might otherwise scare easily embarrassed bidders away. Other times, price is the issue. When the auction is for something enormously expensive, like a $120,000 diamond necklace, many bidders would prefer not to let the whole eBay community know that they can afford such things. So to attract bidders, sellers of high-priced goods often make their auctions private.

In a private auction, the identity of anyone who bids remains a secret. During the auction, only the high bid shows, not the ID of the bidder, as shown in Figure 1-19. There's no way to search specifically for private auctions, so you won't know whether an auction you're interested in is private until you look at the auction page. If you bid on a private auction, you can view your *bidder status* (see whether you're the high bidder), but you can't check out who's bidding against you. When the auction is over, eBay sends contact information to the high bidder and the seller so they can complete the transaction. At that point, anyone can see the bid history on the auction page, but only in terms of what bids were placed and when. You still can't see bidders' eBay IDs. Otherwise, private auctions work just like any other.

Note: When you search by bidder, private auctions don't appear in the search results. And feedback left for private auctions doesn't show an auction number, so you can't see the auction the feedback refers to.

Figure 1-19:
Private auctions keep the identity of all bidders a secret, both while the auction is running and after it has finished. If buyer and seller exchange feedback, "private" appears instead of the item number in the Feedback Forum.

Mature Audiences

eBay allows auctions for adults-only items, called *MA* (for *mature audiences*) *auctions*. Most of these auctions have to do with sex, and eBay takes steps to ensure that children and those who might be offended by MA items won't view them.

Note: The Mature Audiences category is not "anything goes." For example, eBay doesn't allow child pornography, obscenity, or hidden-camera videos—all of which are illegal.

First, eBay makes it hard to stumble across MA auctions by accident. These auctions don't appear in main areas of the site, such as the Featured Items area of the eBay home page. Second, anyone who wants to view an MA auction must have a credit card number on file; this requirement serves as age verification.

If you want to view MA auctions, go to eBay's home page and look in the left-hand Categories menu for Everything Else. Click the link, and on the Everything Else category page, click the Mature Audiences link. eBay prompts you for a password and presents you with terms of use. These terms include verifying your age, promising not to show MA pages to minors, agreeing that you're not offended by items of an adult nature (or you'll leave the MA area if you find yourself becoming offended), and promising to abide by all relevant laws. Click Continue if you agree to these terms. If you don't have a credit card number on file, you can enter one in the next step. If eBay does have your credit card number, you can search, view, and bid on MA auctions. Many MA auctions are private auctions (see page 28).

Note: MA auctions have some other restrictions placed on them: sellers can't set these auctions up as Buy It Now auctions or use PayPal (page 52) as a payment method.

Preapproved Bidder Auctions

A seller can create a list of preapproved buyers or bidders and apply it to an auction. If you're not on the list and you click the Place Bid button, you won't see the usual page that lets you type in your bid amount. Instead, eBay responds with a notice asking you to contact the seller by email. The seller can then choose to add you to the preapproved list and you can get in on the action.

Sellers sometimes block bidders who live in countries they don't ship to, who have a negative feedback score, or who've been reported as a nonpaying buyer by more than one seller in the past month. If you're in any of those boats, you won't have much chance of talking the seller into letting you bid. In addition, many sellers won't add you to their preapproved list if you have fewer than 10 feedback comments or any recent negative feedback. (For more on feedback, see page 40.)

Warning: Be careful if you're looking at a preapproved bidder auction run by a seller you don't know. Some scammers take advantage of preapproved bidder auctions to get eBayers' email addresses and try to sell them something offsite. Only they don't actually have anything to sell–they just want your money. *Never* agree to an off-eBay transaction–you lose eBay Buyer Protection (page 72), the right to file an Item Not Received report (page 71), even the right to leave feedback (page 40). For more on this kind of scam, see page 130.

Dutch Auctions

Dutch auctions aren't about windmills and wooden shoes. Also called a *multiple-item auction*, a *Dutch auction* is an auction that lists a number of identical items. Several bidders can win this kind of auction, not just the single high bidder. Dutch auctions let you buy items in quantity for a low price—sometimes for even less than you actually bid. You'll find Dutch auctions for all kinds of items, from tulip bulbs and beads to digital cameras and MP3 players.

How a Dutch auction works is a little confusing until you get the hang of it, but it's a great way to pick up a bargain or two—or even more, depending on the quantity up for grabs.

In a Dutch auction, you specify how many of the items you want and what you're willing to pay for each. The highest bidders win, but they pay only the price offered by the lowest successful bidder. Confused? You won't be after you take a look at Table 1-1. In this example, a seller is offering five disposable cameras for sale; the opening bid is set at $1.50 per camera. Five eBayers bid on the auction.

***Table 1-1.** A Dutch Auction for Disposable Cameras*

Bidder	Number Desired	Bid
A	2	$4.00
B	1	$3.75
C	1	$3.50
D	3	$2.00
E	1	$1.50

As in all auctions, those willing to pay the most win. In Table 1-1, the seller has five cameras to sell, so these will be distributed among the highest bidders, starting with whoever bid the most. Working from the highest bidder down the bid ladder, bidder A wins two cameras and bidders B and C win one apiece. Bidder D would like three cameras, but there's only one left, so that's all bidder D can buy. Bidder D is the last bidder who qualifies for a camera, so his is the bid that wins—the lowest winning bid. Because in this case $2.00 is the lowest winning bid, bidders A, B, C, and D all get their cameras for that price, no matter what they were willing to pay. Note that $2.00 isn't the lowest bid, it's the lowest *winning* bid. Bidder E, whose bid is below that $2.00 cutoff, is out of luck, because all the cameras were gone before her bid could be considered.

Note: Winning bidders in Dutch auctions can refuse partial quantities. So bidder D in Table 1-1 can buy one camera at $2.00 or none at all—without penalty. If you don't get the quantity you bid on, you don't have to complete the transaction.

Sellers sometimes label their Dutch auctions in the item description: Search for "*dutch auction*" to find one. You can also find Dutch auctions from the Advanced Search page: Enter your search terms, then scroll down to "Multiple item listings" and type in a number. When you've found a Dutch auction, look for the word Quantity under "Start time" to find out how many items the seller has up for sale.

For more on Dutch auctions, including strategies on how to win without overpaying, see page 110.

Live Auctions

Timed auctions are exciting, but for some bidders nothing beats the back-and-forth competition of a live auction. eBay's live auctions put you right on the floor of auction houses around the world. You bid against other Internet bidders and bidders physically present at the live auction. You can place an absentee bid before the auction begins if it's happening while you're at work or asleep, or you can watch the auction and bid in real time. Figure 1-20 shows you the eBay Live Auctions home page (located at *http://pages.ebay.com/liveauctions*).

Figure 1-20:
Find the eBay Live Auctions site at http://pages.ebay.com/ liveauctions. Start dates and times appear for each auction under Upcoming Auctions. To see the auction catalog (a list of items up for sale, with photos), click the title of an auction. Any registered eBayer can watch a live auction in progress (click the View Live button), but if you want to bid, you have to sign up. Click the Bid Now button to sign up for an auction in progress or the Sign Up button for one that hasn't started yet.

During the auction, a window shows a picture of what's up on the block, as well as its estimated worth and the current high bid. Instead of an auctioneer yelling, "Going, going, gone!" the window displays the words "Fair Warning" when the auction is about to close. The action is fast-paced, with bids flying in from the Internet and the auction floor.

My eBay–Your Shopping HQ

Hours of searching and scrutinizing auction pages can send your head spinning like a special effect in *The Exorcist*. Once you've found two or three possibilities out of four gazillion auctions, how do you find them again? How do you remember which kewpie doll you bid on when there are 300 up for sale? And how do you know if you're still the high bidder or if someone's snatched the kewpie from your clutches?

To keep you organized, eBay creates a page for you and you alone (Figure 1-21). Your *My eBay page* shows you items you're bidding on, auctions where you've been outbid—and auctions you've won and have to pay for. And that's just for starters. You can reach My eBay by heading to the top of any page on the site, finding the navigation bar, and clicking the My eBay Button.

Note: You must be *signed in* to eBay to see your personal My eBay page. But if you sign out, no problem: just click the My eBay link at the top of the eBay home page. Instead of the My eBay page, you see the Sign In screen. Type in your eBay ID and password, click Sign In Securely, and your My eBay page appears.

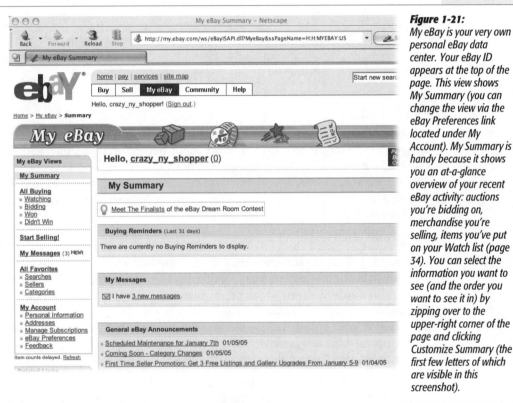

Figure 1-21:
My eBay is your very own personal eBay data center. Your eBay ID appears at the top of the page. This view shows My Summary (you can change the view via the eBay Preferences link located under My Account). My Summary is handy because it shows you an at-a-glance overview of your recent eBay activity: auctions you're bidding on, merchandise you're selling, items you've put on your Watch list (page 34). You can select the information you want to see (and the order you want to see it in) by zipping over to the upper-right corner of the page and clicking Customize Summary (the first few letters of which are visible in this screenshot).

Your My eBay page is an invaluable headquarters. It lets you keep track of the specific auctions you're interested in—whether you're bidding, selling, or just watching—and do other important stuff, too, like update your account information and save searches for when you're in the mood to power-shop. With all these goodies, My eBay provides a handy home base for exploring the site.

On the left-hand side of the page is My eBay Views: a menu of all the different parts of your My eBay page. You can customize the way your My eBay page appears by choosing from this menu. The next sections explain your choices.

My Summary

My Summary is shown in Figure 1-21, and it's the page that appears whenever you log in and click My eBay. My Summary gives you an overview of your recent searching and trading activity: the items you're currently bidding on (if any), how many items you've won (and lost), how much you've spent on eBay so far, and so on. My Summary is a good choice for getting a bird's-eye view of what you've been up to on the site.

Tip: If you'd like to set up a different view to greet you whenever you visit My eBay, find the My eBay Views menu on the left-hand side of the page, and then click eBay Preferences. Scroll down the page that opens until you find the section called My eBay Preferences, and then make your selection from the "Default opening page" drop-down list.

All Buying

Imagine heading for the mall with an assistant whose job it is to keep track of everything you buy, everything you think about buying, and even the sale items you miss out on. You could use that information to fine-tune your shopping list—know the best prices, the best stores, the best times to shop. The All Buying section of My eBay is just such an assistant: it records your activity related to shopping and buying.

Here's what you'll find in All Buying:

- **Watching.** If you want to keep track of an interesting item but you're not quite ready to bid on it—perhaps you're waiting to see just how high the price gets—you can *watch* the item, which means that the item, its current high bid, the number of bidders, and the amount of time left in the auction appear in this section of your My eBay page—along with a Bid Now button in case you want to stop watching and get in on the action. To learn how to add an item to your Watch list, click "Watch this item" in the upper right of any auction page.

- **Bidding.** If you've jumped into the fray and bid on something, information about the auction shows up here: the current price, whether you're the high bidder, and how long before the auction ends.

- **Won.** This section records your triumphs—auctions you won as the highest bidder. These auctions appear for up to 60 days or until you decide to remove them.

- **Didn't Win.** This section shows items you bid on but didn't win. Viewing this information not only reminds you what you've been shopping for, it also shows you what the prevailing bid was, so you can adjust your bidding next time around.

Start Selling!

When you first register with eBay, you can bid on items, post on discussion boards, and search the site. If you want to sell, you have to go through another registration process. This link lets you register as a seller. To learn how to sign up to sell on eBay, see page 154.

My Messages

If you've ever had a spam filter swallow an important email, you'll be glad to know that eBay's doing something to make sure that your eBay-related emails never suffer that fate. My Messages, shown in Figure 1-22, started as a way for eBayers to receive official eBay announcements about the site.

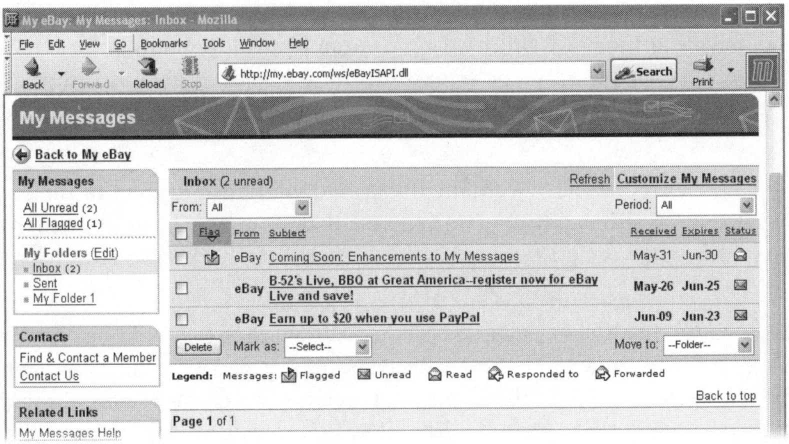

Figure 1-22:
Your My Messages Inbox lists all incoming eBay-related communications. You can flag, delete, or transfer any message; just turn on the checkbox next to one or more messages and take one of the actions at the bottom of the message list. From the left-hand My Messages menu, you can view only messages you haven't read or the ones you've flagged. Your Sent folder stores a copy of every message you send through My Messages. You can copy messages from the Sent folder to store in other folders, but you can't move or delete Sent messages.

In mid-2005, eBay enhanced My Messages in three important ways:

• **Account-related messages.** Instead of just general announcements, official communications from eBay related to your individual account (such as invoices, notices of a password change, and so on) now appear in My Messages. *Spoof emails*, official-looking emails sent by crooks hoping to steal your account information, have become the bane of the Internet (see page 137 for more on spoof emails). If you get an email that looks like it's from eBay but suspect it's a spoof, check My Messages. All eBay communications about your account appear in your My Messages Inbox. If it's not in there, it's not from eBay.

- **Answers from Customer Support.** If you've emailed eBay with a question or problem, the response appears here.

- **eBayer-to-eBayer communications.** One of the biggest causes of negative feedback is miscommunication. When you use My Messages to contact another eBayer, eBay sends two copies of your message—one to the person's My Messages inbox and the other to his registered email address. Now you can be sure that your trading partner gets your emails.

My Messages lets you create and use up to ten personal folders to store your messages, so you can organize your communications in any way that makes sense to you.

All Favorites

Here you can save searches, sellers, and categories that interest you. Saving searches buys you time and effort when, for example, you're hunting for baseball cards to add to your collection or an out-of-print DVD for a gift. You can run the same search over and over, whenever you want, without having to type in keywords.

You can save searches by keyword, or if you find yourself returning to the same seller's auctions again and again, you can save that seller as a favorite—and even receive emails when the seller lists new items. (See Search for Items by Seller on page 80.)

To save a search, under My Favorite Searches, simply click the "Add new Search" link. A form opens, much like the Advanced Search (page 19), letting you choose search criteria. Fill it out, run the search, and then on the search results page in the upper-right corner, click "Add to Favorites." Once you've saved a search, it appears on your All Favorites page with an "Edit Preferences" link that lets you adjust its search criteria.

Figure 1-23 shows how to save a favorite category search to streamline the time you spend searching, making it easier and faster to find the things you want. For example, if you collect antique Buddha figures, you can save a category search that, with one click, will show you what's newly listed in the Antiques/Asian Antiques/Statues/Buddha category.

To find a favorite category you've saved, go to your My eBay page, scroll way down to the section called Shortcuts to My Favorites, and choose the Select a Category drop-down list. If you prefer, you can get to your favorite categories from the left-hand My eBay Views menu: under All Favorites, click Categories. Finally, your favorite categories also show up on the Advanced Search page under Favorite Searches.

My Account

This view contains the nuts and bolts of your eBay account. If you move or change your phone number or email address, you want to make sure that trading partners can still find you. You can also subscribe to eBay services or change your notification preferences—how often you hear from eBay, and about what.

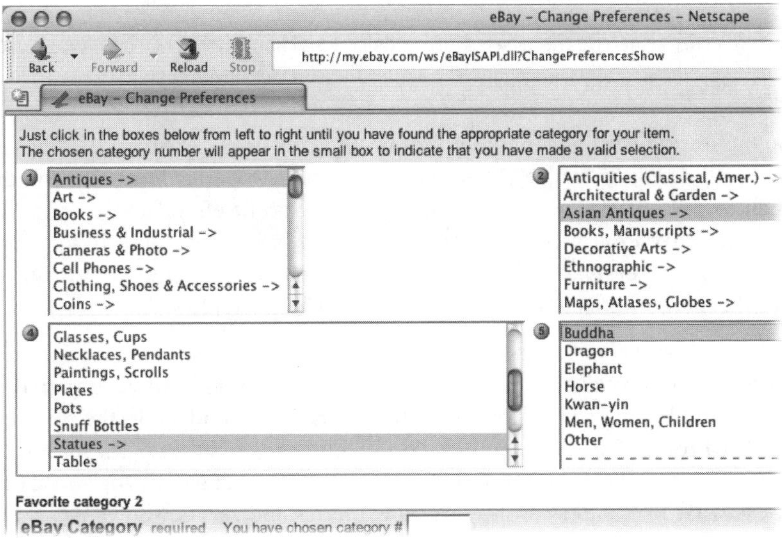

Figure 1-23:
To get here, from My eBay, click Category → "Add a favorite category." Select a general category in box 1. Relevant subcategories open in box 2. If there's an arrow next to your choice, eBay has more subcategories to choose from; your cursor jumps to the next box, and more categories appear. When you've got to the point where there are no more subcategories, eBay's assigned number for that category appears in the box at the top. You might have to go through several subcategories to find the specific type of item you want. When you're done, click Submit at the bottom of the page.

Here's what you can look at or change under My Account:

- **Personal Information.** View or edit the information you submitted when you registered: your eBay ID, password, email address, mailing address, and any financial information. If you've created an About Me page (page 191), you can change that here, too.

- **Addresses.** View or change your eBay registration address, the address where you receive payments, and your shipping address. For most people, these three addresses will be the same.

- **Manage Subscriptions.** This page is where sellers can sign up for and manage various services eBay offers, including eBay Stores (page 259), Selling Manager (page 332), eBay Blackthorne (page 334), and Picture Manager (page 203). You must have a seller's account and, in some cases, a certain amount of feedback to subscribe.

• **eBay Preferences.** Some people like to hear from eBay constantly. Others prefer to keep their inbox relatively email-free. Choose Notification Preferences to customize when and about what eBay can contact you. You can receive an email to let you know when an auction you're watching is going to end soon, when you've been outbid, when you've received feedback or need to leave it—or not. It's up to you. Most notification options are already turned on, so be sure to visit this page and fine-tune your preferences.

Tip: If you'd rather not receive telemarketing calls and direct mail from eBay, scroll down to the bottom of the Notification Preferences page and turn off both checkboxes under Other Contacts.

You'll also find Authorization Settings on the eBay Preferences page. This section reminds you if you've OK'd any third parties to perform actions on your behalf on the eBay site. Examples include installing the eBay Toolbar (page 89) or signing up to put a counter on your auction page (page 208). If you don't want any third parties messing around with your eBay account, turn on the "Revoke this authorization" checkbox, and then click Apply.

• **Feedback.** For every eBay transaction you participate in, you have an opportunity to give and receive *feedback*, rating the transaction as positive, negative, or neutral, and leaving a brief comment that's permanently added to the receiver's Member Profile. This page reminds you if you haven't left feedback for a trading partner and shows you any recent feedback others have left for you. Feedback is what makes eBay work—it's how buyers and sellers who've never met know they can trust each other. So when you've finished a transaction, leave feedback to let the world know how it went. For more information on how feedback works, see page 40.

Note: If you're registered with PayPal (page 52) or if you're registered as a seller, information about your PayPal account and any selling activity—such as auctions you're running or fees you owe—also appears on your My Account page.

CHAPTER 2.

Bidding, Paying, and Following Up

Most of the time, if you want to buy something on eBay, you can't purchase it outright. Instead, you have to *bid* for it at auction. Bidding means that you vie with other potential buyers to offer the most for an item. If this system sounds like it's designed to bleed money out of you, think again. Auctions can help you get screaming deals.

Note: The exception to the bidding rule is Buy It Now auctions, described on page 26.

On the other hand, if you're not savvy about bidding, you could wind up paying $40 for a $3 SpongeBob comic book. Or, worse, you could find yourself unable to purchase what you want at any price.

This chapter shows you how to bid on eBay auctions with confidence, giving you the lowdown on:

- What feedback is, why it's important, and how to use it to tell if a seller is trustworthy—*before* you bid.

- How eBay's bidding process works.

- How to place a bid.

- How to pay for auctions you've won.

- When and how to leave post-auction feedback.

- How to avoid common buying problems.

Is This Seller Trustworthy? How to Read Feedback

When you're trying to figure out whether a deal really is as good as it looks, studying the auction page (page 19) is a great place to start. But smart buyers dig deeper—and eBay's *Feedback Forum* lets you do just that. If the software that keeps auctions running 24/7 is eBay's heart, feedback is its soul.

After all, why are zillions of sellers, scattered all over the globe, willing to hand over their jet skis and their grandmother's fine china to someone they wouldn't know from Adam? And why are zillions of buyers comfortable forking over money based on a couple of $2 \times 3''$ photos and a three-line description?

In a word, trust. And on eBay, that trust is established through *feedback*.

In the Feedback Forum, both buyer and seller take a minute after their transaction is complete to rate their level of satisfaction. Through ratings and comments, they tell the world how it was to deal with their trading partner: wonderful ("My black-light Kiss posters arrived fast and in perfect condition"), so-so ("Can't complain"), horrible ("The &^*(%@! bum never paid!"). Feedback paints a picture of an eBayer's moral character, affecting whether a buyer will buy from a seller and whether a seller will accept a prospective buyer's bid.

So spending a few minutes in the Feedback Forum to read and understand a seller's feedback can help you avoid getting ripped off. For example, a feedback score of 90, or a string of comments like, "The 'perfect' Cabbage Patch doll I paid for was missing both arms," suggests that you should reconsider doing business with a seller. (The box on page 42 tells you how to interpret feedback scores.)

Here's how feedback works. After each auction, eBay asks the buyer and the seller to leave comments about how smoothly (or how horribly) the transaction went. Comments are positive, negative, or neutral and can be no longer than 80 characters. You can leave feedback only for actual, completed transactions, which helps keep feedback accurate. A seller's friends can't pad his feedback with phony compliments about items they never bought, and his competition can't shoot him down with bogus complaints.

Feedback is voluntary, but most eBayers participate. After all, most people use the Feedback Forum themselves to separate the sheep from the wolves, so they know their opinion counts—and will help smart eBayers (like you) know whom to trust. (See page 59 for a discussion of why *you* should leave feedback, when, and how.)

To see a seller's feedback from the auction page (Figure 2-1), click the seller's ID, the number in parentheses that follows the ID, or the "Read feedback comments" link.

Any of these links takes you to the *Member Profile* for that eBayer, shown in Figure 2-2. The Member Profile page is where you read feedback—the good, the bad, and the ugly.

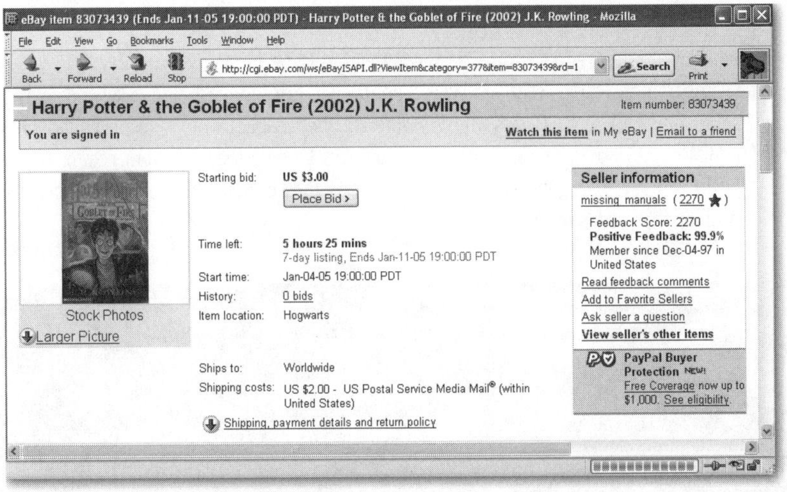

Figure 2-1:
On the right of every auction page is the "Seller information" box. Click the seller ID, the number after the ID, or the "Read feedback comments" link to go to that seller's Member Profile page, where you can get the lowdown on the seller's eBay reputation.

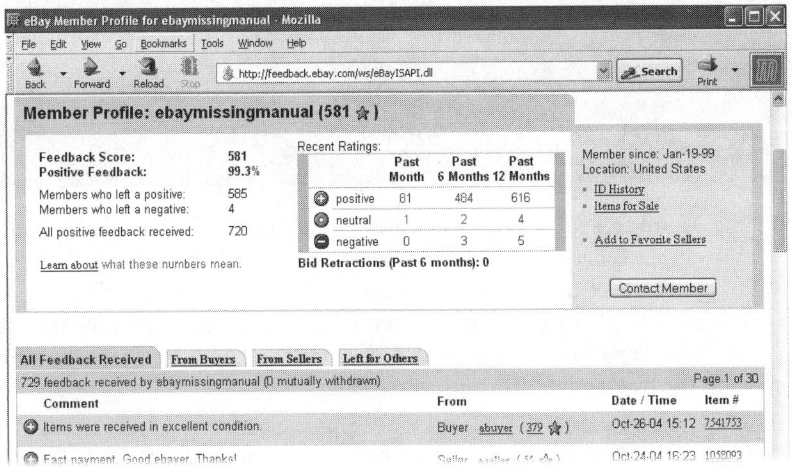

Figure 2-2:
The Feedback Score tallies positive and negative comments for all transactions. This eBayer has received 585 positive comments and four negatives, so the feedback score is 581. To help put these numbers in perspective, consider the math: eBay calculates the percentage of positive comments out of all feedback received—in this case, 99.3 percent, which is a decent score.

Tip: eBay lets you change your ID. If you want to see other IDs the eBayer has had in the past, click ID History on the right-hand side of the page. Feedback travels with a new ID, though, so a seller can't dump bad feedback merely by changing the name on her account.

The feedback score reflects how many trading partners have been happy with their transactions with this eBayer. For every positive comment, you get one point. Each negative comment subtracts one point from your feedback score. Neutrals don't affect your feedback rating one way or the other. The box below explains how to deconstruct feedback scores like a pro.

Note: To count toward the feedback score, each comment must be from a unique eBay ID. If you buy five separate items from the same seller and leave a positive feedback for each one, eBay adds only one point to the seller's feedback score. (That's why, in Figure 2-2, the feedback score is 581, even though that eBayer has a total of 720 positive comments.) eBay does this to keep feedback from getting artificially lopsided—a buyer with an ax to grind, for example, can't buy tons of items from a seller with the sole intention of crashing that seller's feedback score.

FREQUENTLY ASKED QUESTION

When 97 Percent Is a Bad Score

What's a good feedback score?

You might glance at the seller information on the auction page, see that the positive feedback is 95.2 percent, and think you're good to go. On the contrary, you should always check the feedback in a seller's Member Profile before you bid—especially any seller whose percentage of positive feedback is below 98 percent.

Ninety-eight percent is the minimum positive feedback rating that eBay accepts for *PowerSellers*: high-volume sellers

who receive special privileges. In other words, 98 percent positive feedback is eBay's cutoff for what makes good customer service. (Some experienced eBayers are even pickier; they won't do business with any seller whose feedback score is lower than his body temperature, 98.6.)

So if a seller you want to do business with has a feedback rating below 98 percent or so, check out the feedback and see if you can determine where those negs came from. If there are a lot of recent negative comments, think twice before placing your bid.

Beneath the Member Profile box, you can read actual comments. Give these a quick scan, even if a seller's feedback score looks good. (You might find a few neutrals, which don't affect the feedback score but often express a complaint.) Each comment shows who wrote it, when the person left it, and the item number of the transaction. Click any link—ID, feedback score, or item number—for more information about the transaction the comment applies to.

Tip: The Member Profile page usually has only 25 comments on it. For some PowerSellers, that could represent this morning's feedback alone. To scan more feedback in less time, scroll down to the bottom of the Member Profile page and set "Items per page" to 200.

Tips for Interpreting Feedback

Don't just glance at the Member Profile and rush back to the auction page to bid. Read some comments. You might be surprised at what you find, like a comment marked positive that says, "Seller sent book but charged $15 for media mail!!!" or

"Photo showed accessories not included in auction. Read carefully." Take a few minutes to understand the information the profile offers. Here are some suggestions:

- **From Buyers.** When you want to get the lowdown on a prospective seller, From Buyers is the tab to click. Here you see whether other buyers have been happy with their purchases and customer service. Look for mentions of any problems with communication or shipping (either speed or packing) and whether the item met expectations. Sometimes a complaint appears buried in a comment marked as positive, such as "Great CD. Took two weeks to ship," or "Check shipping cost before you bid." Keep an eye out for such comments. A pattern might indicate a problem you'd rather not deal with.

Warning: If you're about to bid on an item listed by someone who has no feedback on the From Buyers tab, you're probably just dealing with an eBayer who's new to selling. However, if the auction is for an expensive item at a ridiculously low price—such as a car, motorcycle, ATV, digital camera, computer, and so on, going for a fraction of what you know it's worth—and the seller has no feedback from other buyers, you may be looking at a *hijacked account*. In other words, a thief has stolen someone's eBay account and is using it to list items with no intention of selling them. Be careful. Check for the other red flags described on page 132. If in doubt, don't bid. Better to miss out on a bargain than to kiss your hard-earned cash goodbye.

- **From Sellers.** Leopards rarely change their spots; someone who won't pay up when she's the buyer probably won't deal square when she's the seller. You can find out whether a potential seller has a history of honoring obligations by clicking this tab. (And when you get the selling bug yourself, From Sellers is the most important tab on a Member Profile page.)

UP TO SPEED

Star Light, Star Bright

The stars that appear with some eBayers' feedback ratings show how *active* that eBayer has been on the site. They have nothing to do with an eBayer's feedback score itself.

Each feedback point counts toward a star. After you've received 10 feedback points, you get your first star—a gold one, just like in school. As you accumulate more feedback, the color of the star changes:

- Gold star: 10 to 49 points.

- Blue star: 50 to 99 points.

- Turquoise star: 100 to 499 points.

- Purple star: 1,000 to 4,999 points.

- Green star: 5,000 to 9,999 points.

When your feedback rating hits 10,000, you're in a whole new league. You get a shooting star:

- Gold shooting star: 10,000 to 24,999 points.

- Turquoise shooting star: 25,000 to 49,999 points.

- Purple shooting star: 50,000 to 99,999 points.

- Red shooting star: 100,000 or more points.

- **Left for Others.** It's always a good idea to see what kind of feedback the seller has left for others; the Left for Others tab shows you at a glance. Feedback should be professional in tone. After all, eBay auctions are business transactions. If an eBayer leaves only nasty feedback or starts calling names like "idiot" or "thief" when a transaction runs into problems, is this someone you want to do business with? Similarly, an eBayer who never bothers to leave feedback is unlikely to leave any for you, so be aware that the auction probably won't help your feedback score.

Tip: Check out the number at the top of the Left for Others tab, which tells you how many feedbacks that eBayer has left. When you're new to the site and trying to build up your feedback score, a seller who's left as much feedback as she's received (or even more) will probably add a precious point to your climbing score.

- **From.** This column lets you click the ID or feedback rating of the comment writer to view the comment writer's Member Profile. You might be able to get a glimpse into the other side of the story or discover that the comment writer has been involved in lots of conflicts with others. Occasionally, you might even find that the comment writer, for whatever reason, just lives to leave negative feedback.

- **Item #.** The item number is in the far right column of the comments. Item number links remain active for 90 days after someone leaves feedback. Click this link to see what else a seller has been selling. If a seller who's been auctioning nothing but scrapbook supplies suddenly lists several SUVs or other expensive out-of-specialty items, be extremely careful. It could be a clue that a scammer has hijacked a legitimate seller's account.

- **Mutual Feedback Withdrawal (MFW).** Above the actual comments is a line that indicates the total amount of feedback and how many comments (if any) have been mutually withdrawn (page 65). A lot of MFWs could point to a seller who leaves *retaliatory negative feedback*—negative feedback left purely in revenge for having received it. The seller then uses the retaliatory neg as leverage to get the buyer to go through the MFW process—when feedback is withdrawn, the comment remains but the negative strike against the feedback score disappears. Really good sellers do not leave feedback without thinking it through, so a seller who has a lot of MFWs is usually someone to avoid.

- **Responses.** If you see a negative comment or two, don't panic. As in all areas of life, things do go wrong. Every eBayer has the right to respond to received feedback. This response shows up right below the comment itself. Sometimes, illness or a personal crisis might lead to a flurry of negative comments. Other times, a single transaction didn't work out, thanks to a shipping problem or communication snafu. In any case, many sellers will take the time to explain what went wrong, as shown in Figure 2-3. Feedback is an eBayer's reputation on the site, so most eBayers take great care to protect theirs. See page 64 to learn how to respond to feedback.

- **Contact Member.** If you want an explanation of something in the Member Profile before you bid, click the Contact Member button on the right-hand side of the page (Figure 2-3). Just remember to keep your question short, courteous, and professional. "Are you really 'a thieving sociopath who'd rip off his own grandmother' like it says in your feedback?" isn't going to reflect well on you.

- **Private feedback.** Any eBayer can choose to hide her feedback from public consumption. You can still view the feedback score, percentage of positive feedback, and numbers of positive, neutral, and negative comments left in the past month to the past year. You just can't see the comments themselves. Figure 2-4 shows what a Member Profile looks like for someone who's chosen to hide his feedback.

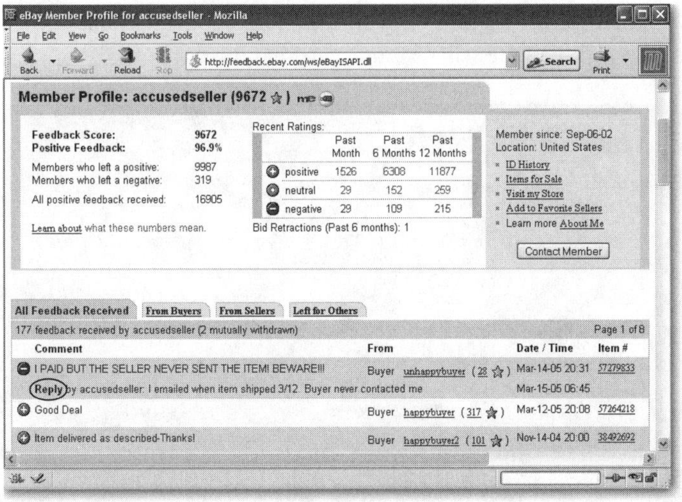

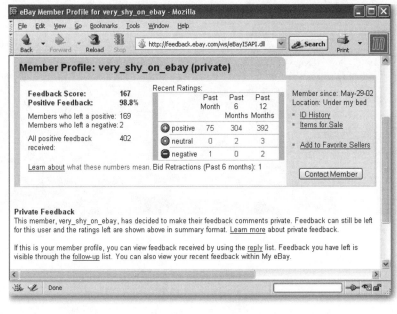

Figure 2-3:
When a trading partner leaves feedback—whether positive, negative, or neutral—the person who received the feedback can use up to 80 characters to write a response. Responses appear just below the original comment. Most eBayers respond only to negative or neutral feedback. It offers the opportunity to give their side of the story when a transaction goes sour.

Figure 2-4:
Most eBayers choose to show the world their feedback, which is the way eBay sets up your account. But you can hide your feedback. Go to your My eBay page, look in the left-hand menu for the Feedback link, and click it to go to the Feedback Forum. From there, the "Hide my feedback" link lets you make your feedback private. If you do so, your feedback isn't private from you: from the bottom of eBay's home page, click the Feedback Forum link, then the "Reply to feedback received" link. After taking these steps, your member profile will look like this.

So why would anyone *want* to hide her feedback from other eBayers? The obvious reason is the one you should be wary of: a seller with private feedback and a positive feedback score of less than about 98 percent is waving a bedsheet-sized red flag at you. You might want to look for another auction or email the seller to find out what the story is.

On the other hand, occasionally an honest seller has a good reason to hide feedback. If another eBayer left feedback that violates eBay's policies by posting obscenities or personal information about someone, the seller who received that feedback might hide all comments (you can't hide just one) while waiting to get the offending comment removed (see page 66 for more about the kinds of feedback eBay will remove). Email the seller to find out what the deal is.

WORKAROUND WORKSHOP

How to Read Private Feedback—Sometimes

When someone makes his feedback private (page 45), his Member Profile page won't show you the comments that he's received or those he's left for others. If a seller with private feedback has had auctions close within the last 30 days, however, you can see feedback that the seller has received or left for others. You just have to do a little sleuthing. Follow these steps:

1. Look in the upper-right corner of most eBay pages to find the Advanced Search link, and then click it to go to the Advanced Search page. On the left-hand side of the page, click the Items by Seller link.

2. Type the seller's ID in the text box and turn on the "Include completed listings" checkbox just below it. Doing so brings up the Items for Sale page, listing current and completed auctions.

3. For any completed auction you find, click the *buyer's* ID. (Look for auctions that ended at least a week or two ago so there's been time to complete the transaction and leave feedback.)

4. On the Member Profile page, click the From Sellers tab. Increase the number of comments on the page if necessary. Type Ctrl+F or select Edit → "Find in this

page," type the seller's ID in the text box, and then click Find. If the seller with the private feedback has left feedback for that buyer, you can read it here.

5. Click the Left for Others tab and repeat the Find process. If this buyer has left feedback for the seller you're checking, you can read it.

It might take a little searching before you find some comments. Feedback is voluntary; not everyone leaves feedback for every transaction. A few never leave it at all. And if a seller with private feedback runs only private auctions, you won't be able to find the IDs of any buyers. But if you want to find out what's up with a seller's private feedback, it's worth spending a few minutes to track down the feedback that seller has chosen to hide.

And if you're a seller looking at a potential buyer with private feedback, you can follow the same steps. Just start with Items by Bidder in the Advanced Search page in step 1, click the ID or feedback rating of the seller in step 3, and click the From Buyers tab in step 4. Troublesome buyers are often notorious for spewing lots of bad feedback, so if you have any doubts about a buyer with private feedback, these steps are definitely worth taking.

Bidding on eBay

eBay's genius is in its bidding system, called *proxy bidding*. Proxy bidding is the automated bidding system that lets you participate in auctions even when you're away from your computer: you put in your maximum bid and eBay bids on your behalf, up to your high bid. Here's how it works.

As Figure 2-5 shows, when you place a bid on eBay, the Place a Bid page shows two bid amounts:

- **Current bid.** This is the high price of the moment; you have to bid a little more than the current bid to join in the auction (eBay shows you the minimum acceptable bid right next to the box where you type in your bid amount).

- **Your maximum bid.** The amount you type in here is the *most* that you'd be willing to pay to win the auction. Your maximum bid is a secret amount—hidden from everyone but you and eBay's computers. In fact, if the price in an auction doesn't go as high as your maximum bid, no one else will ever know how much you were willing to pay.

Figure 2-5:
When making your bid, you must type in at least the amount listed to the right of the text box, but you can type in the maximum amount you're willing to pay. If you're unsure that you're bidding correctly, click "Learn about bidding" in the lower-left corner (not shown here) for a quick pop-up tutorial.

When you type in your maximum bid, eBay checks that amount against the minimum bid. If your bid is at or higher than the required minimum, eBay accepts the bid, and you become the high bidder by one *bid increment,* the minimum price increase for an acceptable bid. Depending on the current price, each new bid must be at least one bid increment higher—for example, if the current bid is $9.99, the bid increment is 50 cents, so the next acceptable bid would be $10.49.

Note: Bid increments increase as the price does, ranging from five cents for items whose current price is less than a dollar to $100 for items currently prices at $5,000 or more. To find out more about bid increments—and how to use them to win an auction by just a penny or two—see page 102.

After you've placed a bid, if another eBayer comes along and bids on the same item, eBay compares the new bid with your secret maximum amount. When two people bid against each other, eBay's computers raise the price one increment at a time until the current price exceeds someone's maximum bid.

For example, imagine you find an ultracool pair of sunglasses with an opening bid of $9.99—a good price, but you'd pay $15.99 plus shipping and still think you got a bargain. When you type in $15.99 as your maximum bid, eBay checks to make sure that you've bid enough to cover the minimum. You have, so you become the high bidder for the sunglasses at $9.99. But eBay remembers that your high bid is $15.99 and will bid up to that amount on your behalf—with no further action from you—if someone else joins the bidding. So when another bidder swoops in— call her sunglasses-stealer—and hopes to win the sunglasses for one puny bid increment more, she types in $10.49 as her maximum bid. eBay accepts her bid, and then checks your secret amount. Your maximum bid of $15.99 is more than one bid increment higher than sunglasses-stealer's max, so eBay raises your bid by one increment. You're now the high bidder at $10.99.

But what if sunglasses-stealer decides to keep bidding and types in a new maximum amount? The same process happens all over again. eBay compares your high bid with sunglasses-stealer's high bid, increasing each by one increment until the bidding goes over someone's maximum. If sunglasses-stealer's maximum bid is higher than yours, bidding will stop at one bid increment above your max of $15.99—staying at $16.49 unless somebody else bids before the auction ends. When someone outbids you, eBay emails you an *outbid notice* explaining that you're no longer the high bidder and inviting you to bid again.

There are three things worth noting about proxy bidding:

- **Bidding always goes up by one bid increment at a time.** If the current price appears to make a big jump, it's because both bidders had a maximum bid significantly higher than the opening bid. eBay increased each bid one increment at a time—but at the lightning speed of computers.

- **eBay's proxy bidding system will never bid more than your maximum bid on your behalf.** If the bidding has gone past your max and you're behind by a few cents, you have to bid again if you want to stay in the action.

- **Unlike live auctions, which keep going until no one's willing to make another bid, an eBay auction goes to the person with the highest bid at the moment the auction ends.** It's not worth trying to save a few cents by lowballing your bid, because you might find yourself outbid at the last moment—at a price that was within your range. Bid your true maximum amount, then let eBay's computers fight it out with other bidders for you until the clock runs down.

Note: A bid is a true offer to buy. Place a bid for $2.00, and you promise to pay $2.00, plus shipping costs, if you win the auction.

FREQUENTLY ASKED QUESTION

Instantly Outbid!

How can I be outbid just seconds after I placed my bid?

If you're bidding in an auction in which there are already other bidders, you might be outbid as soon as you've OK'd the amount you're willing to pay. How can this happen? Are those other bidders hovering like vultures over their computers, refreshing the auction page every few seconds, just so they can outbid you?

Unlikely. Your real opponent is proxy bidding. Remember that when you bid, eBay invites you to specify the maximum amount you're willing to pay for the item, but this amount won't necessarily be your opening bid. Instead, eBay keeps track of the amount you're willing to pay and automatically places bids for you, according to predetermined bid increments, up to your maximum amount.

Imagine you spot a good deal on an antique wooden fishing lure. You're willing to pay up to $200 (plus shipping) to add it to your collection. The current high bid, made by fishing-lure-guy, is only $49.99 and the bid increment is $1.00,

so you've got to bid at least $1.00 more than the current bid. You type in a bid for $50.99. Within seconds, you've been outbid, and fishing-lure-guy's high bid has zipped up to $51.99.

When you made your bid, eBay's computers checked to see whether any other bidders had a higher maximum bid. Fishing-lure-guy did, so eBay automatically raised his bid to beat yours.

If you bid again, specify the maximum amount you're willing to spend—in this case, $200. Now eBay keeps track of your maximum bid and raises your bids accordingly as the situation changes. You might find that you're the high bidder at $98.99. That means that fishing-lure-guy's maximum bid was $97.99. Is the lure yours? Maybe, maybe not. eBay notifies the other bidder that he's been outbid, and he might come back and raise his maximum bid. Or other fishing-lure fanatics might jump in. You never know who's won until the auction's over.

Placing a Bid

eBay gives you two ways to place a bid from the auction page. Scroll to the top of the auction page and click the Place Bid button, or save yourself a precious mouse click by heading to the "Ready to bid?" section near the bottom of the page and typing your bid into the "Your maximum bid" text box.

Tip: When you're new to eBay, start small. Learn how the system works before you make your first big purchase. Scammers often look for new eBayers, preying on their lack of eBay experience to lure them into buying an expensive—and nonexistent—motorcycle or diamond watch. For more on common scams and how to avoid them, see page 132.

If you want to start *really* small, eBay offers a test auction where you can practice bidding to get comfortable with the process before you do it for real. Type http://*pages.ebay.com/education/tutorial/course1/ bidding/index.html* into your browser's address bar or, from the Help page, select A–Z Index → P → "Proxy bidding" → "test auction."

If you click the Place Bid button, eBay takes you to the Place a Bid page, shown in Figure 2-5. Read the description to make sure the item you're bidding on is the one you want. (If you've been browsing lots of auctions, things can get a little confusing.) Check out the current bid, and then type your bid in the text box. Click the Continue button to confirm your bid.

Warning: Typing in a bid and clicking Continue *does not* mean you've bid. You must confirm the information you're submitting by clicking the Submit button on the Review and Confirm Bid page.

eBay reminds you that your bid is a contract and that the seller, not eBay, is responsible for the auction listing. Clicking the Submit button means you agree to all that (even though you already agreed to these things when you registered). Now, with your cursor hovering over the Confirm Bid button, is the time to consider whether you really want or need or can afford that set of platinum-rimmed pasta bowls.

Tip: If you notice a mistake in your bid on the Review and Confirm page—like you thought you typed 12.99 but now eBay is telling you that your maximum bid is $12,299—click the Back button on your browser and type the correct bid in the text box, then click Continue. Check to make sure that the new amount is the amount you want to bid.

The Bid Confirmation page tells you that eBay has accepted your bid and whether you're the current high bidder, as shown in Figure 2-6. Make sure that your maximum bid really is the most you're willing to pay. If you bid low and tell yourself you'll place a higher bid later, you could lose to a *sniper*—a bidder who swoops in during the closing seconds of the auction and outbids everybody. For more on sniping, including how to do it yourself, see page 104.

Tip: When you place your bid, add a few cents—$12.53 instead of $12.50, for example. To see why a couple of cents can make a big difference in who wins an auction, see the section on bid increments (page 102).

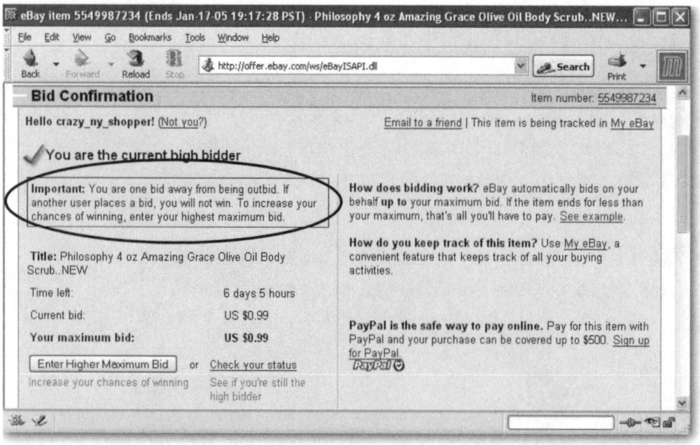

Figure 2-6:
If the current bid is the same as your maximum bid, eBay warns you that you're in danger of being outbid. You'll lose the auction if just one more bidder comes along.

When to Bid Again

Just because you bid on an item doesn't mean you'll win the auction. If someone else bids higher, you're knocked out of the game—unless you bid again.

How do you know when you've been outbid? Two ways:

- **You can tell eBay to fire off an automatic email notification telling you you've been outbid.** The email tells you the current high bid and provides a link to take you right to the auction page, so you can snatch that Elvis bobblehead doll away from the interloper who's bidding on your auction. See page 37 on how to set your notification preferences.

- **You can check the auction page from time to time.** The auction page always displays the latest bid, so you can tell at a glance whether it's higher than your max. You can also keep an eye on the auction's status in your My eBay page (page 32) under Items I'm Bidding On, although My eBay is notoriously slow to update in running auctions. Better to find the auction in My eBay, then click its title to get up-to-the-minute bidding news.

Tip: New eBayers are more likely than seasoned bidders to get caught up in a *bidding war*, where emotions (rather than market value) drive bids through the roof. Don't let excitement over an auction cause you to bid more than you're willing to pay. You can find tips for avoiding impulse bidding on page 97.

After the Auction

You've bid on a collection of rare Godzilla action figures or a musical cake plate and won your first auction. What happens now? When do you get your stuff? The first step, of course, is paying for it. And the sooner you pay, the sooner your prize will show up on your doorstep.

Note: Most sellers expect payment within three to seven days of the auction's end—this should be spelled out on the auction page. Before you place a bid, always check the seller's terms to find out how long you have to pay.

Paying the Price

When you've won an auction, eBay sends you an email to notify you of your triumph. This email gives you the seller's email address and provides a payment link. You can click the link to go to the checkout, or you can get there by logging in to eBay, going to your My eBay page's Items I've Won section, and clicking the Pay Now button.

Note: If you were watching the item before you won the auction (page 34), it appears in two places on your My eBay page: Items I'm Watching and Items I've Won.

If you're signed in, a Pay Now button also appears on the auction page, as shown in Figure 2-7. (To sign in, go to the top of the eBay home page and click the Sign In link).

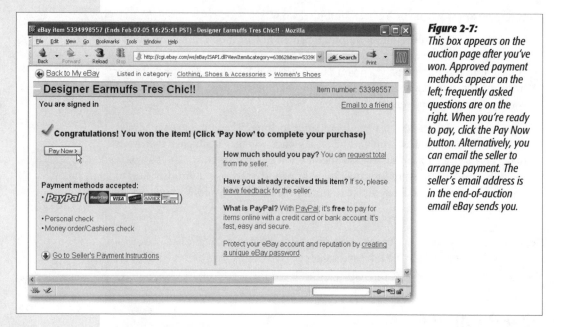

Figure 2-7:
This box appears on the auction page after you've won. Approved payment methods appear on the left; frequently asked questions are on the right. When you're ready to pay, click the Pay Now button. Alternatively, you can email the seller to arrange payment. The seller's email address is in the end-of-auction email eBay sends you.

Paying with PayPal

Most (but not all) sellers accept payment through PayPal, a money transfer company owned by eBay. PayPal lets you transfer funds from your credit card or bank account directly to the seller.

Most buyers love PayPal because it's easy and fast: from My eBay or the auction description page, you click the PayPal link and pay for your item within minutes. Information about the auction, including item number, seller, and amount, is already filled in; all you have to do is select the source of your funds (credit/debit card or bank account) and click the Send Money button. That's it: you've paid. No muss, no fuss—and it's free, too. (Free to buyers, that is; PayPal charges sellers a transaction fee. See page 165 to find out more about PayPal's charges for receiving funds. Even with the transaction fee, sellers like eBay because offering it means they don't need a merchant account with a bank in order for buyers to use credit cards to pay them.)

Note: If you pay through PayPal, many of the things you buy on eBay are eligible for up to $1,000 worth of buyer protection coverage (page 72). PayPal Buyer Protection doesn't cover motor vehicles: no cars, motorcycles, RVs, or airplanes. Sellers in Live Auctions and the Mature Audience category can't designate PayPal as a payment method, so Buyer Protection excludes those auctions, too.

There's only one catch: you have to register with PayPal before you can use the service. Fortunately, registration is free, easy, and you only have to do it once. The next section shows you how.

A Little PayPal History

In 1998, Stanford graduate Peter Thiel and Max Levchin, a Russian immigrant just a couple of years out of college, started PayPal as a way to beam money transfers securely between wireless devices, like cell phones and PDAs. Consumers didn't show much interest in that idea, and the pair turned their attention to the Internet. At the time, although online purchases were popular, paying for them often presented a problem. Back then, most eBay buyers paid for their items with checks or money orders—and waited a looong time for their merchandise to arrive.

Thiel and Levchin got the idea of transferring money via email, and they went to work on the technology that would become PayPal. All a customer needed was Internet access, an email address, and a credit card or bank account. Their technology could transfer the money to anyone, anywhere, as long as the recipient had an email address. It was fast, simple, and secure. As an added inducement, the company offered a $10 sign-up bonus to new customers in its early days.

The idea took off like a rocket. PayPal opened for business in October 1999 and had 10,000 customers by the end of that year. Just two months later, that number had increased 10 times. Today, there are more than 70 million PayPal accounts in 45 countries around the world.

PayPal was a natural choice for online auctions because it allowed buyers to transfer money quickly and at no added cost, while sellers could receive credit card payments without having to open a merchant account. The speed of its transfers also accelerated business on eBay by opening up the possibility of instantaneous payment—no longer was there any need to wait for checks to arrive in the mail and then wait some more for them to clear at the bank before an item could ship. In July of 2002, eBay bought PayPal for $1.5 billion. It's now the most popular method of payment on eBay and integrated fully into eBay.

Registering with PayPal. PayPal registration is quick and painless. All you need to get started is an email address and either a credit card or a bank account. You can pay for your first auction as soon as you've signed up.

To register, go to *www.paypal.com,* and then click the Sign Up Now link. (Or go to the bottom of eBay's home page, then click the PayPal link to pull up the PayPal home page, and then click Sign Up Now.)

Figure 2-8 shows how to get started. Choose which kind of account you want:

- **A Personal Account** lets you send and receive payments. You can't receive payments made by credit card, just direct transfers and eChecks (page 55) from a bank account. Perfect for eBayers whose main interest is shopping, personal accounts are free.

- **A Premier Account** lets you send and receive payments and also lets you receive credit card payments. For this type of account, PayPal charges a fee when you receive money. You can select this option during the sign-up process for a personal account. If you want to sell on eBay but not to start a full-blown eBay business, a premier account is a good choice, because most buyers want the option to pay with a credit card.

• **A Business Account** offers the benefits of a personal premier account under the name of your business. It also allows multiple logins for larger businesses. This kind of account works well for high-volume and specialized sellers who are running a retail business on eBay.

Figure 2-8:
To get started with PayPal, select the country in which you live or where your business is based. If you select a business account, you must provide contact info for customer service and the business owner, in addition to the business itself.

To complete registration, fill in the form asking for your name, address, and phone number; type in your email address and create a password; choose two security questions for password retrieval; and then OK the User Agreement and Privacy Policy.

After you've submitted the form, PayPal sends you an email to confirm your email address. Reply to it, and you're in.

Whenever you send money, PayPal gives you two payment options: a credit card or a bank account. A credit card is the quickest way to get started, and many buyers prefer this method because their credit card offers additional purchase protection.

Tip: Providing your credit or debit card number offers another advantage: PayPal matches up the billing address with your registration address and *voilà*—you have a PayPal confirmed address. And that's a very good thing: many eBay sellers ship only to confirmed addresses.

Setting up your bank account to pay for online purchases, which works a lot like a debit card or a check card, requires a little more patience. After you've given PayPal your account number and your bank's routing number, PayPal makes two small deposits in your account. (Nothing to get excited about—just a few cents. But you don't have to give them back.) Call your bank to find out the exact amounts, and then log in to PayPal to verify the amount of each deposit. This process proves to PayPal that your account is valid; from then on, you can use your bank account to make PayPal payments.

Confirming a bank account with PayPal makes you a verified PayPal member. Verification proves to other eBayers that you're who you say you are, making others more confident in dealing with you. In addition, PayPal imposes a $2,000 sending limit on nonverified accounts. Once you reach that limit, you can't send any more money until you get verified.

Note: You can use your bank account to pay by direct debit (for an immediate money transfer) or by *eCheck*, which is an electronic version of a bank check that takes three or four days to clear. Using an eCheck lets you start spending Great-Aunt Gertie's birthday check while you're waiting for it to clear.

Once you have a PayPal account, it's easy to pay for the eBay auctions you win. When there's a PayPal link on the auction page, just follow it. Information about the auction, including item number, seller, and amount, is already filled in. Select your payment method, and then click the Send Money button. That's it—you're done. Now you can start checking the mail for your sad-faced-clown-on-velvet artwork to arrive.

Other payment methods

Most sellers accept several forms of payment—and a few don't take PayPal (usually because they don't like PayPal fees). Depending on the individual auction, you have a number of options for forking over the money:

- **Credit card.** Some sellers accept credit cards directly, but this method is relatively rare on eBay.

- **Money order.** Money orders are a popular payment method because a money order, bought with cash up front, clears more quickly than a personal check, and the buyer retains a record that payment was made. If you pay by money order, you have to know where to send it, so you also have a traceable address for the seller.

Note: Some sellers only accept money orders bought through the U.S. Postal Service because they're tough to forge.

- **Cashier's check.** This payment method works similarly to money orders. Some sellers prefer cashier's checks to personal checks because they're less likely to bounce—you have to pay for a cashier's check before the bank will issue it to you. They're like a money order issued by your bank.

- **Personal check.** If you want to pay with a personal check (on the off chance the seller accepts checks), be prepared to be patient. You've got to wait for your check to get to its destination, for the seller to stop by the bank and deposit it, and then 10 days or so for the check to clear—all before the seller will ship your item. Not a good method for buyers craving instant gratification.

• **BidPay.** BidPay, shown in Figure 2-9, was developed by Western Union specifically for online auctions. With BidPay, you can use a credit or debit card to send funds directly to the seller's U.S. checking account, or you can have BidPay mail a money order. This method is convenient because the buyer's part of the transaction takes place online—if the seller insists on a money order, you don't need to trudge out and stand in line to buy the money order, stick it in an envelope, and drop it in the mail. BidPay's Pounds Sterling Cheque option is also a convenient way to pay U.K. sellers who don't accept PayPal. The drawback is that BidPay charges buyers a service fee; the minimum fee is $1.95.

Note: BidPay doesn't accept MasterCard as a means of payment.

Figure 2-9:
BidPay's home page lets buyers calculate the fee for using its service. You can deposit money directly into a U.S. checking account, send a money order by first-class mail, or, for an extra fee, by next- or second-day air. The service isn't cheap; for this sample $30.49 payment ($25.99 winning bid plus $4.50 for shipping), BidPay's fee is $3.95.

Even though their names are similar, don't confuse PayPal and BidPay. With PayPal, the seller pays the transaction fee—all the buyer pays for is the item, shipping, and (if it's offered and you want it) insurance. With BidPay, the buyer pays the fee. Why tack on an extra service fee to your total when you have other options?

• **Escrow.** Using an escrow service is the best way to pay for expensive items. If you buy, say, a diamond bracelet for $10,000, you're probably a little leery—with good reason—of writing a five-figure check to someone you don't know. And PayPal only protects purchases up to $1,000. For anything over $1,000, smart buyers use an *escrow service*. Here's how it works: you send your payment to the escrow service, not directly to the seller. The escrow service notifies the seller that they've received payment, and the seller ships the item to you. After you've received the item, looked it over, and approved it (for that diamond bracelet, you might also get a jeweler's appraisal), you have the escrow service release your payment to the seller.

Escrow.com, shown in Figure 2-10, is the only U.S. escrow service recommended by eBay. (For eBay-approved international escrow sites, see the list at *http://pages.ebay.com/help/confidence/payment-escrow.html#escrow*.) For a fee (a percentage of the purchase price, which is paid by the buyer), Escrow.com holds your money until you've received and inspected the item. If you reject the item, you must return it to the seller, of course—but you still pay the escrow fee and the return shipping fees.

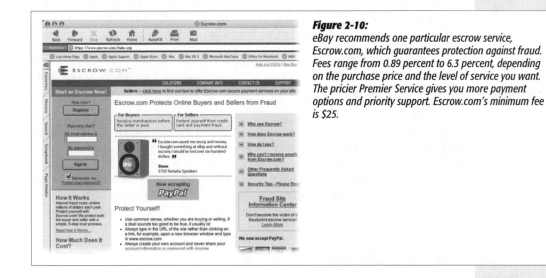

Figure 2-10:
eBay recommends one particular escrow service, Escrow.com, which guarantees protection against fraud. Fees range from 0.89 percent to 6.3 percent, depending on the purchase price and the level of service you want. The pricier Premier Service gives you more payment options and priority support. Escrow.com's minimum fee is $25.

Warning: Some particularly clever scammers have created fake Web sites for phony escrow companies, luring buyers into believing that they were dealing with a reputable escrow service when in fact they were just putting money into the scammers' pockets. To play it safe, stick to Escrow.com. For more on this kind of scam, see page 141.

- **Cash.** Would you send cash through the mail to a total stranger? Don't do it for the sake of an eBay auction, either. Too much can go wrong, leaving you with no recourse.

- **Wire transfer.** Companies like Western Union and MoneyGram provide this service. With a wire transfer, you send money to a bank or agent, and the recipient picks up the money in person. Western Union emphasizes that you should use wire transfers to send money only to someone you know—definitely *not* to a complete stranger for an online auction.

Warning: eBay recommends against using instant wire transfers. If something goes wrong, you have no recourse, even if you used a credit card to send the money. In fact, eBay actually prohibits sellers from listing wire transfer as the sole method of payment for an auction. If a seller insists that you pay via instant wire transfer, report that seller to eBay (go to Help → Contact Us → "Report problems with other eBay members"). A seller who insists on a Western Union payment is usually a seller who's trying to scam you. See page 132 for more on scams.

The exception on wire transfers occurs in European countries, where *bank-to-bank* wire transfers are a common method of payment. These are different from instant wire transfers, because the money goes into a traceable bank account, rather than being picked up in person by someone who may or may not be who they claim.

Where's My Stuff? Communicating with the Seller

At the mall, some shoppers love to chat; they'll talk about anything—the weather, their kids, the cat's latest trip to the vet—with just about anyone: the next person in line, the cashier, the bag boy. Others like to pay up and get out.

Same thing goes for the store's staff. Some shopkeepers thrive on the personal touch; they know their customers by name and go out of their way to say thank you. Others prefer to make the sale and move 'em out without so much as a "Have a nice day."

eBay's no different. With so many sellers from all over the world—stay-at-home moms selling outgrown baby outfits, harried employees trying to grow their eBay sales so they can quit their day jobs, full-time eBay powerhouses, and everything in between—it's impossible to predict how a given seller will close the sale. While after-the-auction communication is a good idea, not everyone takes the same approach. This section tells you what you can do as a buyer to keep the lines of communication open.

From buyer to seller: what to say

If you use PayPal, you don't have to do a thing. When you've made a payment, PayPal emails the seller for you, sending a payment notification and your mailing address. You're all set.

Tip: Always save the item number and your trading partner's eBay ID until the transaction is complete. You need these to get contact information or to report a problem. This information appears both in the end-of-auction email eBay sends you and on your My eBay page under Items I've Won (for 60 days or until you delete the auction).

If you're paying by check or money order, it's a good idea to email the seller to say so, and then get in touch again when you've mailed the payment. (eBay's email notification, telling you that you won an auction, contains the seller's email address; you can also use the "Ask seller a question" link from the auction page.)

Tip: You can get full contact information, including a phone number, from the Advanced Search page: Advanced Search → Find Contact Information.

Will you hear from the seller? Possibly. Keeping customers in the loop is good business practice. Some sellers contact auction winners immediately after the auction; some only get in touch if there's a problem. Many high-volume sellers use software that automatically sends out email to each winner. (You don't need to respond to such an email unless there's a request that you do so.) If you pay with PayPal immediately after an auction, you might not hear from the seller at all until the package arrives at your door. It all depends on that particular seller's way of doing business.

First-time buyers often get nervous if they don't hear from the seller within minutes of the auction's end. Give the seller a little breathing room. The only time you should start to worry is if you've emailed to ask a specific question and you don't get a response within a day or so. (Keep in mind that sellers need an occasional break from work just like the rest of us, so be patient on weekends and holidays.) Otherwise, make your payment and wait a week for your item to arrive. If it hasn't come within seven to ten days, *then* contact the seller.

Sometimes you just need to pick up the phone and hear the reassurance of a human voice. You can get a seller's telephone number from the Advanced Search page: Advanced Search → Find Contact Information. Be sure to have the item number and the seller's eBay ID at hand; eBay won't send you this information unless you're in a transaction with the other party. (Look for item number and seller ID in the Items I've Won section of your My eBay page or in the email eBay sent you at the auction's end.) Clicking Find Contact Information gets you an immediate email with the seller's phone number. At the same time, eBay notifies the seller that you've requested his contact info; that email contains your own contact information.

Having Your Say: How and When to Leave Feedback

Feedback is important for two reasons, and as a smart shopper, you already know one of them. If you've used the Feedback Forum to check out a seller's reputation before you bid, you may already have avoided a costly auction disaster by steering clear of a seller whose Member Profile is brimming over with those little red disks. Thanks to other eBayers who've taken the time to leave feedback, you can buy with confidence. And now that you've completed a purchase, it's time to return the favor.

The other reason feedback is important is that it gives *you* credibility as a buyer. Perhaps you've come across a few auctions warning, "I'll cancel all bids placed by zero-feedback bidders!" Sellers, just like you, want to be sure they can trust the other party. And, really, why should they trust *you*? You know you're an honest buyer, but they can't see who's hiding behind that big$pender321 or shop-til-1-drop eBay ID. (And later, if you decide to sell on eBay, a good feedback score will make other eBayers want to buy from you.) So you need to collect some feedback, reach for that first gold star (see the box on page 43), to show the eBay community you mean business.

> **Note:** Feedback appears on individual eBayers' Member Profile pages (Figure 2-2).

In fact, if you think of eBay as a community, you can also think of leaving feedback as your civic duty. You do your bit to spread the word about good and bad sellers. In return, you get a reliable way to tell the good guys from the scammers. And, when someone leaves you positive feedback, not only does it increase your standing in the community, it just plain feels good.

> **Note:** *Don't* use feedback to communicate with the seller. You get one chance to leave feedback per auction; don't waste it on something you should be handling in email. Sellers will get justifiably annoyed with you if you leave a neutral feedback saying something like "Just wondering if you've sent my iPod yet"–you've lost them a feedback point. Communicate with your trading partner through email, not through the Feedback Forum. If email doesn't seem to be getting through, you can get the seller's phone number from eBay (as long as you're involved in an active transaction with the seller). Go to Advanced Search → Find Contact Information and fill in the item number and seller's eBay ID.

TROUBLESHOOTING MOMENT

Buyer Activity Limits

Here's one more reason to build up your feedback score. eBay places *buyer activity limits,* which can restrict your bidding and buying, on low-feedback accounts. You'll know if eBay has slapped a buyer activity limit on you because you won't be able to bid.

eBay is a little cagey about exactly what buyer activity limits are and exactly who might get slapped with restrictions. In fact, eBay refuses to publish the actual rules. But if you're new to the site (or even if you've been around for a while but you have fewer than, say, five feedbacks), here are some activities that might restrict your ability to bid:

- A whole bunch of winning bids in current auctions—and no, eBay won't say exactly what constitutes "a whole bunch."

- An unusually high number of auctions won in a short time—again, eBay doesn't define these terms.

- A high dollar amount being bid on a bunch of auctions at once.

- A lot of items that you've won but haven't paid for yet.

For example, if you've got three feedbacks so far and you've won auctions worth, say, $5,000 in a couple of days and you're currently winning another $3,500 worth of auctions, eBay *might* limit your ability to bid on anything else.

eBay is keeping mum about exactly what buyer activity limits are and exactly when they apply because it's caught between a rock and a hard place on this issue. On the one hand, half of all Unpaid Item (UPI) complaints are against bidders with a feedback score below five, and eBay wants to protect sellers from clueless bidders. On the other hand, everyone started out with a feedback score of zero, and eBay wants to encourage new buyers to spend as much money as they can stand to spend on the site.

To avoid buyer activity limits, build up your feedback score by buying a few items at a time. Don't go crazy and spend your whole paycheck the first afternoon you shop on eBay.

How to leave feedback

The time to leave feedback is after the money and the goods have changed hands, after you've resolved any problems, or when it's clear that you won't be able to resolve those problems—in other words, when the transaction is absolutely positively over and done with. If you receive your item in a reasonable amount of time and are happy with it, leave positive feedback for the seller. You may or may not receive feedback in return. Some sellers wait until the buyer has left feedback first to show that they're happy with their purchase. Other sellers (usually high-volume sellers) leave feedback in batches every couple of weeks.

Tip: If you're new to eBay and you need to boost your feedback score, a good way to determine whether an eBayer is likely to leave you feedback is to check his or her Member Profile and read the feedback left for others. If there's nothing there, don't expect to get any feedback. Look for sellers who've left more feedback than they've received—a good sign that they know the importance of feedback.

To leave feedback, go to My eBay (page 32). On your My eBay page, under Items I've Won, find the auction you want to leave feedback for and click the Leave Feedback link. This link takes you to the Feedback Forum: Leave Feedback page. eBay automatically fills in the eBay ID and item number for which you're leaving feedback.

Alternatively, you can look on the left side of your My eBay page for My eBay Views, and then click the Feedback link there. The page that opens shows recent feedback you've received and any auctions you haven't left feedback for. Click the Leave Feedback button to go to the Feedback Forum, shown in Figure 2-11.

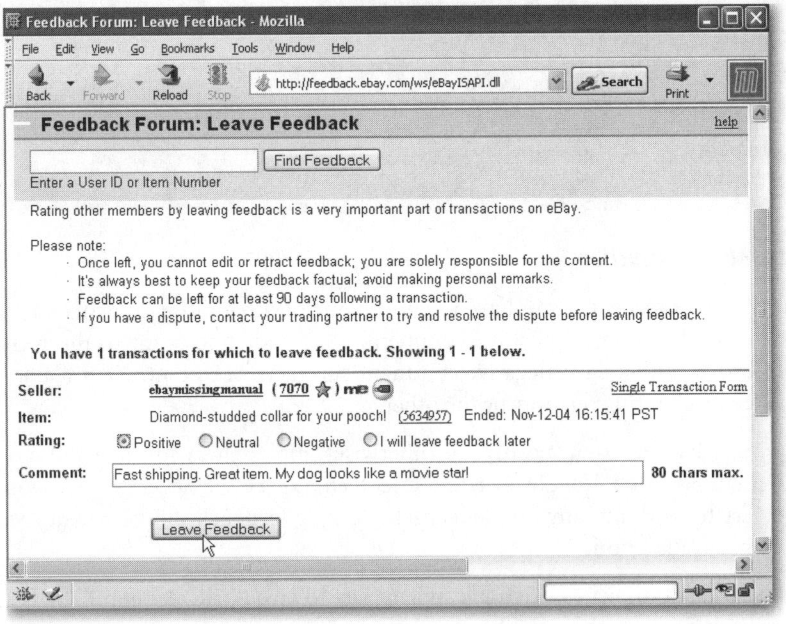

Figure 2-11:
The cardinal rule of feedback: be professional. Focus on the facts and don't indulge in name-calling or personal digs. If you use obscenities or publicize personal information or Web addresses in the Feedback Forum, eBay might remove your feedback. You can't retract feedback after you click that Leave Feedback button, so choose your words with care.

Tip: Here's yet another way to get to the Feedback Forum: from your My eBay page, under Items I've Won, click an auction's title to go to the auction page and then click the Leave Feedback button. Taking this route lets you review the auction page and make sure you're leaving feedback for the right transaction.

Below the ID and the item number is where you leave feedback. You can rate a transaction as positive, negative, or neutral. Your comment can be 80 characters, maximum.

On the Feedback Forum page, eBay reminds you of a few things:

- **Say what you mean.** You can't change or delete feedback once you've left it.

- **Make every effort to resolve disputes before heading for the Feedback Forum.** You have about 90 days (sometimes a little longer) to leave feedback.

- **Stick to the facts of the transaction.** Don't let things get personal—avoid name-calling and your keyboard's Caps Lock key (using all capital letters looks like you're yelling).

Note: Always double-check that the auction you're about to leave feedback for is the one you intend. Because feedback is so crucial to the eBay community, you don't want to accidentally leave negative feedback for a flawless transaction or positive feedback for a disaster.

WORKAROUND WORKSHOP

How to Leave Feedback More than 90 Days After the Auction Has Ended

Many eBayers don't realize that it's possible to leave feedback beyond the 60 days that the auction appears on your My eBay page or the 90 days that an auction link stays live in your Member Profile.

To leave late feedback, you must have the other person's eBay ID and the item number at hand, so be sure to hang on to these; they're in the email eBay sends you when you've won an auction.

From your My eBay page, click Feedback → Leave Feedback → Single Transaction Form. On the page that opens, type in the eBay ID and the item number, then fill out the feedback form as usual.

How to rate a transaction

When you leave feedback, you have to choose one of three ratings: positive, negative, or neutral. For every positive comment, eBay adds one point to the recipient's feedback rating. Each negative comment subtracts one point. Neutrals don't affect a feedback rating one way or the other.

Once you've left feedback (positive or otherwise), most sellers consider the transaction final. So don't leave a negative and *then* expect the seller to give you a refund. Try to work out any problems first—leaving feedback should be your very last step in a transaction.

Here are some examples of when it's appropriate to give positive, neutral, or negative feedback. Some of them might surprise you:

- **Positive.** You're satisfied with how the auction went. If you're the buyer, the item was as described on the auction page and arrived well packed and in a reasonable amount of time. If you're the seller, the buyer paid in good time.

- **Positive.** The item was not as described on the auction page or arrived damaged, but the seller agreed to replace it or to refund your money. That's good customer service, and it deserves praise.

- **Positive.** You didn't read the auction page carefully, and the seller is charging shipping and handling fees you think are too high, or else the item arrived with scratches or scuffs *described in the auction* that you missed when you glanced at the item description. You're the one at fault—not the seller—if you didn't scrutinize the terms and the item description. Bidding on an auction means that you agree to all terms set forth on the auction page.

- **Positive.** If you're the seller and a buyer's personal check bounced, but the buyer made up for it by paying promptly via another method.

- **Neutral.** It's hard to know when to give neutral feedback. eBay's own Help section doesn't offer any guidelines about leaving a neutral. If your transaction partner was rude or difficult to deal with but the transaction did take place, a neutral might be in order. Similarly, if you had to file a report with eBay to push the other person to complete the transaction, but they did complete it, you might consider a neutral.

Warning: Many eBayers consider a neutral almost as bad as a negative, and some will leave a retaliatory negative if you give them a neutral rating. It's not fair, it's not professional, but it happens. When you're tempted to give a neutral, consider not leaving any feedback at all instead.

- **Negative.** Your trading partner refuses to complete the transaction. If this happens, you should allow a reasonable amount of time to pass and file the appropriate report with eBay (see page 71 for an item you didn't receive or page 184 for a winning bidder who wouldn't pay). Sometimes, all a "forgetful" trading partner needs is a little reminder from the eBay powers-that-be. If such a reminder doesn't work, though, leaving a negative feedback will warn other eBayers about doing business with this person.

Leaving feedback comments

Comments let you tell what really happened during an exchange. A positive rating is all well and good, but a comment like, "Knock-out customer service—and they hid salt-water taffy in the packaging!" paints a useful picture of your experience.

In your feedback comments, consider naming the item that changed hands. That way, even after the link to the auction page disappears, other eBayers reading feedback will know what the auction was for. "Great egg boiler!" is much more specific than "great item!" Knowing what you bought or sold can be helpful to eBayers involved in similar transactions. Wouldn't you think twice about buying a pricey pickup truck from someone who's sold nothing but patented egg boilers for the past year?

It takes a little time to get a feel for what kind of feedback is appropriate. If you're researching sellers by reading their feedback, you'll soon learn how typical feedback reads—and what sticks out like a sore thumb. Inappropriate feedback reflects more poorly on the giver than the receiver.

Note: There are a few things you *can't* say in feedback: no obscenity, no personal information or links to Web pages, no references to any official investigation (by eBay, PayPal, or law enforcement). For more details, including how to get eBay-forbidden feedback removed, see the box on page 66.

FREQUENTLY ASKED QUESTION

Negging vs. Reporting

Why should I file a report if there's a problem? Won't someone with a lot of bad feedback get kicked off eBay?

Negative feedback is a last resort, not a way to solve a problem. If someone refuses to follow through on a transaction, report that person to eBay. Reporting eBayers who misuse the site is far more important than leaving negative feedback; eBay doesn't monitor the comments in the Feedback Forum, so the only way to make your complaint known to eBay itself is to file a report (pages 71 and 184).

If you do, eBay may designate the culprit "No longer a registered user" (NARU), which is eBay-speak for getting kicked off the site. A nonpaying bidder who has several Unpaid Item (UPI) disputes reported by different sellers in a short time will be NARU'd. Similarly, sellers who break the rules— like not sending an item you paid for or trying to lure you off eBay to complete a sale—face penalties that range from warnings to getting NARU'd.

eBay does automatically NARU eBayers whose overall feedback score drops to -4. But for a high-volume seller with thousands of sales each month, it's possible to do terrible business and still *stay* in business; as long as the seller gets a few more positives than negatives, his feedback score will never drop all the way to -4. eBay will never know that there's a problem unless burned buyers send in a report.

Responding to feedback

As a buyer, you get to leave feedback for the seller. But the seller also gets to leave feedback for *you*—and every once in a while, you might be surprised by a negative comment that appears to come out of left field.

It used to be that whoever left you feedback had the last word. You could leave that person feedback in return, of course, but your comments would be over on their Member Profile. Anyone reading feedback left for you wouldn't get your side of the story unless they looked for it. You didn't get a chance to explain.

eBay fixed this problem by allowing follow-ups to feedback. For every feedback you receive, you have the option of posting a response. The person who left you feedback can follow up their original comment with a second one. Those are the limits, though: one response from the receiver and one follow-up from the giver. eBay doesn't want feedback turning into a discussion board with long back-and-forth threads. Figure 2-12 shows you what a response and follow-up look like.

To respond to a feedback comment, go to My eBay → Feedback → "View all feedback" → "Reply to feedback received" to see your feedback. In the far-right column of the comment you want to reply to, there's a Reply link. Click it, and then type your reply into the text box. Replies can be a maximum of 80 characters, so make each one count.

Figure 2-12:
If you get negative feedback, don't panic. Just respond to it, explaining what happened, so other eBayers can see both sides of the story. A calm, factual response looks a lot better than accusations hurled in all caps. Even though this eBayer got a negative, the response and follow-up reveal who's being unreasonable here.

Agreeing to disagree: mutual feedback withdrawal

Sometimes eBayers (but not you!) post negative feedback in the heat of the moment and *then* manage to resolve the dispute that prompted it, leaving them wishing they hadn't been so quick to slam the other person in the Feedback Forum. You can't take back feedback you've left, but if you have a change of heart, eBay gives you the option of *mutual feedback withdrawal (MFW)*, which means that the rating disappears from the comment and no longer affects the feedback score, but the comment itself remains. It's mutual because both parties must agree, and both parties get their feedback withdrawn. Here's how to do it:

1. **Contact the other person.**

   Feedback withdrawal has to be mutual, so it's a good idea to let the other person know you're starting the process before you do anything on the eBay site. If you both agree to withdraw the feedback, the other steps are easy. But if the other person refuses to withdraw feedback, the other steps are pointless.

2. **Find the Mutual Feedback Withdrawal form.**

   From your My eBay page, choose Feedback → "Go to Feedback Forum" → "Feedback disputes" → "mutual feedback withdrawal."

3. **Type in the item number for the feedback you wish to withdraw, and then click Continue.**

   If you don't have the item number handy, you can find it on your Member Profile page (click your eBay ID), in the far-right column of the piece of feedback you're withdrawing.

4. **Explain why you want to withdraw the feedback.**

   The page that opens shows you the feedback given and received (if any) for this transaction. Make sure the auction is the right one. Then type a message into the text box, explaining to the other person why you want to withdraw the feedback you left. Click Continue.

5. **Let eBay do its stuff.**

eBay contacts the other person, who must agree to withdraw the feedback. If eBay receives the other person's consent within 30 days after the posting of the comment or 90 days after the end of the auction (whichever is later), eBay withdraws the feedback.

TROUBLESHOOTING MOMENT

Feedback Is Forever—or Is It?

In general, feedback that you leave or get is part of your permanent record on eBay. Even if you change your eBay ID, your feedback carries over from the old ID to the new one. You can hide your feedback, but even private feedback isn't all that private to someone who knows how to ferret out the comments. And mutual withdrawal doesn't remove a comment—just that comment's effect on your feedback score.

Are there any circumstances under which eBay will remove feedback? A few. If a comment violates eBay's feedback policy, you can petition eBay to have it removed. But eBay's conditions are strict; they'll remove only the following kinds of feedback:

- Feedback with language that's obscene or racist. (Most garden-variety name-calling, from "liar" to "thief" to "scam artist," does not fall under this category.)

- Feedback that contains a link or reference to a non-eBay Web site.

- Feedback that reveals personal information about another eBayer, such as the person's real name, street address, phone number, or email address.

- Feedback that refers to an investigation by eBay, PayPal, or a law enforcement agency.

- Feedback that was left for one eBayer when another was intended, but only if identical feedback has already been left for the correct eBayer.

- Feedback that was left by someone ineligible to use eBay or whose contact information is invalid.

- Feedback that was left by someone who bid on an item not to buy it, but solely to be able to leave negative feedback.

- Feedback that is considered libelous or slanderous by the courts—accompanied by a court order to prove it.

If you'd like to remove feedback that meets one or more of these conditions, go to Help → Contact Us → "Report problems with other eBay members" → Feedback Concerns, and choose the type of feedback problem you're having. Click Continue, and then click the Email link. Fill out the form, giving all the information eBay requests, such as the other eBayer's ID and the item number of the auction. (You can get both of these things from the actual feedback comment.) You can speed up your request if you copy and paste in the rule that the feedback violates.

If the feedback meets eBay's criteria, eBay will remove it. But be aware that eBay's definition of what's vulgar or harassing might not match yours.

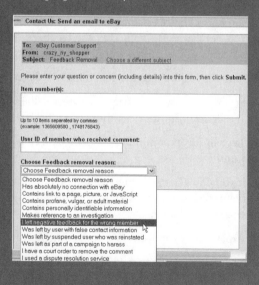

When eBay withdraws feedback, it adds a note to the comments in the affected Membership Profiles, saying that the rating was mutually withdrawn, and the positive, negative, or neutral symbol disappears.

Note: You can request no more than five MFW requests per 30 days. (And if you need more than this, there's something wrong with your approach to feedback. Go back and read the guidelines to feedback ratings on page 62.)

Occasionally, you might go through the mutual-feedback-withdrawal process for an auction where only one party has left feedback. For example, perhaps your check really *did* get lost in the mail, and a seller left you negative feedback. Then your check shows up, with postmarks from Kankakee to Kokomo, and the seller realizes you were telling the truth and wants to cancel the neg. You haven't left feedback yet, but the only way to withdraw the neg is to go through the MFW process. After you've gone through that process, the case is closed—on both sides. You can't leave feedback for the seller.

Note: You might hear that an organization called Square Trade can get feedback removed. This isn't true. Square Trade is a mediation service recommended by eBay for settling disputes. It's free if you use Square Trade to facilitate direct negotiation, but if you decide to bring in a professional mediator, you pay a fee. And since February 9, 2004, Square Trade can only get feedback comments *withdrawn*, not removed.

Buyers' Woes and What to Do About Them

Shakespeare knew that "the course of true love never did run smooth"; sometimes, the course of commerce takes a bumpy road, too. Most eBay transactions begin and end without a hitch. But the eBay world isn't perfect. This section describes some common problems buyers face and what to do about them.

The Seller Cancels Your Bid on Your Very First Auction

Sellers have the option of canceling bids or blocking bidders from their auctions. They don't have to give a reason. Some sellers are wary of new buyers with no feedback and will cancel bids from zero-feedback buyers if they see them. From a new buyer's point of view, this stinks. How can you earn feedback if you can't even bid?

You have a couple of options.

One option is to email the seller (use the "Ask seller a question" link on the auction page). Explain that you're new to eBay but you understand the rules and are serious about bidding. Emphasize that you know that a bid is a binding agreement and you intend to follow through if you win. This sort of communication will convince many sellers that you're sincere and will lead them to let you to bid on the auction.

Note: Sellers can set their auctions to automatically block bids from buyers with a negative feedback score or who live in countries the seller doesn't ship to.

The other option is to build up your feedback rating by buying several inexpensive items quickly, paying up even more quickly, and leaving good feedback for the seller. (BIN auctions, on page 26, are great for building up a history on eBay—a couple of clicks and you've bought the item, and you don't have to wait a week for an auction to end.) After a sale, you can politely request feedback from the seller with an email that says something like, "I received the rainbow-striped toe socks today and was very pleased. I've left you positive feedback and hope you'll do the same for me." As long as you pay promptly and focus on good communication, your feedback rating should increase.

Tip: Don't plague a seller by sending daily emails demanding feedback. Some sellers leave their feedback in batches, so it might take them a while to get around to yours. Others choose not to leave feedback at all. Remember that feedback is voluntary. And if you make a pest of yourself, you might get an unwanted negative.

You Made a Mistake in Your Bid

Sometimes, in the heat of the moment, you make a mistake in your bid. Typing 3599 when you meant to type 35.99 can be an expensive mistake. Or you might make a bid and then think of a question to ask the seller, but the seller doesn't answer your emails and you're starting to have doubts about dealing with this person. Or you go back to check out an auction to see whether you're still the high bidder, and the seller has edited the item description to say, "Oops! I typed in 14K gold but the ring is 14K gold-*plated*." If you make a mistake while bidding or change your mind about the auction, is it too late to take your bid back?

You can retract a bid, but only in certain circumstances:

- **You made a typographical error.** If you typed in the wrong amount, you can retract your bid, but you must specify the correct bid immediately after the retraction. If you retract your bid for this reason without submitting a new bid and eBay finds out, you could be NARU'd—suspended from eBay. (How would eBay know? The seller might report you.)

- **You can't contact the seller.** This reason doesn't refer to a seller who's simply slow to respond to emails. If a phone has been disconnected or an email is returned to you as undeliverable, then you can use this option.

- **The seller changed the item description on you.** If the auction page changes to show that the item you thought you were bidding on isn't what the seller has up for sale, you can retract your bid.

Note: Buyer's remorse isn't a valid reason to retract a bid. Once you've bid on an item or clicked the Buy It Now button, you can't change your mind just for the heck of it. That's one big difference between eBay and the local mall—you can't simply return something if you decide you don't really want it.

To retract a bid, go to the navigation bar and click "services," scroll down the Services page to Bidding and Buying Services, and then click the "Retract your bid" link. (eBay asks you to sign in or confirm your password.) Most of the Bid Retractions page is a lecture on why you shouldn't do what you're about to do. At the bottom of the page is the Bid Retraction form, shown in Figure 2-13.

Tip: If you want to retract a bid, try contacting the seller first and asking them politely to cancel your bid. The seller has no obligation to do so and will probably refuse, but sometimes a sympathetic seller will help you out. If the seller cancels your bid, you won't have to worry about a bid retraction appearing in your Member Profile.

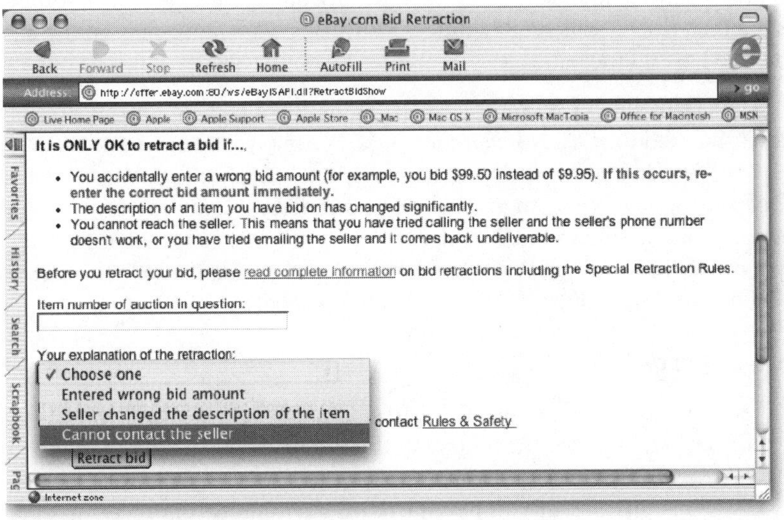

Figure 2-13:
To retract a bid using this form, type in the item number (from the auction page), select your reason for retracting, and then click the Retract Bid button. Avoid retracting a bid unless you have a valid reason—bid retractions become public knowledge, and they don't endear you to sellers.

Bid retractions come with a ticking clock. If you placed your bid more than 12 hours before the auction is due to end, you can't retract it during the last 12 hours of the auction (although you may be able to sweet-talk the seller into canceling it for you). If you placed your bid during the last 12 hours of the auction, you must retract it within one hour of when you placed it, or the bid stands.

Sometimes retractions are unavoidable. But don't take back your bid unless you really have to. A count of the bid retractions you've made during the past six months shows up in your Membership Profile, as shown in Figure 2-14, for all the world to see. Too many bid retractions will make sellers block you from their auctions. You can also get NARU'd if another user (like a disgruntled seller) reports you for having too many retractions.

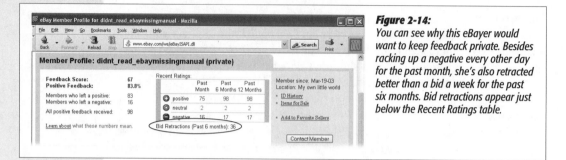

Figure 2-14:
You can see why this eBayer would want to keep feedback private. Besides racking up a negative every other day for the past month, she's also retracted better than a bid a week for the past six months. Bid retractions appear just below the Recent Ratings table.

You Don't Hear from the Seller After the Auction

Buyers, especially rookies, can be understandably impatient to get their stuff. But here's another way in which eBay differs from the mall—no instant gratification. You have to have a little patience.

eBay suggests that the buyer and the seller establish contact within three business days after the auction ends. Note *business* days. For many sellers, eBay *is* their business. They want to relax a little on evenings, weekends, and holidays, just like everyone else. So if you win an auction on Friday night, Monday is day one of the contact period. For similar reasons, if you don't receive a response to your email within a couple hours of sending it, chill out and give it some time. The seller may be in a different time zone or may not live at the computer.

When to contact the seller

Even after you wait the recommended three days, not all sellers will get in touch with you. Some simply ship the item after they've received payment. Having little or no contact with the buyer isn't the best way to do business, obviously, because it makes customers anxious. If you haven't heard anything within three or so days after you've paid, email the seller to ask whether your item has shipped.

Tip: The email you receive from eBay at the end of the auction contains the seller's email address. If you didn't save this eBay email, you can contact the seller by going to My eBay → Items I've Won, and then clicking the seller's ID, which takes you to the seller's Member Profile page. From there, click the Contact Member button. Or go to the auction page of the item you won and click "Ask seller a question."

If time keeps passing without a response, you can request the seller's contact information and try to get in touch by phone. See page 58 to find out how to get the phone number of an eBayer you're doing business with.

Tip: Spam filters are great for keeping the junk out of your inbox, but sometimes they trap legitimate email. If you don't get a response from a seller to email you've sent from your own address, your emails might be disappearing into a spam filter the seller (or the seller's Internet service provider) set up. Try calling, or use the Contact Member button on the seller's Member Profile page to send your email. Emails sent via eBay go both to the seller's email address and to the My Messages section of the seller's My eBay page.

When to report the seller

If you call and email and still can't contact the seller, it might be time to file an Item Not Received report, found through the Help page's Security Center link (Figure 2-15). You should try to contact the seller for at least two weeks after the auction ends before you file a report, though; eBay won't even let you file a report until 10 days have gone by.

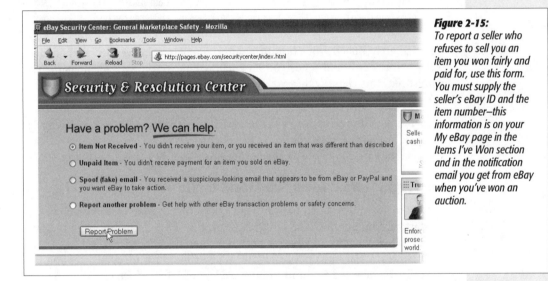

Figure 2-15:
To report a seller who refuses to sell you an item you won fairly and paid for, use this form. You must supply the seller's eBay ID and the item number—this information is on your My eBay page in the Items I've Won section and in the notification email you get from eBay when you've won an auction.

If you've paid and the seller hasn't sent the item and won't respond to your attempts to make contact, take these additional steps:

- **File an eBay Item Not Received (INR) report.** eBay gives you up to 60 days after the auction ends to file a fraud alert. Don't miss that 60-day deadline, though, or you're out of luck. If you need to report a fraud, find the auction in your My eBay page, and then click the "Report an Item Not Received" link.

  If you paid with PayPal, start your complaint process with eBay. When you've finished filling out the "Item Not Received" form, eBay sends you to PayPal, where you can let PayPal know about the problem. Later, if PayPal finds in your favor, it issues a report to eBay about the seller. But if you skip the eBay process and go straight to PayPal to get your money back, eBay will never know there was a problem. Since INR reports are what get a bad seller kicked off eBay, it's important to go through eBay's channels first.

- **Notify your payment provider.** If the seller has accepted your PayPal payment, you must file your claim with PayPal within 45 days of the transaction; PayPal allows up to three Buyer Protection claims per buyer per year. If the seller hasn't accepted the payment, you can simply cancel it. With BidPay, you can cancel your money order request if it hasn't been marked "approved" or "mailed" on your BidPay History and Status page. If you used a credit card, the purchases you make on eBay are covered by the card issuer's standard protections, so you might be able to chargeback the payment. If you paid by personal check, call your bank to see whether the check has cleared. If not, you can usually stop payment.

Note: If you used a credit card to pay via PayPal, file your claim through PayPal before you contact your credit card company. If you don't follow PayPal's procedure, PayPal could suspend your account. Later, if PayPal denies your claim, you can still call your credit card issuer and see if they can help.

- **File an eBay Buyer Protection Program claim.** After you've filed a fraud alert, eBay processes it and sends you an email telling you how to file a claim. You must file your claim within 90 days of the auction's end. Again, don't let that deadline slip by!

When you buy, it's nice to know that eBay has procedures in place to protect your purchase. Most of the time you won't need them, but if you encounter a rare deadbeat seller, be sure you know what your options—and their deadlines—are.

You Bought It Now when You Meant to Bid

The way to avoid this dilemma is to read what's on your computer screen before you start clicking buttons. The Buy It Now process is very different from bidding. When you bid, you type in your maximum bid and then confirm it. When you use Buy It Now, you have no opportunity to specify a bid. Instead, eBay takes you to a page called Review and Commit to Buy (see Figure 2-16), which lists the item title and number, the BIN price, additional charges (shipping/handling and insurance), and payment methods. eBay also reminds you that you're making a commitment to buy the item when you use BIN. Even the button you click reflects the binding nature of what you're about to do: rather than Confirm Bid, it says Commit to Buy.

So if you goof, it's possible that you just clicked a series of buttons without reading carefully, thinking you were bidding or putting the item into a shopping cart. Fine. But don't expect the seller to accept that as an excuse. When you click the Commit to Buy button, you're agreeing to a legally binding contract. Most sellers will hold you to your purchase; if you don't pay, they'll file an Unpaid Item (UPI) dispute, which will result in an Unpaid Item strike against you. Too many strikes from

different sellers and you're out of the game—you get NARU status and are suspended from using the site.

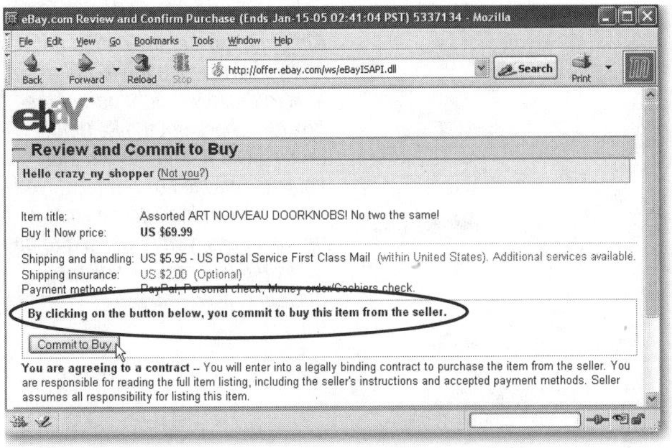

Figure 2-16:
eBay gives you plenty of warnings that you're really about to buy something when you click the Buy It Now button. Always be sure to read the page carefully so you know what you're about to do when you click the button.

Note: An Unpaid Item strike doesn't affect a buyer's feedback rating, but buyers and sellers both can leave feedback for auctions involving unpaid items. UPI strikes are a private, administrative matter between a nonpaying bidder and eBay, but unhappy sellers can—and do—speak up loudly in the Feedback Forum when someone doesn't pay.

Occasionally, a sympathetic seller might take pity and agree you don't have to pay. But you can still expect that seller to file a UPI dispute against you—it's a necessary part of the process for the seller to recoup the fees eBay has collected for the completed auction. When you get an email asking if you agree to a "mutually agreed" UPI dispute resolution, say "yes." Otherwise, you'll end up with a UPI strike *and* an unhappy seller on her way to the Feedback Forum.

You Were Outbid—But Then You Won

Winning an auction you "lost" sounds impossible, but it can happen. When you're outbid and you don't want to go any higher, the natural thing to do is to look for and bid on another, similar item. After all, someone outbid you on that first crystal chandelier, and you really need one for next month's ball. But be careful—you might end up with two crystal chandeliers when your ballroom has space for just one.

Here's how it works. Say you were outbid. If the winning bidder retracts his bid or the seller cancels the high bid (perhaps because it was made by a buyer who's given the seller trouble in the past), you might find yourself in the #1 spot again—when you'd thought you were out of the running. In fact, eBay warns you this might happen in its outbid notice, shown in Figure 2-17.

The moral? If you're outbid, wait until the auction ends before you bid on another auction for the same thing.

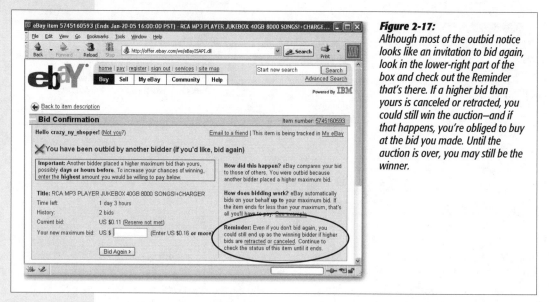

Figure 2-17:
Although most of the outbid notice looks like an invitation to bid again, look in the lower-right part of the box and check out the Reminder that's there. If a higher bid than yours is canceled or retracted, you could still win the auction—and if that happens, you're obliged to buy at the bid you made. Until the auction is over, you may still be the winner.

You Bid Against Yourself

Sounds like a sitcom plot—but it's actually just an aspect of proxy bidding (page 47), in which eBay's computers bid on your behalf. There's no particular recourse for it, but here's the backstory.

Say you're already the high bidder, but you're going to be on a sun-drenched beach in Tahiti when the auction ends (*sans* laptop, naturally) and you want to raise your high bid before your flight leaves to make sure you get the item. You go back to the auction page and submit a new bid. Even though you were already the high bidder, the current bid jumps to a higher amount the second you place the new bid.

What happened? One of the following scenarios:

• If the auction is a reserve auction (page 25) and your new bid meets or surpasses the reserve price, your current bid jumps to the reserve.

• If you and another bidder offered the same dollar amount, but you're the high bidder because eBay processed your bid first, your bid goes up by one bid increment (somewhere between $0.05 and $100, depending on the price of the item you're bidding for) to put you firmly in the lead.

• If you lead the auction by less than one full bid increment over the second highest bidder, when you submit a new bid, eBay increases the amount of your current bid to equal a full bid increment over the next highest bid. For example, say your previous maximum bid was $14.92, and that's the current high bid. When you raise your maximum bid to $20.00, eBay increases your bid to $15.00 to make it a full bid increment over the next highest bidder's $14.50. That's not a big deal when you're in the range of 50-cent bid increments, but be aware that bid increments increase as prices climb—up to a maximum of $100 (ouch!) for items costing $5,000 or more.

Note: Learn more than you ever thought possible about bid increments on page 102.

Finding—and Getting— Bargains

Spending money on eBay is a snap. What's tricky is learning how to do it *wisely*.

Two things stand between you and smart shopping: more listings than you can shake a mouse at, and scads of eager bargain hunters. To get an edge, you have to search better than the competition, and you have to bid smarter. This chapter shows you how.

Here's what it covers:

- How to find the hidden bargains that other shoppers miss.
- How to comparison-shop for the best deal.
- How to avoid impulse buying (and the buyer's remorse that goes with it).
- How to *snipe* (win an auction at the last minute).
- How to boost your odds of winning Dutch auctions.
- How to find deals off eBay's beaten path.

Tips and Tricks for Serious Searchers

Smart searching involves more than typing a couple of words into a text box and clicking the Search button. Sure, a simple search gives you a list of results—but that's what every other shopper on eBay is getting, too. You're out to find the bargains others miss. Chapter 1 illustrated the basics of searching. This section turbocharges your searches.

eBay has so many items—more than 10 million auctions are running on any given day—that searching can quickly become difficult and frustrating. For example, a search that seems straightforward, like NASCAR, can bring up thousands of items you probably never even thought of: not just the tickets you were looking for, but pet bandanas, bracelet charms, cell phone casings, calendars, pillows, and tons more. You can refine your searches to pinpoint items by learning how to work the system.

Speak the Search Engine's Language

Precision-tune your search by telling eBay's search engine exactly what you want. You can use symbols to make searching easier:

- **Quotation marks.** Put quotation marks around any two or more words to force them to appear as a phrase in the results. For example, typing in *boots* gets you around 65,000 or so results: cowboy boots, ski boots, rain boots, work boots—the list goes on and on. Type *"ankle boots"* and the search engine cuts to the chase, winnowing out 62,000 or so results you don't want, so you can focus on the auctions you do want.

Tip: Narrow your search even further by clicking the most appropriate link in the Matching Categories menu on the left-hand side of the page. Doing so restricts your results to auctions listed in that category.

- **Asterisk.** The asterisk is an immensely useful *wildcard* character, which stands in for a letter or letters. It's great if you don't know the exact spelling of something. Search for *"Engelb* Humperdin*"* to find that rare Englebert Humperdinck LP for your mother's birthday. eBay doesn't allow wildcard searches with fewer than two letters. But given the six trillion results you'd get from typing, say, *m**, that's not usually a disappointing limitation.

Tip: If you're searching for a keyword that could be either singular or plural, don't bother to use an asterisk. eBay automatically expands your search to include singular and plural versions of common keywords. So if you're in the market for one or more teacups, type in *teacup* to have eBay show you auctions for just one cup and for those offering a cupboard full. If, however, you don't want eBay to perform this service for you—if, for example, you're looking for a single teacup to complete a set, use quotes to get the search the way you want it: *"teacup"*. Putting quotes around a single word forces eBay to search for that word exactly the way you typed it.

- **Minus sign.** Put a minus sign in front of a word or phrase you want to *exclude* from your search. If you're a Francophile rather than a hotel-chain-heiress fan, type *Paris -Hilton* and see how much junk disappears from your screen.

Note: Make sure there's a space before that minus sign. Otherwise, the word becomes *part* of your search, rather than excluded from your search.

- **Parentheses.** To find possible variations of a word, put them in parentheses to have eBay search for both versions. Separate the terms with a comma but no spaces. A collector of medieval battle axes who searches for *(medieval,mediaeval,midevil)* gets results whether the seller used the American spelling, the British spelling, or a terrible but common misspelling. A recent search for all three terms produced nearly 100 more listings than searching for *medieval* alone.

Tip: Use a minus sign with parentheses to exclude multiple terms from your search. If you don't want your search for a cell phone to bring up auctions for cell phone cases or flashing keypads or antennas, type *"cell phone" -(case,flashing)*. Don't let a space sneak in between the minus sign and the open parenthesis.

Search for Items by Bidder

After you've spent some time on eBay, you're likely to notice another bidder or two with tastes or interests similar to yours. eBay lets you tag along as they hunt for bargains, by searching for items by those bidders' eBay IDs. Searching by bidder is a great way to use others' search skills to find items and see what others are willing to pay for them.

First, find the eBay ID of a bidder you want to shadow. One way to do this is to look on your My eBay page (page 32) for an auction you didn't win (in My Summary, scroll down the page until you find Items I Didn't Win, or, from the eBay Views menu, look under All Buying and then click Didn't Win), click the item's title, and notice the ID of the winning bidder. Another way to find the ID of a bidder worth tailing is to spend a little time researching completed auctions for items you want. In the upper-right corner of any page, click the Advanced Search link. Type your item in the Search page's text box, then turn on the "Completed listings only" checkbox before you click the Search button.

Note: You have to be registered and signed in to search for items in completed auctions.

As you look through the search results, watch for auctions that ended successfully with one or more bidders. Check out these auctions by clicking the item title. Under the auction's "Start time" is its History: click the number of bids listed there to get a detailed report of who bid how much. (Of course, getting a bid report won't work for private auctions, where bidders' IDs are hidden. See page 28 for the scoop on private auctions.) After you've looked at a few items, you're likely to notice a repeat bidder or two. Make a note of their IDs, and you're ready to go shopping right along with them.

With a bidder's ID in hand, you're ready to find out what else that bidder is shopping for. From the Buy page (or under the Search box at the top of most pages), click the Advanced Search link. On the Search page that opens, look in the menu on the left-hand side for Items by Bidder, and then click that link. Type the

---

bidder's ID in the text box, select your options, and click the Search button. Figure 3-1 shows you how it works.

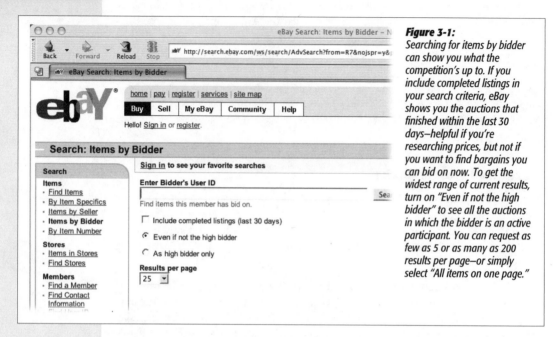

Figure 3-1:
Searching for items by bidder can show you what the competition's up to. If you include completed listings in your search criteria, eBay shows you the auctions that finished within the last 30 days—helpful if you're researching prices, but not if you want to find bargains you can bid on now. To get the widest range of current results, turn on "Even if not the high bidder" to see all the auctions in which the bidder is an active participant. You can request as few as 5 or as many as 200 results per page—or simply select "All items on one page."

Using this technique, you can find all the yodeling CDs your shadow bidder is currently trying to buy, scoot to the appropriate auction pages, and do your best to outbid him. He all does the legwork, you end up with a great CD collection. What better way to cut down on your own search time?

Note: Items by Bidder shows only those auctions in which the eBayer has placed a bid. The search doesn't show you the items she's watching—only those she's bidding on.

Of course, other eBayers can search for items using *your* eBay ID. If your significant other knows your ID, don't bid on an anniversary gift and expect it to be a surprise.

Search for Items by Seller

Whether you're a collector or just always on the lookout for a good deal on tennis shoes, you might find the same seller's name appearing again and again in your search results. Keep track of what that seller is offering by searching for items by *seller*.

Searching for items by seller lets you spot sales trends and use them to your advantage. Does the seller seem overstocked on a particular item? If the seller has had many auctions for the same item end with few or no bids, you might be able to buy that item for the starting price with a last-minute bid, or the seller might lower the price soon. Has the seller raised or lowered the price recently? Does demand seem higher or lower on certain days of the week? Knowing the answers to such questions tells you when to bid, and how much.

To add this trick to your bag, first find the seller's eBay ID, which is on the right side of any auction page in the Seller Information box. Click Advanced Search, then, in the left-hand Search menu, click Items by Seller. Type the seller's eBay ID into the text box and click Search, as shown in Figure 3-2.

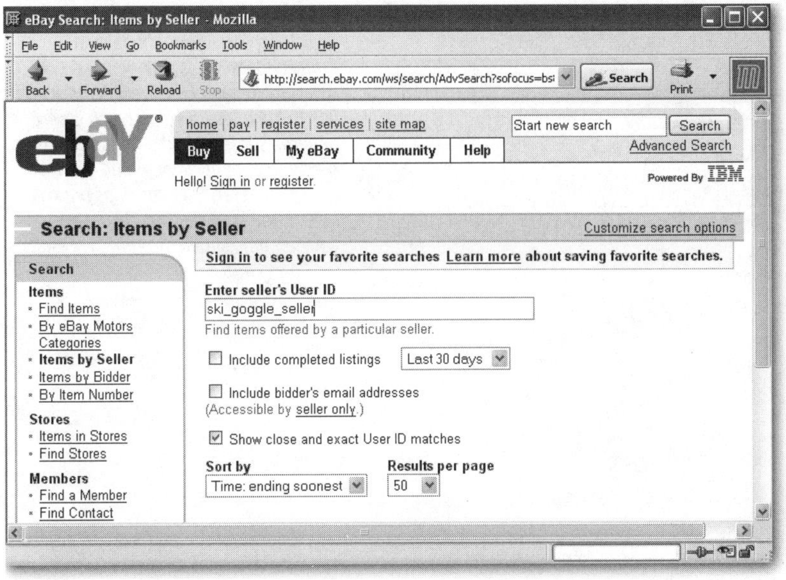

Figure 3-2:
Turn on the "Include completed listings" checkbox if you want to see the winning prices for items similar to one you're considering. How much have those ski goggles gone for in the last month or the last week? You can choose from 5 to 200 results per page and sort by time or price. If you're not sure of the seller's ID, leave "Show close and exact User ID matches" checked to get a list of similar IDs in your results. If you know the ID for sure, turn off this checkbox to return only an exact match.

If you're thinking long-term relationship with this seller, save this search as a favorite (described in the next section). Open one of the seller's auction pages, look in the right-hand "Seller information" box, and then click Add to Favorite Sellers.

Have Searches Find You

Wouldn't it be cool if you could send an automatic request to every single eBay seller every single day, saying, "*Now* does anyone have any size 20, terry cloth, pink poodle skirts for sale? How about *now*?"

In fact, you can. Here's how it works. You can save almost any search as a favorite, which means that eBay remembers the search terms you typed in and saves them so you can redo the search without all that extra typing. To play favorites with your searches, simply look on any search results listing, on the right side just above the results list, for the Add to Favorites link. Click it to display the Add to My Favorite Searches page and save the current search as a favorite. Saved searches are accessible from your My eBay page (page 32) or from the Search page.

After you've saved a favorite search, you can opt for daily email notification of new items that meet your search criteria. On the Add to My Favorite Searches page, turn on the checkbox that gives the OK to email you when pink poodle skirts (or whatever you're searching for) become available. Use the drop-down list to set your preference about how long you'll receive notifications: from one week to one year (Figure 3-3).

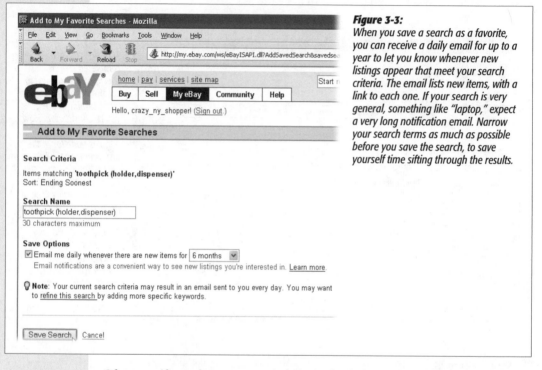

Figure 3-3:
When you save a search as a favorite, you can receive a daily email for up to a year to let you know whenever new listings appear that meet your search criteria. The email lists new items, with a link to each one. If your search is very general, something like "laptop," expect a very long notification email. Narrow your search terms as much as possible before you save the search, to save yourself time sifting through the results.

Of course, if you change your mind about the daily emails—enough poodle skirts already!—you can edit your preferences to cancel them. Go to your My eBay page and click All Favorites. Find the favorite search you want to change, click Edit Preferences, then make the changes you want.

Search Within a Price Range

If you're on a budget, you can limit your results to a certain price range. Click the Advanced Search link and enter your keywords in the text box. Look down the page for Items Priced, and enter your minimum and maximum amounts. Then click the Search button to have eBay give you results within the price range you specified.

Note: Of course, the prices of the items in your results list are the *current* prices. Prices do tend to go up as the clock ticks down, so a wristwatch that was within your price range when you first ran the search might skyrocket into the price stratosphere by the time the auction ends. If you want to view only *fixed-price auctions* (auctions that end the second someone is willing to meet the seller's asking price), click the Buy It Now tab at the top of the search results page. (Read more about Buy It Now auctions on page 26.)

Think Globally, Search Locally

The Advanced Search page lets you do another cool trick: you can limit your search to find only items that are close to home. Finding local auctions is useful when you're shopping for something large or bulky and would rather pick it up yourself than pay exorbitant shipping costs. Sometimes, you can also find a seller with a brick-and-mortar store you can visit in person.

Note: If you want to pick up your purchase in a local auction, OK your plans with the seller *before* you bid. If the auction page says nothing about local pickup, click the "Ask seller a question" link to make sure the seller will let you pick up the item in person. Some won't.

After you've clicked Advanced Search, scroll down to the bottom of the page until you find "Show only." In this section, turn on the checkbox next to "Items within" and type in your Zip code if it's not already there (it should be if you're registered and signed in). Then use the drop-down menu to determine the searching distance, from 10 to 2,000 miles—although 2,000 miles might be a little far for local pickup. When you click the Search button, your results show a new column, Distance, that indicates how close the seller is to the Zip code you typed in. If you don't get enough results, try increasing the distance by an increment or two.

GEM IN THE ROUGH

Advanced Search Options

Advanced Search offers a range of options for refining your searches:

- **Location.** Find items that are located in or available to a specific country. If you're in the U.S., there's no need to use this option—unless you're planning to travel to Taiwan for your Star Wars action figures.

- **Currency.** Most eBay auctions are conducted in U.S. dollars. But eBay is growing throughout the world; auctions in British pounds, Australian dollars, and Euros are all common. This option lets you shop by a particular currency.

- **Multiple-item listings.** If you're looking for groups of items sold in lots (also known as *Dutch auctions*, page 30), use this option to indicate how many you're looking for.

- **Show only.** Restrict your search to fixed-price Buy It Now auctions (page 26); items whose sellers accept PayPal (page 52); items listed as gifts (if you

see the blue gift box icon, it means some sellers—not all—include gift wrapping and express shipping); new listings or listings ending within a specified time; or number of bids. Number of bids is probably the most useful of these options, because it can find either hot items with lots of bids or overlooked items that may be underpriced.

You can also search for auctions offering *Anything Points*, eBay's rewards program (page 113) or auctions that give a portion of the proceeds to charity.

Don't get carried away with all the options on the Advanced Search page. The more parameters you set, the narrower your results. If you're not getting the results you want from your searches, try setting fewer parameters. You might really want a Terminator 2 pinball machine priced between $5.00 and $50.00 that you can pick up by driving 10 miles or less and pay for with Euros left over from your vacation—but if that's yielding nothing, try eliminating your parameters one by one.

Find What Other Shoppers Miss

One good way to find items overlooked by other shoppers is to try alternate spellings and misspellings. Even if you think that your search term is such a common word that no one would misspell it, try some variations anyway. Typos happen, and one letter can make the difference between an item with dozens of lofty bids and a bargain. If you're a collector, try searching for *"art decco"*, *"art noveau"*, or *"deppression glass"* (all misspellings). Looking for good buys on clothing? Search for *Abercombie, sequence* (for *sequins*), or *"Manolo Blanik"*. A search for *satelite, saphire, karioke, projecter, tredmill, Titliest,* or *"Harry Poter"* might bring up some interesting results—with little or no competition in the bidding. You get the idea. Play around with spelling—dropping, adding, or transposing letters—to find popular items hidden from others' searches.

Tip: You can save a lot of time by automating your searches for misspelled items. The free typo finder at *www.fatfingers.co.uk* generates a huge list of misspellings based on the keyword you type into its search box; when you click Find, up pops an eBay search results page showing those misspelled items. You can tell Fat Fingers to filter out the correct spelling (to narrow your results) or to choose only Buy It Now items or only auctions that accept PayPal.

There's one exception to using typos to find good deals: some sellers of fake designer goods purposely misspell the designer's name in the title to hide auctions from members of VeRO, eBay's verified rights owner program. VeRO allows copyright holders and other intellectual property owners to report and cancel auctions that trample on their rights—designer fakes, unauthorized sellers, unlicensed use of copyrighted material, and so on. So searching for *Viutton* or *Burbery* might not get you a deal—just a cheap (and illegal) knockoff. For more on designer fakes and VeRO, see page 132.

Tip: Save your favorite searches by category, so you'll get an alert for all new items listed in that category, whether or not the item's title has misspellings. For example, if you're a philatelist always on the lookout for cool-looking Australian stamps featuring your favorite marsupial, you can receive notification whenever someone lists new items in the Stamps/Australia/Kangaroos category. To save a search category, see page 36.

Going, Going, Gone!

Picture a packed auction house, the tension mounting as the auctioneer prepares to slam down the gavel and declare a winner. On eBay, it's the clock that declares the winner. And it's exciting to find bargains by racing against the clock, looking for deals as auctions are about to end; Figure 3-4 shows you how.

If no one else has bid, you can snap up the goods for a rock-bottom price with no competition. Or, if others have already been bidding, you can snipe the auction (page 104) in the last few seconds. Either way, finding a last-minute auction and getting in on the action is the closest thing eBay offers to instant gratification.

Tip: Even in a last-minute auction, though, remember to check the seller's feedback and the shipping costs to save yourself a potentially expensive mistake.

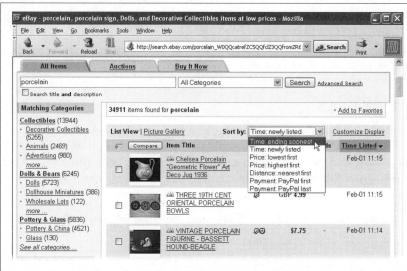

Figure 3-4:
To find auctions that will end soon, do a search for what you're looking for. When the results page appears, click the drop-down arrow in the "Sort by:" box and then choose "Time: ending soonest." At the head of the re-sorted list, you'll probably find numerous auctions with just a minute or two left to go.

Tip: You can also find items ending soon by going to any Search Results page and looking under the Search Options listed on the left-hand side of the page. Turn on the "Listings Ending within 1 hour" check-box, and then click Show Items.

Buy It First, Buy It Now

In a regular auction, getting in the last bid can put you at an advantage; Buy It Now auctions benefit from the opposite strategy. To find BIN items at a good price, you want to get there first and snap them up before anyone else spots the deal.

To do so, from the Buy page (which you find by heading to the eBay navigation bar and clicking Buy), type your search term into the box, and then click Search. On the search results page, click the Buy It Now tab (to show only BIN auctions); then sort the results by "Time: newly listed." Then scan the list for the best prices.

Watch the Clock—and the Calendar

eBay never sleeps, but the rest of the world has to. You can often find bargains by looking for auctions that end when most of the U.S. is snug in bed; demand decreases during hours when few people are online. Often, auctions ending between midnight and 5:00 a.m. eBay time (also known as the Pacific time zone) have few or no late bids. You don't have to be a night owl to take advantage of this lull. Either place your bid using proxy bidding (page 47) the night before the auction ends, or use an automated sniping service (page 107) to place your bid for you.

Similarly, the prices of many items increase or decrease according to the season. When an item is hot in the stores, it's likely to be hot on eBay, too. But shopping for snowshoes in July or for Halloween decorations in April can yield some good buys.

Tip: Summer, when many people take vacations or spend their free time outdoors, is eBay's slowest season. It's a good time to hunt for bargains, whatever you're shopping for.

List It Again, Sam

About half of all eBay auctions end without a single bid. When that happens, sellers can relist the unsold item once without paying any new fees. A seller who really wants to move that plaster bust of Beethoven might lower the starting price when he relists it. As a bargain hunter, you can make eBay's relisting policy work for you by being ready to make a bid when a seller relists. Here's how:

1. **At the top of any page in the eBay site, click the Advanced Search link.**

   The Search: Find Items page appears.

2. **Type in your search term.**

   "Plaster bust" or whatever.

3. **Turn on the "Completed listings only" checkbox to search auctions that are over and done with, and then click Search.**

   On the results page that appears, look for items that ended with no bids. (In other words, look for a 0 under the Bids column.) If you see something of interest, click the title to look at the auction page, where you can check to see whether the item has been relisted. Figure 3-5 shows you what to look for.

Warning: Don't try to contact the seller to buy the item off eBay. If he reports you, trying to make an off-eBay deal can get you kicked off the site.

Have Sellers Search for You

Want It Now is eBay's version of the want ads. The idea is simple: boost your own searches by posting what you want in a special section of the site. Sellers can then scan the ads and notify you if they have what you want. Instead of spending all day chasing down that dogs-playing-poker print, you can sit back and let it come to you. (Great in theory—but in practice, Want It Now still leaves a bit to be desired. Check out the note on page 89.)

Note: You need a feedback score of 5 or higher, or else a credit card on file, to post to Want It Now.

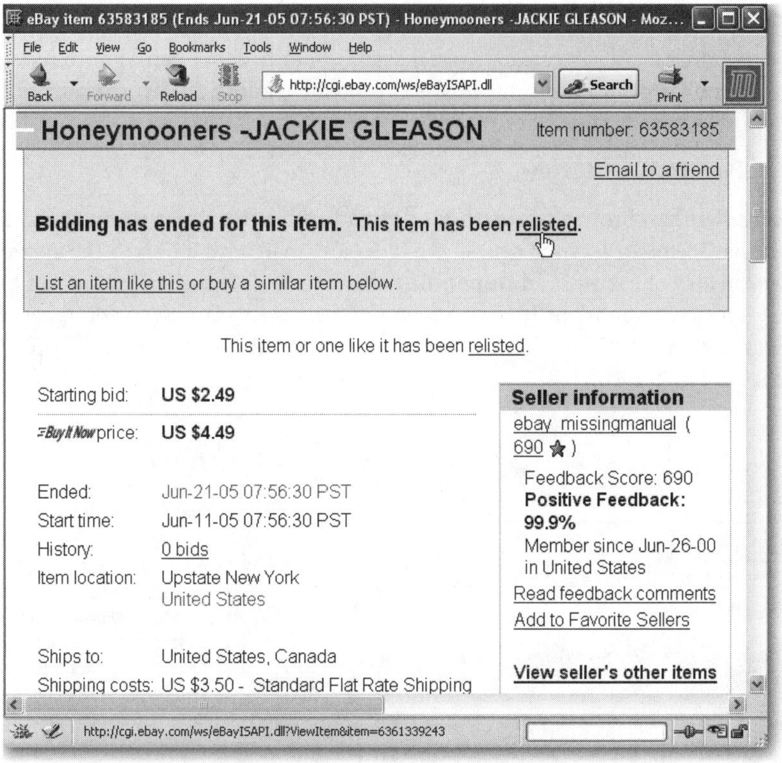

**Tips and Tricks for
Serious Searchers**

Figure 3-5:
*When you click either of
the two "relisted" links on
the page of an auction
that's ended, eBay takes
you to the current
auction for the same
item. Often, you'll find
that the item no one bid
on before is up for
auction again, this time
with a lower starting
price. If the item hasn't
been relisted, look under
the seller's ID and click
the "View seller's other
items" link to see if the
seller has anything
similar on offer.*

Here's how you can post a want ad in Want It Now:

1. **Point your Web browser to** *http://pages.ebay.com/wantitnow.*

   Figure 3-6 shows you the Want It Now page that appears.

2. **Click Post To Want It Now.**

   Doing so takes you to the page where you can compose your ad.

3. **Write your want ad.**

   Give your ad a title (up to 55 characters) and a description (up to 500 characters) that spell out in detail what you're looking for: size, color, year, brand—
   whatever's appropriate and important to you. It's a good idea to give your price
   range, as well. The more specific your ad, the better your chances of finding

exactly what you want. Don't bother to put words and phrases like L@@K or
"Please HELP!!!" in your ad; focus on keywords that will help sellers searching
Want It Now to match up what you want with what they've got.

4. **Select the category that best matches the item you're looking for.**

Use the same top-level category you'd search in to find the item. For that dogs-
playing-poker print, for example, you'd probably choose the Art category. eBay
will post your ad to this category within Want It Now.

5. **Click Post To Want It Now.**

Now sellers can browse or search for your ad. When a seller is running an auction that seems to fit your needs, you'll get an email with a link to the auction.
You can also check your ad from time to time to look for sellers' responses that
way. To view your Want It Now ad, go to *http://pages.ebay.com/wantitnow* and
under the Post To Want It Now Button, click the "in one place" link (you can
see it in Figure 3-6).

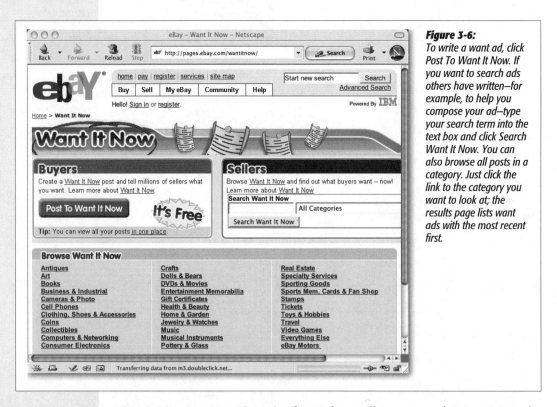

Figure 3-6:
*To write a want ad, click
Post To Want It Now. If
you want to search ads
others have written—for
example, to help you
compose your ad—type
your search term into the
text box and click Search
Want It Now. You can
also browse all posts in a
category. Just click the
link to the category you
want to look at; the
results page lists want
ads with the most recent
first.*

Want It Now posts remain active for 60 days. Sellers can search Want It Now by
category or keyword. Sellers who see your ad and are offering what you want can
let you know the item number of their auction; eBay sends you a link to the auction in an email. A link also shows up in your Want It Now listing, as you can see

in Figure 3-7. The seller doesn't know your eBay ID or email address (the only personal information that appears with your Want It Now ad is your feedback score, location, and length of eBay membership), so you don't have to worry about being plagued with spam just because you invited sellers to contact you.

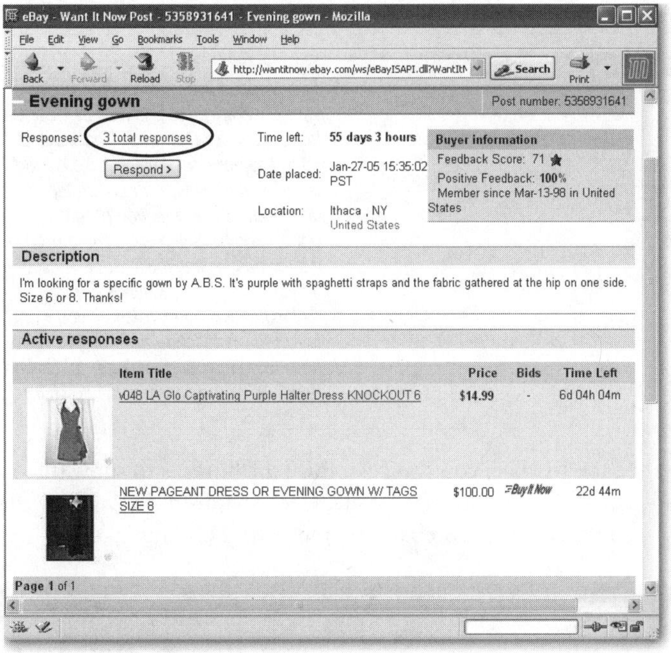

Figure 3-7:
To get to an auction from your Want It Now post, simply click the auction title. If an auction ends (either by running out of time or through Buy It Now), the link to it disappears from your Want It Now post. That's why this example lists three total responses at the top of the page but shows links to only two auctions.

Note: Want It Now is still evolving; it's not yet a terribly useful feature. Many ads go unanswered; others attract inappropriate responses, like when you specifically ask for an 8×10 green-and-gold Persian rug and get a response advertising 50 square yards of pink shag carpeting. Checking out auctions that miss your ad by a mile wastes time. Still, if you're trying to buy a one-of-a-kind item and your search results aren't turning up much, it's worth giving Want It Now a try.

The eBay Toolbar

The eBay toolbar is free software you can download and install to add an eBay navigation bar to your Web browser—*if* your Web browser happens to be Internet Explorer. Installing the eBay toolbar lets you search eBay, keep track of auctions, and go to your My eBay page with a single click, wherever on the Web your browser happens to be. The toolbar makes it easy to find bargains and keep an eye on the bidding—even alerting you when an auction nears its end—so that great deal on a digital camera doesn't slip away while you're busy downloading tunes for your MP3 player.

Note: To install and use the eBay toolbar, you must be running Internet Explorer 5.01 or higher on a PC with Windows 98 or a more recent version of Windows. Mac fans and people who prefer other browsers are out of luck.

Figure 3-8 shows you what the toolbar looks like.

Figure 3-8:
To download the eBay toolbar, go to your My eBay page and look in the left-hand menu for Download Tools. Select eBay Toolbar, and then click Download eBay Toolbar Now. Your computer downloads the installation program (called ToolbarSetup.exe); you must run it to actually install the toolbar. (Based on your computer's settings, either a dialog box will open, asking if you want to run the installation program, or you'll have to go to your downloads folder and double-click the program to launch it.)

Once you've installed the toolbar, you can customize the buttons to show the ones you use most and hide the ones you leave alone. Click the drop-down arrow next to the eBay button, and then select Toolbar Preferences and Customization.

FREQUENTLY ASKED QUESTION

Is the eBay Toolbar a Double Agent?

Is the eBay Toolbar spyware?

Some eBayers hesitate to use the eBay toolbar because they're worried that it contains *spyware*, stealth software that collects information about your Web browsing habits and sends that info back to its source—without your knowledge or consent. Does your eBay toolbar spy on you and let eBay know when you're shopping other sites and what you're looking for?

eBay's official answer is no. Early versions of the toolbar did track which toolbar buttons eBayers used most frequently, but (according to eBay) not sites browsed or other Web activity. eBay claimed that collecting this information helped its staff to understand how eBayers used the toolbar and how to optimize it. Nowadays, eBay says, the toolbar doesn't collect even that information. eBay insists that the only information it gets from your toolbar is when you choose to report a potential spoof site. In other words, you

have to click Account Guard → "Report this as a Suspicious Site" in order for your toolbar to send information to eBay.

Some people are concerned, however, about what the toolbar is *capable* of collecting. The spyware-removal software Spybot Search & Destroy defines the eBay toolbar as a threat and, if you run Spybot S&D, removes the toolbar from your computer. According to the Spybot S&D Web site (*www.safer-networking.org*), the eBay toolbar transmits information, like the keywords you type when you do a search, to the marketing firms Mediaplex and DoubleClick; either of these companies could potentially track your online activity. Such tracking would be in violation of eBay's own privacy policy, but so far eBay has declined to comment on this issue.

The question boils down to how much you trust eBay, how useful you find the toolbar—and how closely you choose to guard your privacy.

The eBay toolbar helps keep you in touch with what's happening on eBay, even when you're busy doing other things. For example, it sends you a bid alert when an auction you're watching is about to end, even if you're not online. Here's a button-by-button overview:

- **eBay.** Click the eBay button to go to eBay's home page. The small arrow next to the eBay logo opens a drop-down menu that lets you sign in or out and zip to various sites within eBay (Buy, Sell, eBay Announcements, the Community page). Use this menu to set your toolbar preferences or to uninstall the toolbar.

Tip: To use the toolbar most efficiently, sign in on *both* eBay and the toolbar itself. Once you've signed into the toolbar, you stay signed in until you sign out. But you have to sign in to eBay separately.

- **Account Guard.** A new feature of the toolbar, Account Guard is how eBay fights back against *spoofed* Web sites—fake sites purporting to be eBay or PayPal that scammers set up in an attempt to steal the identities and accounts of law-abiding, unsuspecting eBayers (page 137) like you. These spoofed sites, often reached through a link in an unsolicited, official-looking email, mimic the real thing but have no connection to eBay or PayPal.

To protect your account, the Account Guard button turns red when you're on a potential spoofed site. (It's green when you're on an official eBay or PayPal Web page and gray if you're on a page that the toolbar can't identify.) But Account Guard does even more. If you attempt to type your password into an unknown site, a warning pops up, as shown in Figure 3-9.

Figure 3-9:
In the eBay Account Guard Alert, click Yes to submit your account information. Click No to cancel your submission attempt. If you suspect that the site is spoofed, click the Report This Site button to let eBay know about it. If the site is one you know is trustworthy, turn on the checkbox at the bottom of the alert. eBay recommends that you have different passwords for each account you have on the Web; it's a good idea never to use your eBay ID and password as your ID and password for accounts at other sites.

Note: If you change your eBay password, you must also change it on the eBay toolbar.

Account Guard is a great addition to the eBay toolbar, helping eBayers protect their personal information from scammers. Only type in your eBay or PayPal ID and password when the Account Guard button is green—never when it's red. If it's gray, use your own judgement—but proceed with caution.

If you have an older version of the toolbar that's missing Account Guard, simply download the new version at *http://pages.ebay.com/ebay_toolbar* to get Account Guard's protection.

Note: You must be signed in to the toolbar for Account Guard to do its stuff.

- **Search eBay.** Clicking this button takes you to eBay's Search page. But you can save a step by typing your search word or phrase into the text box to the left of the search button. Then click the arrow to the right of the search button and select the kind of search you want. You can search for items by title, title and description, eBay stores, completed items, category, subcategory, and more. See Figure 3-10.

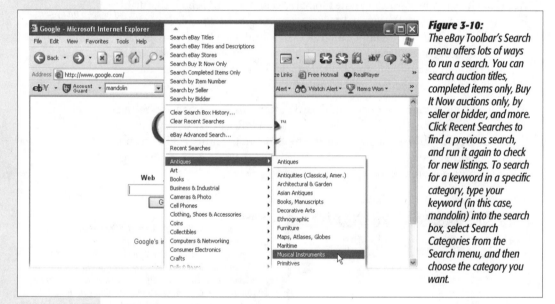

Figure 3-10:
The eBay Toolbar's Search menu offers lots of ways to run a search. You can search auction titles, completed items only, Buy It Now auctions only, by seller or bidder, and more. Click Recent Searches to find a previous search, and run it again to check for new listings. To search for a keyword in a specific category, type your keyword (in this case, mandolin) into the search box, select Search Categories from the Search menu, and then choose the category you want.

- **My eBay.** Click this button to jump to your My eBay page.

- **Bid Alert.** When you've made a bid in an active auction, use the Bid Alert button to remind you when the auction is about to end; it will pop open a window on your screen, even if you're offline. Even better, if you're online, you can click a link in the window to head directly to your auction.

To set a bid alert, click the arrow next to the eBay button and then select Toolbar Preferences and Customization. Here you can set your reminder time (10, 15, 30, 60, or 75 minutes before the auction's end), turn audio notification off or on, and set how long the pop-up alert will stay open. The really cool thing about bid alerts is that you don't have to have a browser window open—or even be online—for your reminder to appear. Even if you're immersed in work and have forgotten all about the auction, Bid Alert will remind you.

- **Watch Alert.** Similar to Bid Alert, the Watch Alert button lets you know when auctions you're watching are going to end soon. You don't have to be a bidder to get watch alerts. Figure 3-11 shows you what a watch alert looks like. You don't need to do a thing to turn on Watch Alert—it automatically monitors what's on your Watch list (page 34) and pops up to remind you when it's time to move in and make your bid.

Figure 3-11:
Watch alerts and bid alerts appear in the lower right-hand corner of your screen, whether you're on eBay, another Web site, or offline. Click the link to open a new window with the auction page and place your bid or keep an eye on the closing minutes. To make sure the list of items you're watching is up to date, click the arrow on the Watch Alert button and then choose Refresh Watch List.

- **Items Won.** This button takes you to the auction page of any item you've won, the Feedback Forum, or the PayPal home page.

Note: If your eBay Toolbar doesn't display buttons for advanced features like Watch Alerts and Bid Alerts, your computer's firewall is probably blocking the toolbar from full Internet access. Most firewalls come with tight restrictions on programs that try to access the Internet. To get the most out of the eBay toolbar, you need to change the settings of your firewall to allow the program "eBay Toolbar Daemon" (also called "eBayTBDaemon") full Internet access. The Help section or the Web site of your computer security software tells you how.

Go Wireless

Even the most avid eBayer doesn't spend her life in front of her computer. Sometimes you've got to coach the kids' Little League games, or take the dog for a run on the beach, or watch a dozen TiVO'd episodes of *Buffy the Vampire Slayer*. But auctions keep going, even when you're on the go. What if, as Fido splashes through the waves after his Frisbee, some bidder in Dubuque is preparing to outbid you on that complete antique silver service for eight? You don't have to rush home and check to make sure you're still winning. You can just pull out your cell phone.

eBay's Anywhere Wireless service lets you search eBay and keep track of auctions you're involved in, no matter where you are. You can search by keyword, seller, or category/subcategory; browse categories and featured items; view your My eBay page; even bid—all from your cell phone or PDA, wherever you happen to be. If you've got service, you've got eBay.

You can get to eBay from your wireless device two ways: either navigate there using your device's Internet menu or open its *minibrowser,* which lets you look at cut-down versions of Web pages, and point it to *http://wap.ebay.com* (most devices let you leave off the "http://" part). Log in and you're ready to search, browse, and buy. Now, when you're waiting in line at the bank or the post office, you can search eBay for bargains instead of fretting about the ones you're missing out on.

Tip: When you use Anywhere Wireless, sign in before you start searching. You can't bid unless you've signed in, and that tiny little keypad makes it awkward to navigate back to the home page, sign in, and then find your item again.

Unfortunately, you can't put an item on your watch list while using your phone to search, although you can go to your My eBay page and view or bid on items already on that list. Another thing you can't do with your cell phone is read sellers' feedback. On the item page, you can see the feedback score but not the percentage of positives, and you can't read feedback comments. For this reason, it's best to use your cell phone to manage active auctions, where you've already done your research and feel confident dealing with the seller.

Searching with Anywhere Wireless

To search for items using Anywhere Wireless:

1. From *wap.ebay.com,* select Search.

   You can search by item number, keyword, or seller ID. Type in the number or word you want, and then select Continue. If you type in a keyword, eBay prompts you to choose a category (or you can select all categories).

2. **Choose an item.**

   The search results page displays item titles. If you select an item to view, you get a stripped-down version of an eBay auction page. There's no photograph on this screen, and you can't look at the bid history or seller feedback.

3. **At the bottom of the auction page, select Description.**

   This page shows you more details: a photo (if the listing has one) and the item description text. No fancy graphics, of course, but you still get most of the important info.

Receiving email notifications from Anywhere Wireless

Anywhere Wireless can email outbid notices, feedback notifications, and win notifications to your wireless device. To sign up, go to My eBay → eBay Preferences. At the top of the page that opens is "Notification preferences"; click the View/Change link. eBay asks you to verify your password. After you've done so, find eBay Wireless Email, and then click Subscribe. Turn on the button by "Send wireless email to the address below" and then type your wireless email address in the text box. Click Save Changes, and you're good to go.

Offsite Searching

Thanks to eBay, a cottage industry now exists, offering a whole platoon of services to improve your online auction experience. Try these offsite search engines and tools to streamline your eBay shopping and make bargain-hunting easier and less time-consuming:

- **Finds-It.** A subscription site located at *www.finds-it.com*, Finds-It lets you run searches and store the results in your own database located on the Finds-It site. When you log in, Finds-It automatically retrieves your stored searches so you can see what's new. This site has two subscription levels: at the basic level, you can save and store up to 250 searches; at the professional level, that limit increases to 1,000. Finds-It charges a monthly fee for its service.

- **ItemScout.com.** This site lets you create a highly detailed search agent that will scour eBay for search terms you specify and report back to you via email; it's more specialized than eBay's own email notifications.

  Searches take place at intervals you determine, from every few minutes to once a day. One of the nice features of this site is that you can specify certain notification parameters, such as if the price exceeds a certain amount, if a new bid comes in, or if the price is still below a certain amount with only so much time left before the auction ends. If you're bidding on a motorcycle helmet, for instance, and you want ItemScout to notify you if the price is still below $50.00 with only half an hour to go, it will. You can also have alerts sent to a wireless device, like your cell phone or PDA. ItemScout.com is a subscription service— you can pay by the month, the quarter, or the year—but offers a weeklong free trial.

- **Clusty.** This is an Internet search engine that *clusters* its results, putting similar items into folders that let you quickly sort through what it finds. Clusty has customizable tabs that let you narrow your search to a specific area of the Web: one of those tabs is eBay. If you search in Clusty's eBay tab for *weasel*, as in Figure 3-12, Clusty organizes the results into folders, such as various book titles, Matchbox cars, ferrets, and so on. Click any folder to restrict your results to what's inside that folder. You can further sort the results by price or the amount of time left in the auction.

Clusty's folders go beyond eBay's categories. If, for example, all you can remember about a book is that it has *weasel* in the title, the best you can do on eBay is to search for *weasel* in the Books category, then go through the results. Clusty drills down deeper in just one step, creating folders based on the titles of books. If you click the "more" link, you get *Pop Goes the Weasel, Never Tease a Weasel, Axis of Weasels, Dilbert and the Way of the Weasel….* Find the title you want and open its folder to compare auctions for that book.

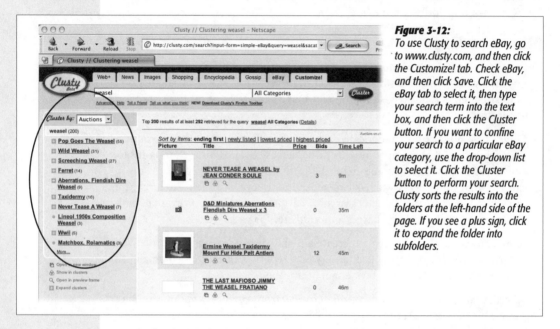

Figure 3-12:
To use Clusty to search eBay, go to www.clusty.com, and then click the Customize! tab. Check eBay, and then click Save. Click the eBay tab to select it, then type your search term into the text box, and then click the Cluster button. If you want to confine your search to a particular eBay category, use the drop-down list to select it. Click the Cluster button to perform your search. Clusty sorts the results into the folders at the left-hand side of the page. If you see a plus sign, click it to expand the folder into subfolders.

- **Pluck.** Pluck is a plug-in you can download (for free from *www.pluck.com*) and install in your browser. Pluck lets you sort your search results by number of bids—something eBay won't let you do. Sorting by bids lets you see what's hot (perhaps the subject of a bidding war) and what hasn't yet shown up on other shoppers' radar.

Note: The Pluck plug-in is available only for Internet Explorer version 6.0 or higher on computers running Windows 2000 or Windows XP.

Take a look at Figure 3-13 to get an idea of what Pluck can do. If you click an auction in the top pane's results list, the bottom pane opens the actual auction on the eBay site, so you can watch an item or bid on it without opening a new browser window, going to eBay, and finding the auction that interests you.

Pluck also offers a Web component, Pluck Web Access (PWA), that lets you keep an eye on your searches from any computer connected to the Internet.

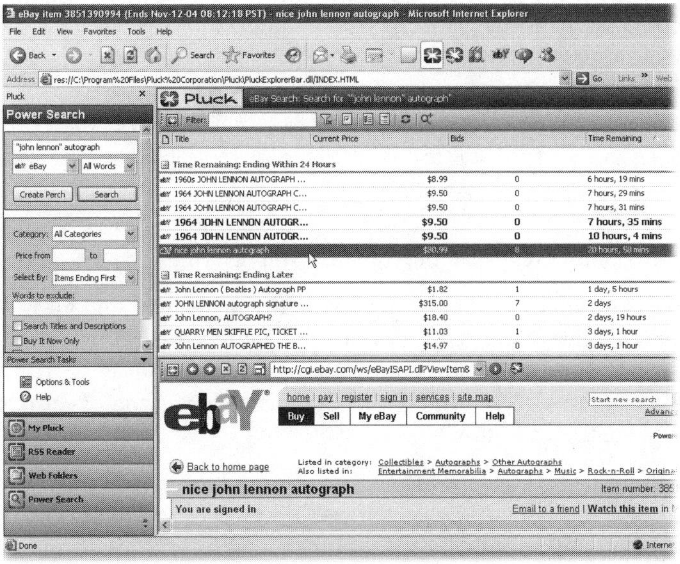

Figure 3-13:
Pluck's dual panes let you view your search results and look at individual auctions without having to switch back and forth between browser windows. You can choose to limit your results to BIN items and auctions accepting PayPal. (Pluck displays prices in U.S. dollars, no matter the currency used in the auction.) Sort results by price, time remaining, or number of bids. To turn your search into a power search, or "perch," click the Create Perch button. Pluck will keep performing the search in the background, updating your results periodically—or you can right-click a particular perch and select Refresh to update it right now.

What's It Worth?

On eBay, it's not uncommon to see the bidding rocket past what everyone knows is a reasonable price. People sometimes pay more at auction for the same item they could buy in the discount store across town. And sometimes the bids might reach, say, $22, even when the *seller notes in the item description* that she has similar items available for a fixed price of $17.99 in her eBay store. What's going on? It's simple: the excitement of a timed auction and the thrill of competitive bidding can make bidders lose their heads and pay more than they meant to.

Don't be part of the headless masses. If you do your research and keep calm, you'll avoid overpaying.

Do Your Research

You don't have to jump into the bidding as soon as you discover eBay. To avoid getting yourself into trouble and becoming the winning bidder at $40,800 for a haunted toothpick, take a step back and click around the site while you collect yourself.

Do these basic things to cool out and get more info on an item. Use eBay's comparison-shop feature (page 99). Put items on your Watch list to see where their final price lands and get a sense of the going rate. Visit a seller's eBay store (page 259) to check whether the seller offers the same item for a fixed price—and how much. Read the discussion boards (page 362) related to the things you want to buy.

Note: If you're concerned that you're going to miss a deal on a unique, never-going-to-be-available-again, ghost-infested item, bear in mind that nearly everything turns up on eBay over and over, given time. To see whether something similar has sold recently on eBay, check the completed auctions, described below.

Next, avail yourself of other resources that can help you determine value:

• **Research closed auctions.** Checking out what similar items have sold for in the past few weeks can give you a good idea of what your item is worth now. To research closed auctions, from almost any eBay page, click Advanced Search, type in your search term, then turn on the "Completed listings only" checkbox before you click the Search button.

Your search results page (Figure 3-14) lists auctions that have ended in the last 30 days. You can sort the results by date, if you want to see how hot the market is right now by checking recent sales against older ones, or by price, if you want to get a feel for the price range or the average price. (You can also sort by distance, which could be a factor if you're looking for a bulky item or hoping to find a seller with a brick-and-mortar store near you.)

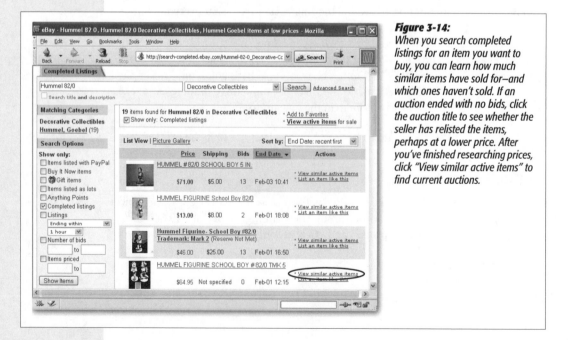

Figure 3-14:
When you search completed listings for an item you want to buy, you can learn how much similar items have sold for—and which ones haven't sold. If an auction ended with no bids, click the auction title to see whether the seller has relisted the items, perhaps at a lower price. After you've finished researching prices, click "View similar active items" to find current auctions.

- **Use a comparison-shopping engine.** There are many resources off the site to help you research prices. For new items, use a comparison-shopping engine like Froogle (*http://froogle.google.com*) or mySimon (*www.mysimon.com*) to get a feel for the item's price range. You can also check out some of the price-analysis tools described on page 118. (For more on comparison shopping on eBay itself, see the next section.)

- **Consult a standard reference.** If you're a collector, you're probably familiar with the standard reference books in your field. These provide a good resource, but in the world of eBay, prices can change faster than printed books can keep up. In some cases, eBay has brought prices down because its worldwide marketplace has dramatically increased supply. You don't have to travel to flea markets or antique stores to find things for your collection, and you can buy from sellers from Anchorage, Alaska, to Zarephath, New Jersey—and beyond—as easily as someone who lives on that seller's block. On the other hand, competition among buyers has also increased, and when an item becomes hot, prices can soar. The upshot: use reference books for a ballpark value, but keep in mind that eBay prices fluctuate a lot more and a lot faster than the books can keep up with.

Tip: Some price guides are now online. Collectors can find good resources at *www.strongnumbers.com* and *www.kovelsprices.com*. Again, take the prices with a grain or two of salt. eBay prices can be significantly lower than the guides indicate—it all depends on who's shopping for what on a given day.

Comparison Shopping

eBay has so many auctions running at once that it can be easy to lose track of what you've seen. The sheer volume of what's on offer can make shopping difficult; by the time you've looked at your seventh or eighth MP3 player, it can be hard to remember exactly which one had the 20 GB storage capacity and an FM radio but was a little cheaper because it was missing the headphones. eBay's Compare feature means that you don't have to fool around with making lists or managing a bunch of browser windows when you want see how several items stack up against each other.

To see the details of several auctions side by side, first conduct a search. The search results page, shown in Figure 3-15, makes it easy for you to select items you want to compare side by side

When you click Compare, a new page opens, showing the items you've selected side by side, as in Figure 3-16. The Compare Items page shows up to four items at a time, each in its own column.

Tip: If you're comparing more than four items and you click the Show All Items link, all the auctions you've chosen appear on the same page, but they're not all visible at the same time. You have to scroll sideways to see them.

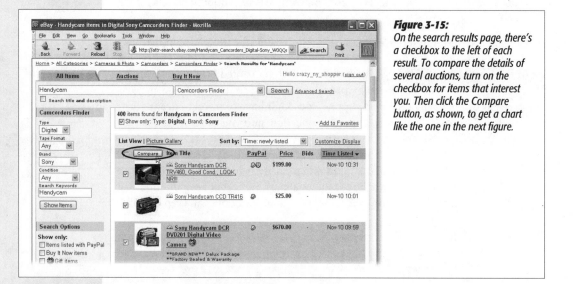

Figure 3-15:
On the search results page, there's a checkbox to the left of each result. To compare the details of several auctions, turn on the checkbox for items that interest you. Then click the Compare button, as shown, to get a chart like the one in the next figure.

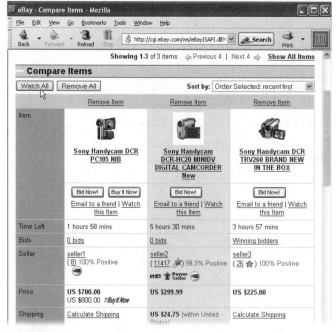

Figure 3-16:
Comparison shopping lets you view information on several auctions side by side. You can sort the comparison by time, price, whether the seller accepts PayPal, alphabetically by seller ID, or by the order in which you added items to your comparison. Information displayed includes time left, number of bids, seller ID and feedback score, current price, shipping, item location, and payment methods. Further down the page, you also get specifications about each product and the seller's policy on returns.

As you narrow your search to the auctions that really grab your interest, you can remove items to focus on the best ones. Click the Remove Item link at the top or bottom of the column you want to ditch.

You can bid on any item by clicking the Bid Now! button, or you can add one or more items to your Watch list: click the appropriate "Watch this Item" link, or click the Watch All button to slam-dunk the whole screen onto your Watch list. If you want to start over, click Remove All.

UP TO SPEED

Price vs. Value

Researching prices gives you an idea of what price the market will bear at this point in time. But sometimes, you might want something for reasons that have nothing to do with its price. It boils down to these questions: "What's it worth?" and "What's it worth *to you*?"

You get the answer to "What's it worth?" when you do your research, as described in the preceding section.

The question "What's it worth to you?" is trickier. Only you can answer it. Sometimes, there might be a good reason to

pay a little more than the market price: to complete a set, to get living-room drapes in precisely the right color, to buy something that reminds you of your long-lost Uncle Ernie, or to get your hands on something you need as of yesterday.

When thinking about what you're willing to pay, take a few minutes to answer both these questions. You'll be happier with your purchases.

Bidding Wars

One way to avoid paying more than an item is worth is to be a bidding pacifist. Bidding wars tend to happen when two or more bidders each get to thinking of the item as their very own. Emotions take over and possessiveness flares up: "No way I'm going to let that bidder have *my* musical beer stein for $83.50!"

Use these strategies to keep from losing your head (and your hard-earned cash):

- **Watch and wait.** The best way to stay out of a bidding war is to wait until late in the auction to decide whether you're going to bid. Put the item on your Watch list (page 34) so you can monitor the situation. When you add something to your Watch list, you've taken a step toward a possible purchase, but you're less likely to think of an item as "yours" if you're just watching it. As the end of the auction nears, you can check the current price and see if the item still looks as desirable as it did when you found it.

- **Let someone else bid for you.** Another way to avoid bidding wars is to use an automated sniping service (page 107). With automated sniping, you make your bid as early in the auction as you like (through the sniping site or software), but the sniping service places that bid in the final seconds of the auction, saving you from getting emotionally involved.

This method seems similar to proxy bidding, but there's an important difference. With proxy bidding, eBay's computers tip your hand by upping your bid the moment someone else places a bid. That means bids can creep up and up well before the auction's end. When you use an automated sniper, the competition is sitting there, thinking they're on top of the bidding, until your bid comes along and zaps them out of the auction in the last three seconds. Sniping means that the winning bid is less likely to reach your top limit, because the clock runs down before the competition can fight back. It's all in the timing.

• **Let it go.** Sometimes a bidding war drives the price higher than you're willing to go. When that happens, don't think you've lost out. If an item sells for a very high price, be assured that other sellers are watching, eager to get in on the demand. Other auctions will appear in quick succession—and often these jump-on-the-bandwagon auctions don't command the high prices that the original did. In other words, you could actually be better off in the long run by paying less for a similar item in the third or fourth or fifth auction. So when you're tempted to bid past your budget, remember this: auctions are like buses. If you miss one, don't worry, because another one will be coming along in a few minutes.

Bid to Win

eBay newbies often complain that it's hard to win the auctions they bid on. Sometimes there's too much competition. Sometimes another bidder wins by just a couple of cents. Other times, a bidder thinks she's winning, then someone outbids her during the last minute of the auction, with no time left for a response. This section shows you the bidding strategies that will help you win more auctions.

How to Win by Two Cents

After you've bid in a few auctions, or even if you're just looking around the site, you've probably noticed that some auctions have bids in odd amounts like $14.53 or $267.32. Bids like this are the work of bidders who've learned to use *bid increments* to their advantage. The bid increment is how much a bid must increase over the current price to register as a bid. For example, if the current price is $14.00 and you try to bid $14.01, eBay won't accept your bid, because it's not a full increment above the current price; you'd have to bid $14.50 or more.

Bid increments are determined by eBay and the current price of the item, as you can see in Table 3-1. As the price of the item passes certain threshold amounts, the bid increment increases.

Table 3-1. Bid Increments: As the Price Goes Up, So Does the Minimum Bid

Current Price	Bid Increment
$0.01–$0.99	$0.05
$1.00–$4.99	$0.25
$5.00–$24.99	$0.50

Table 3-1. *Bid Increments: As the Price Goes Up, So Does the Minimum Bid (continued)*

Current Price	Bid Increment
$25.00–$25.99	$1.00
$100.00–$249.99	$2.50
$250.00–$499.99	$5.00
$500.00–$999.99	$10.00
$1,000.00–$2,499.99	$25.00
$2,500.00–$4,999.99	$50.00
$5,000.00 or over	$100.00

So how can you beat out another bidder by just two cents? The minimum bid increment is five cents; won't eBay reject any bid that doesn't win by at least that amount?

The answer lies in the proxy bidding system (page 47). The secret is that your bid has to be at least one full increment above the price that's current *at the moment you place your bid*. As long as you meet that requirement, your bid can be any amount you want, and eBay's computer will take your bid up to its max, but not above. So when a bidding battle erupts, if your maximum bid is just a few cents higher than another bidder's max, eBay takes the higher bid—yours.

For example

Here's an example. If the opening price for a video game is $9.99 and you make a maximum bid of $15.99, eBay's proxy bidding system bids the smallest amount possible on your behalf, while keeping your secret maximum bid hidden. In this case, the opening bid of $9.99 is the smallest bid possible, so your current bid is $9.99. When another bidder comes along (call her game-raider), she sees your current bid of $9.99 but has no idea of what your maximum bid might be. All game-raider has to do is place a bid that is one or more bid increments higher than the *current* bid: $9.99. As long as she meets that requirement, she's free to type in any amount as her own maximum bid. The maximum bid is a hard-and-fast limit—it says "Absolutely no more than this amount"—and eBay can't stretch that maximum amount just to make it to the next bid increment.

So if game-raider types in $16.01 as her maximum bid (two cents more than your max), those two cents count. A proxy bidding battle takes place behind the scenes, raising the bidding by one increment each round, until someone's maximum is surpassed, in this case making game-raider the high bidder. Thanks to proxy bidding, whoever has the highest maximum bid takes the lead. In this case, your maximum bid is $15.99, and proxy bidding won't bid for you beyond that amount. But even though game-raider's is just a little higher, the higher bid prevails.

If game-raider had typed in $17.01 as her maximum bid, the current bid would show as $16.49: one bid increment over your max of $15.99. eBay raised her bid one increment, keeping her upper limit a secret. If you came back and bid $16.99, the high bid would be $17.01—game-raider's max is still higher than yours—and you'd still be outbid by two cents.

The moral of the story

The key here is to realize that bid increments come into play *at the time a bid is placed,* not after the dust settles in a proxy bidding battle. As long as your bid is one full increment over the current price when you make the bid, it does not have to be a full increment over your competitor's maximum bid—it just has to be higher.

So instead of getting beat out by two or three cents every time, use bid increments and maximum bids to your own advantage. To beat another bidder by a couple of cents, don't think in even numbers—always add two or three cents to your maximum bid.

Tip: Adding a few cents to your maximum bid is particularly effective when you're sniping. The next section explains sniping in detail.

Don't Be a Nibbler

Sometimes new buyers try to win an auction by the smallest amount possible. This practice, called *nibbling,* involves making lots of small bids—just an increment or two over the current price—and hoping to hang on to the high bidder spot.

Nibblers are usually outbid. They don't bid what they're willing to pay, just what they're hoping to get away with. Any other bidder who is willing to pay what the item is actually worth will almost always win out over a nibbler. All the nibbler does is drive up the price that the winning bidder pays.

Not only that, but a nibbler's bidding habits are extremely easy to spot. If a smart bidder sees a nibbler steadily bidding and rebidding $1 more until the nibbler finally takes the lead, the smart bidder knows *exactly* what it'll take to snipe the auction out from under them, winning by a hair in the final seconds.

The best and most basic bidding strategy is to bid the maximum you're willing to pay. You'll win more auctions that way, and often for less than your maximum bid.

Swoop in and Snipe

Last-second bidding is called *sniping*, and 15 percent of all eBay auctions are won within the last minute. If you've ever been sniped, you know how frustrating it can be when someone swoops in at the very end of an auction and outbids you—often by a small amount. You might have been willing to go back and bid another dollar or two, but thanks to the last-second action of the sniper, you didn't have time. On the other hand, you can use sniping to your advantage by outbidding other buyers when an auction is down to the wire.

Note: Sniping is controversial, but it's perfectly legit. eBay recommends letting the system handle your bids in a regular proxy bid, but it lets eBayers snipe to their hearts' content. (Sniping merely uses eBay's proxy bidding system to place bids as late as possible in an auction.)

Snipe it manually

If you've never sniped an auction, you should try it at least once. It's exciting—you don't know until the last tick of the clock who wins or for how much—and when the dust settles and you're the winner, you get to savor the thrill of victory. Even if sniping isn't your idea of fun, trying it for yourself lets you experience for yourself how the competition operates.

If you're going to be at your computer when the auction ends, here's how to snipe manually:

1. **Decide on your maximum bid.**

   Figure this out well before the auction's end, taking shipping, insurance, tax (if any), and any other costs into account.

2. **With about 10 minutes left in the auction, check out the auction page.**

   If the bidding has already gone higher than your max, this isn't the auction to snipe.

3. **Open a second browser window.**

   Resize each of your two windows so that you can see them side by side on your screen. In each window, open the auction page for the item you want to snipe, as shown in Figure 3-17.

4. **Get ready to make your bid.**

   In one of the windows, click the Place Bid button (sign in if eBay asks you to) and type in your maximum bid. (Keep in mind that the current high bid is not necessarily the high bidder's *maximum* bid.) Click Continue, but stop there. Don't click Confirm Bid until you're ready to snipe.

5. **In the other window, refresh the auction page to see how much time is left and whether any bidding action is going on.**

   When the clock is ticking down to the last minute, it's time to sit up and really pay attention. You might be tempted to watch the auction from your My eBay page, but don't do this if you're going to snipe. My eBay updates more slowly than you can update progress on the auction yourself by watching the auction page and frequently clicking your browser's Refresh or Reload button.

Tip: If you're dialing into eBay (rather than using a high-speed connection), you may find it easier and faster to click to the Bid History link and refresh *that* page instead of the actual auction page. The Bid History page has almost no graphics, so it loads very quickly, keeping you up to speed with what's happening in the auction.

---

6. **Keep refreshing the auction page, watching as the time ticks down to seconds.**

7. Snipe it!

In the last 10 seconds or so, click the Confirm Bid button in the second window, where your bid is waiting. If your bid is higher than any other late bids, you've just sniped an auction!

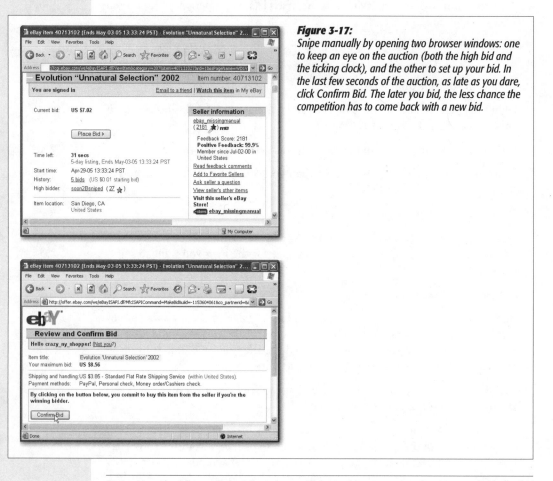

Figure 3-17:
Snipe manually by opening two browser windows: one to keep an eye on the auction (both the high bid and the ticking clock), and the other to set up your bid. In the last few seconds of the auction, as late as you dare, click Confirm Bid. The later you bid, the less chance the competition has to come back with a new bid.

Note: Manual sniping works best if you have a high-speed Internet connection. You can hold your bid until the last few seconds, confident your bid will make it to eBay's servers in time. If your Internet connection is on the slow side, give yourself a few extra seconds to place your bid.

As you watch the auction, you might find that bids start coming in during the last couple of minutes. A lot of bidding action might make you revise your snipe bid—or convince you to try again with a different auction.

Tip: If you think the whole sniping thing is more frustrating than fun, check out Appendix B. It lists other auction sites, some of which extend the auction time when a bid comes in during the last few minutes, giving all bidders a chance to respond to any would-be sniper before the auction ends.

Snipe it automatically

Even if you get a kick out of do-it-yourself sniping, you can't always be at your computer when an auction is about to end. Happily, sniping services are available that will snipe on your behalf. When you sign up for a sniping service, you give the service your eBay ID and password so that the automated sniper can log in and bid for you in the final seconds of the auction. (If sharing your secret info freaks you out, see page 108 for the down-low on downloadable sniping software.)

Many sniping services offer more than just last-minute bidding. For example, if you just *have* to have an iPod and you just *have* to have it for $200 even, you can create a bid group—the sniping service will place snipes on one iPod auction after another until you win for $200 or less, then automatically cancel any pending snipes (so you don't end up with three iPods). You can also find search tools and tracking services on many sniper sites, and some offer buttons you can add to your Web browser's toolbar that will let you set up a snipe without even leaving eBay. If you're interested in an automated sniping service, check out several (most offer a free trial), ask eBay acquaintances about their own favorites, and then decide which one is best for you.

Tip: One advantage to using an automated sniper over eBay's regular proxy bidding is that if you change your mind before the auction ends, you can cancel a snipe right up until a few minutes before the auction's end. With proxy bidding, your bid is a promise to buy.

Here are some popular sniping services (prices and policies, of course, may change):

- **eSnipe** (*www.esnipe.com*). After a free trial period, eSnipe charges one percent of your winning bid (minimum 25 cents, maximum $10) whenever it successfully snipes an auction for you. If you don't win the auction, eSnipe doesn't charge.

- **AuctionSniper** (*www.auctionsniper.com*). Your first three wins are free. After that, AuctionSniper's fee scale ranges from 25 cents to a maximum of $5, based on your winning bid.

- **EZ sniper** (*www.ezsniper.com*). Three successful snipes free, then a per-win percentage fee between 10 cents and $10.

- **BidSlammer** (*www.bidslammer.com*). This site calls itself a "win management service": It integrates searching, tracking, and sniping. BidSlammer's Auction Tribune lets you create a list of searches, tracks your searches across 200 e-commerce sites (not just eBay), and emails you results once a day. The free trial is three snipes; then the fee range goes from 10 cents to $5 per win.

- **Bidnapper** (*www.bidnapper.com*). Available by subscription after a 10-day free trial, Bidnapper adds a few features: seller profiles strip out all the positive feedback and show you just the negative (when you're looking for troubling patterns); a feedback automator means you can leave feedback from the Bidnapper site; and Bidnapper's search feature, the Shadow, lets you search by keyword or bidder to set up your snipes—if someone keeps winning auctions you're bidding in, the Shadow lets you target that bidder and start sniping his auctions. Subscriptions range from $6.95/month to $45.95/year, or you can buy blocks of snipes.

- **PhantomBidder** (*www.phantombidder.com*). Two-week free trial with unlimited bids. Besides a subscription plan, PhantomBidder offers fixed-price sniping: you pay $6 for 10 bid credits (you spend one bid credit for each auction PhantomBidder wins on your behalf) or $10 for 20 bid credits. PhantomBidder lets you leave feedback from its site, and it lets you snipe all international eBay sites except Korea's.

- **HammerSnipe** (*www.hammersnipe.com*). This one is free for occasional, basic sniping—up to three snipes per week—but every time you log in, you have to navigate past a couple of pages urging you to subscribe or donate money before you can set up your snipe. And if you want advanced options, like bidding on a group of auctions or the ability to specify when your snipe will hit, you have to subscribe to HammerSnipe's "priority service," which starts at $8.95/month. HammerSnipe offers a free toolbar called PowerTool that allows one-click sniping as you browse auctions. You can download PowerTool at *www.hammertap. com/powertool*.

- **AuctionStealer** (*www.auctionstealer.com*). AuctionStealer tracks an unlimited number of auctions and lets you make up to three free snipes each week. You can bid on multiple items, view past snipes, and cancel a snipe at any time if you change your mind. Or you can upgrade to priority service to snipe in bid groups, specify your precise snipe time, and snipe as often as your heart desires.

Tip: Merlin Software's JustDeals (*www.pctechzone.com*) is a Windows-based search-and-buy engine that combs through Buy It Now auctions—and only BIN auctions—to find you the best price. Tell JustDeals what to look for and how much you want to spend, and let it do your bargain-hunting for you. The program will notify you with a desktop alert, an email, or a text message to your cell phone (your choice). It can even buy the item for you before someone else finds the deal. It's kind of like having an automatic sniper for BIN auctions.

If you don't feel comfortable sharing your eBay ID and password with a third party, you're not locked out of the automated sniping game. You can download and install a snipe program on your computer. Many of these programs offer other functions, such as search filters and auction tracking, in addition to sniping. Even though you don't have to be at your computer to snipe using these programs, you do have to leave your computer turned on so it can connect to the Internet and start sniping. Prices vary; BidSage (for Windows) and JbidWatcher (for Macs) are free. The following downloads are for Windows, except where noted:

- Final Bid (*www.v-com.com*)

- AuctionSleuth (*www.auction-sleuth.com*)

- Auction Sentry (*www.auction-sentry.com*)

- Snipe (*www.telience.com*)

- BidSage (*www.auctionsagesoftware.com*)

- MaxiBidder (*www.colourfull.com/maxi.html*); for Macs

- JbidWatcher (*www.jbidwatcher.com*); for Macs

If you're really interested in automated searching and sniping, you may want to check out the Auction Software Review (*www.auctionsoftwarereview.com*). Shown in Figure 3-18, the Auction Software Review evaluates dozens of sniping services and programs. The site charges $9.99 for a lifetime membership; in return, you get candid opinions on what does and doesn't work. The Auction Software Review covers software related to selling, searching, feedback, and more—not just sniping.

Figure 3-18:
Joining the Auction Software Review Web site is a good idea, whether you're looking for the fastest sniper or the most flexible tracking database. The left-hand menu shows the kinds of tools available. Besides reviews of software for buyers and sellers, the site offers eBay statistics, discussion boards, and FAQs and articles about buying and selling. Some of these resources are free; others are for members only.

Other Proxy Bidding Strategies

The idea behind proxy bidding (page 47) is that you bid the most you're willing to pay, hoping to get the item for less but resigning yourself to letting it go if someone else bids more than your maximum bid. eBay recommends that you bid early, bid your max, and hope to win. This sounds great in theory, but all too often, you find yourself outbid by 50 cents in the closing seconds of an auction, realizing too late that you wouldn't have minded paying another dollar or two.

Tip: One eBayer described his proxy bidding strategy like this: don't bid for a bargain and hope to win. Bid to win and hope for a bargain.

Of course, sniping, described in the previous section, is one way to work the system. But if you're not comfortable with that method, you're not left in the cold. For the absolute best chance of winning an auction, tweak eBay's official recommendation just a bit and follow this simple three-step strategy:

1. **Figure out your true maximum bid.**

   In timed auctions, it might feel like the last bid wins, but this isn't necessarily true. The *highest* bid wins, no matter when someone placed it, as long as it comes in before the clock's done ticking. So the first thing to do is figure out your true highest bid. Research the item, online or at the local mall, to determine a reasonable price. And don't forget to factor in any shipping or insurance costs. Then, ask yourself: would I be willing to pay just 50 cents more? A dollar more? Two dollars? Five? When you can't imagine paying a penny more (even if someone else would), that's your maximum price.

2. **Time your bid late in the game.**

   If the auction still has several days to run, don't bid yet. No need to call other shoppers' attention to an item you want. You, savvy shopper, want to bid as late as you can in the auction. (When other buyers are scanning their search results page, it's human nature to want to check out the auctions that already have some interest. If someone's made a bid, at least one person thinks the item is worth buying—that fact makes it worth closer inspection.) If you're going to be asleep or at work when the auction ends, there's no need to stay up late or cut out of a staff meeting so you can post your bid in the last five minutes. But put in your bid as late as is reasonable, given your schedule.

3. **Let the system work its magic.**

   eBay's proxy bidding system bids the minimum amount required on your behalf: either the starting price (if no one else has bid), or one or more bid increments (if there's already a bid on the item). As new bids come in—even from snipers—eBay's proxy system continues to bid for you, little by little, until you win the item or the price sails past your maximum (in which case, you don't want it anyway).

How to Win Dutch Auctions

Dutch auctions might look like a free-for-all, with lots of people bidding on numerous items, but what they really offer are bargains for a few lucky winners. In a Dutch auction, a number of identical items are for sale, and they go to the highest bidders until the quantity runs out. The cool part is that all winning bidders pay only the price that was bid by the *lowest* winning bidder. (For more on how Dutch auctions work, see page 30.)

Think of it this way. There's a line drawn in the sand. All the winning bidders are on one side of the line; all the losers are on the other side. The closer you stand to that line, the higher your chances of being nudged over to the losing side. So when you join in the bidding on a Dutch auction, you want to bid a little higher than you have to, to make sure you're on the winning side of the line when the auction ends.

Here's an example. You're shopping for an ink cartridge for your printer. You find a Dutch auction for the right brand and model number. The seller has four available. The opening bid was $9.99, the lowest winning bid at the moment is $10.99, and the current highest bid is $15.99. The auction has only half an hour left to run, and you're in competition with six other bidders. Table 3-2 shows how the bidding stacks up.

Table 3-2. *Dutch Auction Bidders*

eBay ID	Bid Amount	Quantity Wanted	Quantity Winning
bidder1	15.99	1	1
bidder2	14.49	1	1
bidder3	12.49	1	1
bidder4	10.99	1	1
bidder5	10.49	1	0
bidder6	9.99	1	0

UP TO SPEED

Winning with Proxy Bidding: An Example

You're looking for a 2,000-count case of fresh paintballs and can buy them locally for about 45 bucks plus tax. You get on eBay, hoping to find them for less. Eventually, you find an auction that looks good: a brand-new, unopened case with a starting price of $19.99. Shipping costs $10 even, so you're looking at $29.99, which is still under the price you're willing to pay. The seller's feedback looks good. This auction is worth going for.

You'd be happy to get the paintballs for $29.99, including shipping, but you'd be *willing* if necessary to pay more than that. If your final cost were $34.99, you'd still be ahead of the mall price by a little more than 10 dollars. It would seem a shame to lose a good deal over a few cents; after giving it some thought, you decide that a total cost of $39.49 is as high as you're willing to go. More than that, and you might as well drive to the mall and pick up the paintballs there.

You subtract the $10 shipping fee from the total amount, making your bid $29.49. The auction has a little over a day to run, and no one has bid yet. You add the paintball auction to your watch list and will take another look when you

get home from work tomorrow, when the auction will be down to its last two hours.

When you check the next day, the number of bids is still zero. Because the auction will close soon, you decide to place a bid of $29.49. You appear as the high bidder, at the opening price of $19.99. If no one else bids, you'll win them for that price. If someone else who's been watching the auction tries to snipe it, however, you've authorized eBay to bid up to $29.49 for you.

In the last minute of the auction, things start happening. Your bid jumps from $19.99 to $20.99—someone tried to beat your opening bid by just 50 cents, but proxy bidding immediately raised your bid by one bid increment to beat the attempted snipe. The price jumps again, but you're still the high bidder. When the auction ends, you've won the paintballs for $23.49. The sniper set his bids too low, trying to win by a few cents, but ran out of time before discovering your bid cap. When the clock ran out, you won. You fended off a sniper and even came in with a little more than the $10 savings you were hoping for.

In this Dutch auction, there are four high bidders: bidders 1 through 4. If the auction were to end right now, bidders 1 through 4 would each win one ink cartridge, and each would pay $10.99—the lowest winning bid. But the auction is still running, and you want to bid. You must bid higher than $10.99. If you bid $11.99, your bid pushes bidder4 across the line into the "loser" pool—but now *you're* the one whose bid is on the line.

Instead, aim higher. You want your bid to be a couple of steps away from that line in the sand. If you bid an amount between bidder2's $14.49 bid and bidder3's bid of $12.49—say, $12.99—you knock bidder4 out of the bidding and nudge bidder3 to the line. If no more bidding action takes place after you make your bid, you and bidders 1 through 3 will each get a cartridge for $12.49.

What if you want two cartridges? You can still bid $12.99 (each), but your bid will knock out bidders 3 and 4 both, because only four ink cartridges are up for auction. That makes you the lowest bidder, and the next one liable to be shoved across the line. If you want two cartridges, consider bidding an amount between bidder2's $14.49 and bidder1's $15.99 to protect yourself from being knocked out of the auction. You could still be out of the bidding if another bidder comes along and bids higher—for instance, someone could come along and bid $17.99 apiece for all four—but the higher you place your bid in the bidding hierarchy, the better your chances of staying in the auction.

Note: As in all auctions, don't bid more than you're willing to pay. You'll pay less than your bid in a Dutch auction if someone else has made a lower winning bid, but this isn't guaranteed. *Your* bid might be the lowest winning bid, so be ready to follow through.

Can you snipe a Dutch auction? Sure. Follow the same strategy of placing your bid a couple of steps higher than the lowest winning bidder, but do so in the closing seconds of the auction. Depending on how many other snipers are around, you'll knock out the low bidder, but you'll still probably get the item for less than you bid.

More Ways to Get a Good Deal

By now, you can track down bargains like a bloodhound and snipe like a sharpshooter. You can get eBay's proxy bidding engine revving like a race car and shoulder your way into Dutch auctions. This section lets you in on a couple of other money-saving tricks.

About Me

eBay forbids sellers from including links to Web pages outside eBay in their auctions. Yet some of these sellers have their own Web stores, often with wider selection and sales worth checking out. How can you find these stores if sellers can't advertise them? By viewing something called an *About Me page* (page 191).

If the word *me* appears next to the seller's ID and feedback rating on an auction page, click it. This takes you to the seller's About Me page. About Me pages are personal Web pages hosted by eBay. Any eBayer can create an About Me page to tell the rest of the eBay community about herself, her hobbies and interests, her family, what she collects or sells. Sellers can use their About Me pages to link to sites beyond eBay. If a seller has a Web store or a brick-and-mortar store, you might find it on their About Me page—expanding your shopping options.

Note: eBay protects only transactions conducted through its site (see page 72 for more on eBay's Buyer Protection Plan). If you buy offsite, you're on your own. Shop only in the offsite stores belonging to sellers you trust, after you've bought from them in an eBay auction or two.

---

eBay Anything Points

Airlines have frequent-flyer miles. Hotels and credit cards have rewards programs for loyal customers. eBay has Anything Points. One point isn't worth much all by itself—just a penny or so—but as they add up, you can use your Anything Points toward purchases you make on eBay.

Earning Anything Points

You can sign up for Anything Points by going to *http://anythingpoints.ebay.com*, shown in Figure 3-19, and then clicking Join Now. eBay prompts you for your password, then asks for the email address you use for your PayPal account.

Note: You must have a PayPal account to use Anything Points. If you're halfway through the sign-up process and realize that you don't yet have a PayPal account, just sign up for Anything Points with your regular email address, then go to *www.paypal.com* (or follow the link from the signup page) and open your PayPal account. See page 52 for more on PayPal.

Once you've signed up, you can start earning Anything Points. Here are a few ways you can get started:

- **Some auctions feature Anything Points for each dollar you bid (as long as you win).** To find these auctions, go to the Anything Points home page (*http://anythingpoints.ebay.com*), and then click the Earn Points from eBay Sellers link.

- **Refer a friend.** If your friend registers with eBay, you earn 500 points.

- **Swap points from other rewards programs (like frequent-flyer miles) for Anything Points.** From the Anything Points page, click the Exchange Points link to find out if your rewards program is eligible.

- **Shop offsite with certain eBay partners and earn points for your purchases.** Follow the Anything Points page's Earn Points from Partners link.

- **Sign up for an eBay credit card and earn points when you use it to buy stuff.** To get info about the credit card, go to the Anything Points page, and then click Earn Points from Partners.

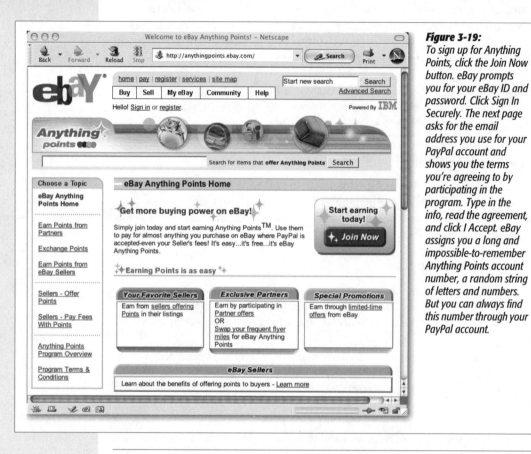

Figure 3-19:
To sign up for Anything Points, click the Join Now button. eBay prompts you for your eBay ID and password. Click Sign In Securely. The next page asks for the email address you use for your PayPal account and shows you the terms you're agreeing to by participating in the program. Type in the info, read the agreement, and click I Accept. eBay assigns you a long and impossible-to-remember Anything Points account number, a random string of letters and numbers. But you can always find this number through your PayPal account.

Tip: If you ever lose your account number, you can find it easily through your PayPal account. Log in to PayPal, then choose My Account → Profile → Redeem Gift Certificates and Points (under Financial Information). This page lists your Anything Points account number and any points you've accrued.

Redeeming Anything Points

Once you've accumulated a nice stack of points in your PayPal account, you can use them to pay for your auctions. It's like getting a new caboose for your Lionel train set for free. To redeem your points, log in to PayPal to pay for something. On the Payment Details page, click Add/Select Redemption Codes or Anything Points. Then continue as usual.

You can even use Anything Points to pay for *part* of a purchase, creating a do-it-yourself discount. After you've applied your Anything Points, just choose your usual funding source to make up the balance.

There are some conditions for spending your points:

- For you to pay for an item using Anything Points, the seller must accept PayPal as a payment method.

- You must purchase the item through eBay, and the auction must use U.S. dollars, Canadian dollars, British sterling, or euros as its currency.

- You must pay through PayPal within 10 days of the auction's end.

- If you have more than one eBay account, you have to make the purchase with the same eBay ID that your Anything Points account is registered to.

Tip: You can also search for auctions offering Anything Points from the Advanced Search page. After you've typed in your search term, scroll down the page and turn on the "Items offering Anything Points" checkbox.

ALTERNATIVE REALITY

The Best Bargain of All

The best deal of all, of course, is getting things for free. You won't find free stuff on eBay, but you will on this site: *www.freecycle.org*. Freecycle is a grassroots network of more than 2,000 regional groups of people who want to give away, not throw away, their excess possessions.

You can post a request for something you're looking for or a notice that you have something to get rid of. The one hard-and-fast rule is that everything listed on Freecycle must be free. There are Freecycle groups all over the U.S. and Canada, ranging from a few dozen members to several thousand, and international groups are on the rise. On the off chance there's not already a group in your region, you can start your own. The Freecycle discussion boards work through Yahoo! groups, so you need a Yahoo! ID and password to sign up. You can get these during the sign-up process.

To join a Freecycle group, follow these steps:

1. Point your Web browser to *www.freecycle.org*.

2. From the menu on the left-hand side of the page, choose a group near you. Groups are organized by country and (in the U.S.) region. Click your general region, and then scroll down the list to find a group near you.

3. Click Join. This opens a blank email in your email program. You don't have to type anything; just send a blank email to the address provided.

4. When you receive an email with instructions on how to join, follow the steps given.

If you click GoTo instead of Join in step 3, click the blue Join This Group! button on the page that opens and sign in (if you have a Yahoo! ID) or register (if you don't have a Yahoo! ID).

Power Buying Strategies

eBay has a recognition program for serious sellers—high-volume, highly rated businesspeople it calls PowerSellers. eBay has no official "PowerBuyers" program, but some shoppers deserve the name.

Power buyers are the ones who really know their way around eBay. They might be collectors snapping up treasures for their collections—coins, comics, Matchbox cars, Beanie Babies, Civil War–era autographs, you name it. Or they might be the big spenders who close big deals, buying houses, cars, and luxury items that most shoppers merely dream about. Power buyers know how to use buyers' tools to streamline their shopping, and they can spot a scam a mile away.

While the previous chapters covered bidding strategies, this chapter shares other secrets serious shoppers use to prevail on eBay, including:

- Tools to help buyers research smarter.
- Software to help collectors organize their collections.
- Strategies for buying jewelry, cars, and real estate with confidence.
- Tips for avoiding common scams.

Tools for Power Buyers

When you're power shopping, you want the information for good buys right there at your fingertips, right now. Is $79.99 a good price for that cell phone, or could you get it for $50 if you waited a couple of weeks? Is that PowerSeller a slow shipper, or does he get a lot of returns? Serious shoppers power up their shopping with *price-analysis tools* to figure out the best price, and they use *feedback filters* to drill down straight to the feedback they need to see. And if, like many hardcore buyers, you're a collector who uses eBay to beef up your collection, there are tools to help you organize your collection.

Price-Analysis Tools

On eBay, the marketplace sets the price of any given item, as bidders vie with each other until only one's left standing at the auction's end. But that marketplace changes daily. Supply and demand both shift as sellers try to jump on hot-item bandwagons and as shoppers spend more time at their computers (around the holidays) or less (summer weekends). A digital camera that sold for $225 one week might sell for $187 the next. To get a picture of eBay price trends, you could sift through completed auctions, record winning prices, and figure out the averages—but why go to all that effort when price-analysis tools will do it for you in a couple of seconds?

Price-analysis tools scour completed auctions and scoop up the closing prices, then use that information to help you decide how much to spend now—or whether to wait until the price goes down. Here are a couple of good price-analysis tools:

- **Terapeak.** The market research gurus at Terapeak (*www.terapeak.com*) offer a free, quick price analysis. Terapeak's search results give you the average eBay price for similar items that sold in the last week and show currently active listings. On Terapeak's home page, head to the Shop Smarter On eBay.com text box, type in the name of the item you're shopping for, select the appropriate eBay category, and then click the Find It button to get results like those shown in Figure 4-1. (Be patient. It can take several seconds for the results to appear.)

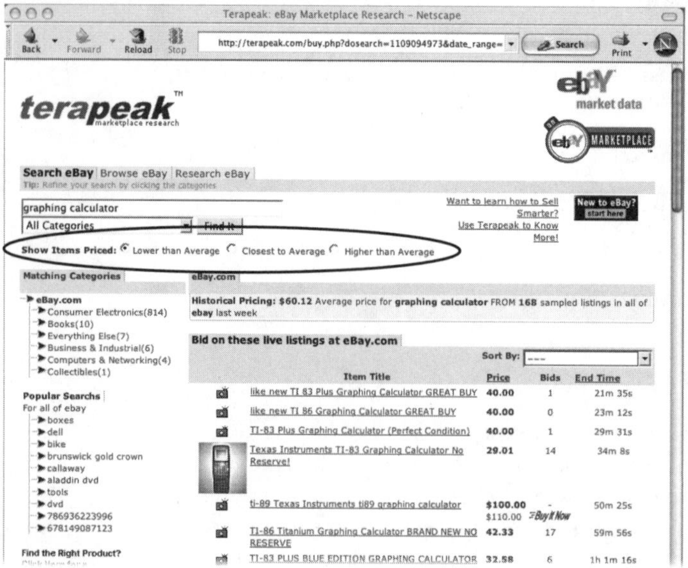

Figure 4-1:
If you're looking for bargains on Terapeak's Search eBay page, you can use the Show Items Priced button to sort your results and find items priced lower than average. (In practice, though, this choice often brings up accessories or brand-new auctions with a low opening bid.) If you want to buy now, select Closest to Average (click Find It again) to see what you're likely to pay. Higher than Average will show you overpriced items—but also high-end merchandise if that's what you're looking for. Click any item's title to go to its auction page.

• **AuctionSmart.** This price-analysis tool (download it at *www.boostauction.com*) works with Windows and Internet Explorer to stack the odds of winning an auction in your favor. Search for an item you want, and then click the Analysis button on AuctionSmart's toolbar. AuctionSmart searches completed auctions and breaks them down by winning bid, presenting a chart that tells you what bid will most likely win the auction. To do AuctionSmart's analysis on your own, you'd need a calculator, a spreadsheet, and a degree in statistics. See Figure 4-2.

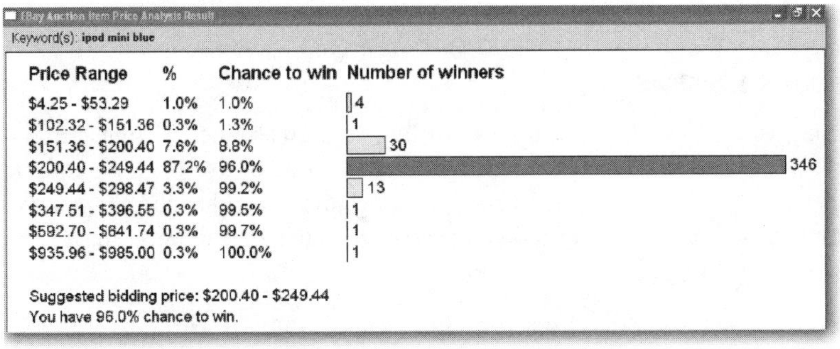

Price Range	%	Chance to win	Number of winners
$4.25 - $53.29	1.0%	1.0%	4
$102.32 - $151.36	0.3%	1.3%	1
$151.36 - $200.40	7.6%	8.8%	30
$200.40 - $249.44	87.2%	96.0%	346
$249.44 - $298.47	3.3%	99.2%	13
$347.51 - $396.55	0.3%	99.5%	1
$592.70 - $841.74	0.3%	99.7%	1
$935.96 - $985.00	0.3%	100.0%	1

Suggested bidding price: $200.40 - $249.44
You have 96.0% chance to win.

Figure 4-2:
AuctionSmart's price-analysis chart show that the vast majority of recent auctions for a blue iPod mini ended with a winning bid between just over $200 and just under $250. If you bid in that price range, you have a 96 percent chance of winning.

Feedback-Analysis Tools

Feedback paints a picture of how a seller conducts his business. In most cases, you'll probably find the simple strategies outlined on page 40 sufficient to analyze a seller's feedback and come to a bid/don't bid decision. But if you're considering purchasing from a high-volume seller, you need more. You need a feedback-analysis tool.

Here's why. High-volume sellers can accumulate a couple of pages' worth of new comments each day, and you could waste precious time combing through pages and pages of feedback comments looking for troubling patterns in a seller's feedback history, like multiple complaints about slow shipping or lousy packing. Feedback-analysis tools save you time by filtering out the positive comments so you can take a hard look at the problems.

GutCheck (*www.teamredline.com*) is a free tool that works with Internet Explorer and Windows 95 or higher. After you've installed GutCheck and you're looking at an eBay auction page, right-click a seller's ID or feedback score and you can choose from these options:

• See the percentages of positive, negative, and neutral comments for all feedback received. eBay displays only the percentage that's positive, but GutCheck breaks it *all* down.

• Filter out the newbies and see what seasoned pros have had to say. You can ignore feedback left by eBayers with a feedback score lower than five (or any number you specify).

• Filter out all positive comments to see only the dirt.

Another feedback checker that lets you filter out positive comments is BayCheck Pro, available at *www.hammertap.com*. BayCheck Pro has more than a feedback filter; it also gives you one-click access to a seller's history, so you can check current and completed auctions at a glance. Save a list of frequently checked sellers to keep an eye on their auctions.

Tip: For a quick check of all the negative and neutral feedback an eBayer has given or received, you don't need to install any software. Just go to *www.toolhaus.org/cgi-bin/negs* and type in the eBay ID you want to check.

Tools for Collectors

Collecting is big business on eBay. According to a 2004 Nielsen survey, about a third of all Americans collect something—and one out of five of those collectors buys, sells, or browses on eBay. Most eBay collectors agree that the site has made collecting more fun and given them access to items they'd never have found otherwise.

If you're serious about collecting, you need to get organized. Not only will collectors' software keep you from going crazy trying to remember what you have and where you put it—and whether you should bid on that Niagara Falls souvenir spoon to round out your collection—but if your stuff is valuable, this software can help you create detailed records for your insurance company.

There are several specialized programs out there to organize your collection, creating records of what you own, how much it's worth, and where you've stashed it. You can even include one or more photos for each record. The bigger your collection (and it can grow very quickly once you get going on eBay), the more helpful you'll find these tools. Each has a different look and feel—take a look at several and see which works best for you.

Here's a selection of what's available.

- Mac fans can use **Complete Collector** to keep tabs on any kind of collection. Complete Collector, available from *www.colourfull.com,* lets you drag and drop photos into your records and has a built-in search feature, so you can look up exactly when you bought that 1939 Lincoln wheat penny and how much you paid for it.

- For Mac fans who collect CDs, DVDs, or books, Bruji offers specialized software for these types of collections: **CDpedia, DVDpedia, and Bookpedia.** If you type in a title, the software connects to an online database to fill in the rest of the information. You can organize your collection in any way you like. For example, Bookpedia lets you organize your book collection by topic, favorite author, genre, and so on, and you can set up your categories to update automatically whenever you add a book that matches a particular category's criteria. You can also make wish lists for items you want to add to your collection and keep track of what people have borrowed from you. Download the software at *www.bruji.com*, shown in Figure 4-3.

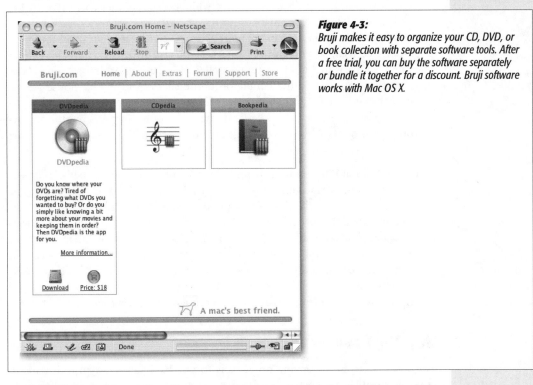

Figure 4-3:
Bruji makes it easy to organize your CD, DVD, or book collection with separate software tools. After a free trial, you can buy the software separately or bundle it together for a discount. Bruji software works with Mac OS X.

- **Collectibles Database,** for collectors of 14 popular kinds of collectibles (including figures, coins, bears, ornaments, and baskets), works on Windows 95 or higher, or on Macs that have SoftWindows or Virtual PC. This software comes preloaded with information about collectibles, including photos. So you don't have to type in the details of each and every Precious Moments figure you own, because the program already has 'em—for more than 2,500 Precious Moments items. You can print reports and graph prices and other trends, as well as buy annual updates to keep your information current. This software is available at *www.collectiblesdatabase.com*.

- Primasoft's **Organizer Deluxe** series (*www.primasoft.com*) offers Windows-based software for specialized collections—books, coins, wine, music, movies, stamps, sports cards, and more. If your collection doesn't fit one of these specialized categories, Collectibles Organizer Deluxe is a more general program useful for a wide range of collectibles. As you create your collection database, you type in the item name, its condition, how much it cost, when you bought it, what it's worth, and any notes. When you search your collection, you can sort the results by title, country, order of entry, category, and more, and you can filter searches to find, for example, which sports cards you bought between December 28, 2004 and February 18, 2005 (and how much you spent on them).

- **Vendi** (*www.vendisoftware.com*) comes with specialized data-entry screens tailored to more than 30 popular categories—breweriana, arrowheads, war memorabilia, dolls, jewelry, and many more—or you can create your own. It offers a 30-day free trial, so you can see whether you like it before you buy. Vendi's coolest feature is that it integrates with eBay. You can import information about an auction you won with a couple of mouse clicks. And if your house gets so full that you have to start auctioning off some of your collection, Vendi helps you keep track of your eBay sales and saves you some eBay fees by storing auction photos on its Web site (see page 203 for more about using Web sites other than eBay to host your auction photos).

- **Visual PackRat Plus** is currently for Windows only (but the company is considering including a Mac version in the next release). Visual PackRat Plus has 36 different editions, each tailored to a popular kind of collectible: Barbies, advertising memorabilia, paperweights, Disney figures, Swarovski, NASCAR, collectible plates, *Star Wars* stuff, and more. You can store up to seven images for each item in your collection, email those images, and organize up to five collections at once (there's an additional charge for each edition you install). Visual PackRat Plus also lets you hook up with eBay to import items you've bought and help you if you decide to sell. It's available at *www.vpackrat.com*.

Hey, Big Spender

The best way to begin buying on eBay is to purchase some low-priced items to build up positive feedback and learn how auctions work. After a while, though, you might be tempted by luxe-level offerings. Before you bid on big-ticket items, there are a few things you should know, like when to use escrow (page 56) and how far eBay and PayPal's buyer protection programs will (or won't) cover you (page 72). But there's more. This section shows you what you need to do before you bid, and it offers specialized strategies for the pricey stuff, like jewelry, cars, and real estate.

If you plan to bid $15,000 or more, you need to contact eBay in advance; eBay requires big-ticket bidders to have a valid credit card number on file or separate confirmation of your identity (explained below). If you haven't registered a credit card number with eBay, you can do so from your My eBay page. (Head to the navigation bar and click My eBay to pull up your My eBay page.) Click the Personal Information link, scroll down to Financial Information, and then click Change. After you've confirmed your password, you can type in information about your credit card.

Tip: If you submitted your credit card info a while ago, make sure the card hasn't expired since then. If it has, update your information.

If you'd rather not give eBay your credit card number, you can have your personal information verified for a $5 fee. When you do so, you get a nifty icon next to your eBay ID to show that you've been verified. From the navigation bar, select Services → ID Verify → Sign Up Now. Be prepared to give your date of birth, Social Security Number, and driver's license number (if you have one; if not, select No Driver's License from the drop-down list). When you click the Continue button, you authorize eBay to check your personal credit profile.

Note: When eBay verifies your identity, you can't change your contact information (address and phone number) for 30 days. After 30 days, you can change this info—but if you do, you lose your verified status. You'll have to go through the verification process all over again if you want it back.

FREQUENTLY ASKED QUESTION

Join the Club

Where can I discuss collectibles with other collectors on eBay?

One of the joys of eBay is that you can find other people from around the world who share your interests. If your friends and family are getting a little tired of hearing about your passion for vintage lunch boxes or mermaid figurines, it's obviously time to make some new friends.

The place to look is in eBay's Collectors Clubs. In these bulletin-board-style discussion groups, you'll find both buyers and sellers in conversation about every aspect of collecting, from questions about particular items to notices of special sales to talk about favorite pieces. Groups also let members conduct polls and post photo albums.

From the navigation bar, click Community. On the eBay Community page, look under Connect for eBay Groups. Click the Groups link, and then click Collectors Clubs to discover a whole new world of fellow collecting fanatics. There are 15 top-level categories, from Antiques to Toys Hobbies & Trading Cards, each with many groups under its umbrella. Click any category to browse its groups.

When you find a group you'd like to join, click its name to open the Welcome page for that group. The Welcome page gives you a description of the group and tells you the eBay ID of the group's leader, when the group began, how many members it has, and the date of the last post. It also tells you whether the group is *public* (any eBayer can join) or *private* (to join, you must receive an invitation or email the group leader for approval).

To join, click the Join Group button. If the group is public, you're in. If it's private, a page opens with a text box that lets you explain why you'd like to join. Type your message, and then click Send Request.

If you don't see a group that interests you, you can start your own: from the navigation bar, click Community → Groups → Collectors Club → Start Group. To start a group, you have to have a feedback score of 50 or higher and have been registered for at least 90 days. For more about eBay Groups, see page 366.

Smart Shopping for Big Spenders

No matter what big-ticket item you buy—from an antique armoire to a brand-new luxury car to a warehouse for stashing all your purchases—follow these guidelines to make sure you're going to get what you pay for:

- **Always check the seller's feedback (page 40) and read the item description carefully.**

- **Check out the seller's return policy (on the auction page).** If you're spending big bucks, you should have time to inspect and authenticate the item before the transaction becomes final. Watch out for no-return policies and *restocking fees*; sellers sometimes charge a fee for taking a return (usually a percentage of the purchase price).

- **Check the auction page to see whether escrow payments are available.** If not, and you want to use an escrow service, use the "Ask seller a question" link to make sure that the seller will go with Escrow.com. Ask this before you bid. Be sure to mention Escrow.com by name to assure the seller that you're not trying to set up a fake transaction.

Warning: The biggest recent trend in online fraud has been fake escrow services. eBay recommends only one service in the U.S., Escrow.com, discussed on page 57. See page 141 for more on scams using fake escrow sites.

- **If you're planning to bid more than $15,000, register your credit card with eBay (page 122).** If you neglect this step, eBay won't accept your bid.

- **Check out the seller's contact information before you pay.** Use the "Ask seller a question" link from the auction page (which sends an email) or, if you're in an active transaction, use Advanced Search → Find Contact Information (which gets you a phone number). If the phone is disconnected or the email you send bounces back, report the contact information as invalid (Help → Contact Us) and don't send any money.

- **Shell out for insurance (page 167).** It's worth it to make sure you'll get your money back if the item arrives damaged or doesn't arrive at all.

- **Never agree to any off-eBay transactions, and never agree to wire transfer as the form of payment.** Wire transfers are untraceable and unrecoverable (see the box on page 144). If the seller asks you to wire money or tries to close the deal off eBay, report them. (Choose Help → Contact Us → "Report problems with other eBay members" → "Problems with sellers," and then select the specific problem. Click the Continue button, and then the Email link. Type your report and click Send Email.)

- **Be ready to authenticate the item—take it to a jeweler, mechanic, rare-book expert, or whoever is qualified to judge what you're buying.** It's ideal, of course, if you can do this before the auction ends, but if you use an escrow service, you can keep your payment in limbo until you've got an expert's thumbs up (or thumbs down).

Jewelry

When you go into a jewelry store, you have a chance to inspect the merchandise (check for flaws or loose settings, try on a piece to see how it looks) before you decide whether to buy. And most stores make it easy for you to return your purchase if you change your mind later on.

Things are a little different on eBay. If you're interested in buying expensive jewelry or watches on eBay, know that many reputable jewelers sell on the site. But problems do exist, including inflated weight estimates, suggestions that the item's quality is better than it actually is, and overblown or phony appraisals. Because many online jewelry sellers aren't certified gemologists, sellers may not realize that their descriptions are misleading. (Or sellers may be shady characters who know darn well what they're doing.)

Either way, the following strategies can help you sift the gems from the dirt:

- **Be familiar with eBay's listing policies.** eBay has established listing policies to make it easier for buyers to know what they're getting. For example, only natural (mined) diamonds meeting industry definitions can be listed in a *diamond* category. Man-made stones must have the word *simulated* or *lab-created* in front of the gem's name; titles must contain phrases like *simulated diamond* or *lab-created sapphire.* Cubic zirconia has its own category and must contain *cubic zirconia* or *CZ* in the title. Similarly, if an item is not solid gold, sellers must state this fact in the auction's title: *gold filled, gold plated, gold electroplate,* and so on. Sellers who fail to meet these guidelines risk seeing their auctions canceled.

  Even with these guidelines in place, you should read the auction description thoroughly. Sometimes a seller will "forget" to state in the auction's title that a gem is lab-created but mention this fact in small print somewhere on the auction page itself.

  If you got taken in an auction that advertised a diamond but sold you a CZ, report it to eBay. Go to Help → Security Center and report the seller for misrepresenting the item.

- **Be prepared to get your own appraisal.** You can find an appraiser through the American Society of Appraisers (*www.appraisers.org*) or the American Gem Society (*www.ags.org*).

- **Ask to use an escrow service.** If your seller will accept payment through Escrow.com—ask before you bid—the site will hold your payment until you've had the item appraised and accepted it.

• **Insist on a fair return policy.** Although using an escrow service affords the best protection, many sellers don't like using them because they feel it protects the buyer but leaves them open to risk: some unscrupulous buyer might replace their genuine piece of jewelry with a fake, returning the fake and keeping both the real item and the payment. If that's the case, make sure that the seller has a return policy you can live with. Look for policies that allow enough time for you to get the item appraised after you've received it, and watch out for restocking fees.

UP TO SPEED

Certification vs. Appraisal

Some of the auction listings on eBay offer jewelry with "certified" stones and show a photo of the certificate. Others describe the jewelry as "appraised." What's the difference?

An *appraisal* is a jeweler's estimate of the item's retail value. Regardless of what the auction claims about appraisals, you should have your own appraisal done by a jeweler you trust to confirm that the piece is worth what you paid for it.

A *certificate* analyzes the specifications of a particular gem, rating what jewelers call the *four c's*: carats, cut, color, and clarity.

- **Carats** are the weight of the stone; one carat equals 200 milligrams. Larger stones are worth more because they're rarer than smaller stones.

- **Cut** describes the stone's shape: round, pear, marquise, oval, princess (square), and so on. A well-cut stone is symmetrical; its facets reflect light evenly to increase the stone's brilliance.

- **Color** involves *hue* (the gemstone's basic color), *saturation* (the color's intensity), and *tone* (the depth of the color). Even diamonds that appear white or clear have color ratings.

- **Clarity** measures the visibility of *inclusions*, tiny flaws or cracks within the gemstone. The lowest clarity rating is I3, in which prominent inclusions affect the stone's appearance; the highest are FL or IF (flawless or internally flawless) and VVS (for very very slightly included). The inclusions in VVS stones are difficult for a gemologist's trained eye to spot, even at 10x magnification.

Just because a gemstone has a certificate doesn't mean it's valuable. It's a good idea to scrutinize the certificate and know where it comes from. To make sure you're getting a valid report, look for these laboratories:

- **Gemological Institute of America (GIA).** Look for the phrase *GIA Gem Trade Laboratory* on the report. The GIA's Web site is *www.gia.edu.*

- **American Gem Society (AGS).** The report should state that an AGS-certified gemologist has compiled it. See *www.ags.org.*

- **EGL USA.** The company began as the U.S. branch of the European Gemological Laboratory but is now independently owned and unaffiliated with EGL labs outside of North America. You can verify EGL USA reports on its Web site: *www.eglusa.com.* Click Online Results, and then type the report number in the box and click Submit. (Many auctions for EGL USA certified items include the report number on the auction page. If not, you can email the seller to ask for it.)

- **International Gemological Institute (IGI).** This site also lets you verify its reports online. To do so, go to the IGI's Web site at *www.igi-usa.com.* From the home page, click English → Update & Duplicate Reports, type in the "SOA number" (which is shown on the report in the text box), and then click View Report. A window opens with a copy of the report, so you can double-check the particulars.

---

eBay Motors

Since its beginnings in April 2000, eBay Motors (Figure 4-4) has been the venue for more than one million car sales and is now the fastest-growing part of the entire eBay site. The Motors division is a nationwide car lot, with everything from collectible muscle cars to basic transportation to brand-new luxury vehicles. Most of the vehicles are sold by dealers, and the average price is just shy of $10,000. To check it out, head to the eBay home page and click the link for eBay Motors, or type *www.motors.ebay.com* into your Web browser.

Figure 4-4:
eBay Motors sells more than just cars. It's the place to look for any motorized vehicle, including go-karts, snowmobiles, speedboats, RVs—even helicopters and airplanes. Be sure to stop by the "How To" Center to familiarize yourself with vehicle auctions before you bid.

You might be nervous about buying a car sight unseen over the Internet. And you'd be right. If you can't kick the tires and look under the hood yourself, how do you know what you're getting?

The first thing to do when you're considering buying a car on eBay is to learn as much as you can about the vehicle. Besides reading the description carefully, something you'd do for any auction, you can check the vehicle's history (page 128) and order a professional inspection (page 128). These options cost money, but if you're seriously thinking about buying a car from a stranger in another state, spending a little money before you buy can save you lots of money later.

Tip: To find car auctions close enough to home that you can look at the car before you bid, click Advanced Search on eBay's home page (*not* the eBay Motors home page, which has a minimum range of 500 miles). Type in the model you want, select eBay Motors as the category, and then scroll down the page to the "Show only" section. Check the box next to "Items within," then select the number of miles you want and type in your Zip code. The results are within the distance you specified.

Run a vehicle history report

A vehicle history report lets you know whether there are any known problems with the car's title, odometer, service record, and more. For example, if the car has been reported stolen or an insurer has declared it a write-off after an accident, a vehicle history will reveal those things.

To run a vehicle history report, head to the auction page of the car you're looking at, and then click the VIN (vehicle identification number). Doing so takes you to AutoCheck (owned by Experian, the credit-reporting company), where you can buy a vehicle history report. (Sellers who offer cars built after 1981 must include the car's unique VIN in the item description; cars built before 1981 don't have a VIN.)

Tip: AutoCheck reports are $7.99 apiece, but if you order several at the same time, you can get up to 10 for $14.99. Helpful if you know you're going to buy a car but are undecided among several choices.

Get an inspection

A physical inspection of the car you're considering can go a long way toward making you feel comfortable that a seller's description is, in fact, accurate.

At your request, SGS Automotive Services (recommended by eBay) will send a technician to do a 150-item check, including interior and exterior photos, of a car you're thinking about buying. Most inspections cost just under $100, and SGS also inspects motorcycles.

Note: An alternative inspection service, CarChex (*www.carchex.com*), offers a 55-point inspection for $79.95.

Know what it's worth

If you were considering buying a car from Ed's Used Cars down the street, you'd look up the going rate in Kelley's Blue Book (*www.kbb.com*). Do the same when you're buying through eBay Motors.

Other industry-standard resources include NADA guides (*www.nadaguides.com*) and Edmunds (*www.edmunds.com*). These sites let you customize your search beyond year, make, and model: you can include factors like mileage, optional equipment, condition, and even the vehicle's Zip code to fine-tune the price you should be paying.

Calculate all costs

In your rush to get a good deal on a hot car, don't forget the costs that go beyond the purchase price. After you buy a car, you still have to deal with your state's tax, title, and registration costs. Also, check to see whether the seller charges any additional fees beyond the purchase price. If the vehicle is in another state, for example, you'll need to factor in the cost of getting it to you (or you to it).

Tip: If you want the car delivered to you, *www.movecars.com* is an Internet directory of auto transport companies that can help you find the best rate.

Arrange financing

It's fun to bid on cars, but after you've played, you've got to pay. If you need financing, you can get it through eBay's financing center (*http://financing-center. ebay.com*) before or after you commit to buy. Rates and lenders vary. In most cases, you can get your application reviewed in less than a minute.

(Of course, you can also arrange financing with your local bank or credit union—if you can do it fast. Most sellers want full payment within a week of the auction's close.)

Watch out for scams

Because car sales typically involve thousands of dollars per transaction, eBay Motors attracts scammers like swarms of geeks to a *Star Wars* premiere. Page 132 reveals a number of general scams, but there are a couple you should be aware of that are common on eBay Motors.

If you bid on a car, motorcycle, ATV, boat, or other vehicle, be particularly careful about Second Chance Offers. A *Second Chance Offer* (SCO) sometimes happens when a buyer backs out of a sale, or when a reserve auction (page 25) ends without meeting its reserve. In those cases, the seller can either relist the item or offer it to another bidder for the highest price that person bid. (Usually Second Chance Offers go to the second-highest bidder, but they can go to anyone who participated.) Read more about fake SCOs, how to spot them, and how to detect them on page 143.

Warning: *Never* accept a Second Chance Offer that comes in an email with "Question from eBay Member" as its subject line. How do scammers get your email address? Sometimes they just guess. If your eBay ID is joesmith989, they'll try *joesmith989@aol.com, joesmith989@hotmail.com, joesmith989@yahoo. com*, and so on. But if you're selling something on eBay, the scammer will use the "Ask seller a question" link in one of your auctions to send you the bogus offer.

Another common scam abuses preapproved bidder lists. The scammer sets up a legitimate-looking auction for, say, a brand-new Mini Cooper, but only preapproved bidders can participate. You email the seller to see if you can get on the list, and the seller comes back with an offer to sell you the Mini for a few thousand bucks. All you have to do is wire the money…. Huh? Doesn't the seller *want* to see how high the bidding will get? Don't be fooled. Every would-be buyer who asks to be on the list gets the same offer you did—because there is no Mini. (And after reading the box on page 144, you'll know it's always a bad idea to pay for an auction with a wire transfer.)

Tip: If you have any questions about buying on eBay Motors—or if an auction looks fishy to you—click the Live Help link at the top of any eBay Motors auction page to chat with an eBay Motors specialist.

Real Estate

Listing real estate on eBay lets sellers reach an international audience of over 50 million potential buyers, and more than 2,000 properties sell via eBay every month. But real estate transactions are complex, and before you bid you should make sure you know what you're getting into.

Although eBay says that its real estate auctions are divided into "binding" and "nonbinding" auctions, no real estate auction conducted on eBay is in fact legally binding, thanks to a plethora of state laws and the complexity of real estate transactions. Here's what the terms actually mean:

- **Nonbinding.** A *nonbinding* real estate auction is basically an ad. The price listed is the seller's asking price, and there's no Place Bid button or bid history. Instead, there's a form at the bottom of the auction page, shown in Figure 4-5, where you can type in your contact info and any questions you might have. Contacting the seller is not the same as making a bid; potential buyers who fill out the contact form don't have any obligation to follow through. It's like calling a realtor about an ad in the paper.

- **Binding.** A so-called *binding* auction for real estate looks just like a regular eBay auction. In these auctions, you're not supposed to bid unless you intend to follow through with the transaction. But because there's so much involved in completing a real estate sale (everything from a property inspection to a title search to obtaining a mortgage) and because laws governing real estate sales vary widely from one state to another, there's no legal obligation to complete the sale. What "following through" means is continuing in good faith. In other words, if you win a real estate auction, you're promising to take the next steps in the transaction. But if the house doesn't measure up to its description or if your mortgage application doesn't come through, you're not obliged to buy.

Note: Buyers and sellers can leave feedback on a binding real estate auction, just like on any other eBay auction. There's no feedback involved in the nonbinding real estate listings advertised on eBay.

Before you place a bid in a real estate auction, take all the steps you would in any other auction. Check out the seller's feedback (given as well as received). Read the auction description carefully, watching for hidden costs. For example, some auctions include a processing fee or closing costs beyond those you pay the bank. In other auctions, you're bidding not on the actual sale price, but a down payment on a much higher price.

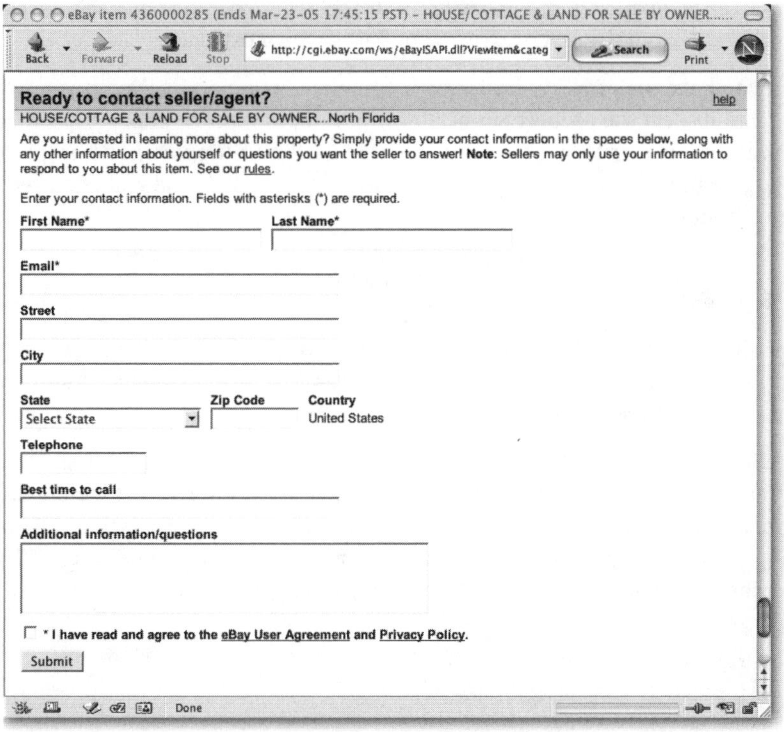

Figure 4-5:
To learn more about a piece of property advertised on eBay, fill out this form. All that's required is your name, email address, and agreement to eBay's terms, but you can also ask questions and provide your phone number and a time to call. The seller can use the information you supply only in relation to this transaction; any other use of your information, if you report it, can get a seller kicked off eBay.

Tip: In the Item Specifics section of the item description, look for a Neighborhood Profile. Click the link to get statistics and demographics about the property's neighborhood, based on Zip code. You can learn about average income, population, and crime rates for the area. All sellers have an opportunity to include a Neighborhood Profile when creating a real estate auction, so if there's *not* a Neighborhood Profile, you should wonder what the seller is trying to hide—a high crime rate? A depressed area where you're unlikely to find tenants? Know what you're getting into before you bid.

Other issues to investigate when buying real estate through eBay include the following:

• Is the title clear? Can you buy title insurance?

• Are taxes up to date?

• Is the property inhabitable as is, or does it need significant renovation?

• Are there any easements or restrictions on the property?

• What type of deed comes with the property? Make sure you're getting a *warranty deed*, which guarantees the title comes to you free and clear.

• What are prices of comparable properties in the same area? (You can look up current listings on *www.realtor.com* to get an idea of prices.)

• Will you have time to apply for a mortgage after the auction ends, or should you arrange financing immediately? Will the seller consider *owner financing*, which means that the seller carries all or part of the mortgage?

• Can you have the property inspected before the auction ends? Even if you can't travel to inspect the property in person, you can pay a professional inspector to look at a property you're seriously interested in. Find a licensed home inspector anywhere in the U.S. at *www.inspectorsguide.com*, or call a local real estate agent for recommendations.

Avoid Scams

Internet fraud is all over the news. And more than 60 percent of online fraud complaints are about online auctions. On the other hand, according to eBay, less than 1 percent of its auctions involve fraud.

Most eBay buyers and sellers are honest; the feedback system soon reveals those who aren't. But the scammers are there. eBay's size makes it easy to hide one fake auction, and the large number of newbies attracted to the site, eager to bid before learning their way around, means a constant supply of new people to con. This section shows you how to avoid becoming one of them.

Note: eBay works hard to shut down scammers on the site. According to Matt Halprin of eBay's Trust & Safety Group, eBay NARU'd over a million accounts in 2004. Not all of those million accounts were scammers, of course; other violations (like moving and forgetting to change your contact info) can result in suspension from the site. And when you consider eBay's gargantuan size, it means more than 99 percent of eBayers do play fair.

---

eBay finds scammers when other eBayers report them. So if you see anything fishy going on, like one of the scams described in this section, go to Help → Security Center and let eBay know.

Designer Fakes

After five months of buying and examining products sold through eBay, Tiffany & Co. estimated that nearly three-quarters of all Tiffany items sold on eBay are fakes. Burberry contends that the number of sham Burberry items is closer to 90 percent. Whether you're looking for jewelry, handbags, watches, designer jeans, sunglasses—anything where the brand matters—be warned in advance that many of the "deals" you'll find on eBay really *are* too good to be true.

Cheap knockoffs of exclusive, high-priced designer goods have flooded the market worldwide in recent years. It's become such a problem that eBay has set up a special program for designers to report (and remove) auctions for fake goods; see the box on page 135 for more about this program, called VeRO.

When you can examine the merchandise in person, you can check for clumsy stitching, misspelled labels, cheap zippers or other hardware, smudged or uneven lettering in authenticity stamps, and other giveaway signs. With an online auction, though, you can't give the goods that kind of inspection until after you've paid. Other than avoiding designer auctions altogether, what can you do?

You can follow these smart fake-busting strategies:

• **First, research the product.** Go to the designer's Web page or an approved online merchant like eLUXURY (*www.eluxury.com*; Figure 4-6) and study the details. Then compare the real thing to the auction you're considering. Are the colors the same? Does the online auction photo hide details that should verify authenticity? Is the stitching even, or does it call attention to itself? A hand-crafted wallet should not look like a mass-produced item.

Figure 4-6:
eLUXURY.com, owned by LVMH (Louis Vuitton, Moet, Hennessey), is an authorized online retailer of many designer brands. It's a good place to inspect the details of high-end retail merchandise, so you can compare those details with pictures of items up for bid on eBay. When you're looking at a particular item, use eLUXURY's alternate views and zoom feature to scrutinize the real thing.

Note: The fact that an item comes with a box, dustbag, or shopping bag doesn't guarantee it's genuine. Not only can sellers fake these items, sellers can also buy them (empty) on eBay.

- **Pass on any auction that fails to include a photo of the item.** If the seller included a photo and it looks good, double-check to make sure it's not merely a copy snagged from the manufacturer's Web site. You want to be as sure as you can that the photo on the auction page is the actual item up for bid. In fact, one photo doesn't tell you all that much. Click the "Ask seller a question" link to request more pictures.

- **Keep an eye out for these telltale clues.** Would you sell a $25,000 Rolex for $19.99? A ridiculously low starting price with no reserve is a clue that the seller doesn't have much to lose, because the item isn't genuine. For another clue, click the "View seller's other items" link. Does the seller have dozens and dozens of listings for brand-new, high-end merchandise? Companies like Louis Vuitton, Chanel, and so on do not wholesale to independent eBay sellers. So where's the seller getting all this stuff?

Tip: To boost your chances of finding an authentic designer item (say, a Gucci handbag), look for a gently used bag offered by someone who's not selling a boatload of Gucci stuff. And odds are that someone selling a real, live, second-hand Gucci bag has started the bidding at a price high enough to recoup some of its original purchase price.

- **Check the seller's member profile and feedback.** If other buyers of similar items complain they've received fakes, it clues you in to what that seller is really offering. A relatively new seller who has tons of cheaply priced luxury goods probably isn't selling the real thing. Even a seller with 100 percent positive feedback can be suspect; did most of it come from members who are no longer registered? Was the positive feedback from buying or selling? What kinds of items? You might want to think twice before bidding on a Louis Vuitton clutch offered by someone whose entire trading history so far consists of buying and selling one-cent recipes.

Tip: After you've checked the feedback, wait a few days and check it again. A fraudulent seller can accrue a lot of negatives in a short amount of time.

- **Trust your gut.** Use some common sense. If someone is selling a Coach bag, claiming to have original tags and a receipt from Bergdorf's, why didn't the person just return the bag to Bergdorf's for a store credit? Why would the seller put it on eBay and lose so much original purchase price? The old "I waited too long to take it back" excuse is baloney. If you had $1,200 on the line, you'd make it a priority to return the item and get your money back, wouldn't you?

When it comes to designer auctions, know that there are a lot of fakes out there—some would say that *most* of the designer products up for auction on eBay are fake—and proceed with caution. If you have any doubts, don't bid.

POWER USERS' CLINIC

VeRO

VeRO, eBay's *Verified Rights Owners* program, works to protect the rights of intellectual property owners: designers, patent holders, copyright holders, and so on. Just as important, VeRO helps protect consumers from paying big money for phony goods.

Here's how it works. When a VeRO member—who might work for a design or music company, or might be an artist or an inventor—reports an item that infringes on the person or entity who owns the rights to that product, eBay removes the listing and warns the seller not to list any similar infringing items.

An example of an infringing product might be a fake Rolex watch, cheap sunglasses purporting to be from Chanel, a forged painting, or a pirated DVD or computer program. A seller who ignores eBay's warning and continues to list infringing items will get kicked off eBay.

Some companies have full-time staff hunting for and reporting counterfeit items up for auction. eBay also does some voluntary monitoring, but it really relies on VeRO members to find the auctions that step on their toes.

What can you do if you find an item you know is fake? Report it. Go to *pages.ebay.com/help/policies/replica-counterfeit.html* to submit a report (copy the item number from the auction page and have it ready). eBay may or may not act on your report—they tend to sit up and take notice most when it's a VeRO member who does the reporting.

Some VeRO members list contact information on eBay, so you can go to them directly. If you can contact the VeRO member whose rights the auction infringes on, you can bet they'll act (and eBay will listen). To find a VeRO member and see if there's a way to get in touch with that member, go to the bottom of the eBay home page, and click Policies → Verified Rights Owner (VeRO) Program → "VeRO Program participant About Me pages." Click a category, such as Apparel, Jewelry, and Watches; Music; or Sporting Good & Memorabilia. If the VeRO member you're looking for is on the list, click its name to see its About Me page and whether there's an email address. If there is, use it to send the VeRO member the auction number. If the VeRO member passes your info on to eBay, the counterfeit item will magically disappear.

Shill Game

Shill bidding is the practice of placing false bids to drive up the price of an item artificially. Sometimes a seller will bid on his or her own items from a second account; other times friends or family members will bid on items they have no intention of buying, just to get the seller a better price. Shill bidders often try to start a bidding war, getting other bidders caught up emotionally until they've bid beyond their better judgment. When the bidding stops, the shill bidder retracts his high bid, leaving another bidder holding the bag.

Shill bidding is annoying and dishonest; rather than letting the marketplace determine the price, shill bidders push it up. And eBayers get cheated out of bargains.

Besides all that, shill bidding is illegal.

One way to avoid shill bidding is to save your bid until late in the auction. If you snipe the auction, shill bidders won't have time to push up your bid.

But what about an auction that already has some bids? Can you determine whether the bidding is legitimate, showing real demand for the item, or artificially inflated? The first place to look is the item's bid history; on the auction page, click the History link (Figure 4-7). Shill bidders tend to put in really high bids (then retract them) or nibble (page 104) at an item until they've revealed another bidder's maximum. These strategies aren't proof of shill bidding, but they're a place to start investigating.

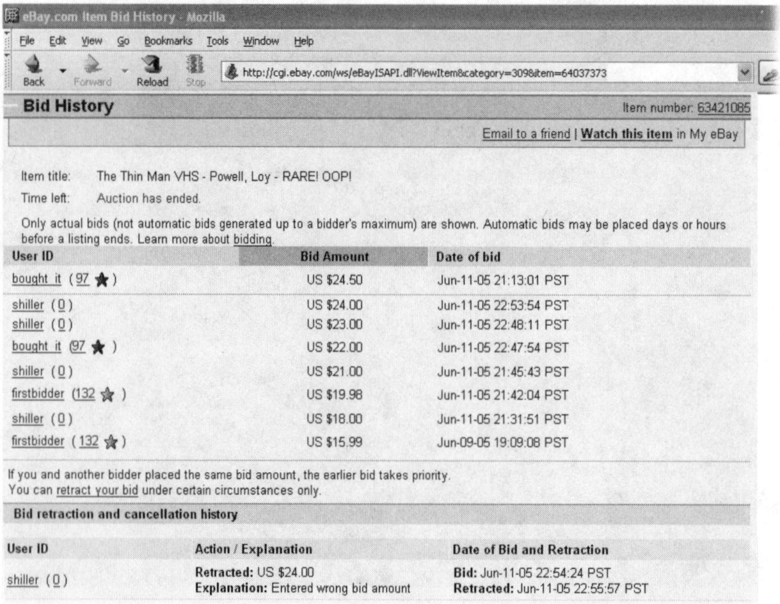

Figure 4-7:
In this auction, shiller waited until a bid was placed, then made small bids to try to keep others bidding. The first bidder dropped out when the bidding got past $20. When a new bidder got involved, shiller kept nibbling the bids up, then dropped out of the bidding 10 minutes before the auction's end. Shill bidders also have a tendency to retract their bids as late as possible in an auction; look for bid retractions under "Bid retraction and cancellation history" at the bottom of the page.

Looking at the bid history doesn't tell you the whole story, though. Some nibblers put in lots of small bids because they don't understand how proxy bidding (page 47) works and they're trying to get a deal. But those nibblers are legitimate bidders who pay for the items they win.

One way to tell the nibblers from the shill bidders is that shill bidders tend to keep putting in small bids until they've made it to high bidder—then retract their most recent bid, leaving another bidder on top of the pile. They do this to make sure that the price gets as high as it possibly can.

If you think a Bid History reveals a possible shill bidder, the next step is to hunt down other auctions the suspect's bid on: hit Advanced Search → Items by Bidder. Type the suspected shill bidder's eBay ID in the text box and check "Include completed listings" and "Even if not high bidder." Maximize the number of results displayed per page, and then click Search; the results may be enlightening. Shill bidders tend to bid only on the auctions of one particular seller; another clue is that a bidder has been on eBay for a long time but never won an auction. See Figure 4-8.

eBay.com Bidder List: shiller - Mozilla

File   Edit   View   Go   Bookmarks   Tools   Window   Help

Back   Forward   Reload   Stop   http://cgi6.ebay.com/ws/eBayISAPI.dll?MfcISAPICommand=ViewBidIte   Search   Print

Current and recent auctions bid on by shiller (0)

For auction items, bold price means at least one bid has been received.

In some cases, shiller (0) may no longer be the high bidder.

1 - 13 of 13 total. Click on the column headers to sort

Item	Start	End	Price	Title	High Bidder	Seller
55505400	Jun-04-05	Jun-11-05 00:21:22	US $30.53	Princess Di - Royal Wedding – int'l stamp set	bidder1 (*)	shillpartner
43593416	Jun-04-05	Jun-11-05 12:32:53	US $15.50	Lavender bath oil! Smells SOOO good!	bidder2 (*)	shillpartner
38700985	Jun-04-05	Jun-11-05 22:01:12	US $30.00	Marilyn Manson poster! Scare your parents!	bidder3 (*)	shillpartner
63421085	Jun-04-05	Jun-11-05 23:12:59	US $24.50	The Thin Man VHS – Powell, Loy – RARE! OOP!	bought it (*)	shillpartner
81172216	Jun-05-05	Jun-12-05 00:51:26	US $25.52	Hand-knit baby booties! Pink!	bidder4 (*)	shillpartner

Figure 4-8:
The shill bidder bids only or predominately on one seller's auctions–and never wins. In this case, the shill bidder bid a variety of auctions up to a high price and then dropped out of the bidding. All the auctions were from one seller.

Shill bidders often have a lot of retractions in their Member Profile. If the shiller becomes the high bidder, she retracts the bid and drops out of the auction, leaving the next highest bidder the winner.

If you find someone you think is shill bidding, report it to eBay using the Help → Contact Us link. eBay will investigate and, if they agree that the bidder is a shill, will NARU the person. Keep in mind, though, that not all unusual bidding patterns show shill bidding. Newbies are often nibblers. Or a buyer might have a particular seller listed as a favorite, returning frequently to that seller's auctions. And a buyer determined to get a particular item, especially below a certain price, is likely to keep bidding on similar items until he or she wins. If you think someone's been trying to push up bids, let eBay check it out.

Spoof Emails

You might have received emails purporting to be from eBay before you ever even registered with the site. These *spoof emails*, fake emails sent by scammers trying to steal personal information, usually report an urgent problem with your account (or sometimes merely request routine maintenance). The emails urge you to verify your account details by clicking a link and typing in your ID, password, and sometimes other information—like your Social Security number, credit card number, date of birth, and so on. Many people are so used to sending personal information over the Internet that they click the link and type in the required info without giving it a second thought. Later, they'll find themselves locked out of their own eBay or PayPal account as the scammer uses it for fraud or for running up credit card charges.

eBay has taken action to combat spoof emails by enhancing the My Messages section of My eBay. Any official eBay communications about your account will appear there; go to My eBay → My Messages to check your Inbox. If the email isn't in there, it's a spoof.

Note: The practice of sending spoof emails with the intent of stealing account information is also called *phishing*.

Detecting spoof emails

Spoof emails like the one shown in Figure 4-9 can look highly authentic, using the eBay or PayPal logo and valid links to the real sites. But several telltale clues, including a generic greeting, grammatical mistakes, incorrect terminology, and a request to hand over account information—all items eBay would never include in a legitimate email—clue you in that the email is bogus. Check out Figure 4-10 to see an example of another dead giveaway common to spoof emails: a non-eBay link.

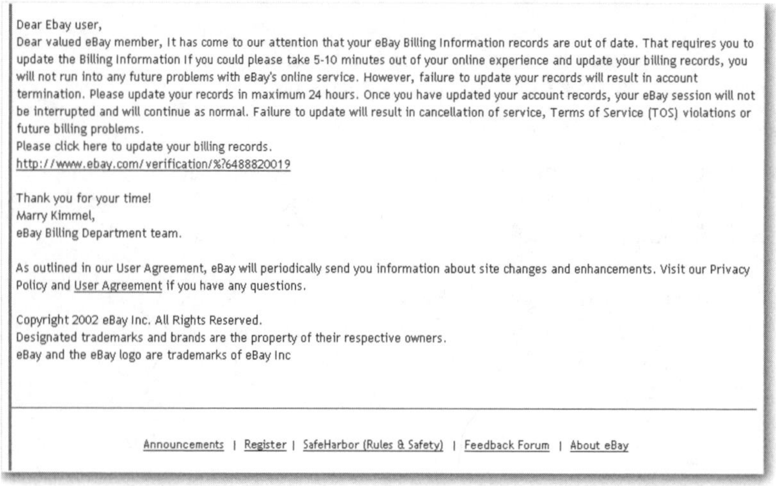

Dear Ebay user,
Dear valued eBay member, It has come to our attention that your eBay Billing Information records are out of date. That requires you to update the Billing Information If you could please take 5-10 minutes out of your online experience and update your billing records, you will not run into any future problems with eBay's online service. However, failure to update your records will result in account termination. Please update your records in maximum 24 hours. Once you have updated your account records, your eBay session will not be interrupted and will continue as normal. Failure to update will result in cancellation of service, Terms of Service (TOS) violations or future billing problems.
Please click here to update your billing records.
http://www.ebay.com/verification/%?6488820019

Thank you for your time!
Marry Kimmel,
eBay Billing Department team.

As outlined in our User Agreement, eBay will periodically send you information about site changes and enhancements. Visit our Privacy Policy and User Agreement if you have any questions.

Copyright 2002 eBay Inc. All Rights Reserved.
Designated trademarks and brands are the property of their respective owners.
eBay and the eBay logo are trademarks of eBay Inc

Announcements | Register | SafeHarbor (Rules & Safety) | Feedback Forum | About eBay

Figure 4-9:
This email has many clues that reveal it's a spoof. eBay doesn't send out emails addressed to "Dear Ebay user"; it greets you by your eBay ID. The letter contains grammatical mistakes, like the phrase "please update your records in maximum 24 hours." The terminology is also wrong. eBay doesn't "terminate" or "cancel" accounts; it "suspends" them. But the biggest clue is the link you're supposed to click to update your billing records. eBay will never, ever ask you for your account information via a link in an email.

Recovering from spoof emails

When you receive an email that you suspect is spoofed, forward it to *spoof@ebay.com* (or *spoof@paypal.com* if it refers to your PayPal account). eBay will get back to you and let you know for sure whether the email is genuine or a fake. The vast majority are fakes. Don't click that link!

If you ever suspect that you've already given your eBay ID and password to a bogus site, you need to do several things *immediately*:

- **Make sure your computer is clean.** When you followed the link in the spoof email, your computer might have been infected with a virus or *spyware* (an unwanted, hidden program that monitors and reports your computer activity to people you haven't authorized). If your computer has picked up a *keystroke logger,* for example—spyware that records everything you type and sends that information to a third party—the scammer will know when you change your password and what you change it to. So before you do anything else, fire up your computer's virus-protection software (like Norton AntiVirus or McAfee Virus-Scan) to scan for and remove any viruses. Lavasoft's Ad-Aware (*www.lavasoftusa.com*) can root out and destroy any spyware hiding on your computer.

- **Sign in to eBay and change your password.** You sign in to eBay by typing *www.ebay.com* into your Web browser's address box and clicking the Sign In/Out link that appears on the eBay home page. If you can't sign in to your account, contact eBay immediately; go to eBay's home page and click Live Help.

- **Report the bogus site to eBay.** To do so, go to the navigation bar and click Help → Contact Us.

- **Contact PayPal, your credit card company, and your bank.** If you gave any information to the bogus site relating to your PayPal account, credit card, or bank account, contact those companies and let them know what happened.

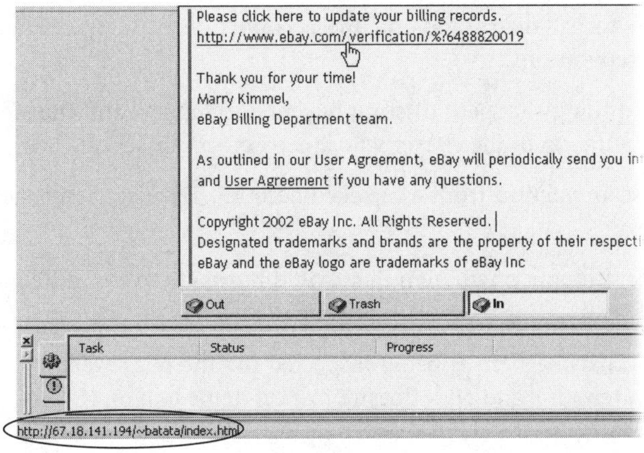

Figure 4-10:
Hovering the cursor over the supposed link to eBay reveals that the link won't take you anywhere near eBay. Look at the bottom of the figure. Those numbers after http:// are a surefire clue. Rather than starting with http:// pages.ebay.com, like a legitimate eBay link, this link takes you to an unknown Web site. The bogus site might look just like eBay, but the information you type in will let thieves steal your identity.

- **Contact the credit bureaus and Social Security.** If you revealed financial information or your Social Security number, notify the three major credit bureaus and the Social Security Administration to put a fraud alert on your information by calling these fraud lines:

  Equifax: 1-800-525-6285
  Experian (TRW): 1-888-EXPERIAN
  Trans Union: 1-800-680-7289
  Social Security Administration: 1-800-269-0271

Tip: eBay has teamed up with Equifax to fight identity theft. eBayers can order discounted credit reports from Equifax to see whether anything odd is up with your credit. Moreover, you can subscribe to Credit Watch for eBay, which alerts you by email when there are changes to your credit report, like new credit cards or bank accounts opened in your name. Check it out at *http://creditzone.ebay.com*.

Sham Auctions

Behind all the spoof emails going around are scammers looking for accounts to hijack. *Account hijacking* is a form of identity theft. When scammers harvest someone's eBay ID and password from a response to a spoof email, they steal that person's eBay account. The scammer might sign in and change the account's password and contact information, locking out the rightful owner of the account. Or, to avoid detection (because eBay sends you an email when you change your password), the scammer might simply use the hijacked account to create phony auctions, with a note in the item description that says something like, "The Ask Seller a Question link isn't working. If you have any questions, email me at scammer@hotmail.com." If the rightful owner doesn't check his eBay account for a few weeks, he never knows what's going on.

Because scammers use hijacked accounts to run fake auctions for items they don't have, they look for established accounts with a decent feedback score. Smart eBayers are unlikely to buy big-ticket items from a new seller with little or no feedback, so the scammers want to get their hands on the accounts of legitimate eBayers who've earned a good reputation.

When they do, two bad things happen: trusting buyers lose money, and the scam auctions destroy the reputation of the eBayer whose account got hijacked.

Don't be fooled by a scam auction from a hijacked account. Here are some signs that an auction isn't legit:

- The seller offers free shipping on an item that would normally cost hundreds of dollars to ship, such as shipping a car from Europe to the U.S.

- The seller promises that the item is being inspected in "the eBay warehouse." (There is no eBay warehouse, and eBay doesn't inspect items sold on its site.)

- The seller has a lot of auctions running simultaneously for identical high-end items. Such auctions could be legitimate, but check for other warning signs, like payment by wire transfer.

- The seller offers to end the auction early, just for you. Think about it a minute. Why would the seller want to end the auction early when the bidding might go higher?

- The seller's feedback shows a sudden change in direction, as shown in Figure 4-11. If someone who's specialized in Beanie Babies since 2001 is suddenly selling speedboats, or if someone who hasn't done a thing on eBay for months or years buys a couple of cheap items and then lists a dozen brand-new laptops, avoid their auctions.

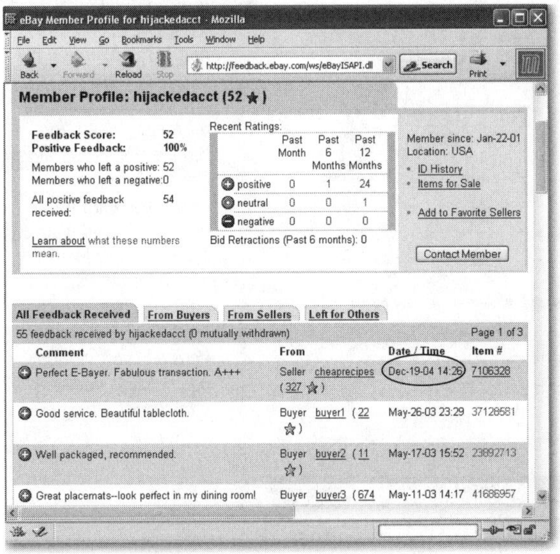

Figure 4-11:
Reading feedback carefully can reveal a possible hijacked account. In this case, after nearly a year and a half of inactivity, the seller has one recent feedback: for the purchase of a 99-cent recipe. (Check out recent transactions by clicking any active item-number link.) Before that, the feedback shows, the eBayer sold table linens. If this ID is now listing big-ticket auctions for items like electronics or motor vehicles, you've got reason to be suspicious.

Tip: On the auction page, click "View seller's other items" to check the seller's other auctions. If the item description says, "I have to sell this plasma TV because my wife didn't like the way it took over our living room," how come the same seller has half a dozen other, identical plasma TVs for sale?

Bogus Escrow Services

An *escrow service* is a third party that people often use in transactions for expensive items. The service holds the buyer's payment (assuring the seller that payment has been made) until the buyer has received, inspected, and accepted the item. Escrow services, described in detail on page 56, allow total strangers to conduct big-ticket transactions with confidence.

For scammers, bogus escrow sites are a synonym for "easy money." As a buyer, you send in your money, trusting that you can get it back if the item doesn't arrive or isn't of the quality you expected. But the item never arrives, the escrow company doesn't answer your emails, and there's no other way to contact the company. Your money is gone.

Fake escrow services have mushroomed all over the Internet. Often they look professional at first glance, as in Figure 4-12. How can you tell whether a particular escrow service is the real thing?

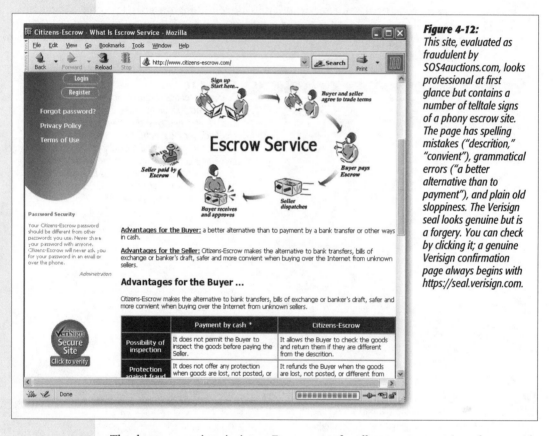

Figure 4-12:
This site, evaluated as fraudulent by SOS4auctions.com, looks professional at first glance but contains a number of telltale signs of a phony escrow site. The page has spelling mistakes ("descrition," "convient"), grammatical errors ("a better alternative than to payment"), and plain old sloppiness. The Verisign seal looks genuine but is a forgery. You can check by clicking it; a genuine Verisign confirmation page always begins with https://seal.verisign.com.

The short answer is to insist on Escrow.com for all escrow transactions, because it's the only U.S. escrow service approved by eBay. If your trading partner tells you they can't or won't use Escrow.com—no matter how good the excuse may sound—don't continue with the transaction.

Note: If you're trading outside the United States, eBay recommends a few international escrow services. To find them, go to the navigation bar and click Help → A–Z Index → E → "Escrow for Buyers." Scroll to the bottom of the page to see the list of recommended escrow services.

Some scammers will try to convince you that Square Trade is an escrow service. It's not. Square Trade (*www.squaretrade.com*) is an independent company that does three things related to eBay: it verifies sellers, it mediates disputes, and it sells warranty plans. Square Trade never takes part in ongoing auctions.

TROUBLESHOOTING MOMENT

Spotting a Fake Escrow Site

Fake escrow services are insanely common on the Internet, set up by scammers who want to fool you into thinking you're protecting your money—while they take it and run. Some of these sites have names similar to Escrow.com, the only U.S. escrow service eBay recommends; others look an awful lot like it. It can be confusing. You might think you're on Escrow.com or an approved international escrow site, but how can you be *sure* that the site you're on is safe?

One sure way is to type *www.escrow.com* into your browser's address bar whenever you want to go to Escrow.com. Don't click a link in an email or from another Web site. Here are some other telltale signs you can look for:

* **Sloppiness.** Watch for misspellings, mistakes in grammar and punctuation, and inconsistent information (for example, a company address in New Jersey and a phone number with an area code in Utah). Legitimate companies make sure that their Web sites are free of these things.

* **Bad or missing contact information.** If the site provides a telephone number for customer support, try calling it. If you can't get through, or if someone answers the phone in an unprofessional manner, be wary. If the site gives no phone number, you probably wouldn't want to do business with that company, anyway.

* **Phony affiliations.** Scam escrow sites often claim affiliation with eBay or Escrow.com. eBay recommends only Escrow.com itself (for North American auctions), and Escrow.com is not affiliated with any other escrow site. Similarly, many sites use phony eTrust or Verisign logos. Just because a site displays one of these logos doesn't mean it's safe; try clicking through to make sure you land on the real eTrust or Verisign site.

* **Wire transfers.** If the only accepted method of payment is wire transfer (such as Western Union or MoneyGram), stay away. The box on page 144 explains why this payment method is risky.

* **Google invisibility.** Phony escrow sites typically pop up, rip off several people, and then disappear—all within a few days. Try going to *www.google.com* or your favorite Internet search engine and searching for the escrow company's name. If there's no listing for the company (or if most of the search results refer to bulletin-board discussions naming the site as fraudulent), you're probably dealing with a phony site.

* **Condemned by SOS4auctions.com.** Go to *www.sos4auctions.com* and search for the escrow site in the database there. SOS4auctions.com is tireless in analyzing escrow sites to identify the fraudulent ones.

If in doubt, you can always ask the experts in eBay's Answer Center. Go to Help → Community Answer Center → Escrow/Insurance, and then either post a question or search the board for the name of the escrow company.

Illegitimate Second Chance Offers

Sometimes the high bidder who wins an auction can't (or won't) complete the transaction. Stuff happens: illness, loss of financing, a stubborn case of cold feet. In these cases, eBay lets the seller send out a *Second Chance Offer* (SCO) to any of the nonwinning bidders. A Second Chance Offer means that even though you didn't win the auction, you can (if you want) buy the item. Sellers can also send Second

Chance Offers if they have two or more identical items for sale or if more than one bidder participated in a reserve auction (page 25) that failed to meet the reserve price.

If you receive a Second Chance Offer, it will be for the amount of your highest bid, even though that bid didn't win the auction. The item will have a new number, and you can sign in to eBay and use Buy It Now to purchase the item for the amount you bid. There's no obligation to accept a Second Chance Offer, but these offers can be a great way to win an auction you thought you'd lost.

The trouble is that scammers manipulate Second Chance Offers to sell items they don't have. In this type of scam, the scammer looks over the bid history and contacts the nonwinning bidders, offering to sell the item at the bid price. But the scammer isn't the original seller and has no intention of selling anything, just grabbing your money.

FREQUENTLY ASKED QUESTION

Wire Transfers: Just Say No

Why is it dangerous to pay using a wire transfer service like Western Union or MoneyGram?

Wire transfers are *always* a red flag. When you wire money, you can't trace who picked it up and you can't get it back. No matter how reasonable a seller seems, don't agree to use a Western Union or MoneyGram wire transfer to pay for an online auction. Ever.

Here's how an online wire transfer works. You register with a service (such as MoneyGram or Western Union), type in your financial information (the credit card or bank account number you're using to pay), and provide information about the person you're sending money to. The wire service issues a reference number (Western Union calls this a *money transfer control number* or MTCN). A person who has the reference number may be able to pick up the payment without showing ID. Or a recipient who has ID and knows the amount and origin of the transfer may be able to pick up the money without giving the reference number.

This means that anyone who has a couple of basic facts about the transaction can pick up the money, anywhere in the world. Believing that you're wiring money to Phil Smith in Dallas doesn't mean that the money is going to anyone named Phil Smith or anywhere near Dallas.

In one common scam, the bogus seller tries to convince a buyer that wire transfers are the safest way to send payment.

For example, the scammer explains that, without the MTCN, there's no way to pick up the money, so the payment sits there safely until the buyer receives the item. However, with an ID (probably forged) and other knowledge about the transaction, the scammer usually can get the money. Or the scammer will send a phony email that looks like it's from eBay, asking for the MTCN to activate the Square Trade buyer protection program—when no such program exists. Sadly, a lot of eBayers fall for it and lose their money.

Sending money via instant wire transfer is like handing over cash. Once the recipient has picked up the money, it's gone. Wire transfers aren't traceable. So if you get ripped off, the scammer simply disappears. When you're buying in an online auction, it's always a good idea keep records until the transaction is complete and you're satisfied. That way, if anything goes wrong, you can document your side of the story. If you pay by instant wire transfer, you're missing a very important detail: who really got your cash.

Western Union and MoneyGram are both legitimate companies. Use them the way they're designed—to send money quickly to people you know and trust. Don't use these services to pay for online auctions. You might as well open the window and toss your money into the street.

How can you tell the difference between a legitimate Second Chance Offer and a scam? Here's a checklist:

- **Real Second Chance Offers come from eBay and have a link to a Buy It Now page.** Also, legitimate Second Chance Offers *never* have "Question from eBay Member" as their subject lines. Bogus ones come from the scammer's email account or ask you to contact the scammer via email to complete the transaction.

- **Real Second Chance items have a reassigned item number.** To check out an item number, log in to eBay (by typing *www.ebay.com* into your browser's address box), click Advanced Search, and search for the item number that was in the SCO email. If it brings up the item as a BIN auction with your price as the BIN price, it's legitimate. If it doesn't, it's a scam.

- **Real Second Chance Offers appear on your My eBay page.** You can check whether a Second Chance Offer is legitimate by heading to the navigation bar and clicking My eBay, then checking out the My Summary view. If you don't see a Second Chance Offer listed there, the offer you received is bogus.

Tip: Scammers promising fake Second Chance Offers are trying to lure you off eBay to complete the transaction, because offsite transactions aren't covered by eBay's protections. Always go directly to eBay to double-check that eBay recognizes the offer.

- **Real Second Chance Offers show the original seller.** Look up the original auction on eBay. Check to make sure that the seller's ID in the original auction matches *exactly* the ID of the seller in the Second Chance Offer. Scammers often count on the fact that the bidder is unlikely to remember the original seller's ID.

- **Real Second Chance Offers link to the relisted item.** The link in the SCO should go to the relisted item with a BIN price, *not* to the original auction.

- **Real Second Chance Offers never involve wire transfers.** The payment options should be the same as those listed in the original auction. Scammers rarely accept PayPal and are likely to insist on instant wire transfer (such as Western Union or MoneyGram). The box on page 144 explains why you should never pay via instant wire transfer.

- **Fake Second Chance Offers often include a list of "five easy steps."** The first step is that the seller notifies eBay about the transaction. In a real SCO, eBay already knows about the transaction; the seller has to set things up through eBay before you can receive the offer.

- **Fake Second Chance Offers often try to reassure the would-be buyer that the auction is legitimate.** Common scams include claims that Safe Harbor or Square Trade has approved the seller or that the seller has deposited a large amount of money in an "eBay managed purchase protection account." Neither Safe Harbor nor Square Trade "approves" sellers, and—you guessed it—there's no such thing as a managed purchase protection account. eBay doesn't hold money for its sellers.

You can help eBay track down the bad guys by reporting any fake SCO you receive. Go to Help → Security Center to file a report.

If Second Chance Offers make you nervous, you can just tell eBay you don't ever want to receive them. On any eBay page, go to the navigation bar and then click My. On your My eBay page, click eBay Preferences, then, next to Notification Preferences, click View/Change. Scroll down the page to "Second chance offer notice," and make sure the checkbox is turned off. After you've clicked Save Changes to save this preference, eBay won't send you Second Chance Offers, so you'll know that any you receive are scams.

Tip: If you receive a fake Second Chance Offer, forward the email to *spoof@ebay.com* or use the Help → Contact Us → "Report fake eBay emails…" form so eBay can investigate.

Part Two:
Selling on eBay

2

Sell Stuff, Make Money

Where else but eBay can you reach millions of customers, find buyers for everything from those old toys in your closet to brand-new diamond necklaces, and accept payment—all while relaxing in your bunny slippers? Selling stuff on eBay is so easy that regular people—that is, folks without prior retail experience—are doing everything from supplementing their income (and cleaning out their basements to boot) to starting full-fledged home-based businesses. Everybody, it seems, is making money selling on eBay.

There's gold in them thar auctions, all right. And with the tips and tricks you'll find in this chapter, you can join the rush. It includes the lowdown on:

- Finding stuff to sell.

- Registering as a seller.

- Figuring out what it'll cost you.

- Listing an item: the Sell Your Item form in glorious detail.

- Deciding on the best time to end an auction.

- Getting paid.

- Packing and shipping properly to reduce dreaded returns.

- Troubleshooting disputes and other problems.

Get the Lay of the Land

If you're new to eBay, take some time to explore the site and buy a few things (Chapters 1 and 2) before you jump into selling. This feeling-out process helps you in two important ways:

- **Buying helps you build the feedback rating you need in order to sell.** When you start out on eBay, your feedback rating (page 40) is zip, zilch, zero. And that's how it should be, because feedback ratings describe transactions—and you, as a brand-new eBayer, haven't yet participated in any transactions.

  The problem is, few experienced eBayers will buy from a seller with no feedback. So, to start building a feedback rating that encourages buyers to do business with you, you have to begin by buying a few items yourself. (They can be inexpensive trinkets.)

- **Buying helps you conduct necessary research.** How do you know how to price your stuff and present it—how to describe it so people want to buy it, what kinds of pictures to include with your item description, and so on—if you haven't spent some time checking out other auctions? The answer is, you don't.

  If you're considering selling furniture, for example, check out a bunch of furniture auctions. Make a note of what sells and what doesn't, and see if you can figure out why. Is the price too high? The description hard to understand? The auction too short for bidders to find it before it ends? Which auctions make *you* want to open your wallet? Which ones make you want to run the other way? Make copious notes, and save them: you'll need them when you decide to list your own items (page 154).

Learn from Others

When you have an item to sell, check out similar auctions that have ended recently. They can teach you the value of your stuff and give you clues on how to sell it for the highest price.

From the top of any eBay page, click the Advanced Search link and then type in keywords related to the item you want to sell. (For example, you might type in "Miles Davis records".) Then turn on "Completed listings only" before you click the Search button. Your results show auctions that ended in the last 30 days. Use the "Sort by" drop-down list to sort the results by end date if you want to see the most recent auctions; sort by price (highest first) if you want to look for pricing trends.

As you look over the results, check to see whether auctions ended with bids. To do so, you can either keep an eye on the Bids column (look for 1 or higher) or look for the boldface green numbers in the Prices column (green prices indicate that an auction ended with at least one bid).

Items that ended without any bids were probably priced too high, but they may have been listed in the wrong category or just ended on a slow sales day. Items with a lot of bids generated excitement; click the item title and take a look at the auction to see if you can learn from the photo, the title, or the description. You can borrow keywords and use other people's listings for inspiration, but don't copy these things verbatim to use in your own auction; that could get you in trouble with eBay.

See if you can find any patterns that show when items like yours are most likely to sell. Do digital cameras move faster on Sunday evening, for example, or toner cartridges for printers on Monday morning? Try setting up your auction to end then to get the best price.

If you notice a cluster of similar items that sold in a particular price range, that price range is your target—for a winning bid.

The starting price you choose might be considerably lower. Check out successful auctions to see the opening bid. Some sellers like to start with a super-low price—usually a penny or 99 cents—to generate interest, relying on competitive bidding to take it from there. Be aware, though, that if you start an auction for a penny and get only one bid, you'll have to sell at that price. Plus some buyers equate super-low starting prices with low quality and won't even look at penny auctions. Don't price yourself out of business in hopes of sparking a buying frenzy.

After you've determined an opening bid and a target sale price, remember to take into account the fees you'll owe (page 152) and what it'll cost you in time and supplies to ship the item. eBay doesn't let sellers charge directly for eBay or PayPal fees (you can't inflate shipping costs or charge extra for these), but there's nothing wrong with adding a small handling charge to the shipping cost.

Don't overdo it. Buyers get justifiably fed up with sky-high shipping charges, but figuring out what it costs you to pack the item, prepare it for shipping, and send it on its way—then factoring that handling charge into your S&H charge—is perfectly reasonable. You can charge whatever you wish for handling, but it's really in your best interest to disclose that charge up front.

What Should You Sell?

Start by selling what you already have—stuff you don't have any use for anymore, but that someone else might treasure. That rocking horse your 20-year-old daughter loved when she was a toddler, say, or the 78 RPM records gathering dust in your garage. (Can you say *vintage*?) Holiday gifts of the I-had-no-idea-they-made-china-this-ugly variety are also a good place to start.

Tip: If you were going to organize a garage sale or list a few things in the classifieds, what would you sell? Use these things to break into selling on eBay.

After you've completed a couple of auctions and know how things work from the seller's side, you can always ramp up your listings. Chapter 7 gives you ideas for

---

where you can find more stuff to sell. But take it slow: if you try to sell more than you can handle when you're still learning, you'll end up with unhappy buyers—and the negative feedback that goes with them.

Also, be aware that there are some things you *can't* sell on eBay. Some of these aren't surprising, such as guns, human body parts (yuck), drug paraphernalia, pirated CDs or DVDs, and lock-picking devices. Others, however, might surprise you. For example, you can't sell a nonworking antique musket; eBay prohibits the sale of any kind of firearm, although you could sell the individual parts. You also can't sell anything that bears the insignia of the KKK, the SS, or the Nazis, including some authentic World War II memorabilia. Pets, gift cards worth more than $500, television shows you recorded, wine (unless you're an approved, licensed wine seller), and designer knockoffs are all taboo.

Before you start selling, take a minute to check out eBay's list of prohibited items: at the bottom of almost any page, click the Policies link and then click "Prohibited and restricted items."

How Much Is It Going to Cost You?

The only free things in life are true love and homegrown tomatoes. Everything else—and that includes selling stuff on eBay—costs.

Exactly how much eBay charges to let you sell on their site depends on the choices you make when you list your item (page 154) and the final price your item goes for when the auction ends. Altogether, eBay charges three different categories of sellers' fees:

- **Insertion fee.** The *insertion fee* is the minimum you pay to list an item, and it ranges from a quarter to just under five dollars, based on the starting price you choose for your item, according to the fee schedule in Table 5-1.

Table 5-1. eBay Insertion Fees

Your Item's Starting Price	Insertion Fee
From $0.01 to $0.99	$0.25
From $1.00 to $9.99	$0.35
From $10.00 to $24.99	$0.60
From $25.00 to $49.99	$1.20
From $50.00 to $199.99	$2.40
From $200.00 to $499.99	$3.60
$500.00 or above	$4.80

- **Listing fees.** These fees buy you a basic listing of seven days or less with one hosted picture. (For details on how to list an item, see page 154.) As soon as you start adding listing options, though—options such as Buy It Now, Picture Gallery, Listing Designer to add a border to your listing, highlighting to make your auction show up in a search results list, more photos, and so on—your fees increase. eBay shows you the total cost of inserting your auction before you submit the listing, so if it looks like fees are getting high in relation to the price of the item, you can revise your listing to cut back on some of the bells and whistles.

Listing fees are nonrefundable, with two exceptions. If the item doesn't sell and you relist it within 90 days, you can get a listing-fee credit. (This is only good the first time you relist the item; if the second auction doesn't sell it, you pay the insertion fees.) The second exception: if someone wins your auction and doesn't pay, you can get a relisting credit after you've reported and resolved an Unpaid Item dispute (page 184).

Note: Some areas of eBay have different fee scales: eBay Stores (page 259), eBay Motors (page 293), and real estate listings (page 302).

- **Final Value Fee.** Insertion and listing fees aren't all eBay charges. There's also a *Final Value Fee* (FVF), which is a percentage of your item's selling price. If the item doesn't sell, of course, there's no FVF. But if it does, eBay figures the FVF according to this schedule:

    — If the selling price is from a penny to $25.00, the FVF is 5.25 percent of that price.

    — From $25.01 to $1,000, you pay $1.31 (5.25 percent of the first $25) *plus* 2.75 percent of the amount that's over $25.

    — If the selling price is $1,000.01 or higher, you pay $1.31 (5.25 percent of the first $25) *plus* $26.81 (2.75 percent of the next $975) *plus* 1.5 percent of the amount that's over $1,000.

All those percentages and plusses get confusing, so here are some examples:

- If you sell a folding camp chair for $12.94, that's below the first cutoff of $25, so your FVF is 68 cents. (5.25 percent of $12.94 is 68 cents.)

- If you sell a pair of Windsor chairs for $272, the price went over that first $25 cutoff. Your FVF is $1.31 (which is 5.25 percent of $25) plus 2.75 percent of the remaining amount: 272 − 25 = 247, and 2.75 percent of 247 is $6.79. Add the $1.31 and the $6.79 together to get your FVF of $8.10.

- If you sell a leather sofa for $1,204, you've passed the second cutoff of $1,000. Your auction went $204 over that second cutoff, so you add 1.5 percent of the extra amount, which is $3.06, to determine the FVF: $1.31 for the first $25, plus $26.81 for the next $975, plus $3.06 for the last $204 makes a grand total FVF of $31.18.

The graduated scale for FVFs seems complicated, but it saves you money when you sell big-ticket items. If eBay charged a flat 5.25 percent on all auctions, the FVF for that $1,204 sofa would be $63.21—more than twice the FVF you pay with the graduated scale.

If all this calculating makes your head spin, don't worry. eBay figures out your Final Value Fees for you and adds them to the insertion fees to determine the total amount you owe. It's worth learning how the system works, though, so you can take into account what you'll pay eBay when figuring out what price you'll accept for your signed, first edition copy of *Black Beauty*.

Warning: Don't forget PayPal. If you have a business or premier account (the kinds that let you accept credit cards), PayPal charges from 1.9 percent to 2.9 percent of the amount you receive when you sell your item, plus $0.30. That's in addition to the fees eBay charges.

Listing an Item

Listing an item means creating a title and description for your item, setting a price, adding a photo, and putting the whole thing up on eBay for buyers to bid on.

But before you do any of that, you have to register as a seller. Even if you're a registered eBayer and have been buying on eBay for a long time, you still have to officially register as a seller before you can list an item for sale. Here's how.

Register as a Seller

You only have to register once, no matter how many items you want to list. And there's no charge as long as you have credit card and a checking account.

To register as a seller:

1. **Head to the navigation bar, and then click My eBay.**

   Your My eBay page (page 32) appears.

2. **From your My eBay page's left-hand menu, click the Start Selling! link.**

   The How To Sell Items on eBay page appears.

3. **Click the Set Up A Seller's Account link.**

   You see a Sell Your Item: Create Seller's Account page similar to the one shown in Figure 5-1.

4. **Click Create Seller's Account to enter your financial information and register as a seller.**

   eBay asks for a credit card or bank account to prove that you're who you say you are. If you don't want to give eBay personal financial information, you can pay $5 to have your eBay ID *verified*. What this means is that eBay checks out your contact information and verifies that it is correct (page 155 tells you more about verification).

A checkmark icon appears next to the ID of verified eBayers on the Member Profile page. Verification is good until you change your contact information—and you can't change that information for the first 30 days after verification, so hold off on that out-of-state move. To have your ID verified, go to eBay's home page, hit the navigation bar, and select Services → ID Verify.

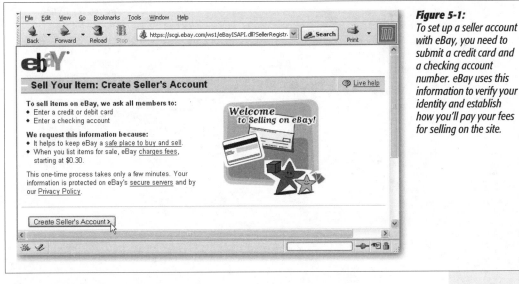

Figure 5-1:
To set up a seller account with eBay, you need to submit a credit card and a checking account number. eBay uses this information to verify your identity and establish how you'll pay your fees for selling on the site.

Choose an Auction Type

After you finish registering as a seller, you can begin to list your items.

Tip: eBay's Sell page (go to the navigation bar and click Sell) offers tons of advice about selling, including how to how to put together a good listing, how to research prices, what eBay tools are available for sellers, how to accept online payments, and much more. There's even an audiovisual tour on how to sell. Use it in conjunction with this book to become a savvy seller.

The first thing you need to do, before you specify the nitty-gritty details about your item, is choose what type of auction you want to run. To choose an auction type:

1. **From the navigation bar, click Sell → Sell Your Item. (Alternatively, from your My eBay page, click Selling Resources; on the page that opens, look under Managing Your Items and click the Sell Your Item link.)**

   The Sell Your Item form appears. On this page, you select a format for your listing.

2. **In the Sell Your Item: Choose a Selling Format page, shown in Figure 5-2, choose what kind of auction you want to run: timed, BIN, real estate ad, or Store listing.**

For your first auction, you'll probably choose a regular, timed auction, so select "Sell item at online Auction." Click Continue to go to the first page of eBay's five-step Sell Your Item process. In step 1, you select a category.

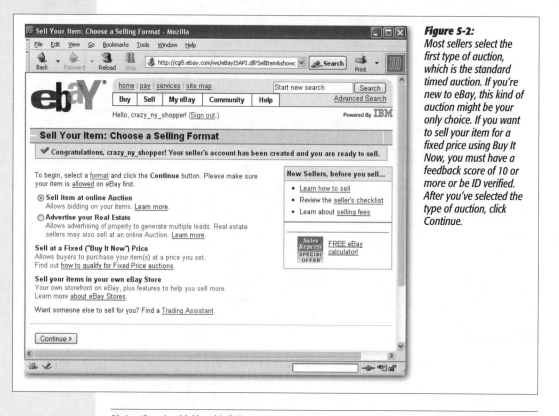

Figure 5-2:
Most sellers select the first type of auction, which is the standard timed auction. If you're new to eBay, this kind of auction might be your only choice. If you want to sell your item for a fixed price using Buy It Now, you must have a feedback score of 10 or more or be ID verified. After you've selected the type of auction, click Continue.

Note: If you're thinking this listing process is too complicated before you've even gotten started, click the Trading Assistant link to find someone else to sell your stuff on eBay for you. Find out more on page 189.

Step 1: Choose a Category

On the Sell Your Item: Select Category page, choose the category you want your auction to appear in: Antiques, Books, Consumer Electronics, and so on. For an example, see Figure 5-3.

When you've got the right category, click Continue to move on to the next page, Sell Your Item: Describe Your Item.

Tip: List your item in two categories to have it turn up in more searches, so more potential buyers will see it. Selecting two categories doubles your listing fees (but not the Final Value Fee you pay when the item sells). To list in a second category, scroll down to the bottom of the Sell Your Item: Select Category page and use the box that says "Choose a second category (optional)."

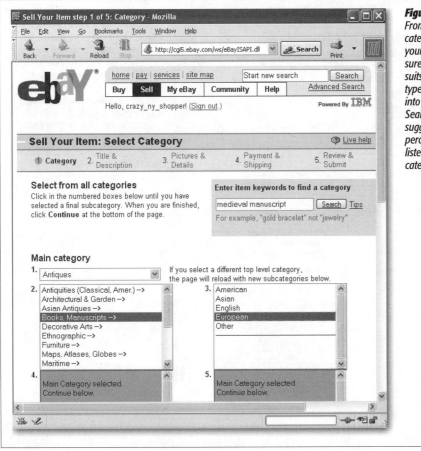

Figure 5-3:
From eBay's list, select the category that best matches your item. If you're not sure which category best suits what you're selling, type the name of the item into the text box and click Search to see eBay's suggestions (and the percentage of similar items listed in each suggested category).

Step 2: Write a Title and Description

After you've selected a subcategory, it's time to write the title and description of your auction on the Sell Your Item: Describe Your Item page, shown in Figure 5-4. The title and description are two of the first things potential buyers notice about your listing, so it's worth taking the time to do a good job. (All other things being equal, "MP3 Player for Sale" won't attract nearly as many bids as "Silver iPod Mini—Brand New in Box," for example.) The next section gives you ideas for creating knockout titles and item descriptions.

Depending on what you're selling, eBay might ask for additional, specific information about the item, such as processor speed and screen dimensions for a laptop, or size, color, and style for a pair of shoes. In the example in Figure 5-4, eBay is asking for details particular to collectible books.

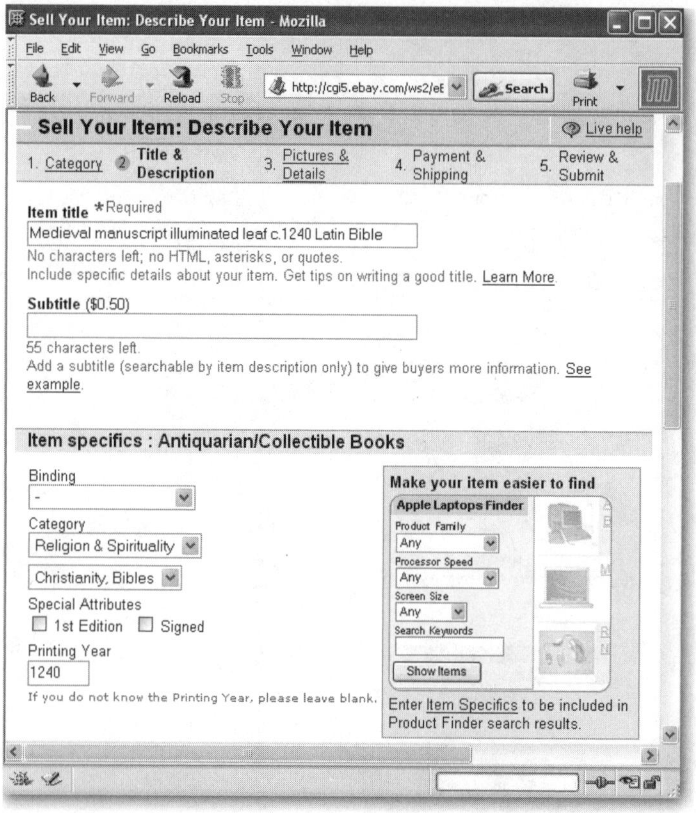

Figure 5-4:
Your item title can be up to 55 characters long. Most buyers search titles (as opposed to titles and descriptions), so load up your title with the keywords buyers looking for your item are most likely to use. You can add a subtitle for 50 cents, but many sellers feel that adding a second line isn't worth the extra expense (subtitles aren't part of title searches). Some categories ask for Item Specifics; if you fill these in, eBay's Product Finder search tool can help buyers zoom in on your auction.

When you're finished with your title and description, click "Spell check" to search for typos, and then click "Preview description" to see how your description will look on an auction page. When you're ready, click Continue, which takes you to the next step, Sell Your Item: Enter Pictures & Item Details.

Writing good titles and descriptions

Creating titles and descriptions that sparkle and pop—that make buyers say to themselves, *"I've just got to have that!"*—is more art than science, but the following top-ten strategies can help.

For titles:

- **Focus on keywords.** Because most searches comb through titles only, you want to get the keywords in your title that buyers are most likely to search for. You've only got 55 characters (and that includes spaces) to play with in your title; don't waste them with nonsense like *L@@K!!!*. Instead, focus on writing a title that will show up in many searches and will make your item stand out from the others. If you were buying, what words would you search for in hopes of finding this item? Put them in your title.

- **Add misspellings.** If the name of what you're selling is often misspelled, try putting both spellings into your title to maximize search results. For example, the title for an auction selling a sapphire ring might say *14K yellow gold sapphire ring saphire* to maximize search hits.

- **Be as descriptive as possible.** Try to use as many of the 55 characters as you can to have your item appear in the highest number of search results. For example, the preceding title for a sapphire ring contains only 37 characters. You could mention diamond accents or the cut of the stone or the lab that certified the sapphire—whatever's relevant and will display your ring listing in more searches.

- **Use capital letters sparingly.** Titles written in all caps can look overexcited and make the title hard to read. Instead, capitalize key words, like the model name or any special feature, to draw attention to them.

- **Add acronyms.** Acronyms like NR (*no reserve*) and NIB (*new in box*) can also get buyers' attention. (For the inside scoop on eBay shorthand, go to Help → eBay Acronyms.)

For descriptions:

- **Keep it short.** For the description, learn the trick of giving specifics without overwhelming buyers with paragraph after paragraph of detail. Buyers simply won't read very long, dense descriptions, especially if they're written entirely in capital letters. You risk losing buyers' interest if your description could serve as the script for an hour-long infomercial.

- **Use bulleted lists.** When buyers are scanning auction pages, it's a lot easier to read a bulleted list of features than to hack through a long, dense paragraph. Appendix B shows you how to use HTML to created bulleted lists.

- **Think like a buyer.** What does someone thinking about bidding on this item *have* to know? What are its features? What, if any, are its flaws? Look at current auctions for similar items and see which listings appeal to you most.

- **Keep it neat.** Your page should look professional and give the facts in an easy-to-read format.

- **Make it personal.** If you're selling one-of-a-kind items, consider giving a little of the item's history. Personalized descriptions appeal to buyers who are looking for something they can't get at the mall.

- **Be honest.** When you're writing your sales pitch, be honest. Don't try to hide any problems or flaws because you're afraid they'll scare away bidders. If you do, you're likely to end up with a dissatisfied buyer who'll demand (and be entitled to) a refund because the item wasn't what you described.

As you build your eBay business, use the item description to sell yourself, too. Showcase your positive feedback by linking prominently to your About Me page (page 191) and your eBay Store (page 259), if you have one. Include a link to your other auctions, as well. A buyer who's checking out this auction is likely to look at your others.

Tip: When you've got an item description you like, copy it and paste it into a text file (WordPad for Windows or TextEdit for the Mac). Later, when you're listing a similar item, just paste the text file back into the item description box of the Sell Your Item form and edit it to fit the new auction. This saves you tons of time and typing.

Step 3: Add Pictures and Details

On the Sell Your Item: Enter Pictures & Item Details page, you set the starting price, length, and other specifics of your auction, as shown in Figure 5-5. There are many areas to consider; you have to keep scrolling down the page to find them all:

- **Starting price.** This is where you set the opening bid that will get your auction rolling. Lower starting prices attract buyers, but there's a danger that the starting price could become the selling price. If you open the bidding for a mountain bike at $1, there's a chance the bike could actually sell for a buck. Some sellers protect their investment by setting a *reserve price* (see next bullet item); others set the starting price at or near the amount they're hoping to get for the item.

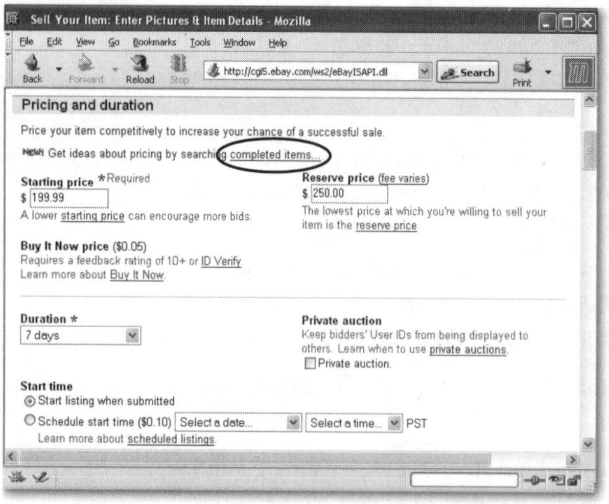

Figure 5-5:
Click the "completed items…" link to do a quick search of similar auctions that ended in the past 30 days. Researching other auctions helps you figure out a starting price. If you set a reserve price, the insertion fee eBay charges you is based on the reserve, not the starting price. You can hide bidders' IDs by making the auction private (there's no charge to do so), but many eBayers feel more comfortable bidding in open auctions. Don't make an auction private unless you've got a good reason, such as a high-priced item or something that people might be embarrassed to bid on.

- **Reserve price.** This option lets you start the bidding low, but sets a secret price that represents the minimum you'll accept for the item. Set a reserve price if there's absolutely no way you can part with an item for less than a certain amount. But be aware that a reserve price will cause many bidders to pass on your auction; why should they bid if they don't know your real price?

Note: eBay charges a fee for reserve price auctions: $1 if the reserve price is below 50 bucks, $2 for a reserve price between $50 and $199.99, or 1 percent of the reserve price for prices more than $200 (with a maximum fee of $100). The reserve fee is on top of regular insertion fees (which are based on the auction's reserve price, not its starting price). eBay refunds the reserve fee if bidding meets the reserve. If bidding doesn't meet the reserve and you use a Second Chance Offer (page 186) to sell to the highest bidder, eBay won't refund the reserve fee.

- **Buy It Now price.** If your feedback score is 10 or higher, you can set a BIN price. If a buyer clicks the Buy It Now button, he commits to buying the item at the BIN price and the auction ends immediately. If a buyer makes a bid rather than clicking the BIN button, the BIN price and BIN button both disappear. So even though buyers can see how much you'd like to get for the item, they might try to get it for less by bidding instead of clicking Buy It Now. And if the auction ends for less than the BIN price you originally specified, you still have to sell to the high bidder.

Tip: If you set a BIN price, you can require any buyer who uses the Buy It Now option to pay immediately. Until the buyer pays, the listing remains active and others can bid or buy. This is a popular way to avoid inexperienced buyers' BIN mistakes. There are a few restrictions: you need a PayPal Premier or Business account, you need to include shipping costs in the auction, and the BIN price can't be over $2,000.

- **Duration.** Auctions can be as short as one day or as long as 10. (You need a minimum feedback score or ID verification to run a one-day auction.) Choose a shorter length if your item is time-sensitive, like concert or sports tickets; choose a longer length if you want to give more people time to find what you're selling. Many sellers like 10-day auctions, even though there's a small fee to run an auction that long, because if you time it right, a 10-day auction runs over two weekends. See the box on page 162 for more about timing your auction.

Note: You can't run a one-day auction for a motor vehicle in the U.S. or Canada.

- **Start time.** Normally, the auction starts as soon as you've checked and submitted your listing. For 10 cents, you can schedule a different start date and time for your auction. Use this option if, for example, your busy schedule dictates that you create your listings at 2:00 a.m. on a Wednesday, but you want your auctions to start (and therefore end) on Sunday evening, thus spanning two weekends.

- **Quantity.** If you're selling one item per auction, the number to put in this box is 1. (eBay only allows up to 10 auctions for identical items from a seller at a time.) If you want to set up a multiple-item (Dutch) auction (page 30), type in the number of items you have for sale here.

Note: To sell items in a Dutch auction, you must be ID verified or meet certain feedback requirements: a score of 15 if you accept PayPal or, if not, a minimum feedback score of 30 and a registration two weeks or older.

Use the Lots tab if you're selling one lot that contains several items. For example, you might have three pairs of jeans to sell, but you want to sell all three pairs together in one sale. Click the Lots tab, then type *1* as the number of lots and *3* as the number of items in that lot. When you preview the auction page, the Quantity field should say "1 lot (3 items each)." The reason this is important is that if you don't use the Lots tab (if you put 3 as the Quantity on the Individual Items tab), you're inadvertently setting up a Dutch auction—which gets confusing for you and your buyers if that's not what you meant to do.

FREQUENTLY ASKED QUESTION

Timing Is Everything

When's the best time to start and end an auction?

eBayers have a lot of theories about this question, but no definitive answers. (If everyone agreed, everyone would start and end their auctions at the same time, and the best time would quickly become the worst time.) Some people think that Sunday evenings are best, because that's when people have leisure time to spend at the computer; others say that's the worst time, perhaps because of all the competition.

Slow times include the wee hours of the morning in North America (from about 11:00 p.m. PST until 4:00 a.m. or so PST) and the first week of each month (when people pay rent and their bills). And every week from Thursday at 11:00 p.m. PST to Friday at 1:00 a.m. PST, eBay does maintenance work on its computers, so that's probably not the time to start or end your auctions.

With the popularity of automated sniping (page 107), ending times matter a little less than they used to. Buyers can instruct the sniping engine to bid on any item in its last few seconds—whenever it ends. The buyer can win your auction

without being anywhere near the computer when it ends. Proxy bidders who make their highest bid and then let eBay do the rest also have no reason to worry about ending times.

One thing you do want is to make sure that your auction runs over the course of a weekend; more people have time to shop eBay then, so it's more likely that buyers will come across your auction. Avoid a three-day auction that starts, for example, on Monday and ends on Thursday.

Play around with different starting and ending times to see what works best for you. Think about when shoppers looking for your item are likely to be at their computers: office managers buy supplies during the work day; kids bug their parents to buy them video games after school (or in the evening when they're supposed to be doing their homework); and hobbyists are likely to look for what they need during their spare time in the evenings and on weekends.

On the other hand, even if you ship only to the U.S., when you include Alaska and Hawaii, that's an area that spans five time zones. Bottom line: don't spend a lot of time worrying about timing your auction to end at just the right minute.

- **Item location.** If the item you're selling is someplace other than where you're registered, you can change location info here.

- **Add pictures.** eBay lets you add one picture to your listing for free; any additional photos cost 15 cents apiece. Supersized pictures (up to twice the size of a standard picture) cost 75 cents; a slideshow, which shows multiple photos in a player at the top of the auction page, costs 25 cents. (See page 198 for info on taking good photos.)

Tip: You can host your pictures on another site to put as many photos as you want in your listing for free. See page 203 for details.

- **Listing designer.** For 10 cents, eBay helps you spiff up your auction with predesigned themes and layouts (Figure 5-6). You can play around with different themes and layouts before you make up your mind, viewing each by clicking the "Preview listing" link. The listing designer is a cheap way to make your auctions look good if you don't want to mess around with HTML.

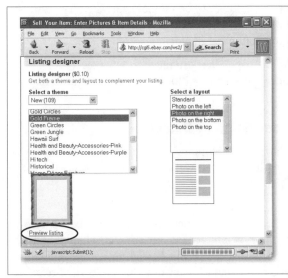

Figure 5-6:
eBay's listing designer lets you choose different frames and layouts to customize your listing. Click the "Preview listing" link to see how your auction page is shaping up.

- **Gallery options.** To get a small picture of your item next to the title in buyers' search results, choose Gallery (which costs an extra 35 cents). Gallery Featured adds a gallery picture and puts your auction in the Featured section at the top of Gallery View search results, but it's expensive at $19.95.

- **Make your listing stand out.** This section lets you use boldfaced font ($1), a border ($3), or highlighting ($5) to make your listing stand out on the search results page. But before you spring for these extras, do some searches and see whether these options really do make a listing stand out enough to justify their cost.

- **Promote your listing.** This section offers eBay's priciest promotion tools: Featured Plus! listings that appear at the top of search results page (for $19.95) and Home Page Featured listings that promote your item on eBay's home page ($39.95 and up). The expense is rarely worth it. Most buyers go straight to the search engine or use automated search tools (page 95) to find what they're looking for—not even glancing to see what's featured on eBay's home page.

Note: You need a feedback score of 10 or higher to use Home Page Featured promotions, and you can't feature adult items, tasteless novelty items, or listings for services or the sale of information there.

- **Gift services.** Popular around various holidays, this option puts an icon of a wrapped package in your auction to show that you think the item would make a great gift. It costs a quarter. (If you're also willing to offer other services related to gift-giving, like wrapping the item, throwing on a nice bow, shipping it to the recipient instead of the buyer, or using express shipping for last-minute gift-givers, say so in the item description.)

- **Page counter.** If you want to keep track of how many people have viewed your item, choose a counter here. Counters can be public or private, depending on the style you choose. They're a good way to keep track of how many people look at your auction in relation to the number of bids.

That's a lot of information for one page! Check to make sure that everything is the way you want it, and then click Continue to go to the Sell Your Item: Enter Payment & Shipping page.

Step 4: Specify Payment and Shipping Details

On the Sell Your Item: Enter Payment & Shipping page, you let buyers know what kind of payments you accept and how much it will cost to get the item to them.

Payment

Payment options include PayPal (page 52), money order/cashier's check, personal check, credit cards (if you have your own merchant account with a bank), and others, like cash or BidPay (page 56). Most buyers like PayPal for its ease and convenience, so it's a good idea to accept it along with any other methods you prefer.

Shipping

The next section of the Payment & Shipping page asks where in the world you'll ship to. Many sellers will ship only to the U.S. because of the extra costs and hassles of shipping internationally (think standing in line at the post office and filling out customs forms); others have been burned by international buyers who turned out to be scammers. (For more on common scams targeting sellers, see page 232.) On the other hand, limiting your shipping range limits potential buyers. Many sellers, realizing eBay is a worldwide market, gladly ship anywhere. If you're selling a bulky item that you don't want to ship at all, you can specify "local pickup only" in this section.

Note: If you ship only within the U.S., *don't* check the box that says "N. and S. America." Checking that box indicates that you'll ship to Canada, Mexico, Guatemala, Colombia, Venezuela, Brazil—any of the countries on the North American or the South American continent (and that includes Central America, too).

WORKAROUND WORKSHOP

PayPal Without Credit Cards

When you're just starting out, you might want to use your personal PayPal account to receive payments. It costs nothing to receive money into a personal account, but these accounts can't accept credit card payments. If you accept a payment by credit card, you automatically upgrade to a premier account—and start paying PayPal fees, which can be as high as 2.9 percent of the money you receive, plus 30 cents.

Even though PayPal charges for premier and business accounts to receive payments, it's a good idea to accept credit cards if you're running many auctions or selling relatively pricey items, because using a credit card through PayPal is how most buyers want to buy. But for occasional sellers, especially sellers of inexpensive goods, a personal account will probably be enough.

If you select the PayPal option as a payment method, though, beware: eBay automatically inserts a PayPal logo that includes a bunch of credit cards. Buyers who see this reasonably assume that you accept credit cards through PayPal, and you can get into a nasty dispute after the auction if you won't let the buyer pay that way.

In fact, flying the PayPal credit card logos when you don't accept credit cards violates the usage polices of PayPal, Visa, and MasterCard, and eBay considers it "search manipulation." If a seller shows the PayPal credit card logos and then refuses a credit card payment made through PayPal, the buyer can report that seller for refusing to sell. And that can be a path to NARU land.

Your options: You can upgrade and pay the extra fees, or you can display a PayPal logo on your auction page *without* the credit cards. Here's how to do the latter:

1. Go to *www.paypal.com* and sign in to your account.

2. Under the My Account tab, click Profile.

3. Under Selling Preferences, click Auctions. If you haven't registered your eBay account with PayPal, you can do so now.

4. Find the column that says Automatic Logo Insertion and make sure it's set to Off. If the setting is On, click it. On the page that opens, turn on the button next to Off, and then click Update.

5. Click the Auction Tools tab, then scroll down to the bottom of the page and click View All Tools.

6. Find Auction Logos – Manual, and then click the Get Started link.

7. Find Standard Logo. It shows the PayPal symbol but not the string of credit cards flying after it. Select and copy all the text in the text box under the logo. Paste it into a document to save it for later.

8. When you're setting up a listing on eBay, paste the text you copied from the PayPal site into the "Item description" text box to insert the PayPal logo into your description. Then, when you select payment methods in step 4 of the listing process, *do not* check the PayPal box. Instead, check "Other—See Payment Instructions…." Explain in your item description that you accept only bank transfers through PayPal. Highlight this info: make it bold or a color that stands out, so that shoppers will notice it.

9. When the auction ends, PayPal won't appear as a payment option on the auction page. Send an invoice through PayPal using your PayPal account's Request Money tab.

You don't have to specify shipping costs in an auction, but it can hurt your auction if you don't. Smart buyers know never to bid without knowing exactly how much they'll pay for shipping and handling. They could always email to ask you, but many will simply move on to find an auction that does state these costs up front. You have two options in spelling out shipping costs:

- **Flat.** This means that shipping will cost the same no matter where the buyer lives. The drop-down menu offers options including various postal and UPS rates. If you're not sure how much it will cost to ship a package, click the "Research domestic rates and services" link to get estimates for various weights, speeds, and distances for both the post office and UPS. Don't forget to add a little for the handling charge; reimburse yourself for the money you spend on boxes and Styrofoam peanuts, and the time you spend packing and sending the item.

- **Calculated.** This option adds a shipping calculator to your auction page, so that buyers can type in their Zip code to find out how much shipping will be. When setting up this option, you indicate the weight and shape of the package and whether to add a handling charge.

Tip: Get a good scale—you can buy one on eBay—so that you can weigh your item (don't forget to include the bubble wrap or plastic peanuts when you weigh it) and get accurate shipping costs when you write the listing. Don't wait until you take a package to the post office. You might find that your guesstimate was way off and end up paying the extra cost yourself.

Whether you choose flat or calculated shipping, you can specify up to three shipping options to offer buyers a choice, as shown in Figure 5-7. For example, you might offer a choice of UPS Ground delivery or Priority or Express Mail via the postal service, letting your buyer choose the shipping speed and the cost. (Page 179 has tips on choosing a shipping service.)

Tip: If you offer expedited shipping, such as Express Mail or UPS Next Day Air, make sure the package is ready to be shipped now. Not tomorrow, not when the buyer has paid, but now. Buyers who pay extra for expedited shipping want their items fast and won't be pleased if it takes you three days to get around to packing up the item and calling the shipping service.

Insurance

This is the section of the Sell Your Item: Enter Payment & Shipping page where you let buyers know whether you require insurance. You don't have to offer insurance at all, or you can make it optional, require it, or factor it into your shipping and handling charge. (See the box on page 167 for a discussion of insurance and why you might want to require it.)

Also, if you charge sales tax to sales made in your state, this is the section where you specify which state you collect for and what the collection percentage is.

Note: Most states require you to obtain a sales tax number and start collecting tax on sales made within any state where your business has a "significant physical presence." To find out if this applies to you, check with your tax consultant or the Sales Tax Institute (*www.salestaxinstitute.com*); look for the Helpful Information link.

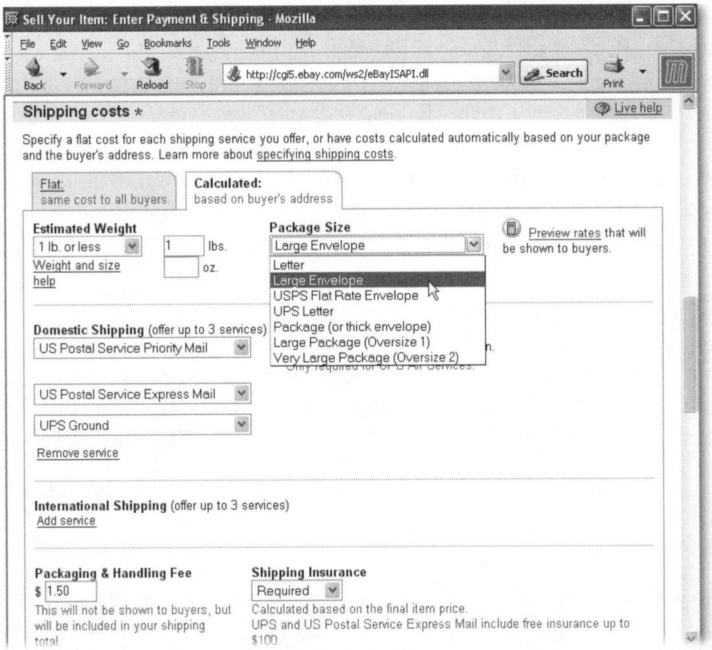

Figure 5-7:
Including a shipping calculator lets buyers enter their Zip code and find out how much it will cost to ship the item to their address; to set one up, use the Calculated tab. Estimate the weight and package size, choose a shipper, and specify whether insurance is optional, required, or unavailable. If you specify a Packaging & Handling Fee, the calculator adds this to the shipping cost to come up with an S&H total; all the buyer sees is the total amount.

Insurance

Should I require insurance on my eBay sales?

eBayers sometimes debate whether insurance really benefits the buyer or the seller. The truth is that it benefits both.

For example, eBay's Standard Purchase Protection Program (page 72) doesn't cover items lost or damaged during shipping, unless the buyer bought insurance in the transaction. But sellers are responsible for getting items to their buyers in good condition. Insurance makes sure that neither buyer nor seller loses out if the item is lost or damaged en route.

When a buyer pays for insurance at the end of an auction, you, the seller, must use that money to purchase insurance for the item when you ship it. Most insurance claims require a receipt to prove you bought insurance, evidence of value

(like the invoice you sent the buyer), and evidence of the problem: if the item didn't make it to the buyer, you may have to submit a letter from the buyer saying so; if the item was damaged, either you or the buyer will have to submit the item itself and all packing materials. After the shipper has investigated, you'll be reimbursed for the amount you insured the item for, usually within 30 days. Check deadlines. For example, the Postal Service won't accept damage claims more than 60 days after the date of mailing.

Many shippers offer free insurance up to $100; check to see whether your shipper does. Another option is to use a third-party insurer like Discount Shipping Insurance (*www.dsiinsurance.com*), which offers low insurance rates and further discounts for high-volume shippers.

Return policy

A *return* is when you ship something to a buyer and the buyer sends it back (returns it, hence the name) and demands a refund or a replacement. If you have a return policy, spell it out in the next section of the Sell Your Item: Enter Payment & Shipping page. Some eBayers won't accept returns; others accept returns for a refund (minus shipping and handling costs), or offer a replacement if an item is faulty or defective. If, after giving the matter some though, you decide to accept returns, it's a good idea to explain in your policy that you won't issue a refund until the buyer has returned the item. (Believe it or not, some buyers think it's perfectly reasonable to demand their money back before they return an item.) Think, too, about whether you want to set a time limit for returns or charge a restocking fee (usually 10 to 15 percent of the sale price). Explain these policies clearly to avoid confusion later on.

Tip: All this might sound like it's better not to accept returns at all. Before you set a "no return" policy, however, take a minute to think like a buyer. What would you find reasonable if you were buying an item like the one you're listing? Keep in mind that even if you clearly specify that you don't accept returns, an unhappy buyer who wants to return his purchase still might leave negative feedback or file a claim with PayPal or eBay to get his money back. So try to come up with a return policy that's fair to you and the buyer both.

Payment instructions

If you want to elaborate on how you want your buyers to pay you, explain in the Payment Instructions section of the Sell Your Item: Enter Payment & Shipping page. For example, if you accept personal checks but plan to hold shipment until the checks clear, say so here. Similarly, if you decide you'll ship only to PayPal-confirmed addresses, make this stipulation part of your terms in this section. No matter what your intentions, you can't hold your buyer to any terms that don't appear on your auction page. Spell it out.

Buyer requirements

You can block certain types of buyers from bidding on your auctions (page 227). The following types of buyers all might present problems you don't want to deal with:

- **Buyers in countries to which you don't ship.** Even if you spell out clearly in your auction terms that you ship only to certain countries, buyers sometimes miss this stipulation. If it's in your auction terms that you don't ship outside the U.S., for example, you don't have to sell to a buyer from another country. But it wastes your time, and perhaps the momentum you had going on the auction, to list the item all over again. Setting this option automatically blocks bidders registered in countries you don't ship to.

- **Buyers with a negative feedback score.** Keep proven deadbeats away from your auctions. You can set up your auctions so that buyers with a score of -1, -2, or -3 (you choose the number) can't bid in your auctions.

- **Buyers with Unpaid Item strikes.** Choosing this option is a good guard against known deadbeat bidders, preventing any eBayer who's received two Unpaid Item strikes in the last 30 days from bidding on your auctions.

- **Buyers without a PayPal account.** eBay estimates that PayPal members have an 80 percent lower Unpaid Item rate than eBayers who don't have PayPal accounts. Restricting your auctions to PayPal members won't guarantee you're paid, but it'll up your odds. On the other hand, some perfectly legit buyers prefer to pay with money orders or checks; blocking these bidders might mean fewer bids.

- **Buyers who may bid on several of my items and not pay for them.** This one is mainly for people who sell expensive items, like cars and diamond jewelry.

Note: If you change your mind about any of these Buyer Requirements after you've set them, you can change them by going to My eBay, clicking Preferences, and then looking under Seller Preferences to find Buyer Requirements. Click the Edit link, make the changes you want, and then click Submit.

When you've completed all the information related to payment and shipping, click Continue. You're finally ready to review your listing and start your auction.

Step 5: Review and Submit Your Listing

Sell Your Item: Review & Submit Listing is the confirmation page. Here you check all your information to make sure it's correct before you submit the listing to eBay. Click "Preview how your item will look to buyers" to get a sneak peek at the listing you've created before your auction goes live; a new browser window opens, and you might notice a mistake or two when you see how the listing in its full glory. You can change any aspect of the auction; look on the far right side of each section for the Edit link. If you spot a mistake in, for example, the item description, click "Edit title & description," make your changes, and then click Save Changes when you're all set.

This page also gives you a chance to review eBay's fees for this listing. If you've spent more than you wanted to, go to the appropriate section and make changes. For example, if you decide that a Featured Gallery listing is likely to cost more than you'll make on the item, click "Edit pictures & details" to remove the Featured Gallery listing charge. When you're looking at your fees, don't forget that eBay also charges a Final Value Fee (page 153).

When you're sure that everything is the way you want it, click the Submit Listing button. A few minutes after you've listed the item, eBay sends you an email to confirm the auction. Check through the details and make sure they're right. If you want to make any changes, you can follow the links in the email or sign in to eBay and revise your auction (page 174).

FREQUENTLY ASKED QUESTION

PayPal Seller Protection

Does PayPal do anything to protect sellers from fraud?

PayPal offers a Seller Protection Policy that covers you for up to *$5,000* if a buyer tries to rip you off (by paying with a stolen credit card, for example). To be eligible for full coverage, you must follow PayPal's guidelines. Follow these practices for *every* sale you make that involves PayPal:

- **Have a Business or Premier account.** Seller Protection doesn't apply to Personal accounts (the ones where it's free to receive money).

- **Get verified.** You've probably already done this to avoid PayPal's sending limit (page 55). In case you haven't, get verified by giving PayPal a bank account number, and then confirming two small deposits that PayPal makes to prove it's your account.

- **Sell tangible goods.** Services (like Web design) and intangible items like eBooks and software downloads aren't covered. It's got to be something you can put into a box or an envelope and load onto a delivery truck.

- **Ship to the address on your PayPal Transaction Details page.** If a transaction is eligible for Seller Protection, it's marked as eligible on the Transaction Details page of your PayPal account. You *must* ship to the address listed for that transaction on the Transaction Details page, or you forfeit coverage.

- **Ship fast.** To get Seller Protection, you have to ship within one week of receiving payment.

- **Get delivery confirmation.** This is in case a buyer claims the item you shipped never arrived. Delivery confirmation means such disputes won't turn into a game of "you-did-not-I-did-so!"

- **If the item you're shipping is worth $250 or more, get a signature receipt.**

- **Accept the whole payment in one transaction.** In other words, insist that the buyer pays once—and pays in full.

- **Don't add an extra charge to cover PayPal fees.** Doing this violates PayPal policies, anyway.

- **When you hear from PayPal, answer immediately.** If you don't respond to a communication from PayPal in three to seven days (the time period depends on the type of claim), you might lose your right to make the claim.

PayPal Seller Protection protects against only buyer fraud, such as when a buyer claims he didn't receive the item and tries to get his money back. If the dispute is about the quality of the item—for example, if the buyer thinks that genuine John Lennon autograph you sold him looks like it was scribbled by a 5-year-old—Seller Protection won't get involved. And it's not available for most international shipments, either. Check PayPal's Help Center to see which countries it covers.

It might take a couple of hours for your listing to appear in eBay's search engines, but you should be able to look at it right away. On the navigation bar, click My eBay to go to your My eBay page and then click the Selling link; eBay shows you the information in Figure 5-8. Auction pages look a little different when you're the seller, as you can see in Figure 5-9.

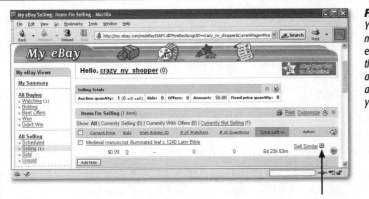

Figure 5-8:
Your My eBay page shows how much time is left before the auction ends. Click the item's title to go to the auction page. The drop-down arrow next to Sell Similar lets you answer questions, make changes to your listing, or end the auction early.

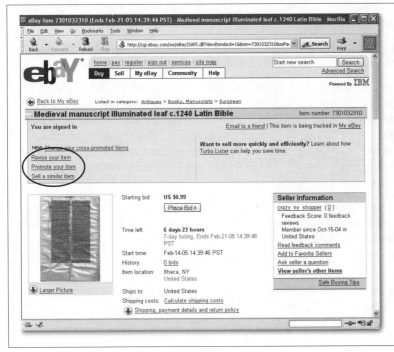

Figure 5-9:
When you're signed in and you view the auction page for an item you're selling, you see a different auction page than prospective buyers. On your version you can revise your listing, promote it (which basically means paying eBay more money), or list something similar right from the auction page. Just click the appropriate link to get started.

During the Auction

You've successfully listed an item, but you can't just sit back and wait for a buyer to send you money. You need to manage your auction while it's running. Keep track of auctions you're running from your My eBay page, where you can see the current price, and, if appropriate, how many bids have been placed, the current high bidder's ID, the number of people who've added your item to their Watch list, and the number of questions you have waiting about the item. Check your auction page to make sure it looks right, respond to buyers' questions, and maybe lower the starting price if you're not getting any bids. This section explains what might come up during an auction.

Finding Your Item

It's easy for one listing to get lost among eBay's millions upon millions of auctions. If you want to check your auction while it's running but can't find it, try one of the following foolproof ways to locate it:

- **My eBay.** Go to your My eBay page and click All Selling. Your auction appears under Items I'm Selling. Click its title to go to the auction page.

- **Item Number Search.** Click the Advanced Search link, then type the item number in the text box and click Search. You can get the item number from the confirmation email eBay sent when you listed the item.

- **Seller Search.** Click Advanced Search → Items by Seller. Type in your own eBay ID and click Search. The results list all of your current auctions.

If you can't find an auction by any of these means, check to make sure that you actually got all the way through the listing process. A quick way to do this is to go to the navigation bar and click Sell. If there's a link that says "Complete your listing," you started a listing but didn't finish it. It could be the missing auction. Click the "Complete your listing" link and follow the required steps. Be sure to click the Submit Listing button on the last page when you're finished so that eBay can register your auction and put it up.

It can take a while—up to several hours—for your auction to appear in shoppers' search results. And if you go back and make changes to your listing, the clock starts ticking all over again. So avoid tinkering with your auctions, changing them two or three times a day, or else buyers will never be able to find them.

Note: eBay has an automatic profanity filter, so if a listing contains any words on the "naughty" list, eBay's search engines won't ever index the auction.

Answering Buyers' Questions

You might get some questions about your item while the auction is running. Typical questions include asking for more details or extra photos, asking about shipping costs or your return policy, wanting to know whether you'll reduce shipping for multiple items (assuming you have more items to sell) or accept a payment method not specified in your auction terms. Every time a buyer clicks the "Ask seller a question" link on your auction page, eBay sends you an email containing the question.

eBay gives you two ways to answer a buyer's question:

- **Respond to the buyer's email address.** Even though questions come through eBay, they arrive with the buyer's email address in the From: field. To answer the buyer directly, just hit Reply as you would when answering any email. (This reveals your email address to the buyer.)

- **Respond via eBay (eBay sends an email to the buyer).** Click the email's Respond Online button, which opens a browser window containing the Respond to Question page. As you can see in Figure 5-10, this page looks a lot like the Ask Seller a Question page, only with a couple of additions.

  If the question is one that will be of interest to a lot of buyers, turn on the "Display this question…" checkbox. You can display up to 100 questions and answers on your auction page, but you can't display any new questions or answers during the auction's last 12 hours. (You can still answer those questions via email, of course.)

Note: Be careful not to violate a buyer's privacy by displaying questions that contain any of the buyer's personal information (full name, email address, and so on). Once you display a question and its answer in a listing, you can't delete them.

If you want to keep your email address private at this stage of the auction, check the "Hide my email address…" box. (The winning bidder, of course, gets your email at the end of the auction.)

If you don't like clicking links in emails (a good policy with so many spoof emails flying around the Internet), you can use another method to get to the Respond to Questions page. Open a Web browser to *www.ebay.com*, click Sign In, and sign in to your eBay account. Then click My eBay to go to your My eBay page and look at the My Summary section. The Selling Reminders section lists all your current auctions that have questions waiting. Select one and click the Respond button. Doing so takes you to the same Respond to Question page shown in Figure 5-10.

Be prompt and courteous when answering buyers' questions. Answer a question even if the answer already appears in your item description. Remember, you're interacting with someone who just might put money in your pocket—so try your best to make a good impression.

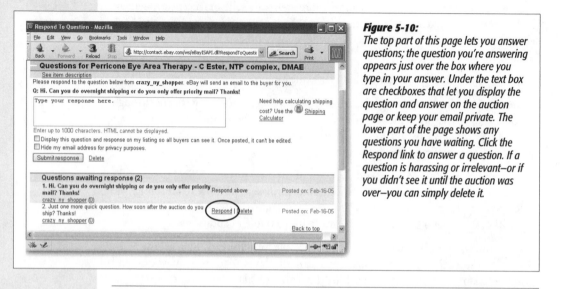

Figure 5-10:
The top part of this page lets you answer questions; the question you're answering appears just over the box where you type in your answer. Under the text box are checkboxes that let you display the question and answer on the auction page or keep your email private. The lower part of the page shows any questions you have waiting. Click the Respond link to answer a question. If a question is harassing or irrelevant—or if you didn't see it until the auction was over—you can simply delete it.

Warning: Even if a buyer asks, don't agree to cancel an auction and sell an item off eBay. Not only is this against eBay policy, you could be dealing with a scammer who wants the transaction to be completely off eBay's radar. If you go off eBay, you lose eBay's protection policies. For example, you can't file an Unpaid Item dispute (page 184) if the transaction didn't happen through eBay.

Revising the Listing

If your auction has been running for a few days and there's no action—no bids yet, no questions in your email, no watchers (or only a couple)—consider making some changes to your listing. For example, maybe a juicier description would spark some interest in your Carrot Top poster. eBay lets you change your listing until you receive a bid or the auction is in its last 12 hours.

To change a listing:

1. **From the navigation bar, click My eBay.**

   Your My eBay page (page 32) appears.

2. **Locate your auction. In the Action column next to the Sell Similar link, click the arrow, and then click Revise.**

   The Revise Your Item page opens with the item number already filled in.

3. **Click Continue.**

   The page that appears should look familiar; it's identical to the Review & Submit page you used to submit your original listing.

4. **Click the section you want to revise, make your changes, and then click the Save Changes button.**

5. **When you're done, click Submit Revisions.**

Here are some strategies you might consider if you're thinking of revising your listing:

- **Extend the auction.** If you don't have any bids, giving buyers more time to find your auction is a logical choice. Auctions can run for up to 10 days (eBay charges 20 cents for a 10-day listing; other lengths are free).

Tip: Because some buyers search by looking for auctions that end soon, try extending your auction several times to make it keep coming up in searches sorted by "Time: Ending soonest." Start off with three days; if there are no bids by the beginning of the third day, extend to five, then to seven. Just remember that you can't extend the auction when it has 12 hours or less left to go.

- **Change your description.** Reread your item description and see if it's missing anything. Is there some way you can make the item sound more exciting? Consider adding a small bonus, like batteries with an electrical item or a sheet of stickers with a kids' book, to make buyers feel that your auction offers extra value.

Tip: To add a little more to your description, go to My eBay, find your auction, and click the far-right drop-down arrow; then click Add To Description. The text you add appears at the bottom of your item description, along with the date and time you added it.

- **Revise your title.** It could be that no one's bidding because they can't find your auction. Take a good, hard look at the title and see if you can change it to make it come up in more searches (see page 194 for title hints). View similar items that have sold in the last 30 days for the price you want; look for any patterns of keywords in the titles that attracted buyers to these auctions.

- **Lower your reserve price.** If you've set a reserve price and no one's bidding, try lowering the reserve—and revising the item description to say so in big bold letters: "New! Lower Reserve!" Or consider revealing the reserve amount in your item description. Many buyers don't like to bid when they don't know the item's real price; they'll just find another auction.

- **Add a BIN button.** This strategy can work if you've got a lot of people watching the auction but no one's bidding. A Buy It Now price that offers a good deal might lure one of those watchers to buy your item.

Ending a Listing Early

Sometimes something happens that prevents you from following through with an auction: you come home to find that your dog has chewed the leg of the reproduction Chippendale chair you were selling, or your spouse has bagged up the lot of designer clothes and donated them to Goodwill. If you need to end your listing early, follow these steps.

Note: You can't end an auction early during its last 12 hours.

1. **From the navigation bar, click My eBay.**

   Your My eBay page (page 32) appears. Locate your listing.

2. **In the far-right Action column is a link that says Sell Similar; next to the link is an arrow (you can see it back in Figure 5-8). Click the arrow, and then select End Item.**

   eBay asks for your ID and password, and then for the reason you want to cancel the listing, as shown in Figure 5-11. If there are bids on your auction when you end it early, eBay gives you the option to cancel those bids. Otherwise, the highest bidder wins when you end the auction.

3. **Select a reason, and then click End My Listing to cancel the listing.**

   eBay cancels the auction immediately.

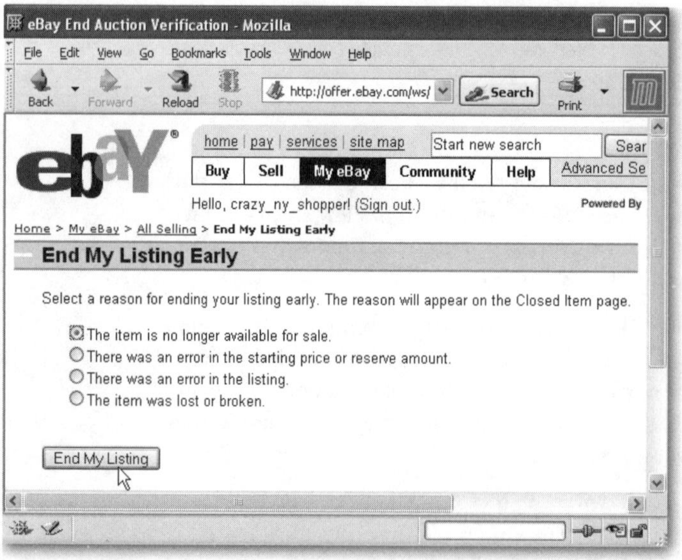

Figure 5-11:
You can end a listing early if the item becomes unavailable, if you specified the wrong price or made some other error in the listing, or if you've lost or damaged the item. The reason you choose will appear on the auction page, which remains visible for 30 days after you end the auction.

After the Auction

Ah, sweet success. A buyer has purchased your vintage Hopalong Cassidy lamp for more than you were secretly hoping to get. Even though the auction is over, you're not done yet. You still have a few details to attend to before you can spend your hard-earned cash.

Invoicing the Buyer

As soon as your auction ends, you get one of two emails from eBay. If your auction ended without any bids, eBay invites you to relist your item. To relist an item, go to My eBay and look under Unsold Items for the item you want. In the Action column, click Relist and follow the instructions.)

If someone won your auction, you get a congratulatory email with the details of the listing, the final price, and the buyer's email address. The congratulatory email contains a link you can use to create and send an invoice to the buyer. (Chapter 9 shows how you can automate the process of sending buyers invoices after the auction ends.)

Getting Your Money

Many buyers pay via PayPal as soon as the auction ends. Others will contact you to let you know they're sending payment through the mail. In either case, it's good selling juju to contact buyers to thank them for payment and let them know when you'll ship the item. New buyers especially get nervous if they don't hear from the seller within a few days of the auction's end.

If a buyer pays via PayPal, you get an email from PayPal letting you know someone has sent you money. Sign in to your PayPal account to accept payment and transfer the funds into your bank account, as shown in Figure 5-12. The minimum you can withdraw from your PayPal account is $10.

If you prefer, you can request that PayPal send you a check. To do so, sign in and select Withdraw → "Request a check from PayPal," then type in the amount you want and select the address where PayPal should send the check. Getting your money out of PayPal by checks takes up to a couple of weeks and costs $1.50.

Withdrawals can't be canceled, but if you decide you want more money in your PayPal account—if you use PayPal to pay your eBay fees, for example—you can add funds to PayPal from your bank account easily and without charge. It's the same process in the other direction. Click the My Account tab, then Add Funds. PayPal takes you through the same process of specifying a bank account and an amount, then transfers the money.

Tip: Transfer money out of your PayPal account to your bank account as soon as your auction ends—or daily if you're a high-volume seller. Doing so makes your money more easily available to you. And if there's a problem with a buyer (it does happen) and PayPal freezes your account, you won't have to go hungry while you're resolving the issue.

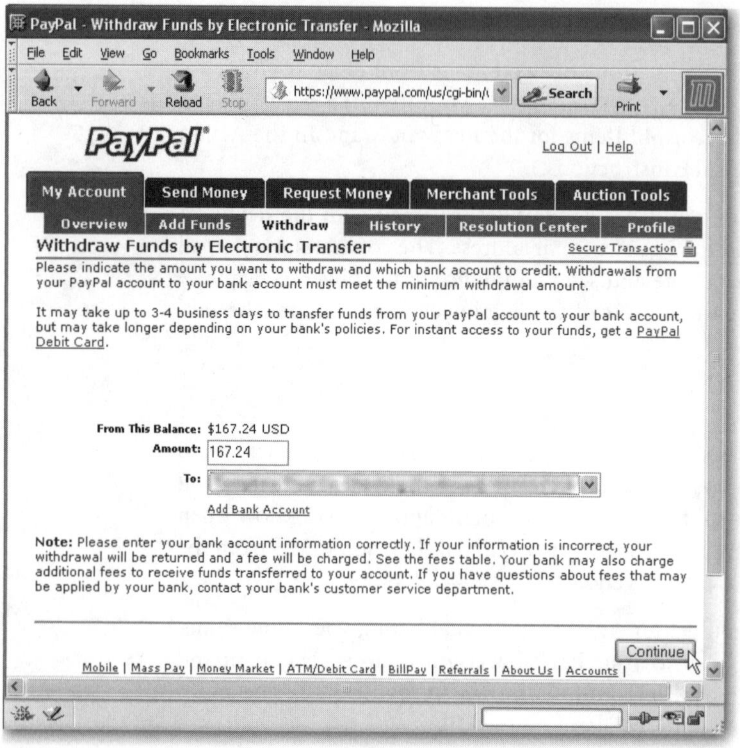

Figure 5-12:
To transfer money from PayPal to your bank account, sign in to PayPal, and select Withdraw → "Transfer funds to your bank account." Type in the amount you want to transfer, choose the account, and then click Continue. Bank transfers take three or four days to process and must be in U.S. dollars.

Packing and Shipping

Two of the three biggest buyer complaints on eBay are poor packing and slow shipping (the other is poor communication). You don't want complaints, of course; you want satisfied buyers who buy from you again and again, tell all their friends how great you are, and leave you positive feedback. Use the tips you find in this section to pack securely and ship wisely—and you may never hear a complaint.

Pack smart

Packing is a lot more complicated than slinging something into a box and sealing it up. You have to pack the item in a way that protects it on its journey from your house to the buyer's. Start by wrapping the item in plastic; you never know when the shipper might be trying to deliver packages in a torrential rain. If the item is small enough to ship in an envelope, use a padded envelope for extra protection, or improvise by wrapping the item in bubble wrap before putting it in a regular envelope.

Bubble wrap and Styrofoam peanuts probably cushion items best—they're a must for fragile items. If you buy on eBay yourself, save the packing materials that come with items you receive to use them when you ship out your merchandise. You can recycle old newspapers by crinkling them up and using them for padding, although the newsprint can be messy, and wadded-up paper tends to compress in transit, so don't use it for fragile stuff. If you have a paper shredder, you can use it to create inexpensive packing material; shred your junk mail, newspapers, and old magazines.

Tip: Many eBay sellers buy their packaging materials cheaply on eBay or get them from other online suppliers like Uline (*www.uline.com*) or BubbleFAST (*www.bubblefast.com*). Also, try calling local gift shops, the ones that stock their shelves with lots of snowglobes, crystal figurines, and other fragile items. When a new shipment comes in, these shops have to deal with tons of packing materials. Sometimes they'll give away boxes, bubblewrap, plastic peanuts, and so on, so they don't have to recycle them.

Make sure you use a heavy cardboard box larger than the item you're shipping. You can often get boxes from local grocery stores or other retailers. Fragile items can benefit from a second box, at least three inches bigger than the first on all sides; put cushioning material between the two boxes to keep the item extra safe.

If you ship via Priority Mail, you can get free boxes from the post office—they'll even deliver them free to your door—but you must use Priority Mail to ship. Figure 5-13 shows some of the free boxes available.

Before you seal your box, give it a gentle shake. If you can hear things moving around inside, add more cushioning. Look at the sides. If they're bulging, your box is too small.

Note: According to the Postal Service, too-small boxes are the #1 cause of items breaking during shipping.

Finally, seal your item securely on all seams. Use packing tape, not masking tape, Scotch tape, or even duct tape. If your item is heavy, use reinforced packing tape.

Pack carefully to save yourself problems with an unhappy buyer. It's better to over-pack than to have the item broken or damaged in transit.

Shipping

It used to be that you had to wait in line at the post office balancing a huge stack of packages to ship your stuff. No more. When your items are packed and ready to go, you can have your shipper come to you.

When choosing a shipper, keep in mind the two factors that determine cost: weight and speed. The heavier your item and the sooner you want it to get there, the more you'll pay. Shop around to find the most reliable shipper at the best price.

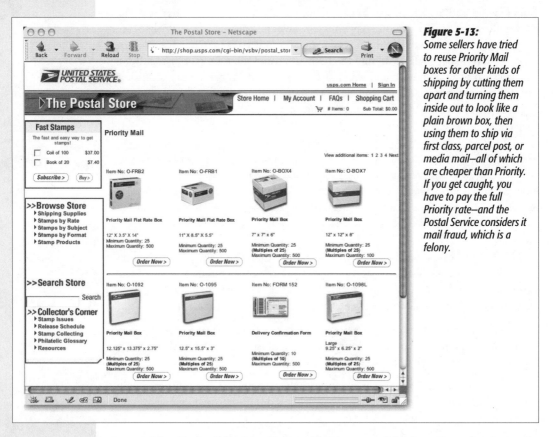

Figure 5-13:
Some sellers have tried to reuse Priority Mail boxes for other kinds of shipping by cutting them apart and turning them inside out to look like a plain brown box, then using them to ship via first class, parcel post, or media mail—all of which are cheaper than Priority. If you get caught, you have to pay the full Priority rate—and the Postal Service considers it mail fraud, which is a felony.

Start with eBay's Shipping Center (Services → Shipping Center), shown in Figure 5-14. Also check out the Web pages of the Postal Service (*www.usps.com*), UPS (*www.ups.com*), Federal Express (*www.fedex.com*), Airborne/DHL (*www.dhl-usa.com*), and other shippers to see what they have to offer. Most offer free shipping supplies and will let you schedule a pickup at home. Many also offer free tracking or delivery confirmation.

Tip: Always make sure that you have some way to track the package or confirm the shipper delivered it. You can use tracking to assure a buyer that the item is on its way. And if a dispute arises, you might need to prove you sent it. This is especially important if you accept PayPal; if a buyer files a PayPal complaint against you saying they didn't get the item, it's totally up to you to prove that they did. Without proof of delivery, the seller *automatically* loses any PayPal nonreceipt dispute.

PayPal also has a convenient shipping center. When a buyer pays with PayPal, you have immediate access to PayPal's shipping tools by clicking the Ship button that appears with the payment details. Select a carrier (the U.S. Postal Service or UPS), print your label and a packing slip, and pay right from your PayPal account.

Figure 5-14:
At eBay's Shipping Center, you can calculate how much shipping will cost with different shippers and shipping options, print labels, track your package, and connect with the Postal Service, UPS, or a freight hauler.

Stamps.com (*www.stamps.com*), shown in Figure 5-15, is another popular site for buying postage online and printing it out yourself, but the software you need currently doesn't support Macs. Mac fans need a Windows emulator to run it (an emulator lets you use Windows software on a Mac). Also, Stamps.com works only with the U.S. Postal Service, not other shippers.

If a buyer purchases multiple items (always a good thing!) and you plan to ship everything in one box, make sure you get only *one* payment for everything. Under PayPal's Seller Protection plan (see the box on page 170), every payment you accept requires its own delivery confirmation number—and you can't get a separate number for each Beanie Baby you pack into a single box. So what do you do if a buyer orders 14 Beanie Babies and has already paid for each one separately? Refund those multiple payments and send an invoice for the combined total of everything he purchased (include shipping fees).

Tip: When you print your shipping labels with any service, use the "stealth postage" option so that the actual postage amount doesn't appear on the printed label. Even if your handling fee is completely reasonable, some buyers go ballistic when the postage shown on the package is a penny less than the amount they paid for shipping. Hide the actual postage cost, and they'll never know the difference.

Figure 5-15:
Stamps.com lets you print out postage from your computer printer. After a free four-week trial, the site charges $15.99 a month for its service. You can print stamps and shipping labels directly onto envelopes, stickers, or plain paper.

Leaving Feedback

Technically speaking, eBay doesn't require you to leave feedback for your trading partner (page 40). But you still need to do it. Feedback helps everyone by describing, for all the world to see, how eBayers conduct their business.

Always leave feedback for the buyer—but not until the transaction is complete. Even if a buyer pays quickly, you're rating the whole transaction. If the buyer bombards you with email after the sale or complains about things beyond your control, you might want to take these things into account when leaving your feedback.

Common Problems

If you sell on eBay, be prepared to deal with the problems that come with the territory. Most transactions go smoothly, but there are a few common problems that, sooner or later, all eBay sellers face. Knowing about them ahead of time will help you deal with them better.

Miscommunication

One of the biggest causes of negative feedback is miscommunication. Over and over again, those little red circles indicating negative feedback precede comments like "Never answered emails." So a simple way to avoid negs is to do your best to be in touch with your buyer every step of the way. Good communication assures both sides that a transaction is going smoothly.

What if you're communicating but the buyer isn't answering? Your email, or the buyer's, may be getting stuck in a spam filter. Spam filters are great at cutting down on electronic junk mail, but they sometimes catch emails you want to read. Check your spam filter regularly before you toss the accumulated junk mail. You might find a note from your buyer.

If you suspect that your emails are getting trapped in the buyer's spam filter, try sending a message through eBay. On your My eBay page, click the buyer's ID to go to their member profile. Click the Contact Member button, and then send a message. Sometimes, messages that go through eBay escape the spam filter that traps other emails. Messages sent through eBay will also appear in the My Messages section of the recipient's My eBay page.

If you still can't get an answer, the next step is to pull the buyer's contact information and try a phone call. Figure 5-16 tells you how to get the 411. When you request an eBayer's contact info, eBay sends them the same information about you.

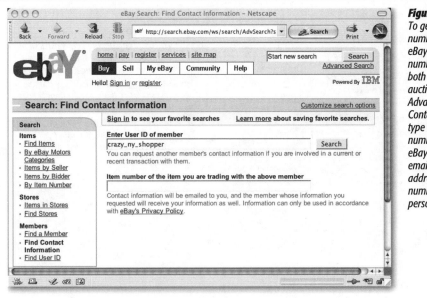

Figure 5-16:
To get a buyer's phone number, you'll need her eBay ID and the item number. You can get both of these from the auction page. Click Advanced Search → Find Contact Information, then type in the ID and item number and click Search. eBay will email you the email address, street address, and phone number on file for that person.

Deadbeat Bidders

Sooner or later, it happens to every seller: someone bids and wins your auction, then disappears without paying. In the meantime, eBay is charging you listing fees and FVFs. What recourse do you have when the auction didn't go as planned?

Report a UPI

File an *Unpaid Item (UPI) dispute*, a formal report telling eBay that the buyer didn't follow through. You can report a deadbeat bidder for not paying any time between seven and 45 days after the auction's end. (Of course, you should try to contact the winning bidder via email and phone before you report him or her to eBay.)

Note: If the deadbeat bidder is NARU'd (no longer a registered user) or registered in an area you don't ship to, you don't have to wait seven days before opening the UPI dispute. (When an eBayer is NARU'd, the words *no longer a registered user* appear next to his eBay ID.)

Here's how a UPI works:

1. **Open an Unpaid Item dispute.**

   From your My eBay page, click Dispute Console → Unpaid Items → Report an Unpaid Item. The page that opens asks for the item number, which you can find in the end-of-auction email or the auction page. The Dispute Console is shown in Figure 5-17.

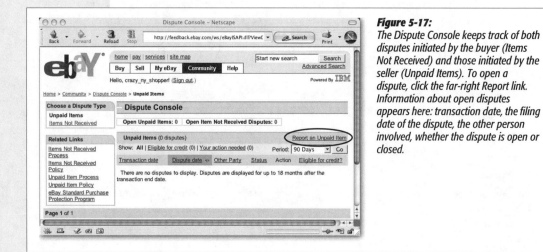

Figure 5-17:
The Dispute Console keeps track of both disputes initiated by the buyer (Items Not Received) and those initiated by the seller (Unpaid Items). To open a dispute, click the far-right Report link. Information about open disputes appears here: transaction date, the filing date of the dispute, the other person involved, whether the dispute is open or closed.

2. **eBay contacts the bidder.**

   Often a reminder from eBay is all that's needed to nudge a reluctant buyer into paying. eBay gives the bidder three response options: she can say she's already paid, she can pay now, or she can communicate with you. eBay even provides an onsite message area where you and the buyer can leave messages for each other without having to worry about email going astray. If the buyer pays, then everyone's happy and you can close the dispute (jump to step 5).

Tip: Don't close a dispute on the mere promise of payment. Wait until you have the money in hand. Once you've closed a UPI dispute, you can't file it a second time, so don't let the buyer off the hook until she's coughed up the cash.

---

3. **The bidder responds—maybe.**

   Disputes are often resolved during this phase. Sometimes, though, the bidder simply ignores eBay's email. Or the bidder might get in touch, only to let you know that she can't or won't pay. In that case, you need to move forward with the UPI process.

4. **Track the status of your dispute in the Dispute Console.**

   If the buyer won't respond or refuses to pay up after a week has passed, you can close the dispute and request a credit of the auction's Final Value Fee. You can also relist the item for free (in the form of a relisting credit), as long as you relist it within 90 days using the "Relist your item" link, either from the closed auction page or in the Unsold Items view of My eBay. You won't get the insertion-fee credit if you start the new auction at a higher price than the original. You also can't get this credit if the deadbeat stiffed you in a Dutch auction.

Note: The relisting credit applies only to the insertion fee, not to extras like highlighting or boldface.

---

5. **Close the dispute.**

   There are three ways you can close a dispute. If the buyer has paid for the item and everyone's happy now, you can let eBay know. If you've communicated with the bidder and agreed to let her off the hook, you can tell eBay that you've agreed not to complete the transaction. In this case, you get an FVF credit and the buyer gets out of the transaction without an *Unpaid Item strike*; too many UPI strikes can suspend a buyer from eBay. The third way to close a dispute is to indicate that you're fed up with the buyer, who's not going to pay. You can do this a week after you've filed the dispute, or sooner if the buyer used the Dispute Console to indicate he's not going to pay. You get your FVF credit, and the deadbeat bidder gets an Unpaid Item strike.

Note: If you want your FVF back, you must close the dispute yourself. Disputes can stay open no more than 60 days after the auction, and if you haven't closed the dispute by then, eBay will close it for you—and keep your FVF.

When you file a UPI, eBay lets the buyer know that the item may no longer be available. So as soon as you file, you can sell the item to one of the underbidders using a Second Chance Offer (page 186), or you can relist the item immediately (but you won't get the relisting credit unless you wait and close the dispute). If the original buyer tries to pay after you've filed the UPI, you don't have to accept the payment.

Offer someone else a second chance

A *Second Chance Offer* (SCO) gives the bidders who lost out on your skateboard another shot to ride it off into the sunset. If the winning bidder backs out, you can send any nonwinning bidder an offer to buy the item at the price that they bid. SCOs are a good choice when an auction had a lot of bidding action but the top bidder turned into a deadbeat.

You can send an SCO from the Bid History of your closed auction, from a link at the top of the closed listing itself, or from My eBay: under Items I've Sold, find the closed auction, click the Action menu, and then select Send a Second Chance Offer. An SCO can last for one, three, five, or seven days before it expires. eBay sends the SCO to the nonwinning bidder you specified and sets up a special BIN listing page with a new item number and a new price. Only you and the buyer who received your SCO can view this page; other shoppers won't be able to find it. If the buyer accepts your offer (by going to the SCO page and clicking the BIN button), you complete the sale in the usual way. Sending a Second Chance Offer doesn't cost anything; if you make the sale, you pay FVFs based on the SCO price.

Note: Sellers can also send SCOs when an auction had bids but failed to meet the reserve price, or when they have duplicate items for sale but haven't chosen to run a Dutch auction.

The Item Doesn't Arrive

Always track your packages—and keep the tracking number handy until the transaction is over and done with. Buyers are happy when you send them a tracking number to let them know the package is on its way; they can follow its progress themselves on the shipper's Web site. And if the package doesn't make it to the buyer, you can get the shipper to track it down or, if a dispute arises, you can submit proof to eBay, PayPal, or a credit card company that the item really did arrive on the buyer's doorstep.

Many shippers offer free tracking as a part of the deal. Others, like the Postal Service, offer delivery confirmation for a small fee (although tracking is free if you're using USPS Global Express Mail). Check with your shipper if you're not sure.

Tip: If you print out your shipping label through eBay (from the navigation bar, My eBay → Items I've Sold → Print Shipping Label), you can use My eBay to track the shipment's progress. Look for the item under Items I've Sold, click the far-right arrow, and then choose View Shipment Status.

But just tracking a package doesn't guarantee the package will make it to its destination. When a package goes astray, the buyer will probably contact you, either directly though email (the usual route) or by filing an Item Not Received (INR) report with eBay (page 71), which shows up in the Dispute Console view in My eBay). First, try to track down the package through the shipper. If that doesn't work, either file an insurance claim, following your shipper's procedure, or offer the buyer a replacement or a refund. As the seller, you're the one who's responsible for making sure the buyer receives the item she paid for. If her rainbow crystal wind chime never arrived, she deserves her money back.

The Item Arrives Damaged

If the item arrives damaged because you didn't pack it well, you have no choice but to refund the buyer's money or replace the item. As a seller, you're responsible for getting the item to the buyer in the same condition advertised in your auction.

As with items that disappear en route, buyers will probably email you first if their Cookie Monster nightlight arrived in pieces. Or they might head straight to the Dispute Console and file a report. (Reporting an item as "significantly not as described" is basically the same process as filing an INR report; see page 71.)

If the damage is due to poor packing—you just rolled up the nightlight in last Sunday's comics and squeezed it into an *almost* big-enough box—you're at fault. You owe the buyer a refund or a new Cookie.

If your packing was fine and the item was damaged by the shipper, insurance will take care of the problem—that is, *if* you insured the package. (Since you're the one who shipped the item, you're the one who files the insurance claim. The buyer paid you in advance for the insurance, but you're the one who purchased it from the shipper.) Without insurance, you're out of luck. Basically, when you didn't buy insurance, you took a gamble that the shipment would arrive OK. If it didn't, you still owe the buyer a refund or a replacement. Once again, it's sellers—not buyers—who are responsible for making sure that the item arrives in the condition advertised in the auction.

Tip: When a buyer claims that an item arrived damaged, don't issue a refund or a send replacement until the buyer has returned the damaged item. No retailer on this face of Earth will refund your money until they have the returned item in hand. Follow this policy—include it in the terms of your auction—or you might find buyers "forgetting" to return the item after you've given their money back.

The Buyer Wants to Return the Item

Just when you thought the auction was over and everyone was happy, the buyer wants to return an item that you've paid eBay (and possibly PayPal) fees to sell. Whether or not the buyer's reason is legitimate, you want to develop a reputation for good customer service as you build your eBay business.

You have several options for handling a return:

- **Accept the return and issue a full refund.** If the buyer paid by check or money order, write the buyer a check. If the buyer paid using PayPal, you can get your PayPal fees back, as long as you issue the refund within 60 days of receiving the original payment. Log in to PayPal and click the History tab of My Account to find the transaction; click Details, and then click Refund. This process issues a full refund to the buyer and refunds any fees PayPal charged you for accepting the money. (You can also issue a partial refund if you're refunding the auction's purchase price but not the shipping, and PayPal prorates your refund accordingly.)

Next, go to eBay and file a UPI (page 184), stating you've given the buyer a refund; the process works the same as a "mutually agreed to cancel" UPI, so the buyer must agree to it. When the buyer agrees, you get your Final Value Fees refunded and a relisting credit with eBay if you decide to relist.

- **Accept the return and charge a restocking fee.** Many retailers charge a 10 to 15 percent fee when buyers return items, called a *restocking fee*. To charge a restocking fee, though, you need to have mentioned it as part of your return policy on your auction pages (page 168).

- **Refuse to accept the return.** As eBay constantly reminds shoppers, a bid is a binding agreement to buy. If a buyer suffers a bout of buyer's remorse, you don't have to accept a return.

Note: If the return is due to some problem with the item that you failed to mention in your auction, you have to accept the return and refund the buyer's money. In this case, it doesn't matter if you said all over your auction page that the item was sold "as is" and that you have a no-return policy. If you didn't disclose a flaw or problem or missing part and the buyer complains that the item was "not as described," it doesn't matter what your return policy is. You'll lose the dispute. Better to accept the return graciously.

You Dealt with a Problem—and Got Negative Feedback for Your Trouble

Sad but true: you can bend over backwards to make your customers happy, but sooner or later you'll still get hit with negative feedback. When a problem arises, some buyers don't take into account whether or not that problem was resolved; they leave a neg for any transaction that wasn't flawless from start to finish. (You see this kind of behavior mostly from newbies who don't yet understand how feedback works.)

Feedback is your reputation on eBay, and it affects your bottom line. Small wonder that an ugly red mark on your otherwise unblemished record can really make you see red. But before you shoot off a nasty email or leave a retaliatory neg, consider these options:

- **Mutual feedback withdrawal.** Contact the buyer and explain that you're disappointed to get negative feedback after you worked so hard to resolve the problem. Point out that problems are inevitable, but you're committed to making buyers happy. Suggest that you start the mutual feedback withdrawal process (page 65) and see whether the buyer agrees.

- **Respond to the feedback.** You can respond to feedback your buyers leave for you (page 64). A seller who responds to negative feedback calmly and factually looks professional. If the buyer says you were slow to ship the item, respond with something like *Pd 3/22, shipped 3/23*. Or if the buyer complains about the item, you can respond *Refund issued 4/1* or *Pls contact me for a refund*. Smart eBayers read feedback and will look at both sides of the story, so tell yours in a professional manner, and you'll come out looking like a pro.

Tip: Many sellers leave positive feedback right after they receive payment, because they feel that the buyer has satisfactorily completed their part of the deal when they pay. Think about waiting, though, until the whole transaction is complete before you leave feedback. That way, if any problems come up and the buyer becomes difficult, you still have recourse.

• **Leave a little feedback of your own.** When you get an unfair neg, it's tempting to leave one in return. Of course, feedback that's purely retaliatory is also unfair, so take a minute to decide on the professional thing to do. You might leave neutral feedback or not leave feedback at all for this transaction. If you must leave negative feedback, don't type in all caps, call names, or use exclamation marks. Just explain what the buyer did wrong.

Leaving negative feedback in return for receiving a neg might make the buyer more amenable to mutual feedback withdrawal—or it might just make the buyer angry. Don't use feedback as blackmail.

WORKAROUND WORKSHOP

No-Hassle Selling

What if you have some things you want to sell on eBay, but you don't want to go through all the work of registering, building a feedback score, taking photos, writing item descriptions, and watching your auctions? You don't have to give up on eBay and head for the local pawn shop or call your newspaper's classifieds department. You can hire a *trading assistant* to sell stuff on eBay on your behalf. Trading assistants are experienced eBay sellers who sell for others on consignment.

Here's how it works. First, find a trading assistant in your area by zipping to eBay's navigation bar, choosing Services → Trading Assistants, and then typing in your Zip code. When you click the Search button, you get a list of trading assistants near you. (If your search comes back with fewer than 20 results, eBay automatically expands the area to find more trading assistants a little farther afield.) The results page gives you each trading assistant's eBay ID, feedback score, city, and Zip code; you can sort by any of these categories. Some have drop-off locations; others will pick the item up at your home. To learn more about particular trading assistants, click their eBay IDs.

Besides saving you time, a big advantage to using a trading assistant is that you use their reputation to sell your items. You're invisible in the transaction, so if your feedback rating has recently taken a hit or you have no feedback score at all, these issues won't affect the sale. To the buyer, the trading assistant is the one selling the item.

For this reason, check out the trading assistant's feedback yourself. Look for someone with at least a few hundred feedback comments and a 98 percent or better positive rating. These are the sellers that eBayers trust—the sellers who know how to close sales and keep buyers happy.

When choosing a trading assistant, keep a few things in mind. Fees vary widely. Most charge a percentage of the final sales price, but commissions can vary from 10 percent to 50 percent, and some charge a flat fee per item, as well. Many will not accept items likely to sell for less than $50. Expect to pay all eBay and PayPal fees related to the sale. Be sure that you understand all charges before you hire a trading assistant—and sign a contract so you're sure of the services you're getting and how much they'll cost you.

Honing Your Competitive Edge

Over a million new listings appear on eBay every single day. Almost any keyword you search for, from *Abercrombie* to *Xbox*, returns tens of thousands of auctions listed by thousands of sellers. With all that competition, why should somebody buy *your* faux-zebra-print slipcovers and not some other seller's?

The answer: because you made your listing stand out from the crowd using the above-and-beyond strategies described in this chapter. (For the basic how-tos of selling, check out Chapter 5.)

Implementing the advice in this chapter can mean the difference between sluggish sales and bidding wars—between selling a couple of things and creating a profitable eBay business. Here you'll find tips for creating more enticing listings, building your reputation, promoting your auctions, avoiding the con artists who sometimes try to take sellers for a ride, and more:

- Selling yourself with an About Me page.

- Making your auctions irresistible.

- Taking terrific photos.

- Boosting your results with auction tips and tricks.

- Sidestepping illegal (if tempting) practices.

- Protecting your auctions from online scams.

It's All About You

You've probably noticed the blue-and-red word *me* that appears next to some eBayers' IDs. Clicking this word takes you to the eBayer's *About Me page*, a personal Web page within the eBay site where eBayers can talk about their families, interests, and hobbies; display photos; link to their eBay auctions, eBay Store (page 259), and outside Web sites; and pretty much present whatever they want to about themselves to the rest of the eBay community.

Smart sellers use their About Me page as a marketing tool, and you can, too. When you're first starting to sell and you don't yet have a lot of feedback as a seller, a good About Me page puts a human face on your eBay ID, making buyers feel more confident about bidding on your auctions. As you build your eBay business, use your About Me page to create a professional presence on the site: direct buyers to your eBay store or your own Web site, state your auction and return policies, quote happy customers, offer a way to sign up for your newsletter, and more.

Before you start designing your About Me page, find a few sellers you admire for the volume of their sales or the way they do business. If these sellers have About Me pages, study them. What appeals to you? What doesn't work? Learn from the pros.

Tip: Because eBayers come in all sizes, shapes, and colors (not to mention nationalities, religions, belief systems, and political leanings), it's a good idea to avoid discussing contentious issues on your About Me page—unless you'd rather get into arguments than generate bids.

You can create your page with your own HTML, or you can use eBay's forms to create your page. Either way, the process requires three steps:

Note: *HTML* stands for hypertext markup language, the lingua franca of the Web. Although it sounds fancy, it's really just a simple coding system for presenting text and other elements on Web pages.

---

1. **From the eBay home page, select services → "About Me page" → Create Your Page.**

   The About Me: Choose Page Creation Option page shown in Figure 6-1 appears.

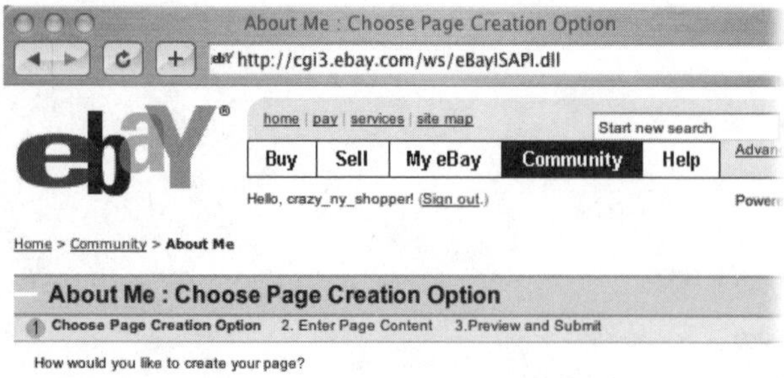

Figure 6-1:
If you know HTML and want to use it to create your own About Me page (for example, if you have a Web store and you want your About Me page to have a similar look and feel), select "Enter your own HTML code" and click Continue; then you can type or paste in your HTML code and preview the page. If you don't feel like messing around with HTML, select "Use our easy Step-by-Step process" and click Continue.

2. **Choose a page creation option.**

If you're an HTML wizard, you may want to create your About Me page using your own custom-crafted HTML code. If that's the case, select "Enter your own HTML code." If you'd rather point-and-click your way to a nice-looking page, select "Use our easy Step-by-Step process." Click Continue.

3. **On the page that opens, type in your page content.**

If you're using your own HTML, type your text and code into the text box, and then click Continue. (You can add eBay-specific HTML tags (see *http://pages. ebay.com/help/account/html-tags.html*) to link to your Member Profile, display how long you've been on eBay, show recent feedback comments, etc.) If you want to use eBay's step-by-step process, fill out the form shown in Figure 6-2. You can include almost anything you want in your About Me page: a photo and description of yourself, links to other sites, information about your current auctions, recent feedback—whatever you like. When you finish, click Continue.

Figure 6-2:
This form helps you to create an organized, easy-to-read About Me page. The top part of the form has text boxes where you can type in a title and a couple of paragraphs of description. Under Show Your eBay Activity (near the bottom of the screen), you can share recent feedback and show up to 200 current auctions. About Me is the only place on eBay where you can add links to your off-eBay Web site.

Note: Although eBay lets you link to your own Web site from your About Me page, you can't use your About Me page to promote off-eBay sales. So don't use it to advertise specials that you're running in your online store.

4. Preview and Submit.

The final step before you finish your About Me page is to preview the page to
see how it looks. If you're using eBay's step-by-step process, you can gussy up
your page by choosing one of three different layouts, as shown in Figure 6-3.
After you select the button next to A, B, or C, a mock-up appears instantly at
the bottom of the page (scroll down to see it). When you're satisfied, click Submit to create your About Me page.

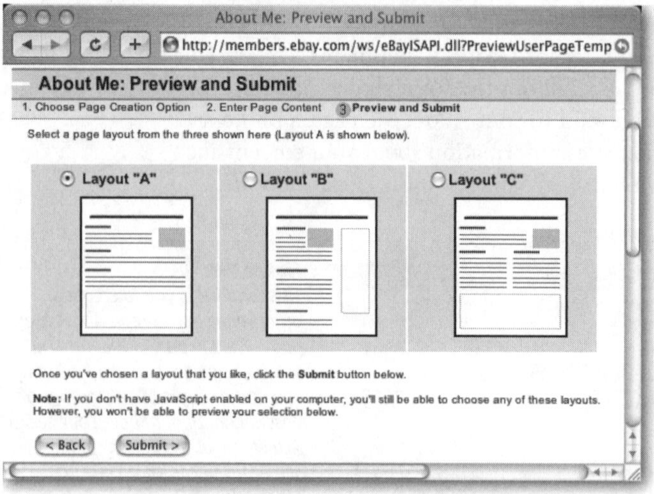

Figure 6-3:
*Choose one of these layouts for your
About Me page. The white rectangle
shows where your current auctions and
recent feedback will appear: at the
bottom of the page or the right-hand
side.*

Build a Better Auction

Chapter 5 took you through the basics of creating a great auction listing. This section gives you tips for making your auctions even harder to resist.

Tempting Titles

The title of your auction is critical because buyers will—or won't—find your auction by searching titles for a particular keyword. For example, if you're selling a
Canon EOS Rebel XT and you title your auction "Digital Camera", people using
"Canon" or "Rebel" as keywords won't find it. So don't just slap your title
together. Do some research to get your auction in more shoppers' search results.

One good place to do that research is through *eBay Pulse*, a section of the site that
keeps track of trends and hot items. You can find it by typing *pulse.ebay.com* into
your Web browser's address bar or, from the eBay home page, selecting Buy →
eBay Pulse. One of the things eBay Pulse tracks is the most commonly used search
terms. On the eBay Pulse main page, you can see what the most popular searches

are for the whole site. Or you can choose a category from the Category drop-down list to see the most popular search terms and most-watched items in that category (Figure 6-4). See which of these hot search terms you can work into your title—but make sure you're not violating eBay's policy against *keyword spamming,* using inappropriate keywords merely to attract attention to your auction (page 223).

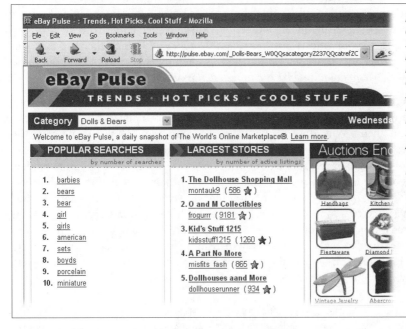

Figure 6-4:
eBay Pulse's Popular Searches list shows you the most searched-for keywords in your category. You can also check out your most serious competition by looking in the Largest Stores box, which shows the eBay Stores with the most listings. At the bottom of the page (not shown) is a list of the most-watched items; study these auctions to figure out why they've attracted so much attention.

In addition to naming your item, use a few attention-getting words in your title. Other good words include *rare, bonus, sexy, mint,* or some eBay-specific acronyms like *NIB* (new in box), *NR* (no reserve), or *VHTF* (very hard to find). For a list of common acronyms used on eBay, go to Help → eBay Acronyms.

Tip: eBay Pulse maintains an ever-changing list of the 10 most-watched auctions on the whole site. Some are just plain goofy (like evil dolls or celebrity images on toast), but all are attention-getters. Study these auctions to see what makes them watchable. By selecting a category on the eBay Pulse home page, you can also view the most-watched items for each category; check out your favorite categories to see how sellers build the auctions eBayers watch.

Irresistible Descriptions

When you look at other people's auctions, you've probably noticed descriptions that are too short to be helpful ("It's a digital camera. It takes good pictures.") and others that are too long to be readable: line after line of densely packed prose that not only tells you the brand and dimensions of a plasma TV but lists every single show the seller's ever watched on it. Buyers want complete information about what you're selling, but they want it in a clear and easy-to-read format. The best item descriptions (page 158) consist of four parts: an attention-getting opening, features and benefits, known flaws, and a call to action. Here's more on each part:

- **Get their attention.** Start with a short statement that echoes and expands on what's in the auction title. Think about why a buyer might be shopping for your item, and then create one line to get that buyer excited about your auction. For example, if your title is *Schwinn Mesa Mountain 19″ Bike Bicycle New!*, you might start off your description with something like this: *This brand-new Schwinn Mesa mountain bike is a proven performer on tough terrain.*

- **Describe features and benefits.** Describe in detail the things that make your item worth buying, and in a way that makes it clear to buyers how the item can benefit them. Why does a buyer deserve your item? How can it make the buyer's life easier or more fun? A diet book, for example, is more than the number of its pages or its sales rank in The *New York Times*. Show potential bidders how buying the book could make life better with an explanation like this: *Follow this program and wear clothes you thought you'd never fit into again.* If your item is one of a kind or an heirloom, give a little of its history to show what makes it unique. Throughout your description, keep paragraphs short and use bulleted lists to make the text easy to read. (There's nothing like a seemingly endless paragraph—especially one written in all capital letters—to drive buyers away.) Of course, the claims you make for your item must be accurate.

Tip: Don't save the best for last—put your item's strongest selling points right up front. Assume that some buyers will stop reading after your first paragraph, and make sure that paragraph says what you need to get across.

- **Don't try to hide flaws.** If there's anything wrong with the item, from a small scratch to a missing part to a broken switch, explain this in a brief paragraph of its own. If an item is used, say so. Don't make excuses; just let buyers know the item's actual condition. An accurate description of any flaws will protect you from claims that the item wasn't the way you described it in the auction. And a scratch or a loose thread isn't always a turnoff; buyers looking for a deal might prefer a slightly flawed item to one that's brand new, if it saves them some money.

- **Finish with a call to action.** End your description by coming right out and telling shoppers what you want them to do. Use active language: *Bid now* or *For great deals, check out my other auctions* or *Add me to your Favorites list!* It's also a good idea to thank the shopper for looking. This simple courtesy shows that you're aware of the buyer—not just the item you're trying to sell.

Tip: Avoid ending the description with a lot of terms, restrictions, and conditions. You don't want to get a potential bidder interested in your auction and then scare them away from actually placing a bid. Instead, put your restrictions and warnings in the "Shipping, payment details, and return policy" section of your auction page.

FREQUENTLY ASKED QUESTION

eBay Keyword Ads

What are eBay Keyword Ads?

When you've searched on eBay, you might have noticed the box or banner ads that appear at the top of the screen, above the Search Results list. These ads are called *keyword ads*; they appear when shoppers search on keywords associated with the ads. They also appear when shoppers browse a related category.

When you click a keyword ad, you're whisked to the ad-owner's eBay Store (page 259) or a list of his current auctions. For example, someone selling consumer electronics like CD systems and MP3 players might choose keywords like *"Sony CD player"* or *iPod* so that his ad appears at the top of the page when shoppers search for those terms. If the shopper clicks the keyword ad, she's then browsing that seller's auctions exclusively.

How much do keyword ads cost?

eBay charges for keyword ads on a *cost per click* (CPC) basis: no matter how often your ad appears, you pay only when someone clicks the ad. In addition, there's no fixed cost per click for keyword ads. Instead, sellers set the price by bidding on the keywords they want to link to. The CPC for a particular keyword is the bid of the next highest bidder plus a penny. Or, if you're the only bidder, you pay just 10 cents per click (eBay's minimum CPC).

For example, you're willing to pay up to $1.50 per click to direct buyers to your eBay Store. Your bid of $1.50 makes you the highest bidder. The next highest bidder has bid $1.20 per click. When someone clicks your ad, you pay $1.21—the next highest bid plus a penny.

The CPC can change as the bids change. For example, if you're the highest bidder at $1.50 per click and the second-highest-bidder drops out of the program, the new second-highest bid might be, say, $1.00, so you'll pay $1.01 per click. eBay rotates the ads according to bids; ads with higher CPCs display more frequently than lower-paying ads.

Will the program increase traffic to my eBay store and auctions?

eBay claims that more than 20,000 sellers have signed up for its keyword program—a tiny percentage of all the sellers on eBay. And many of the ads are for things like Anything Points, or the PowerSellers program—suggesting that individual sellers haven't found them worth the cost.

To check out whether your competition is buying keyword ads for the items you sell, from the eBay home page select Services → eBay Keywords → Keyword Suggestion Tool. Type in a keyword that relates to your product (along with an eBay-generated verification code), and click Go. eBay not only suggests various keywords; you can click the View link to see the current bids for various keywords. You can also see the ad that goes with each bid. Do an Advanced Search (Advanced Search → Items by Seller) to check a seller's past auctions and see whether the advertising seems to help sales.

When you're deciding whether or not to bid on a keyword, think like a buyer. When searching for products on eBay, do you look at the keyword ads or go straight to the Search Results list?

If you do want to try it out, sign up at Services → eBay Keywords → Get Started Now!

Photos That Sell

There's no doubt your description is important—it can generate the excitement that turns a shopper into a bidder—but unless you have a good photo, shoppers may never even read your scintillating prose. (You add photos during step 3 of the Sell Your Item form; see page 160.) Most buyers check out the photos in the search results list before they decide whether or not to look further into an auction. If your photos are out of focus, poorly lit, cluttered, or otherwise hard to make out, it probably doesn't matter how good your description is; you're going to lose potential bidders.

You don't have to take a photography class to learn how to take compelling, attractive photos of your eBay items. Follow the tips in this section, and with a little practice, you'll be taking photos like a pro.

Choosing equipment

You don't have to go so far as to set up a professional photo studio in a corner of your dining room, but having the right equipment does help you take sharp-looking photos. Here's what you need:

- **Camera.** To take photos, you obviously need a camera. A digital camera is the easiest solution, because you can transfer images to your computer as soon as you've taken the shots. (If you prefer to work with a film camera, you'll either need a scanner to get the pictures onto your computer, or you'll have to go to a photo processor to get your pictures copied onto a CD or uploaded to the Internet.)

  You don't need to get the fanciest, highest-resolution camera on the market. In fact, a resolution of 640×480 pixels is plenty because people will be looking at your photos on a computer screen, and smaller images load faster than those with millions of pixels. So if you'll be using the camera just for your eBay listings, there's no need to spend the extra money for high resolution you won't use.

Tip: If you're going to be taking shots of small items, like jewelry or coins, look for a camera that has a *macro lens*, which lets you take close-ups without losing focus and produces an image about the same size as the subject.

- **Scanner.** A *flatbed scanner* (the kind that looks like a photocopier, with a large glass panel where you lay the item you want scanned) is great for getting photo prints into your computer. You can also use it to make digital images of anything that's flat, like a book cover or an autographed playbill.

- **Tripod.** A tripod will help you align the shot and keep the camera steady to prevent blurring caused by moving or jiggling the camera.

- **Lighting.** Good lighting is also important for photos: too much can wash out the subject, while too little will make it look dark. Some sellers invest in professional studio lighting, but you can take good photos with a couple of lamps (see step 3 on page 200).

- **Background.** You don't want someone scrutinizing your sofa's plaid upholstery while ignoring the item you propped there for the photo—so choose a solid-colored neutral background (a sheet can do the trick in most cases). Solid black is good for light-colored objects; beige, white, ivory, or light gray work well with darker or brightly colored items.

WORDS TO THE WISE

Successful Selling

Advertising copywriters know that consumers respond more strongly to some words than to others. Writing coach Dawn Josephson of Cameo Publications (*www.cameopublications.com*) has identified the top 21 selling words. Work as many of these as you can into your item description and watch the bids multiply:

- **Words that refer to the buyer's point of view.** *You/your* is one of the most important selling words you can use, because referring to the buyer (rather than to yourself as seller) helps you to keep the buyer's perspective in mind. After all, the buyer needs to know why he or she should buy this item, not why you want to sell it. *Yes* is another motivating word that people love to hear; it opens a door to action or getting what you want. Josepheson also recommends using the *buyer's name* whenever possible. This isn't possible in your item description, because you don't know who'll be looking at your auction, but it is possible—and important—in communicating with buyers and potential bidders. When you have a buyer's name, use it.

- **Words related to money.** The word *money* itself attracts buyers; so does *save*. Put them together to show how your auction can save buyers money, and you've got their attention. *Free* is another attention-getter. If you can offer free shipping with Buy It Now or throw in a free gift, say so in your description.

- **Benefits to the buyer.** Many selling words fall into this category, including *benefit, easy/easily, quick/quickly, fun, new, more, now, how to,* and *solution*. Remember that you want to write from the buyer's point of view. Explaining the benefits your item offers can motivate shoppers to click the Place Bid button. Other benefit-suggesting words include *health/healthy* and *safe/safely*. An auction for a cuckoo clock won't have anything to do with health, but you certainly can explain why it's safe to buy from you.

- **Confidence in your product.** If you're confident buyers will *love* your product, say so. Offer a *guarantee* that your item will give buyers the *results* they want. Another good word is *proven*, which suggests that your item has passed some sort of effectiveness test.

- **Groups of three.** Psychologically, the number three is a very satisfying number. (Examples in everyday speech abound: "Every Tom, Dick, and Harry…" "Lather, rinse, repeat." "Do not fold, spindle, or mutilate.") You can put this principle to work in your eBay auctions by listing features and benefits in groups of three: *This flash drive stores your data quickly, easily, and securely,* say, or *Be stylish, trendy, and fun in this flirty dress*. You can also phrase your call to action in a group of three: *Click Buy It Now, get free shipping, and start enjoying your new camera*.

Getting a great shot

Taking great pictures is more than just pointing and clicking. For eBay-worthy photos, you need to consider background, position, and lighting, and then edit the image on your computer. For photos that sell, follow these steps:

1. **Prepare the background.**

   Keep the background uncluttered. Drape fabric under and behind the item; choose a neutral color that will make the item stand out. You can also add texture to the background by taking a picture against wood (such as a butcher-block table) or moiré fabric, but always keep in mind that your item is the important element. Don't let the background overwhelm the subject.

Tip: For jewelry, don't photograph someone wearing the ring, earrings, bracelet, or necklace. A shot that's close enough to show the item's details will also show—unappealingly—the close-up texture of the wearer's skin. Unless you're a whiz with image editing and can airbrush the model, stick to photographing the piece against a neutral background.

---

2. **Position the item carefully.**

   Most items look best at an angle; it gives a three-dimensional item depth, as Figure 6-5 shows. Or you can take photos from several different angles to show all sides of your item. To shoppers, getting to look at lots of pictures is the next best thing to picking up an item and turning it over in their hands.

Figure 6-5:
To give bidders the whole picture, try making a composite photo that shows several different angles, instead of showing just one shot from front and center. It's the closest you'll get to 3-D in an eBay auction. Another strategy is including multiple shots, each showing a different view.

3. **Adjust lighting.**

   Natural light is best for taking photos. Try setting up your shot next to a window. (If the sunlight coming through the window is harsh, diffuse it with a thin white curtain.) To avoid deep shadows, use two light sources placed opposite each other. Try not to rely on your camera's flash, which can create obscuring shadows or unwanted glare in photos of shiny objects.

Tip: To get good detail for small items, like coins or jewelry, use a light diffuser. You can buy a professional-quality light diffuser, called a cloud dome, from *www.clouddome.com*, or you can make your own. Cut the bottom off a translucent plastic gallon-size milk jug. Place the jug over the item you want to photograph, and then shoot the picture through the opening in the top (the place where the milk pours out). If you need more light, set up a desk lamp on each side of the milk jug.

4. **Set up your camera.**

   Using a tripod keeps the camera steady when you snap the photo. It also holds the camera in place when you switch items, so you don't have to reposition it every single time you set up a new item. Once you get the focus set, you can take pictures of a whole bunch of items without having to stop and readjust the focus.

5. **Take the shot.**

   The big advantage a digital camera has over a traditional film camera is that, with digital, you can see the results of your shot right away. If the image doesn't look right, you can delete it; adjust the lighting, the item's position, or its distance from the camera, and try again.

Note: Make sure you use your camera's shutter release button correctly. On some digital cameras, you press the button only halfway to focus and set the exposure. Then, after a second or so, you press the button the rest of the way down to take the picture. If you press the button down all the way in one fell swoop, you might end up with a picture that's out of focus or over- or underexposed. Review the first few shots carefully and adjust your button-pressing technique, if necessary.

6. **Edit the image.**

   After you've taken the best shots you can, scan or upload the images to your computer. Then open an image-editing software program such as iPhoto or MS Paint and edit the images to get rid of muddiness, cut out unnecessary space, and save the image as a JPG file (see the next section and the box on page 203 for more on image editing.)

Image editing 101

Your computer probably came with some kind of software that lets you work with images. Mac OS X has iPhoto, and Windows has MS Paint. Both of these programs let you perform basic image-editing tasks, like cropping, resizing, and touching up your images and adjusting contrast and brightness. If you've never used your computer's image editor, play around with it a little to learn what it can do—*before* you find yourself in the middle of creating an auction, trying to get a picture to look right. (The box on page 203 tells you more about image editors.)

Note: For detailed help with iPhoto, check out *The Missing Manual* for the version of the program you have.

To tweak your pictures to make them look just right for your listing, consider these techniques:

- **Batch conversion.** This technique lets you change a whole group of files at once.

- **Brightness.** This setting determines how much light the image seems to give off. If you increase the brightness, the image will become whiter and lighter; decreasing the image makes it darker. You'll know if you increased the brightness too much, because the image will look washed out.

- **Contrast.** Adjust the difference between light and dark tones to make the image easier to see. Increasing the contrast makes the light parts of the image appear lighter and the dark parts darker.

- **Crop.** Cut out unnecessary background space around the item to focus viewers' attention on your item. Cropping an image also makes it smaller, so it will show up faster in your listing. Just be sure to leave some space around the item; cropping too tightly makes the image seem crowded into its space.

- **Format.** There are many different kinds of image formats, but you really only need to know about one. Save your images in the .JPG (pronounced "jay-peg") format, which is the best for displaying photos in eBay auctions. JPG files are *compressed*, which means that they're smaller than images saved in other formats—a plus when you want your photos to show up quickly on your auction page.

- **Resize.** Make your images smaller so that they'll fit on a listing page.

- **Rotate.** Flip your image vertically or horizontally, or rotate it from left to right.

More Photos, More Bidders

The more buyers see of an item, the more confident they are in bidding. Multiple photos show that your auction has nothing to hide. If you want to include several photos with your listings, you have a couple of options: you can insert them into your eBay listing directly using the Sell Your Item form (page 163), or you can *host* your photos (that means store them) on another Web site and tell eBay to grab the images from the other site and display them as if they were part of your auction page.

Tip: Extra photos help some auctions more than others. If you're selling a one-of-a-kind item that buyers would want to examine in minute detail, like a car or a collectible figurine, include lots of photos. But if you're selling something mass-produced, like a book, CD, movie, or new-in-box item, one picture should be sufficient.

Host your photos on eBay

On the Sell Your Item form, eBay lets you display one picture for free; after that, you pay 15 cents apiece for any pictures you want to add. eBay also limits the size of your photos, charging extra for the "super-size" feature that lets buyers click a thumbnail photo to see a larger version.

In 2004, eBay introduced Picture Manager, a photo-hosting service that's also part of eBay. For a monthly subscription fee (which varies according to how much storage space you need), you can store your photos, manage them from My eBay, and include up to 12 pictures in your listing without that pesky 15-cent-per-picture fee. You can subscribe to Picture Manager at *http://pages.ebay.com/picture_manager*.

Host your photos off eBay

You don't have to host your photos on eBay, though, and there are cheaper places to do it (see the box on page 205). Do a Google search for "free image hosting" and browse through the approximately one gazillion results to see what's available. Make sure that the image-hosting site supports auctions; not all of them do.

The Best Image Editors

When you're ready to move beyond the basics and get fancier with image editing, you might want to spring for one of the commercial image-editing programs available. Not every eBayer needs one, but if you take a lot of photos—you'll probably find them worth the price.

- **Photoshop (*www.adobe.com*).** This is the choice of pros and the best image editor around. It's available for both Macintosh and Windows, but it's expensive and probably more than you need for eBay.

- **Photoshop Elements (*www.adobe.com*).** This software comes in the package with many digital cameras, so check to see whether you already have it. It's a scaled-down version of Photoshop that works well for many eBay sellers. (If you need help with this program, check out *Photoshop Elements: The Missing Manual*.)

- **Paint Shop Pro (*www.corel.com*).** This one's for Windows only and isn't in the same league as Photoshop. Its less-expensive, cut-down version, which has everything you'd need for editing eBay photos, is called Paint Shop Studio.

- **The GIMP (*www.gimp.org*).** This editor's name stands for the GNU Image Manipulation Program. It works with Macintosh, Windows, and Unix—and it's free.

In addition, Mac fans can choose from a list of free and low-cost image viewers and editors at Tucows. Go to *www.tucows.com*, and then click the name of any program to get download instructions. Some popular choices include BME, Bosco's Foto Trimmer, HBImageProcessor, and imageX.

When you've found an image host that you like, follow its instructions for getting your images onto its server. Then, when you list an item on eBay, during step 3 (Sell Your Item: Pictures & Details) under Add Pictures, click the "Your own Web hosting" tab, as shown in Figure 6-6.

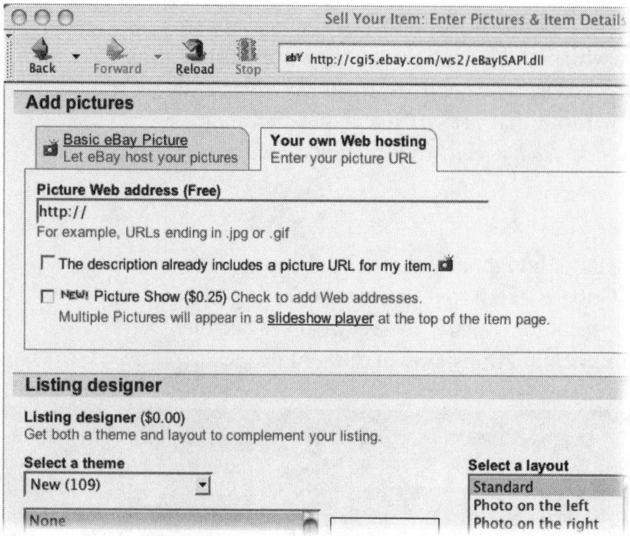

Figure 6-6:
In the "Picture Web address (Free)" box, type in the full Web address of the photo you want to display. It'll look something like this: http://myimagehost.com/myfolder/ myimage.jpg (myimagehost.com is the name of the Web site that hosts your pictures; myfolder is the name of your folder on the image-hosting site; and myimage.jpg is the name you've given to the photo you want to display.) If you don't fill in a Web address here, turn on the checkbox next to "The description already includes a picture URL for my item" to get the little green camera next to your auction in search results.

To have eBay display the photos you've uploaded to your image host, you give the auction site a snippet of HMTL that tells it to find your photos elsewhere and make them appear seamlessly on your auction page. The HTML code for displaying a photo is simple:

```
<img src="http://myimagehost.com/myfolder/myimage.jpg">
```

(include the angle brackets, and put the actual Web address of your image inside the quotes).

Using this code, you can insert as many images as you like into your auction page. In step 2 of the Sell Your Item form (Describe Your Item), include the HTML code in the item description you write (the photos, not the code, will appear on your auction page). If you want rows of photos, put a break tag <br> between two rows (include the angle brackets).

Tip: While you're learning, click Preview frequently to ensure the auction is shaping up the way you want it to.

Super-size me

For a fee, eBay lets you display a picture that viewers can click to jump to a larger version. But if you've opted to use another image host, you can get the same effect, as shown in Figure 6-7.

To make this magic happen, first create two versions of each image: a small one and a large one. Give each an appropriate name, such as *photo1.jpg* and *photo1_ small.jpg*. Then upload both images to your image-hosting service.

Figure 6-7:
A bit of HTML inserted into your auction description produces this tasty result. When a viewer clicks the small picture, a new window opens, showing a larger version of the same picture. Write whatever text you want for the caption; just replace the example's "Click thumbnail to get the big picture!" with whatever you want the caption to say.

UP TO SPEED

The Hosts with the Most

If you're looking beyond eBay for image hosting (so, for example, you can display multiple photos without paying extra for each one), where should you host them? A good place to start is with your own *Internet service provider* (ISP), the company you pay to access the Internet. Many ISPs offer free Web hosting to their clients; contact your ISP's customer service department to find out whether yours does.

If your own ISP doesn't work out, there are plenty of companies out there just dying to host your images. When you're researching possible image hosts, make sure that the images can appear in your actual auctions. Some sites make shoppers click a link to see pictures, and anything that asks a shopper to do a little extra work is a bad idea. (The only clicking they're likely to do is the Back button.)

Here's a list of popular sites that host auction images for a fee. (Prices vary, and some offer a free trial period):

- Andale (*www.andale.com*)
- Auction Assist (*www.globalarray.net/auction/index.asp*)
- Boomspeed (*www.boomspeed.com*)
- inkFrog (*www.inkfrog.com*)

- My Easy Pics (*www.myeasypics.com*)
- Nucite Image Hosting (*www.nucite.com*)
- PixHost (*www.pixhost.com*)

The following sites offer free image hosting. Some offer a free basic package and, if you need more space, a fee-based upgrade. (One thing to watch out for if you opt for a free service: many free services support themselves by forcing you—and anyone who views your photos—to endure flashing, blinking ads, which probably won't win you any points with prospective bidders. Choose your image host carefully and make sure any ads don't interfere with your auctions.)

- FreePictureHosting (*www.freepicturehosting.com*)
- ImageShare (*http://solisearch.net/ims/login.php*)
- MyImageHub (*www.myimagehub.com*)
- One Image Host (*www.oneimagehost.com*)
- Photobucket (*www.photobucket.com*)
- Village Photos (*www.villagephotos.com*)

Next, type this HTML into your auction description (in step 2 of the Sell Your Item form: Describe Your Item):

```
<a href="http://myimagehost.com/myfolder/photo1.jpg" target=_blank>
<img src="http://myimagehost.com/myfolder/photo1_small.jpg" border=0>
<br>Click thumbnail to get the big picture!</a>
```

You can add to your item description a bunch of small photos that a viewer can click to enlarge. To create a simple table of clickable thumbnails, each with a caption, use this HTML—just type it into your item-description form where you want the table to appear:

```
<table cellpadding=10 cellspacing=0 border=0>
<tr><td align=center>
<a href="http://myimagehost.com/myfolder/photo1.jpg" target=_blank>
<img src="http://myimagehost.com/myfolder/photo1_small.jpg"></a>
<br>Caption for photo 1.
</td>
<td align=center>
<a href="http://myimagehost.com/myfolder/photo2.jpg" target=_blank>
<img src="http://myimagehost.com/myfolder/photo2_small.jpg"></a>
<br>Caption for photo 2.
</td></tr>
<tr><td align=center>
<a href="http://myimagehost.com/myfolder/photo3.jpg" target=_blank>
<img src="http://myimagehost.com/myfolder/photo3_small.jpg"></a>
<br>Caption for photo 3.
</td>
<td align=center>
<a href="http://myimagehost.com/myfolder/photo4.jpg" target=_blank>
<img src="http://myimagehost.com/myfolder/photo4_small.jpg"></a>
<br>Caption for photo 4.
</td></tr>
</table>
```

Tip: To get a version of this code that you can cut and paste into your form (and then edit), head to MissingManuals.com, click the link for Missing CD-ROMs, and then click the link for this book. There you'll find a downloadable copy of this code.

Figure 6-8 shows the result.

Tip: For HTML basics, see Appendix B. For tutorials and other resources that help you snazz up your auctions with HTML, visit the HTML Factory at *http://auctionhelp.htmlfactory.us/home.htm*. Or post a question on the HTML/Photos board in eBay Discussion Boards (page 362) or the Answer Center (page 368).

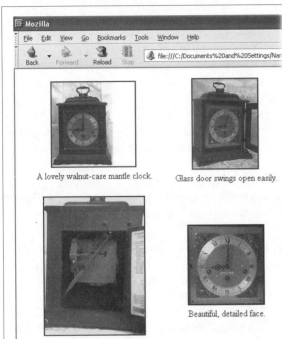

Figure 6-8:
Put your thumbnails into a table to organize them in an attractive presentation. Use captions to add extra information and personality to your photos.

Auction Tips and Tricks

There's a lot of conflicting advice out there about what works on eBay and what doesn't. While it would be nice if there were a sure-fire plan that could take you from newbie to PowerSeller (page 279) in a couple of months, the best way to learn what works for you is by starting with the tips in this section—and then adapting them as you discover which work best.

Best Category, Best Price

Try listing the same items in different categories to see where they perform best—getting the most bids and highest prices. Some categories are straightforward. If you're selling a Dell Inspiron laptop, you're going to list it under Computers &

Networking → Laptops → Dell. But what if you make and sell one-of-a-kind teddy bears? Do you list them under Collectibles → Animals → Bear, or Dolls & Bears → Bears → Other Bears, or both? Does depression glass sell better when you list it under Antiques, or under Pottery & Glass? How do you know where buyers are most likely to look? The following two strategies can help.

- **Compare completed auctions.** Look at completed auctions for similar items and note which auctions had the most bids. To do so, from the eBay home page, click Advanced Search and search for similar items, being sure to turn on the "Completed listings only" checkbox before you click Search. Sort the results by "Price: highest first," and look for items that generated lots of bids and sold for a good price. Then check the auction listings to see which categories the hot sellers were listed in—the info is right above the title and item number on the auction page. Knowing where buyers are likely to look for your items helps you list them in the categories most likely to generate bids and get a great price.

Tip: When you list similar items in different categories to see where they perform better, use a *hit counter*, which keeps track of how many people look at your auction, to see which categories get the most hits. You can add a hit counter in step 3 of the Sell Your Item form (Enter Pictures & Details).

- **Check out the hot list.** Another way to find hot categories is to research eBay's *hot list*. Each month, eBay puts together a report, called the Hot Categories Report, that tracks bidding activity by category. Take a look at the latest hot list by heading to the navigation bar and clicking Sell; look on the right-hand side of the page and then click The Hot List. You can find out where demand exceeds supply and which categories' items tend to attract lots of bids. Figure 6-9 shows a sample page of the hot list.

WORD TO THE WISE

Avoid Auction-Page Gimmicks

Some eBay sellers try to make their auction listings stand out by using gimmicks, like music that plays when a shopper opens the auction page; animated pictures; or text that blinks, shakes, or scrolls across the page.

Ever try to read a Web page while an ad flashes at you or sings that you're the 10,000th visitor? Unexpected noise and jittery graphics are highly annoying. These gimmicks can also increase the time it takes for your auction page to

appear on a buyer's computer screen. Most eBay shoppers aren't patient, spending just a few seconds on an item page before deciding whether to bid or move on. If your auction is slow to load or if it contains gimmicks that a shopper finds more irritating than charming, that shopper will quickly hit the Back button and keep on looking.

Instead of gimmicks, rely on good pictures and a clear, exciting description to psych up your bidders.

Note: eBay considers categories "hot" when the Level 4 category (see Figure 6-9) attracts at least 100 bids per week, when the bid growth from one month to the next is 1 percent or better, and when bid growth exceeds listing growth by at least 1.5 times.

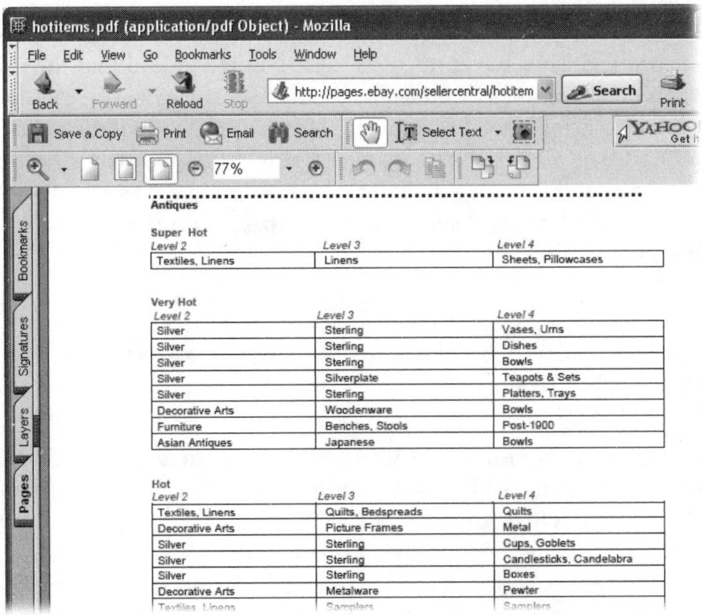

Figure 6-9:
There are three levels of "hot," and all of them indicate how much faster bids are growing than listings: "super hot" means a month-to-month percentage-point spread of 35 or better between listing growth and bid growth; for "very hot" that spread is between 15 and 35; and "hot" means a spread of up to 15. For example, in the "super hot" subcategory of sheets and pillowcases, bids might be up 60 percent over the previous month while listings have increased only 20 percent during that time (there's a 40-point spread between them). In the "very hot" silver urns and vases subcategory, bids might have grown 40 percent while listings only grew 23 percent (a 17-point spread). The "hot" quilts subcategory might have seen bids up by 88 percent while listings increased by 80 percent (an 8-point spread).

Meet or Exceed Buyers' Expectations

A buyer's satisfaction with your auction depends only partly on whether you packed the item well and shipped it right away. Most of how a buyer feels about the transaction comes from whether or not the whole experience—from the moment she first glimpsed that photo of a vintage umbrella stand to the moment she stepped back to admire it all loaded up with her family's umbrellas—lived up to her expectations. Meet the buyer's expectations, and you've got a satisfied customer. Exceed those expectations and you've got a very happy customer. But fail to meet them—watch out. Unhappy buyers can make your life miserable, from emailing you incessantly to leaving negative feedback to filing complaints.

"But that's not fair," you might be thinking. "How am I supposed to know what some buyer in Wichita or Des Moines or Anchorage expects?" And, technically, you'd be right: you can't read minds. What you *can* do is set up your auctions in a way that keeps expectations reasonable. That way, most buyers will be satisfied or happy.

Here are some tips to help buyers keep their expectations down-to-Earth:

- **Keep it real.** When you sell, you want to get buyers excited enough to click the Bid Now button. But don't exaggerate to make the item sound better than it really is. If the item is used, say so. Don't call it "like new" unless you really couldn't tell the difference between your item and one fresh out of the box.

- **Include measurements.** It can be hard to tell from a 3 × 4″ photograph how big an item is in real life. Your buyer might be disappointed to find that the pendant was much smaller or the vase much larger than she thought. You can show an object's size by placing it next to another object in the photo; if the pendant is next to a quarter or a ruler, it's easy to get a sense of the pendant's size. Or grab a tape measure and take measurements up, down, across, and around—it's nearly impossible to have too many—and state these measurements in your item description.

Tip: Clothing sizes are notoriously inconsistent: one designer's size 6 is another's size 10. Don't rely on the size tag in clothes sales. Measure the item (sleeves, bust, waist, length, inseam, and so on) and make those measurements part of the item description.

- **Little things mean a lot.** Nonsmokers care whether or not an item has resided in a smoke-free environment, and people with allergies might be glad to know your home is pet-free. Other things that might mean little to you but everything to some buyers include intact tags or extra buttons in clothing, original box or other original packaging, manuals, price tags, manufacturer's marks—anything you can think of that comes with the item itself.

- **Display more than one picture.** Including several photos taken from several different angles lets buyers scrutinize the item more closely. Then they won't be surprised that the jacket is a little longer in the back or the teddy bear doesn't have a tail. To create a picture display using *thumbnail* images that the viewer can click to make full-size, see page 204.

Tip: If you're selling clothing, press the item before you photograph it—a big mass of wrinkles isn't going to excite potential buyers. After the auction, do your best to make sure that the item arrives looking as much like the photo as possible. Use tissue paper between folds and don't cram the piece of clothing into a too-small envelope. A buyer who bid on a sharp-looking outfit won't be happy to pull a limp, wrinkled mess out of the package.

- **Contact the buyer at auction's end.** Many buyers, especially newbies, expect some kind of contact with the seller after the auction. It can be a bit nerve-wracking to win and pay for an auction and then hear nothing back. The best way to satisfy this expectation and keep the buyer calm is to contact the buyer as soon as possible after the auction ends. You can send a personal email, or you can use auction-management software (Chapter 9) to automate the process for you.

- **Explain your feedback policy up front (and follow through).** Some buyers feel that once they've paid, they've completed their side of the bargain and deserve positive feedback right away. If a buyer emails you and asks for positive feedback before the transaction is complete—that is, before the buyer has received the item and let you know all's well—simply explain that your policy is to leave feedback once you're sure that the buyer is happy and there are no problems with the item. This sounds like good customer service to the buyer—and it protects you from giving premature feedback to a buyer who pays promptly but morphs into a monster later in the transaction (insisting on a refund against your return policy, making spurious claims that the item arrived damaged or didn't arrive, and so on).

The More Auctions, the Merrier

Even when you're just testing the waters as a seller, avoid listing only one item at a time. If one auction you're running looks good enough to bid on, many buyers will click the "View seller's other items" link to see what else you're offering.

You can also take advantage of *cross-promotions,* using one auction to advertise other auctions, when you list more than one item. eBay sets things up so that the checkout page of one auction includes links to your other auctions. You don't have to do a thing to take advantage of this feature—just make sure you're selling several items at once. You can opt out of cross-promotions (through My eBay → Preferences), but why would you want to? A buyer who's decided to buy one item from you is a buyer ripe to buy another.

eBay's Checkout page, where buyers begin the payment process after an auction, displays cross-promotions with the total checkout amount. However, if you didn't include all your payment details in step 4 of the Sell Your Item form (Payment & Shipping) when you created the listing (page 164)—for example, if you didn't specify shipping costs—the Checkout page won't show cross-promoted auctions. So make full payment details a part of each listing.

Tip: To make cross-promotions more effective, offer a shipping discount on multiple purchases (page 212). It can be just the enticement a buyer needs to buy something else from you.

Donate Some of Your Profits

Charity is good for the soul. And, believe it or not, it can be good for your wallet, too: you can actually make more money by giving some away. eBay makes it easy by offering *Giving Works* auctions (page 310), auctions whose proceeds (or some percentage thereof; the minimum donation is $10) go to a nonprofit organization. Supporting a nonprofit feels good. And it can feel even better when you realize that donating part of the selling price to charity can give your auctions a big boost.

eBayers love shopping for a cause. The company boasts that Giving Works auctions average 40 percent higher selling prices and 50 percent better sell-through rates than regular auctions. High-profile celebrity auctions for charity skew those numbers a bit, but the fact remains that shoppers are willing to spend a little more when they know their money supports a good cause.

Buyers can restrict their searches to Giving Works auctions only, and these auctions prominently identify both the cause and the percentage of the sale that goes to support it. So not only can you close more sales for better prices, running some Giving Works auctions can actually increase your visibility and build your customer list. That's smart marketing.

Offer Incentives

You can make your auctions stand out by offering a deal that's just a little better than everyone else's. For example:

- **Shipping discount for multiple items.** eBay buyers complain about inflated shipping costs, but they love sellers who offer a shipping discount on the purchase of two or more items. Not only does this kind of shipping discount save you the hassle (and cost) of having to pack and ship items separately, it gives buyers a real incentive to buy several items from you at once.

  To offer a shipping discount to buyers who buy more than one item from you: from the eBay home page, select My eBay → eBay Preferences. Under Seller Preferences, find "Offer combined payment discounts," click Change, and then specify your discount policy. Be sure to feature your combined shipping discount in your item descriptions.

- **Free shipping with Buy It Now.** If you take shipping costs into account when you set your BIN price, you won't lose any money this way—and the allure of a BIN price with no post-sale shipping tacked on will attract buyers.

- **Price discount for multiple purchases.** Another kind of discount to consider is a price discount. Some sellers offer a five or 10 percent discount on the second (or third or fourth) item purchased within a certain time frame. (Just remember that eBay will charge you Final Value Fees, FVFs, on the final sale price, whether or not you knock a little off your invoice for multiple purchases.)

- **Throw in a bonus.** If you're selling a damask tablecloth, include a set of matching napkins as a bonus. If you're selling a camera, offer to tuck a carrying case in the box, gratis. Be sure to feature the words *WITH BONUS* (or something similar) in your auction's title to attract attention. A buyer who thinks she'll get something extra is a buyer who's likely to bid.

Offer Anything Points

Anything Points (page 113) are a kind of eBay-only currency that buyers can use to pay for things they buy on the site. As a seller, you can offer Anything Points to buyers who win your auctions. Offering Anything Points just might be the incentive that makes a shopper bid on your Bavarian beer stein, and not on someone else's.

Anything Points are worth a penny each—and guess who pays that penny. Yup, the seller who offers them. So if you offer five Anything Points per dollar and a buyer wins your beer stein for $45, you pay $2.25 for the Anything Points the buyer receives. Charges for Anything Points appear monthly on your eBay Account Summary in the My Account view of My eBay.

To offer Anything Points with your auctions, first list some items. Then go to the Anything Points Offer Manager (*http://anythingpoints.ebay.com/offer.html*) and log in. Tell the Offer Manager how many points you want to offer (between one and ten) for each dollar a buyer spends.

Sell in Lots

If you have an item that doesn't sell after a couple of auctions have run their course, try grouping it with other items in a lot. For example, a skirt that didn't sell on its own might be more attractive when paired with a top, and maybe a piece of costume jewelry. Or a light meter that hasn't attracted any bidders on its own might work better with a camera, tripod, and carrying case as part of a complete photographer's kit. The trick here is to think creatively to make the whole—the outfit, the photographer's kit, or whatever—appear more than the sum of its parts.

Note: If you group items together to sell in one auction, make sure there's a reason for them to *be* together. An auction for a Winnie the Pooh cookie jar plus a light meter, or a copper birdbath and a pair of mittens, is going to strike buyers the same way it strikes you: just plain odd.

How to Get More Feedback

It can be frustrating to spend a lot of time creating exciting auctions with good prices, packing items carefully, and shipping them fast, only to find your buyers don't bother to leave you positive feedback. No matter how hard you work to provide great customer service, it takes a while to build the feedback that's so critical to your reputation (and to your bottom line as a seller). Feedback is optional, and not all buyers will leave it.

To increase your chances of getting positive feedback, give the best customer service you can and keep the lines of communication wide open. Pack a note with the item saying, "Thank you for your purchase—I hope you'll enjoy it. Please let me know that it arrived safely." This encourages the buyer to touch base with you—and many buyers will do that by leaving you positive feedback. (And if there's a problem, good communication encourages the buyer to contact you to work things out, rather than heading straight to the Feedback Forum to leave a negative.) It's also acceptable to send a quick email asking whether the buyer has received the item and is happy with it. However, *don't* pester your buyers for feedback. Sending email after email begging for feedback can easily backfire. More than one eBayer who's done so has ended up with a negative that says, "Here's the feedback you kept bugging me for, you pest!"

Tip: Don't leave feedback for a buyer until the entire transaction is over and done with. A transaction isn't over when the buyer pays, it's over when you know the buyer has the item and is happy with it. If you leave positive feedback too early and a problem arises—like the buyer turns into a screaming harpy who insists that you refund her $4.99 even though she won't return the rhinestone-studded sunglasses she bought from you—you'll regret you left that feedback prematurely.

Big-Time Marketing Strategies

Many successful business owners will tell you never to let a single day go by without doing at least one thing to market your business. They're right. If you put consistent, continuous effort into marketing your business, it will grow.

Marketing is nothing more than identifying, reaching, and communicating with people willing and able to buy from you. Many of the things you do in the course of an auction involve marketing. For example, when a potential bidder asks you a question and you come right back with a polite, helpful answer, that's marketing. When you leave positive feedback for good buyers, that's marketing. If you send out a newsletter or email promotions, that's marketing. Below are more ways to market effectively.

Identify—and Reach—Your Market

Your market isn't where you sell—it's to whom you sell. After you've been selling for a while, take some time to analyze your market. Look at who's bought from you and check out their buying habits (Advanced Search → Items by Bidder). By looking at other auctions your buyers have participated in, you can get some ideas for things you might do to improve your auctions, like add more photos or offer a multiple-item discount. Or you might notice a product you hadn't considered that would complement yours; is there anything that your buyers tend to buy in other auctions that you don't offer? Do the same kind of research with low bidders who bid on your auctions but didn't buy. Did they buy a similar item elsewhere? What made them buy in that auction and not yours? Price? Shipping cost? Auction description or picture? BIN vs. regular auction?

Read the feedback buyers leave for you. Sometimes positive feedback contains veiled complaints, like "Never answered my emails but did send my saxophone" or "I wish I'd read the shipping charge before I bid"; if you see a pattern of this, address the problem. Or you might notice a pattern of praise, something that your buyers think you do particularly well, like super-fast shipping or extra care in packing. If you see many of your buyers are happy with some aspect of your products or service, highlight that in your auctions.

Market research teaches you two main things:

• Who your buyers are.

• What they want.

Do everything you can to get as clear a picture as possible of your target market in these two areas. Then you can go out and get 'em.

On eBay, some buyers will come to you. But to build your customer list, you've got to go out and find your target audience, wherever it may be. Here are some ideas for reaching your target market:

- **Run limited-time promotions.** When they can hear the clock ticking, buyers don't want to let a good deal slip through their fingers. Use your newsletter or eBay Store to advertise limited-time specials or auctions with an unusually low starting price.

Tip: If you're running a sale, like a one-cent special on a long list of DVDs, you can use eBay's Home Page Featured promotion to get eBayers shopping all your auctions. Home Page Featured is expensive—$39.95 per listing to get on eBay's home page and at the top of search results lists. Instead of choosing this feature for all your auctions, choose it for just one (to go along with eBay policy, it has to be a real auction and not merely a promotion). Then write your item description to let shoppers know you're holding a huge sale and get them excited about your other listings. Include prominent links to your other auctions and your eBay Store. You'll pay just one Home Page Featured charge, and your other auctions will get piggyback publicity.

- **Let eBay pay your advertising costs.** Well, some of them, anyway. eBay's Co-operative Advertising Program reimburses 25 percent of your advertising costs if you're a PowerSeller (page 279) *and* you're either a Trading Assistant (page 273) or the owner of an eBay Store (page 259). You get more business; eBay picks up part of the tab. To participate, you have to register with Co-op Advertising (go to *www.ebaycoopads.com* and then click the Registration Form link), and eBay must approve your ad. When your ad runs, you submit a form to eBay to get your money.

- **Become a favorite.** Any eBayer can add your ID to her list of favorite sellers when she looks at your auction page. Make it easy for potential buyers to do so by putting a link right in your item description that will take them to the Add to My Favorite Sellers and Stores page. Inserting this HTML into your item description when you create a listing (replace *yourID* with your actual eBay ID) does the trick:

```
<a href="http://cgi1.ebay.com/aw-cgi/eBayISAPI.
dll?AcceptSavedSeller&amp;sellerid=yourID86&amp;sspageName=DB:FavList"
target=_blank>Add me to your favorites list!</a>
```

- **Network.** If your business has a physical presence—a table at flea markets or a brick-and-mortar store—use that business to let people know about your eBay business. Create flyers featuring your eBay Store and drop one in the bag when a customer makes a purchase. Carry business cards with you and hand them out every chance you get. Ask friends who have Web pages or blogs to put up a button (page 221) that links to your auctions or your eBay Store.

- **Market your expertise.** Teach classes (page 277) or write an article for a local or trade publication on how to sell on eBay. Use the exposure to let people know about your business.

- **Barter.** If you're a Trading Assistant, offer a discount or your services to people involved with local or regional organizations—the president of the local landlords association or the lady who sends out the newsletter for the regional writers group—in exchange for advertising space in their trade publication or newsletter.

Get Some Buzz Going

Word of mouth is the best marketing tool out there. Get people talking about your business, and they do your marketing for you. You can start a buzz one customer at a time—or you can shoot for national-level exposure by getting your auction in the news.

Here are some ways to get people talking about your auctions:

- **Ask them to.** People love to brag about getting a terrific deal. Tuck a note into your packages asking the buyer to tell their friends about your auctions.

- **Get on eBay Pulse.** eBayers love to see which auctions are on eBay Pulse's Most Watched Items list (*http://pulse.ebay.com*). These are the 10 auctions that are on more eBayer's Watch lists than any others. Some of the auctions are pure marketing genius—like the guy who got hundreds of dollars in bids for an empty gum wrapper by describing how he started the auction on a bet and then adding updates as the bidding went wild. Study the top auctions to see what gets people excited. In your item description, ask bidders to add you to their Watch list. The more who do, the better your chances of making eBay Pulse.

- **Piggyback on a popular auction.** When you see an auction on eBay Pulse, click Ask Seller a Question to send the seller one of your auction numbers and ask him or her to mention it on the popular auction. If you're charming enough, you might get a link. (This works best if your linked auction is related to the popular auction somehow, or if the proceeds of your auction are going to a good cause through Giving Works; see page 310.)

- **Write a "serial" auction.** One recent craze on eBay has been "mystery" auctions, where a seller puts a box, trunk, suitcase, or other container up for sale without revealing the contents. (Per eBay policy, the auction is for the container only; the contents are a bonus.) When the bidding reaches certain levels—say, every hundred dollars—the seller reveals a clue about the contents of the box. Shoppers love to come back and read the clues, and bidders are motivated to push the price to the next level. You can adapt this strategy to other auctions, as well. For example, you could tell the sob story of how the cameo brooch up for bids was a wedding present from your great-grandfather to your great-grandmother, who wore it pinned over her heart every day until that tragic buggy accident—promising the next part of the story when the bidding reaches a new level.

- **Stop the presses!** You've probably seen eBay auctions in the news—from the Virgin Mary grilled cheese sandwich to a "haunted" cane to the guy who sold advertising space on his forehead. More serious auctions also make the news if an item is extraordinarily rare or important. If you've got an auction with a news angle, you can try to get it into the press. Start locally. Contact your town's newspaper and talk radio stations. If it's a slow news day or your story is attention-getting enough, a wire service might pick up your story. Several companies (such as *www.ereleases.com* or *www.eworldwire.com*) will write and distribute a national press release for you, but the service is expensive; it can cost hundreds of dollars. And there's no guarantee that the media will report your story after you shell out.

Tip: If you've got a weird and wacky auction that deserves attention, like the tennis shoes Elvis wore in junior high or a cookie that's a dead ringer for Bill Clinton, get your oddball auction some attention by notifying popular Web sites that publicize way-out auctions, such as Who Would Buy That? (*www. whowouldbuythat.com*) and Bizarre Bids (*www.bizarrebids.com*).

Promote, Promote, Promote

With millions of items up for grabs on eBay at any given moment, you need a good strategy to drive buyers to your auctions. In other words, don't sit around waiting for buyers to come to you—reach out and find them by promoting your auctions.

Newsletters

A newsletter is an inexpensive way to keep your auctions in the minds of past customers. When you send your invoice, or after a buyer has left you positive feedback, offer the opportunity to subscribe to your newsletter to stay informed of your auctions, great deals, and special offers. You can send newsletters weekly, monthly, or whenever you get around to it.

Note: Any newsletter you send has to be an *opt-in* newsletter: buyers must sign up for it themselves and be able to unsubscribe easily at any time. Otherwise, someone might report your newsletter as spam and get you in trouble with eBay.

A newsletter should offer value to its readers. Instead of simply promoting your auctions, include tips or news that relate to your specialty. For example, if you sell children's clothes, include parenting tips or cute stories about the neighbor's kids. Occasional contests, surveys, and subscribers-only promotions also have appeal. In other words, give your subscribers a reason to read your newsletter that goes beyond browsing your current auctions.

eBay Store owners (page 259) can organize mailing lists and send out newsletters through eBay (see the box on page 219). You can also start your own Group on eBay (page 366) and use it to email eBayers who join. But consider going off eBay to create your newsletter; then you can use the newsletter to promote your Web site, not just your eBay sales. One of the best and easiest ways to create and distribute a newsletter is through Yahoo! groups (it's free). Subscribers must go to Yahoo! to sign up, so it's definitely an opt-in list, which means eBay won't accuse you of sending out spam. Whenever you've got a newsletter ready to send out, you can email it to every member of your Yahoo! group. Here's how.

Go to *www.yahoo.com*, and then click Groups → "Start a group now." Sign in (or click Sign Up if you don't already have a Yahoo! ID) to begin this process:

1. **Choose a category, as shown in Figure 6-10.**

   Pick a topic that relates to your sales niche. You can get really specific with subcategories (such as Family & Home → Parenting → Moms → Working Moms), or you can click "Place my group in…" if you don't want to go any deeper into the subcategory structure.

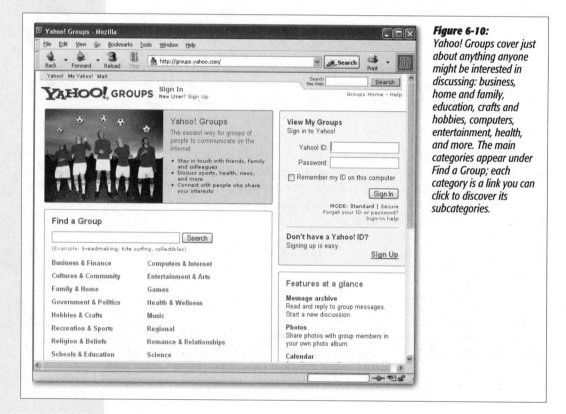

Figure 6-10:
Yahoo! Groups cover just about anything anyone might be interested in discussing: business, home and family, education, crafts and hobbies, computers, entertainment, health, and more. The main categories appear under Find a Group; each category is a link you can click to discover its subcategories.

2. **Describe your group.**

In this step, you select a name for your newsletter, like Kathie's Collectibles Corner or Mad about Barbie, and write a description that lets subscribers know what they're signing up for. Will your newsletter feature secret sales, subscribers-only deals, or articles about, say, how to grow more beautiful roses or build a better model airplane?

3. **Select your Yahoo! profile.**

If you have more than one Yahoo! ID, you can select which one you want to use to administer your newsletter. (If you have just one Yahoo! ID, type it in here.) You also specify the email address you want to use for correspondence related to the newsletter and type in a security code. If you click Continue, Yahoo! creates your group.

4. **On the page that appears after you've created your Yahoo! group, turn the group into a newsletter by clicking the Customize Group button.**

Here you choose options about who can join and whether or not to restrict posting. To make your group a newsletter, answer the question "Who can post messages to your group?" with "Only group owner."

Yahoo! assigns your group its very own Web page. To find it, go to the Yahoo! home page and click Groups. Sign in to Yahoo! (if you're not signed in already), and Yahoo! shows you all the groups you're a member of under My Groups. Click the group's name to go to its page. You can use the Web page to archive past issues of your newsletter, display photos, conduct polls, and more. The Web page's left-hand menu has a Management link: click it to invite or approve new members, edit content and appearance, or delete your group.

GEM IN THE ROUGH

Good News(letters) for eBay Store Owners

If you own an eBay Store (page 259), you can use eBay's Email Marketing program to reach buyers. Here's how it works. Every eBay Store owner can create up to five email lists. When a buyer adds you to his list of favorite sellers, he can opt to subscribe to your newsletter. You can't send more than one mailing a week, but you can make your newsletter whatever you want it to be. Try including special offers, new listings, and other news to keep your readership reading.

To start an email list, from the navigation bar select My eBay → Manage Your Store. Find the Promotions sections, then click Email Marketing, and then follow the instructions. Depending on the level of your store, you get a certain number of free emails you can send each month:

- **Basic store.** 100 free emails per month.

- **Featured store.** 1,000 free emails per month.

- **Anchor store.** 4,000 free emails per month.

Whatever the level of your store subscription, emails beyond the monthly limit cost a penny apiece.

The Email Marketing section of your Store Manager also tracks each newsletter's success on the Sent Email page. Use these reports to find out how many recipients opened your newsletter, the click-through rate, and how many bids and BINs resulted from each newsletter.

---

eBay Groups

Thousands of eBayers join hundreds of eBay Groups to discuss their special interests. If you specialize in a particular kind of merchandise, starting your own eBay Group (page 366), or even posting actively in already existing group, establishes you as an expert and attracts collectors or people with an interest in your specialty. You can build a customer base and make friends at the same time.

Tip: If you start an eBay Group or a newsletter, let potential subscribers know by linking to the group/newsletter sign-up page from your About Me page and your eBay Store.

Want It Now

Check Want It Now ads (page 86) to see if anybody's specifically looking for the stuff you're selling. From the Want It Now main page (*http://pages.ebay.com/wantitnow*), use the Search Want It Now box to search ads. If you see an ad from someone looking for a cookie jar shaped like a teddy bear—and you just happen to have one for sale—you can send the poster your auction number through eBay by clicking the Respond button at the bottom of the Want It Now ad. On the next page, click Respond To Post, as shown in Figure 6-11. Keeping up with Want It Now ads is a handy way to target bidders who are out there searching for auctions just like yours.

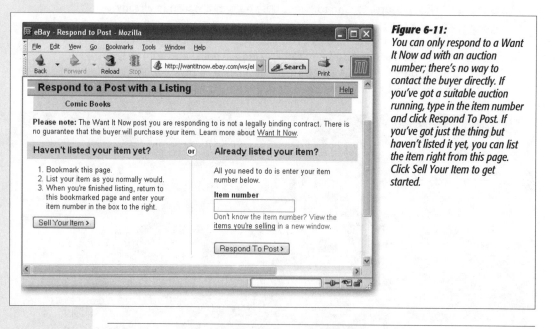

Figure 6-11:
You can only respond to a Want It Now ad with an auction number; there's no way to contact the buyer directly. If you've got a suitable auction running, type in the item number and click Respond To Post. If you've got just the thing but haven't listed it yet, you can list the item right from this page. Click Sell Your Item to get started.

Note: When you respond to a Want It Now ad, your auction should be pretty close to what the buyer is looking for; if the ad is for a mint 1984 Stanford yearbook, don't respond with a 1967 yearbook from Princeton. If your item is close, however, but not quite word-for-word the same as the Want It Now ad (a 1984 Stanford yearbook with pencil moustaches drawn on the entire graduating class), send the auction number, anyway. Let the buyer decide whether what you're selling is what they're hunting for.

Your own Web site

Create an off-eBay Web site to bring potential buyers to your eBay auctions. Your offsite Web page doesn't have to be an official store with catalogs and shopping cards; it can be anything you want it to be. If you're an expert on comic books, for example, you can have fun writing up a Web site that shares your expertise—and links to your current comic-book auctions and (if you have one) your eBay Store (page 259).

Tip: If you participate in email lists and discussion groups (page 366) related to your area of expertise–a great way to build your reputation and let other eBayers know about your auctions–remember to add the URL of your Web site to your email signature. If you do, folks who like what you have to say can click through to your Web page easily.

When you have your own Web site, the simplest way to link to eBay is to add a button to your page. To do so:

1. **From the eBay home page, click Services → "Add link buttons."**

   Figure 6-12 shows you the page that appears.

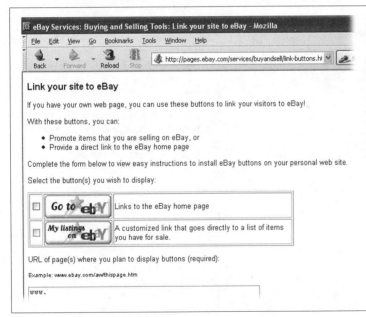

Figure 6-12:
You can add a button to your Web site that links to the eBay home page or to your current auctions. Select the button you want (you can choose one or both) and type your Web page's address into the text box. Then you have to scroll way down the page, past the long License Agreement and its terms (you did read all that, right?) and click I Agree to continue.

2. **Turn on the checkbox beside one (or both) of the button options.**

   You can create a button that links to the eBay home page (not so useful), to your auctions on eBay (more useful), or both.

3. **In the text box, type the complete URL of the Web page to which you want to add the buttons. Then scroll down to the bottom of the page and click I Agree.**

A page containing a customized HTML snippet appears.

4. **Cut and paste the HTML snippet into the HTML code of the Web page where you want the button to appear.**

You need to follow your usual routine for uploading and testing your newly edited Web page.

Creating a link from your Web page to your eBay Store (page 259) is easy. Each Store has its own Web address: something like *www.ebaystores.com/storename*. Create a hyperlink (page 419) from your Web page to your store to help buyers find your auctions.

Tip: When you join the free eBay Affiliates program (page 374), you make money every time someone follows a link from your Web page to eBay and registers or bids. In addition, you get access to the Affiliates Toolbox. Go to Services → eBay Affiliate Program → Toolbox to see what goodies the Toolbox holds. To add your current eBay auctions to your own Web site, you want the Editor Kit, shown in Figure 6-13. On the toolbox page, click the Editor Kit link. The cool thing about this tool is that it lets readers see your actual auctions right from your Web page; they don't have to click a button to see what's on your auction block.

Figure 6-13:
The Editor Kit lets you insert an eBay Search box on your own Web page and show live auctions. Most of the fields are self-explanatory. When you've finished, the Editor Kit generates a sniplet, a piece of JavaScript code that you copy to your Web page and upload to the site that hosts your page.

Just Say No

So far, this chapter has described a bunch of ways to tweak your auctions to increase your visibility and your profits. This section looks at some bright ideas that, when you think it through, turn out *not* to be so bright. Some of these practices are illegal (shill bidding); others are against eBay policy (keyword spamming and fee avoidance). Avoid all these practices to keep your eBay record (and your conscience) clean.

Shill Bidding

Shill bidding (page 135) is bidding on your own auction, or having an accomplice bid for you, to drive up an item's price. For example, a seller might have two eBay IDs and use one of them to bid, or convince a friend or family member to bid on an item with no intention of buying it. Shill bidding can be tempting when lots of people are watching an item but no one's bidding—just one false bid to get things rolling—or when bidding is slow and it looks like an item will sell for a lot less than the seller thinks it's worth.

No matter how tempting, shill bidding is illegal. In 2001, for example, the federal government charged three men with running an art fraud ring on eBay; the accused listed fake paintings and then bid on each others' auctions to drive up the price, defrauding buyers of hundreds of thousands of dollars during a year and a half of shill bidding. Even if the feds never come after you, if eBay catches you shill bidding, you'll be suspended from the site.

Keyword Spamming

Trying to attract buyers to your auction by putting popular but inappropriate keywords in the title is called *keyword spamming*, and it's against eBay policy. Sellers often use keyboard spamming to make their items appear in a wider range of search results, even though what they're offering isn't exactly what the buyer is looking for. A title like *Brand new wallet COACH VUITTON BURBERRY PRADA* is an example. One wallet can't be from all those designers, but the seller wants his title to show up in the search results lists of people searching for *wallet*—and also of anyone searching for any of those designers by name.

eBay contends that keyword spamming is unfair to buyers—that a seller is wasting a buyer's time with a title that promises something that the seller doesn't, in fact, have to offer. There are several kinds of keyword spamming, and eBay frowns on all of them:

- **Comparison.** Your title must describe what you're selling, not compare it to something you're not selling. For example, a title like *Commercial Mixer Like KitchenAid for LESS* is a problem. The auction is not for a KitchenAid mixer, but the seller is trying to attract bidders looking for a KitchenAid appliance. Comparisons don't have to use the word *like*, either. Titles like *Even cuter than a Beanie Baby!*, *Cartier quality at a Kmart price*, or *Swimsuit NOT Calvin Klein Anne Cole* also violate the policy.

Note: There's an exception to the no-comparison rule. You can compare your item to one similar item, but only in the item description (not the title) and only as long as it's crystal clear that you're not selling the item you're using for a comparison. So writing "This mixer has 12 speeds compared to the Kitchen-Aid's 10 and comes with more attachments" is OK as long as the comparison appears in the item description—and as long as it's true.

- **Lists of related words.** This restriction applies to both titles and descriptions. In a title, you're limited to 55 characters, so you can't make really long lists there. But it's against eBay policy to fill up your item description with long lists of words that are there for no other reason than to attract the attention of shoppers who are searching by both title and description. For example, if you're selling wedding invitations, don't include a list of words like this in the description: *wedding invitations bride bridal groom gown veil tiara reception marriage cake honeymoon church organ aisle engagement ring bouquet flowers bridesmaid favors,* and so on. Your auction might turn up in more searches, but it'll just annoy buyers who are looking for something entirely different.

- **Misleading titles.** This policy covers some of the previous taboos but also anything else that could potentially confuse buyers or lead them astray. For example, you might be offering free shipping to buyers who use the Buy It Now option. If that's the case, make sure your title states that the free shipping applies only to a BIN sale. Don't say *Super white Xenon headlights! Free shipping!* Say *Super white Xenon headlights! Free shipping w/BIN!*

If you look, you can probably find running auctions that violate each of these rules. Can *you* get away with it? Maybe for an auction or two, but sooner or later, you'll get caught. If you misuse the brand name of a VeRO member (page 135), for example, it's only a matter of time before that member reports you to eBay. And if you violate the keyword-spamming policy and eBay finds out about it, eBay will end your auction, and you'll lose your listing fees. If you keep doing it, eBay will suspend your account.

Note: The same keyword-spamming policy also applies to Want It Now posts (page 86).

Stealing Photos

It takes patience, practice, and the right equipment (page 198) to take great digital photos. So when you see someone else's auction for the same item, and it has that perfect photo you wish you could take, you might be tempted to "borrow" the other seller's photo. No matter how good that photo looks, though, don't do it. Copyright laws apply to the Internet just as they apply to other media. If your competitor discovers that you've stolen her photo (or her words), she'll report you to eBay and have your listing removed. And because smart sellers constantly keep an eye on the competition, chances are high that you'll get caught. Use others' listings for inspiration and ideas, but take your own pictures and write your own description.

Violating VeRO

At any given moment, there are thousands of designer knockoffs and pirated items for sale on eBay. eBay can't monitor every auction, but it does work closely with rights holders to find and shut down auctions that violate trademarks, copyright, and other intellectual property rights. And rights holders who participate in eBay's VeRO program (page 135) are very active in protecting their rights.

If you're selling something you have no right to sell, like a movie you recorded from your TV, the VeRO member who holds the movie's copyright can ask eBay to shut down your auction. If your auction is shut down for a VeRO violation, you can't relist the item.

Warning: Here's another reason not to mess with VeRO members' goods: eBay will, on request from a VeRO member, reveal the name, address, and phone number of any seller that the VeRO member suspects is infringing on his intellectual property rights. All the VeRO member has to do is make a formal request. And many will use that information to serve you with legal papers.

Whatever you do, don't relist a potentially infringing item until you have eBay's OK to do so. If you do, you risk suspension from eBay.

Note: VeRO participants are humans, and all humans occasionally make mistakes. VeRO members must provide contact information, so you can contact the company to resolve the dispute. If you don't hear back, contact eBay (go to Help → Contact Us → "Ask about selling or billing" → "My listing was removed by eBay" → "Request from a copyright/trademark owner to remove your listing"), explain the situation, and ask for help getting in touch with the VeRO member.

Avoiding Fees

No doubt about it—eBay's fees take a hefty bite out of your profits. And if you accept PayPal, you pay even more. Some sellers would love to market their wares to eBay's zillions of buyers without bothering with pesky little annoyances like Final Value Fees. eBay has a name for this practice: *fee avoidance*. It means that the seller is trying to circumvent fees he or she legitimately owes. From eBay's point of view, your selling fees are *your* responsibility, not the buyer's, and trying to avoid them gets you into trouble.

Kinds of fee avoidance include the following:

- Ending an auction early in order to sell a bidder the item directly and cut eBay out of the deal.

- Ending a reserve-price auction early because it doesn't look like bids will reach the reserve.

- Padding shipping and handling charges (see the next section for more about this practice).

- Putting contact information into an auction title so that buyers can contact the seller off eBay.

- Requiring the buyer who wins the auction to buy something else. For example, a certificate for cheap airfare that requires the buyer to pay for three nights in a particular hotel.

- Running auctions that aren't Dutch auctions but should be. For example, when the seller asks the winning bidder to indicate how many items she wants, even though the auction was for just one.

- Running auctions for catalogs, from which the buyer can buy items off eBay.

Bidders often report fee avoidance, especially if they're angry at having to pay more than they thought they would (or angry at seeing an auction end early because the bidding wasn't high enough to justify the fees). Sellers who have a fee-avoidance complaint against them can expect a warning, temporary suspension, or permanent suspension.

Padding S&H Charges

It's worth looking at this kind of fee avoidance on its own, because it's a widespread practice—and one with a very broad gray area. All sellers—and most buyers—would agree that it's reasonable to compensate the seller for packing materials and time spent packing and mailing an item. That's the *handling* part of the shipping and handling charge. But the controversy begins when you ask, "What's reasonable?"

Some sellers figure that a dollar and a half or two dollars on top of postage is a decent handling charge. Other sellers try to anticipate all possible costs associated with the auction (eBay fees, PayPal fees, postage, shipping materials, time spent packing and hauling stuff to the Post Office) and bundle these costs into the S&H charge. Still others figure out the actual shipping charge, double it, and add a couple of dollars for good measure. Then there are the blatant fee avoiders, who'll start an auction for, say, a digital camera at a penny but charge $150 for shipping and handling. If the camera sells for $20, the seller pays a Final Value Fee of only $1.05; if it had sold for what the buyer is actually paying ($170), the seller would owe eBay an FVF of $3.92—nearly four times as much. A few bucks might not sound like a lot, but when you multiply those few bucks by the millions of auctions eBay hosts, you can see why avoiding fees through inflated shipping costs is a big deal.

Inflated shipping charges are a top complaint of buyers. Even stating the S&H cost on the auction page doesn't necessarily protect you; many buyers bid before they read all the auction terms, and they'll yell if they feel ripped off. If your handling charge adds too much to the cost of postage—such as charging $15 for shipping when the postage shows you paid $3.85 for Priority Mail—expect complaints. Some buyers will report you for fee avoidance; others will leave negative feedback. Neither result is worth the few bucks you get.

Protecting Your Auctions

It's not enough to post an auction and then check back in a week to see who won. In addition to managing your auctions (answering questions, adding photos, or adjusting the price if bidding starts off slow), you need to keep an eye out for trouble. This section describes potential problems that can crop up during an auction, and what you can do about them.

Blocking Unwelcome Bidders

Some bidders seem more interested in messing with auctions than in winning them. They win auctions but don't pay, or they bid from a place you can't ship to. Fortunately, you can head some of these bidders off at the pass by preventing them from bidding on any of your auctions—in other words, blocking them.

Blocking groups of bidders

One way to avoid problem bidders is to use your eBay Preferences to block types, or groups, of bidders you don't want participating in your auctions (Figure 6-14). You can block the following groups of bidders from participating in your auctions:

• Bidders registered in countries you don't ship to.

• Bidders with a negative feedback score.

• Bidders who've received two Unpaid Item strikes in the past month.

• Bidders who are currently winning your other auctions or have won some of your other auctions in the last 10 days (you can restrict this block to low-feedback bidders).

• Bidders without a PayPal account.

Looking at the kind of bidders you can block, you might wonder why anyone would want to prevent someone from making multiple bids on their auctions. Repeat buyers are good, right? Usually, yes. But there are a couple of situations when it makes sense to block a bidder who's blitzing your auctions. Newbies who don't understand how auctions work often "shop" by placing bids on a bunch of identical items, then try to get out of paying when they win more than one. Preventing these buyers from making multiple bids can protect your auctions while they learn the ropes. Also, sellers of expensive items sometimes prefer getting to know their buyers one at a time, so they to restrict the number of items one buyer can purchase before they buy again.

To block groups of bidders:

1. **From the eBay home page, select My eBay page.**

   Your My eBay page (page 32) appears.

2. **On the left-hand side of the page, click the eBay Preferences link you find.**

   The eBay Preferences page appears.

3. **Under Selling Preferences, find Buyer Requirements and click Change.**

   The Buyer Requirements page appears.

4. **Select the groups of bidders you want to exclude from your auctions.**

   A check in the box means that bidders meeting that description (such as bidders in countries you don't ship to) won't be able to bid on any of your auctions. Click Submit when you're done.

Note: Lots of sellers would like to block bidders with a feedback score of zero, but eBay won't let you do this automatically. After all, the reasoning goes, everyone on eBay had zero feedback when they started out. If zero-feedback bidders make you nervous, your only option is to watch who's bidding and then cancel any bids from eBayers with no feedback (page 40), then add each of those individuals to your blocked-bidder list (see the next section). You can state in your terms of sale (TOS) that you don't sell to zero-feedback bidders, but that won't prevent them from placing a bid. More than that, a TOS saying zero-feedback bidders are unwelcome can chase away the bidders you do want; some experienced eBayers will read your TOS, think you're being elitist and unfair, and find another auction to bid on.

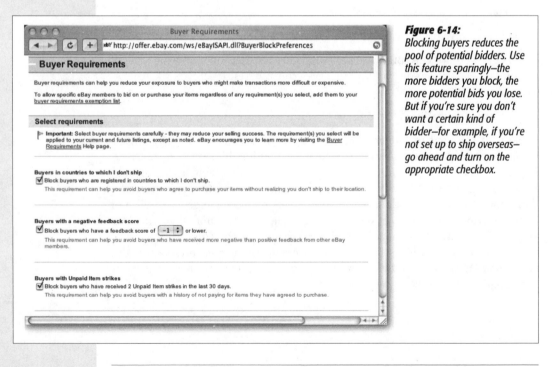

Figure 6-14:
Blocking buyers reduces the pool of potential bidders. Use this feature sparingly—the more bidders you block, the more potential bids you lose. But if you're sure you don't want a certain kind of bidder—for example, if you're not set up to ship overseas—go ahead and turn on the appropriate checkbox.

Blocking individual bidders

eBay also lets you create a *blocked-bidder list* (BBL) that prevents specific eBayers from participating in your auctions. Use this option when someone has given you trouble in the past—for example, if they refused to pay for an item they won.

1. **On the navigation bar, click My eBay.**

   Your My eBay page (page 32) appears.

2. **Click eBay Preferences → Buyer Requirements: Edit → "buyer requirements exemption list" → "Add an eBay user to my Blocked Bidder/Buyer List."**

   The "Blocking a bidder/buyer" page appears (Figure 6-15).

3. **In the box, type the ID of the eBayer you want to block.**

   If you're putting more than one buyer on your BBL, separate IDs with a comma or just hit the Enter key to give each ID its own line. When you're finished, click the Submit button.

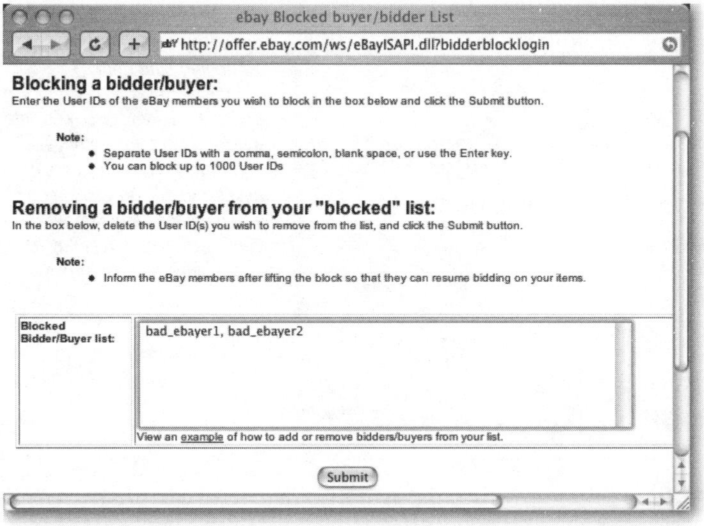

Figure 6-15:
If you want to block someone from bidding but they've already placed a bid, you have to cancel the bid first (see next section), then add their eBay ID to your Blocked Bidder list.

If you're *really* paranoid, you can sell only to bidders you already know. Preapproved bidder lists work best if you've been selling for a while and have gotten to know a group of bidders you trust who keep coming back to your auctions. If you send a newsletter to your customers, for example, you can announce a special sale just for them, and run that auction with only your subscribers as the preapproved bidders.

Letting only a select few bidders participate in your auction may feel safer, but it limits your options. Would-be bidders who aren't on the list can email you for approval, but many won't bother. They'll just find another auction where they feel welcome. Besides, experienced eBayers know that scammers love preapproved auctions (page 30), so they avoid auctions where the bidding isn't open to all.

Here's how to set up an auction for preapproved bidders only:

1. From the eBay home page, select Help → Selling → Managing Your Item → Managing Buyers → Pre-approved Bidders List → "create a list of pre-approved buyers."

2. The page shown in Figure 6-16 appears.

3. Click "Add a new item."

4. On the Pre-Approve Bidders/Buyers page that appears, type in the item number (the auction you want to edit) and the eBay ID (or list of IDs) you want to block.

5. Click Submit Item.

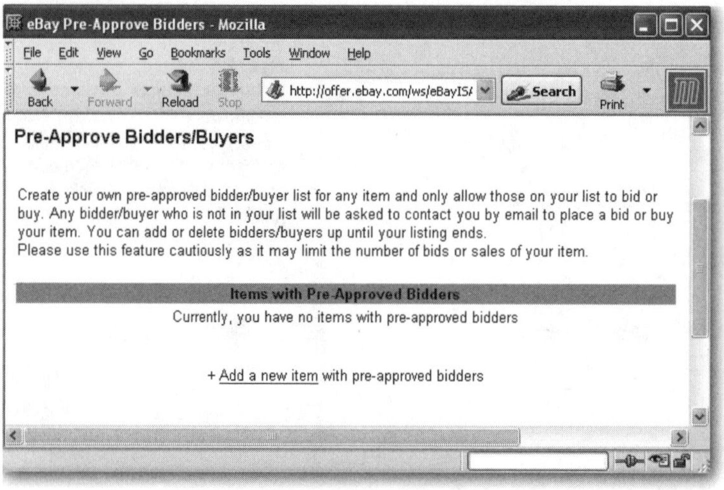

Figure 6-16:
To create a list of preapproved bidders for a particular auction, go to Help → Selling → Managing Your Item → Managing Buyers → Pre-approved Bidders List → "create a list of pre-approved buyers." From there, you can create a new list or edit an existing one. You need the item number of your auction and the eBay IDs of the bidders you approve.

Canceling Bids

Occasionally, you might notice a bidder in your auction who makes you nervous. Maybe you're selling something expensive, and a zero-feedback bidder who registered yesterday has bid what seems like a ridiculously high price. Or maybe the high bidder has OK feedback overall but recently has been collecting negatives for nonpayment and has retracted a dozen bids in the past six months. Or you notice the bidder has a history of leaving nasty feedback over petty issues. Or you check to see what else the high bidder is currently bidding on (page 79) and see that not only is she bidding on your Xbox, but on eight others—and is winning three. Any of these suspicious bidders is unlikely to follow through if they win your auction, leaving you high and dry. The solution? Cancel the bid.

Note: Even though eBay offers only a couple of examples of when it's a good idea to cancel a bid, you can cancel anyone's bid for any reason you like. But once you've canceled a bid, you can't change your mind; you can't reinstate a canceled bid.

To cancel a bid, go to Help → Selling → Managing Your Item → Managing Buyers → Cancel Bids → "cancel bids" and fill out the form shown in Figure 6-17. When you finish, click Cancel Bids.

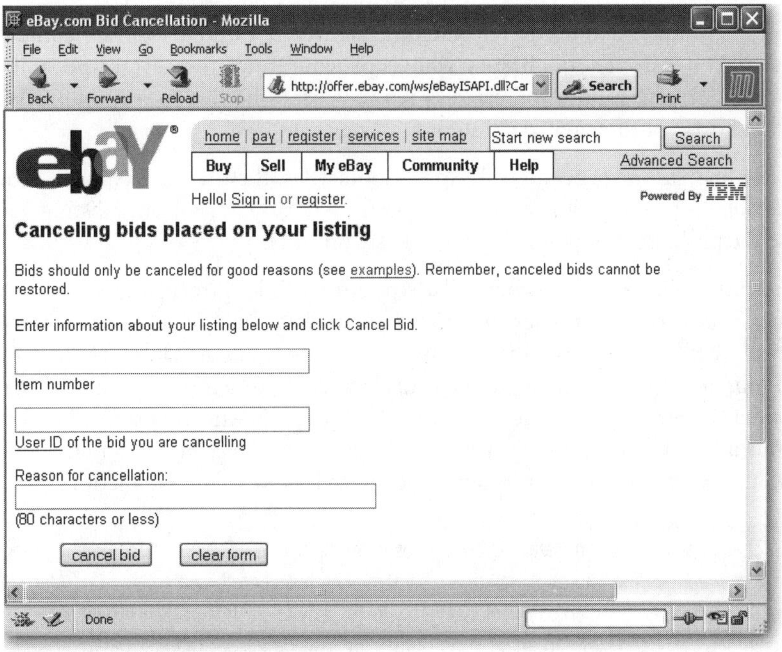

Figure 6-17:
To cancel a bid, you need the item number, the bidder's eBay ID, and a reason for the cancellation. Your reason appears in your listing's Bid History. Reasons to cancel a bid might include "Insufficient feedback," "Uncomfortable with bidder's feedback practices," "Could not contact bidder," "Too much recent negative feedback," and so on.

Tip: If you plan to cancel the bids of eBayers with zero feedback (or a score of less than 10 or whatever cutoff you choose), say so in your listing's terms of sale (TOS). That way, low-feedback bidders won't be surprised when you suddenly dump them from your auction.

Use bid cancellations wisely. Canceling a bid is the opposite of building a long-term relationship with good customers—it's more like throwing someone out of your store. You might want to email the bidder before you cancel a bid to give him a chance to explain whatever's making you nervous. And after you've canceled a bid, it's good form to email the bidder and let her know why. In the end, if you decide that this bidder is someone you just don't want to deal with—ever—add their ID to your Blocked Bidder list (page 229).

Note: If you're ending a listing early (page 176), eBay gives you the option to cancel all bids as part of the process. If you end a listing early *without* canceling the bids, you've agreed to sell to the high bidder at his or her current bid.

Defending Your Auction

It takes a lot of time and effort to get your auction looking just right. So when you come across someone else's auction that looks *just* like yours—another seller has stolen your photo, your description, or both—you have a right to get mad.

You also have a right to report the auction thief to eBay and get the stolen listing removed. You can report eBayers who copy your title, the text of your item description, or your photo; you can also report sellers who link to your offsite Web page that hosts your images (page 203).

From the eBay home page, go to Help → Contact Us, then select "Report a listing policy violation or prohibited (banned) item" → "Copying of your listing" and choose the problem that you're having. Click Continue.

When a lazy seller steals another seller's photo by linking to pictures hosted on another site, the offended seller sometimes gets revenge by uploading a new image: a similar item smashed to smithereens, another item altogether (such as a diamond solitaire replaced with a gumball-machine ring), or a heartfelt confession ("I am a thief. I tried to steal a picture from good_seller42, who's replaced the image with this admission of my guilt"). If you decide to avenge yourself on an auction thief in this way, don't forget to change the image link in your own auction!

Tip: To discourage thieves from stealing your photos in the first place, use your image-editing program to put a *watermark* on your photos. A watermark is text superimposed on the photo; you can still see the item, but the photo is clearly marked as belonging to you. It's easy to create a watermark; any image editing program lets you add text to an image. State something like ©*my_ebay_ID* or *Property of honest_ ebayer,* and image thieves will look for another auction to rob.

Scams to Watch Out For

Just as scammers prey on new buyers (page 132), they also target new sellers. If you're selling expensive merchandise, you can pretty much count on being approached by scammers. Knowing their angles will help you steer clear of trouble. And every seller, large or small, sooner or later runs into someone who tries to get something—*your* something—for nothing. This section describes common ploys aimed at sellers and how to deal with them.

The Check's in the Mail

Deadbeat bidders write great fiction. They'll go to great lengths to sell you a heart-wrenching story of the troubles they've been suffering—and why this means they can't pay for the item they won. On the other hand, tragedies *do* strike, and it would feel pretty awful to accuse a nonpaying bidder of lying and then find out that all sixteen of her children really do need emergency operations.

This situation is probably the least serious but most common of all the scams. It's a scam simply because the bidder is lying to get out of an obligation. Knowing what to do when a nonpaying bidder with a good story asks to back out of an auction can be a tough call. You've got your eBay fees to consider, but you also want to develop a reputation for good customer service—and an unhappy bidder who's won an auction can leave negative feedback even if he or she is a complete deadbeat.

The best approach is to deal with this situation on a case-by-case basis. You might insist on payment and use eBay's UPI dispute process (page 184) to back you up— the bidder forks over payment or gets an Unpaid Item strike. In other cases, you might choose to strike a deal with the bidder to let it go if she reimburses you for eBay fees. Still other times, you might open a UPI dispute and then close it with "We've agreed not to complete the transaction." (If the buyer agrees, this option refunds your FVFs, makes the item eligible for a relisting credit, and doesn't leave a UPI strike against the buyer.)

Tip: If you don't believe the nonpaying bidder's sob story, put the bidder on your blocked-bidder list (page 229) so you won't have to listen to any more of his tragic tales.

Phishing for Sellers

The term *phishing* refers to official-looking (but totally bogus) emails designed to weasel personal and account information out of you, the recipient. A recent type of phishing email has been appearing in sellers' inboxes lately. These fake emails look just like the emails you get when someone clicks "Ask seller a question" to email you a question about a running auction—except the email doesn't really come through eBay. It comes direct from a scammer who's trying to hijack your account.

The spoof email typically says something like, "I paid for the item. When will it ship?" and provides a link you can click that looks like a link to the auction page. But the link doesn't take you to eBay; it takes you to a scam site that tries to get information about your account. In some cases, clicking the link also loads a Trojan horse or other kind of virus onto your computer.

If you get an email like this from a buyer and you're not sure what auction the buyer is referring to, don't click any links inside the email. Open your Web browser, type *www.ebay.com* into the address bar, sign in, and go to your My eBay page. If you have a legitimate question waiting from a buyer, it will show you there.

Tip: Check My Messages in your My eBay page. All messages sent through eBay appear there.

Another phishing email directed at sellers offers to make you a PowerSeller. Because eBay does invite sellers who qualify to become PowerSellers via email, this can be confusing. You can check two ways to see whether the offer is legit: From your My eBay page, check My Messages. If eBay has sent you a message, you'll find it there. Or sign in to eBay and go to Services → PowerSeller Program, and then click the big green PowerSellers Sign-In! button, shown in Figure 6-18.

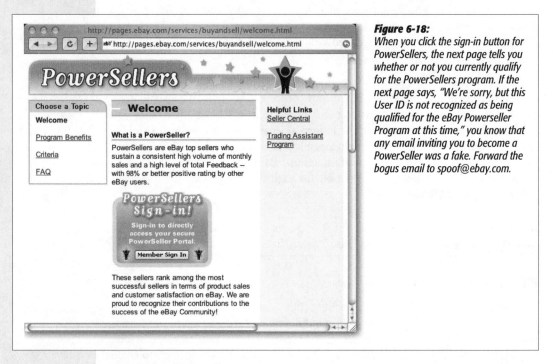

Figure 6-18:
When you click the sign-in button for PowerSellers, the next page tells you whether or not you currently qualify for the PowerSellers program. If the next page says, "We're sorry, but this User ID is not recognized as being qualified for the eBay Powerseller Program at this time," you know that any email inviting you to become a PowerSeller was a fake. Forward the bogus email to spoof@ebay.com.

"Damaged" Goods

Sometimes, you *know* you packed an item carefully, but the buyer will insist that the item arrived in pieces or is not working. This is why requiring shipping insurance is a good idea. If you have an insurance receipt, the buyer has to cooperate with you to get a refund. Buyers who are trying to pull this scam—blaming you for damage that either doesn't exist or is not your fault—will pressure you to give them a refund before the shipper investigates the insurance claim. Don't give in. If the only way that the buyer can get a refund is to participate in the insurance investigation (the buyer has to take the item and the packing materials to the shipper), dishonest buyers suddenly change their minds.

In the same vein, some buyers will claim that an item is damaged or not as described and want you to refund their money immediately. What they're trying to do is get a free item; they keep your perfectly good item *and* get their money back. Don't refund until you have the item back in your hands. Spell this out in your auction's return policy, and these scammers might steer clear of your auctions.

Tip: Buy an ultraviolet pen and UV reader so you can invisibly mark your items (you can get these supplies right on eBay). If a buyer insists on a refund for a "damaged" item that you know was just fine when you shipped it, tell the buyer to return the item so that you can check for the secret mark you put on everything you sell. Your buyer might suddenly decide to keep the item, after all.

Another variation on this theme is switching a good item for a bad one: a buyer purchases something from you, say a new camcorder, to replace a broken one they already own, then tries to "return" the broken one to you for a refund, claiming the camcorder you sent didn't work. The way to beat this shell game is to keep good records. If you're selling electronics, for example, photograph your items' serial numbers and keep them with your sales records, so you have proof of what you sold.

Fake Escrow Sites

A legitimate escrow site protects buyers and sellers: the seller doesn't ship until payment is with the escrow service, and the buyer can make sure the item arrives and is the real thing before releasing payment. But scammers use fake escrow sites to trick buyers and sellers both. (For escrow scams involving buyers, see page 141.) For this reason, some eBay sellers won't do escrow transactions at all.

WORD TO THE WISE

WHOIS That Knocking on My Door?

Scammers can be very persuasive—it comes with their con-artist territory. You might find yourself communicating with someone who appears to have a perfectly valid reason to avoid Escrow.com, and wonder whether you should go ahead with the transaction to save a big sale.

The best path is to insist on Escrow.com or no escrow service at all, but you can check out an alternative escrow site doing a WHOIS search. This kind of search clues you in about when a Web site was registered and who owns it. Network Solutions offers a free, easy-to-use domain name lookup. Go to *www.networksolutions.com* and click WHOIS. Type in the name of the Web site you're checking, make sure that Domain Name is turned on, and click Search.

If the site exists, the page that opens will give you the lowdown on when it was created and registered, and the name, address, and phone number of the registered administrator. If it's only a few days or a few weeks since the Web site's birthday, you can assume that it's not a legitimate escrow site. Scammers love to use stolen credit cards

to set up their fake sites, so another warning sign is a site registered to an individual (as opposed to a corporation) or a registration address in a different state from where the site claims it's located. The scammers steal a credit card account and use it to set up a fake site that the card's rightful owner doesn't even know about.

Finally, if you can't find any registration info because it's hidden, run the other way. What legitimate business would want to keep that information secret?

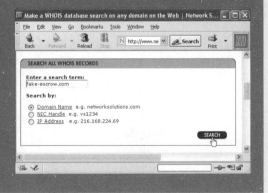

Here's how escrow scams target sellers. A buyer bids on an expensive item, like a computer or a piece of jewelry, and insists on using an escrow service. The fake buyer often acts nervous about the transaction and the seller's honesty. This puts the seller on the defensive; the seller wants the transaction to go smoothly and keep her good reputation on eBay intact. When the buyer suggests using an escrow service, the seller often agrees, figuring it's safe for both parties. The buyer, however, insists on choosing the escrow service, and you can bet it's not Escrow.com or one of the international escrow services recommended by eBay (Help → A–Z Index → E → Escrow for Sellers).

The seller agrees to use the buyer's escrow service, registers on the site, and soon gets an email from the escrow company, saying payment has arrived and it's OK to ship. The seller ships the item. Days pass, and there's no news. The seller goes to the escrow service's Web site, only to find the site has disappeared. There is no escrow service. The buyer set up a fake site to steal the seller's item.

Not only has the seller lost the item, he probably opened himself up to identity theft when he registered with the fake escrow service, which might have asked for his email address, home address, and bank account or credit card info.

The upshot? You can refuse to use escrow at all. But that might scare away legitimate buyers who want the security of escrow when they're spending big bucks. If you decide to accept escrow, protect yourself by always insisting on Escrow.com (or an eBay-approved international escrow service).

The I'll-Ship-It-Myself Scam

Sometimes a buyer insists on using his own shipper. This can seem legitimate; many people have accounts with FedEx, UPS, or DHL/Airborne, and using their account can save them a few bucks on shipping charges. It's a safer bet, though, to stick with the terms of your auction. If your buyer has stolen someone else's shipping account info, when the shipping company catches up with what's happening, they'll charge you for sending the package.

Overpayment

In this scam, a potential buyer contacts the seller with an offer to purchase the item at a good price, sometimes using the Buy It Now button and sometimes asking the seller to end the auction early for a high price. The buyer often (but not always) claims to be an "agent" working on behalf of a "client." Or the buyer might claim that he or she is buying the item as a gift.

The buyer wants to send the seller a cashier's check for an amount that's substantially more than the agreed-upon price. The buyer offers one of several possible explanations for this: the extra money is for shipping and the seller should send the item via the chosen shipper, or someone owes the buyer money and the buyer wants that person to send the whole amount to the seller, or the buyer wants to include a cash gift with the item. The buyer frequently offers the seller a percentage of the overpayment for the seller's "trouble." This appeals to sellers who want to make a quick buck beyond their auction proceeds.

When the cashier's check arrives, the buyer pressures the seller to wire the excess amount at once and ship the item as quickly as possible. The matter is extremely urgent and must be taken care of right away. And the matter *is* urgent (to the scammer): the seller is holding a forged cashier's check, and the buyer wants to steal the seller's money and item before the seller finds out.

It can take a while for a bank to discover that a cashier's check is a forgery, particularly if the check is supposed to be from a bank outside the U.S. Many banks make deposited funds available immediately if your account has as much as or more than the amount of the check. But making the funds available is *not* the same as the check's clearing. And that's how these scammers rip off the seller. You think the check has cleared, so you wire the funds and ship the item. Later, you find out that the check was a forgery—and the money you thought was in your account has disappeared.

Tip: To get an amusing education in this type of scam, visit *www.bustedupcowgirl.com/scampage.html*. The woman who owns this site got so tired of being approached by scammers that she started playing with them, coming up with all kinds of explanations for delaying the sale. Then other sellers started contributing their own stories. You can read email exchanges between scammers and on-to-them sellers, from the initial approach to the final *gotcha!*

If you receive an email from someone asking you to accept overpayment and wire the difference to someone else, run the other way. Don't answer the email. Block all future emails from that person, add their eBay ID to your Blocked Bidder list (page 229), and report them to eBay (Help → Security Center).

Going from Hobby to Business

You've cleaned out every closet and scoured the attic, the basement, *and* the garage. You've gotten rid of perfectly good, going-to-waste stuff you'd never use—and made some money for your efforts. You've built up your feedback score (page 40) and perfected your listing-creation technique (page 154). Now you want to get into selling in a *serious* way.

You're interested in finding inventory to sell, reaching even more buyers, and doing a little paperwork. (Well, okay, you're not actually interested in doing paperwork, but you *are* interested in keeping the tax man off your back as your eBay sales increase.)

You've come to the right chapter.

More than 400,000 Americans make all or a significant part of their income on eBay. This chapter shows you how to become one of them, turning your eBay hobby into a part- or full-time business. Here are the topics it covers:

- What to sell—and where to find it.

- How to define your business: sole proprietorship, partnership, or corporation.

- Doing the paperwork, from writing a business plan to licenses and tax issues.

- Opening an eBay Store.

- Selling internationally.

- Selling on consignment.

- Becoming a PowerSeller.

What Should I Sell?

In taking the next step with an eBay business, the big question on every seller's mind is "What should I sell?" This big question is really two smaller questions:

- Which products offer a good sell-through rate and a good profit?
- Where can I get my hands on these items?

Note: A *sell-through rate* is the percentage of your auctions that end in sales.

New sellers often post to online forums, asking more experienced sellers for the secret of success: what do they sell and where do they get it? If you think about it for a couple of seconds, you can see that this method of market research won't get you very far. Why would your future competitors want to give free information to someone whose goal is to cut in on their business? It ain't gonna happen. Fortunately, this section helps you answer those questions.

Research the Market

To find what sells—and what doesn't—spend some time doing research. If you've sold a number of items already, you'll have a sense of which ones attracted attention and which ones didn't. Use eBay's hot list (page 208) to look for categories with lots of action. Keep checking the list over several months to look for patterns. When you've identified a hot category that interests you, spend some time searching completed auctions in that category.

Are iPods generating lots of bids while other MP3 players languish? Does it look like a category is getting overcrowded—supply going up to the extent that demand starts tapering off—so that the category could go from hot to freezing cold in a couple of months? Does the item sell better at a specific time of the year (think snow tires and swimsuits) or when auctions end on a certain day of the week? Whatever you want to sell, taking the time to familiarize yourself with the market and analyze its trends will position you to use that market to your advantage.

Note: Third-party research tools (page 344) can help you get serious about selling.

Finding Merchandise

Merchandise is everywhere. With a little creative thinking and an awareness of what sells, you can find stuff to sell as far away as the other side of the globe or as close as next door.

Note: Besides the sources offered here, you can find things to sell by offering to sell for others on consignment (page 273).

Secondhand trash and treasures

Anyone who's ever shopped at a tag sale, flea market, or thrift shop has harbored hopes of finding an unrecognized treasure among all the junk. It can take some searching, but consider the following venues as places to find stuff to resell on eBay:

- **Tag sales.** People who have tag sales (also called yard sales or garage sales) just want to get rid of the things they don't use or don't need and make a little money in the process (maybe they're too lazy to sell their castoffs on eBay). So you often can find underpriced items being sold by people who don't know what they could get for them. In addition, it's almost a tradition at tag sales to try a little haggling; don't hesitate to make an offer or see if you can get two items for the price of one. Be sure to show up early to get first dibs on the best stuff.

- **Thrift shops.** Stores run by charity groups such as Goodwill, the Salvation Army, and local churches offer good deals to the discerning shopper. You might have to hunt a bit to find the really good buys. And keep in mind that used clothing, a staple of these shops, usually sells for thrift-store prices on eBay, so be careful not to buy up a pile of used clothing that you can't make money on.

Warning: Use caution when buying designer items from thrift shops. You don't know where those goods came from, and they're often counterfeit.

- **Flea markets and antique shops.** Either of these can be a terrific source for collectibles and one-of-a-kind items—if you know what you're looking for. Most flea market and antique dealers know their stuff, so expect to do a little hunting for bargains.

- **Estate sales and local auctions.** An estate sale is designed to sell off property from the estate of someone who has passed away; estate sales may be held as auctions. Local auctions can be a great place to pick up deals; you'll probably be bidding against other eBayers there. Don't forget that there's usually a commission on top of the price you bid. Arrive early to snap up the best buys; as the auction proceeds, people who haven't bid yet start to feel pressure to participate, so later lots often generate more bidding and higher final prices.

- **Dump & Run.** If you live near a college or university, watch for a Dump & Run sale. Students who are cleaning out their dorm rooms at the end of the school year throw out an amazing amount of stuff, from furniture and kitchenware to books to linens and clothing—some of it brand new. One student, Lisa Heller, was amazed at the waste and started Dump & Run as a way to keep perfectly good items out of landfills and raise money for nonprofit organizations at the same time. Before they head home for the summer, students deposit unwanted items in Dump & Run boxes, rather than the trash. Volunteers sort through the items and hold a massive tag sale, usually in the fall at the start of a new school year. Prices can be unbelievably low. To find a sale near you, go to *www. dumpandrun.org* and click Upcoming Sales.

Tip: Don't forget about government auctions. Government agencies frequently sell off surplus or confiscated goods. Two good sources of information about these auctions are Government Liquidation (*www.govliquidation.com*) and Bid4Assets (*www.bid4assets.com*). On the Bid4Assets home page, look on the left-hand menu under Specialty Auctions to find sales of tax-defaulted property, government surplus, and goods seized by U.S. Marshals.

Wholesalers and liquidators

Wholesalers are middlemen; they buy merchandise directly from a manufacturer and sell it to retailers. Wholesalers usually sell in bulk and don't want to deal with the general public (in other words, the average eBay seller). So if you want to buy wholesale, it's a good idea to have a state sales tax number or reseller certificate (page 255). Visit your state's Web site (go to *www.google.com*, search for the name of your state, and scan the results list for the official home page) to learn how to obtain a tax number.

You can find many, many wholesale directories online. One that was set up especially for eBayers is *www.wholesaleforebay.com*. Other popular directories are *www.wholesalecentral.com*, *www.wholesale411.com*, and *www.vendio.com* (click Seller Resources).

Tip: If you're a member of a wholesale club, like Sam's Club, BJ's Wholesale Club, or Costco, you can find items on sale at the club and resell them on eBay.

Liquidators buy surplus merchandise in bulk and then resell it. The merchandise liquidators offer could be store returns, factory seconds, closeouts, or overstocked items. If you buy from a liquidator, you'll be buying in bulk; some sell by the pallet, others by the truckload. Make sure you have room to store all that merchandise. You should also ask why a liquidator is necessary in the first place. If a store couldn't sell that truckload of toasters, are you sure you'll be able to?

If you're interested in buying from liquidators, consider subscribing to Closeout News (surf to *www.thecloseoutnews.com*), shown in Figure 7-1. Each month, more than 4,000 companies advertise their closeouts, overstock, and discontinued items in this publication.

A popular liquidation Web site is Liquidation.com (*www.liquidation.com*). This is an auction site where you bid for lots of items, ranging from clothing to computers and accessories to jewelry to power tools. Salvage Closeouts (*www.salvagecloseouts.com*) sells items for a fixed price and has an eBay department to help and advise eBay sellers. (On the left-hand menu, click eBay Recommendations.) Overstock.com, whose auction site is one of eBay's main competitors, also offers fixed-price items in bulk through its Club O Gold program, which offers deeper discounts on Overstock's prices and cheaper shipping for an annual fee. Go to *www.overstock.com* and click Join Club O Gold to sign up.

Here are some other liquidators' Web sites:

- Closeout Central (*www.closeoutcentral.com*)

- TDW Closeouts (*www.tdwcloseouts.com*)

- Merchandise U.S.A. (*www.merchandiseusa.com*)

- GB Retail Exchange (*www.retailexchange.com*)

- American Merchandise Liquidators (*www.amlinc.com*)

- AAA Closeouts Network (*www.aaacloseoutsnetwork.com*)

Tip: You can also shop right on eBay for wholesale items you can turn around and sell yourself. Click Buy → "See all categories," find a category that interests you, and check out its Wholesale Lots subcategory.

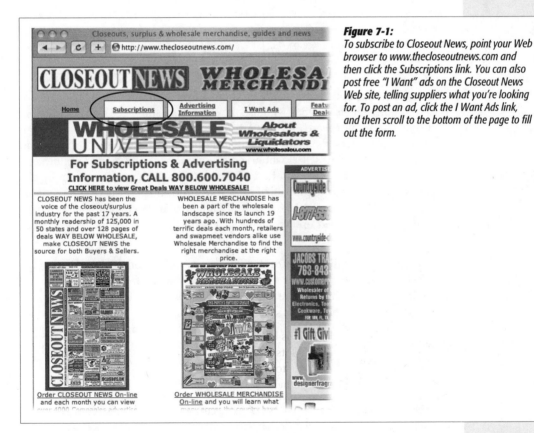

Figure 7-1:
To subscribe to Closeout News, point your Web browser to www.thecloseoutnews.com and then click the Subscriptions link. You can also post free "I Want" ads on the Closeout News Web site, telling suppliers what you're looking for. To post an ad, click the I Want Ads link, and then scroll to the bottom of the page to fill out the form.

Drop shippers

Drop shippers are wholesale companies that ship an item directly to the buyer after your auction. You choose a satellite radio from the drop-shippers catalog or Web site and list it on eBay. Someone buys the radio and pays you for it. Then you notify the drop shipper to ship the radio to the buyer. If you're short on space, this can be an ideal arrangement; you can sell merchandise without cluttering up your house (and your garage and your basement) with inventory.

But if the good thing about drop shippers is that the merchandise you sell never has to pass through your hands, it's also the potentially bad thing. It's *your* reputation on the line with each auction. If the drop shipper drops the ball (instead of your shipment), you're the one who'll receive disputes, complaints, and negative feedback—and the buyer has every right to be mad at you if the item you sold is out of stock or simply doesn't arrive.

Tip: To find out whether a drop shipper is reliable, do a trial run. Try ordering an item or two yourself (you can always resell them on eBay). Then notice how long it takes for the order to arrive, and whether the item is in good shape and well packed. If the shipment doesn't live up to your own standards as a buyer, keep looking.

One way to check out a particular drop shipper before you start using their service is to find other sellers on eBay who use the same drop shipper. This isn't as tricky as it might seem: just search for items you know the drop shipper sells (from the eBay home page, type the name of an item in the Start New Search text box and then click Search). Most sellers who use drop shippers use the shipper's photo and description of an item, so if you find a bunch of very similar auctions run by different eBay sellers, you've probably found your drop shipper. Check out the feedback these sellers have accrued. If you find lots of recent complaints about shipping speed, canceled orders, or the quality of the merchandise, you need to find a better drop shipper.

Beware the lists and directories of drop shippers available on eBay and across the Internet. The people who offer those are making money from selling a list, not from drop shipping. By the time you get your hands on the list (the same list that dozens of others are buying), it's likely to be full of useless, out-of-date information. Also, some of the names on the list probably aren't even legitimate drop shippers; there are plenty of middlemen out there who pretend to be drop shippers but in fact do nothing more than forward your orders to a real, live drop shipper—taking an unnecessary bite out of your profits.

Tip: Avoid drop shippers who charge a "setup" fee. Drop shippers typically charge $2 to $4 per shipment for handling; setup fees or other surcharges are a sign that you're probably not dealing with a legitimate drop shipper.

There's only one drop shipping directory published by a certified eBay provider. Worldwide Brands (*www.worldwidebrands.com*), shown in Figure 7-2, employs a staff of full-time researchers who have created a list of drop shippers (and who update it daily). There's a one-time fee to gain access to the list, but Worldwide Brands guarantees that each drop shipper on its list has its own warehouse, has manufacturer authorization to sell the products, and will ship single items. If you discover otherwise, Worldwide Brands will refund the money you paid to use their list.

Figure 7-2:
Worldwide Brands offers information about drop shippers and wholesale suppliers. From the left-side menu, you can also download a free eBook on starting an Internet business, try out a market-analysis research tool, and subscribe to a weekly newsletter for entrepreneurs running an e-business from home.

It might take some time to find a good drop shipper, and you should be aware that hundreds of other eBayers are also out there looking for a good drop shipper who ships the very same items you want to sell. It's hard to gain a competitive edge when other sellers are getting the same deal you are.

Tip: When working with a drop shipper, do frequent checks of the shipper's inventory. Sometimes someone will come along and buy up all the remaining stock of an item—and you don't want to be running an auction for any item the drop shipper no longer has.

eBay's policy on drop shipping falls under what it calls "pre-sale listings." eBay defines a *pre-sale* as the sale of any item that you don't physically possess at the time you post the listing. Pre-sale listings must mention that you don't have the item in hand and must guarantee delivery within 30 days of the auction's end. If you want to accept PayPal for a pre-sale, things get a little more complicated. PayPal allows pre-sales "on a limited basis," but you must guarantee shipment within 20 days. And if you want to use PayPal's Seller Protection Policy (page 170), you have to ship within a week of the auction's end. Slow drop shippers will trip you up here.

Note: If shipping takes more than seven days, PayPal doesn't allow drop shippers for sales of computers or routers.

Manufacturers

Sometimes you can buy merchandise directly from the manufacturer, getting rid of the need to go through a wholesaler or a drop shipper. When you've decided what kind of product you want to sell, contact some manufacturers directly (use a search engine like *www.google.com* to find the company's Web page and contact information) and ask whether they'll sell you items to resell. If the manufacturer agrees, you can save significant money over wholesale prices.

Another way to find manufacturers is through Andale Suppliers (*www.andale.com*), a free service shown in Figure 7-3.

Figure 7-3:
To find suppliers through Andale, go to www.andale. com and then click Research Tools. If you haven't registered with Andale, register now. (To do so, click the Register button at the top of the Andale home page; then, on the page that appears, scroll down to the bottom and click Continue With Registration). After you've registered, use the Andale Quicklinks menu at the top of the page to select Suppliers by clicking the Search button. You can search for whatever items you want to acquire by manufacturer, wholesaler, or one-time sale.

Attending trade shows also gives you access to manufacturers. A *trade show* is a convention where manufacturers' sales reps exhibit their goods. Trade shows cover a particular section of the market, such as electronics, toys, books, gift items, and so on. Know what you want to sell before you go to make the trip worth your time. Also, some shows feature wholesalers and distributors, who may be more open to dealing with small resellers than some large manufacturers.

Tip: Trade-show producer VNU Expositions maintains a list of upcoming trade shows at *www. merchandisegroup.com*. At their Web site, you can also sign up for MarketWatch, a free e-newsletter for buyers and sellers of novelty and gift merchandise.

Doing the Paperwork

Welcome to the ranks of the self-employed! Whether you're selling full-time or as a sideline, when you're doing business on eBay, you get to be your own boss. The freedom is heady, but it's not without responsibility: you have to keep good records, learn a little bookkeeping, and comply with the legal and tax requirements of self-employed sellers. This section shows you how.

Note: Although this section offers basic information, be sure to consult an accountant or tax professional for guidance on the tax laws that apply to entrepreneurs.

Write a Business Plan

The old adage, "Fail to plan and you plan to fail" is never more true than in business. If you're serious about hanging out your own shingle, you need to create a *business plan.*

Think of a business plan as an outline describing the goals you want to accomplish with your business, and how you intend to accomplish those goals. You want to include things like how much money you want your business to make (and when), how much money you plan to invest, what marketing strategies you intend to use, what kinds of customers you intend to go after (and how you intend to reach them)—that sort of thing.

The great thing about a business plan is that putting one together forces you to think through your business from beginning to end—*before* you quit your day job and invest your life savings. In other words, you get to see on paper, from the comfort of your favorite armchair, whether or not your eBay business has a good chance of succeeding.

If you need another reason to get out paper and pencil, be aware that if you find yourself looking for a business loan, you'll need a business plan to get financing.

If you do decide to write a business plan (and you really should), here are the sections you should consider:

- **Description.** What's the scope of your business? What makes it or your products unique?

- **Marketing.** Who are your potential customers and how will you reach them? Who is your competition? How will you make your products stand out?

- **Finances.** This section includes income statements and your business's balance sheet (page 253).

- **Management.** Is your business bigger than a one-person show (or do you expect it to be)? Who is responsible for various tasks? How many part- or full-time workers do you expect to hire right away? In the future?

Tip: A business plan doesn't just give you an edge in managing your business; it helps you plan for the future. Use your business plan to measure your progress as your business grows, marking both milestones and missed goals. Revise the document as you meet goals and develop new ones.

For more information about writing a business plan, check in with the Small Business Administration (*www.sba.gov*), as shown in Figure 7-4, or BPlans.com (*www.bplans.com*). Both sites offer a wealth of free information; BPlans.com also sells Business Plan Pro, a Windows-based business-plan-writing program.

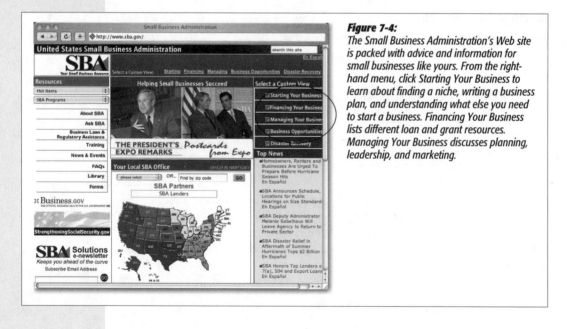

Figure 7-4:
The Small Business Administration's Web site is packed with advice and information for small businesses like yours. From the right-hand menu, click Starting Your Business to learn about finding a niche, writing a business plan, and understanding what else you need to start a business. Financing Your Business lists different loan and grant resources. Managing Your Business discusses planning, leadership, and marketing.

What Kind of Business Are You?

When your eBay hobby grows into a business, you designate it as one of three legal structures: sole proprietorship, partnership, or corporation. This section tells you what these terms mean and looks at the advantages and drawbacks of each.

Note: The Internal Revenue Service's Web site offers information about different business structures and associated tax issues at *www.irs.gov/businesses/index.html*, shown in Figure 7-5.

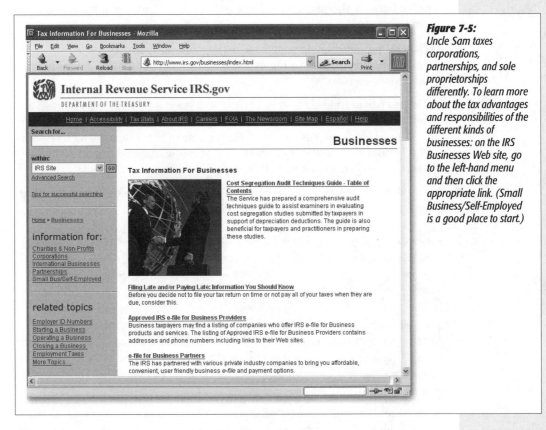

Figure 7-5:
Uncle Sam taxes corporations, partnerships, and sole proprietorships differently. To learn more about the tax advantages and responsibilities of the different kinds of businesses: on the IRS Businesses Web site, go to the left-hand menu and then click the appropriate link. (Small Business/Self-Employed is a good place to start.)

Sole proprietorship

This is the simplest business structure, and for that reason alone, it is the most popular for eBayers. In fact, if you're selling things on eBay (for yourself, not as someone else's employee), you're already a sole proprietor. In a sole proprietorship, one person owns and operates the business. That makes you the one and only boss. Taxes are easier for a sole proprietorship than for the other structures, because you report business income and expenses on your personal income tax return. That means that any losses from your business can offset other income.

The main drawback to a sole proprietorship is that you're personally liable for the obligations and debt of your business. That means that you could lose your personal assets (like your home) to business debts or legal claims against the business. Also, a sole proprietorship usually runs on the owner's resources; it's harder to get banks to lend you money for this kind of business.

Partnership

Being a sole proprietor can be exhausting: you own the business and get all the benefits, but you also take on all the responsibilities. Sometimes, it's better to get by with a little help from your friends. There are two kinds of partnerships:

- **General partnership.** In a general partnership, all partners are active in the company and responsible for its debts. This model is the more common for small businesses.

- **Limited partnership.** This structure has both general partners, who manage and run the business and assume financial responsibility, and limited partners, who are simply investors with no say in the running of the company and no liability risk beyond their initial investment. You don't usually see new or small businesses set up as a limited partnership.

Partnerships offer a tax advantage because the company doesn't pay tax on its income but passes profits and losses on to individual partners.

Note: One kind of partnership of interest to many eBayers is called a *husband/wife trading partnership*, a kind of general partnership that offers tax savings to married couples. If you're married, you don't have to file any special papers to establish this partnership. Ask your accountant for more information if you think this model could benefit you.

The main disadvantage to a partnership is the same as for a sole proprietorship: partners are personally responsible for business liabilities. And dissension among partners can cause problems, because each partner can act on behalf of the partnership, which could cause problems for the business and the individual partners.

To form a partnership, contact a good lawyer. A lawyer who's had experience with partnerships can help you draw up the agreement, as well as help you to ask questions and forestall problems you may not have thought of.

Corporation

The main advantage of a corporation is that it protects your personal assets by separating your business from the actual people who own and operate it. This shields you from being personally liable for your company's debts and obligations. In addition, if you have or expect to have employees, you can put together benefits packages for them: health insurance, a pension plan, and so on. You can extend those benefits to yourself, too.

On the other hand, corporations are complex. Because a corporation is a separate legal entity from the people who own and run it, it must comply with a separate set of regulations and tax requirements. Corporations require more money, time, and paperwork to set up and maintain than partnerships or sole proprietorships. Plan on hiring a lawyer and an accountant.

There are many kinds of corporations. But if you're thinking of incorporating, you'll probably be interested in one of two kinds, described in the box below.

If you want to incorporate, you must file with your state: either through the secretary of state's office or another office that registers corporations. A lawyer can guide you through all the forms and red tape, but can cost up to a couple thousand dollars, depending on your area.

POWER USERS' CLINIC

Types of Corporations

If you're considering forming a corporation, there are two types you're most likely to investigate. Warning: this information is dense and legalistic.

- **S corporation.** This corporate structure, meant for businesses with fewer than 75 shareholders, offers liability protection to the business owner. Income and losses are passed to shareholders and reported on their individual tax returns, so in a new business with early losses, shareholders can offset any such losses against their personal income. There are, however, a number of drawbacks to forming an S corporation. For example, this kind of business is subject to greater legal and tax costs than partnerships or sole proprietorships are. In fact, S corporations are, in a sense, taxed twice: you pay both corporate tax and individual tax on dividends.

Forming an S corporation, like any corporation, takes time (sometimes months) and money, and you'll have higher ongoing costs for legal and accounting fees. Limitations on stock can cause difficulties when you want to raise money.

- **Limited liability company (LLC).** This structure aims to combine the benefits of a corporation with the benefits of a partnership. The company's owners and managers receive the limited liability and tax benefits of an S corporation without the S corporation restrictions. For example, an LLC has no limitation on the number of shareholders. Income and losses pass through to the owners and count toward their personal tax returns. As in a partnership, any member of the LLC can participate in running the business. Rules governing LLCs vary from state to state; not all states offer the same advantages.

Keep Good Records

If you're in business for yourself, good record keeping is a must. You can go low-tech (stuff receipts and other pieces of paper into a shoebox) or high-tech (use a spreadsheet like Excel, Lotus 1-2-3, or Quattro Pro), but when you're figuring out income, deductions, and expenses, you need to know where the money went.

Tip: Mac fans looking for a spreadsheet program should check out NeoOffice/J, which is free, open source software for Mac OS X. You can download NeoOffice/J from this Web site: *www.planamesa.com/ neojava/en/download.php.*

In a nutshell, these are the records you need to keep track of:

- **Income.** This aspect of record keeping can get confusing, because as an eBay seller, you probably have income arriving in several different ways: PayPal, personal checks, money orders, possibly even credit card companies. What's important is to make sure that you record the same information, no matter how the payment comes in. Keep track of the transaction date, who's paying (the name and address of your buyer), the type of payment (PayPal, check, and so on), and the amount you received.

- **Business expenses.** This category includes inventory (the money you spend to acquire the items you sell), of course, but there's more to it than that. Expenses related to your eBay business can include the fees you pay for Internet access, packing and office supplies, travel to auctions and antique centers to purchase inventory, subscription fees for business-related publications and services, other fees you pay to independent contractors to help with Web design, packing, shipping, and more. Whatever the expense, keep a record of its date, type, and amount, and the name of the person or company you paid.

- **Business assets.** *Assets* are equipment you own and use to run your business. Assets might include your computer and its accessories, the digital camera you use to take photos for your auctions, a postage scale if you have one, and so on. The records you should keep regarding business assets include the type of equipment (name and model number), the date you bought it, the amount you paid for it, and how much time you use the asset for personal purposes. (In other words, you can't count the hours you spend using your computer to play Minesweeper, or, if you're going on vacation, you'll probably grab your digital camera, rather than reserving it exclusively for eBay-related photos.) When it comes to tax time, though, you can only deduct the depreciated cost of an asset based on how much you use it for your business (page 253).

Account for Yourself

If you own your own business, *accounting*—keeping track of your business's income and outgo using special IRS-approved rules—is a necessary evil. You can either do your own accounting or pay an accountant to do it for you. Even if you decide to hire an accountant, though, you still want to read through this section (if for no other reason that to keep your accountant honest).

From an accounting point of view, there are two ways to figure your finances: cash-based accounting or accrual based accounting. Here's what each term means:

- **Cash-based.** With cash-based accounting, you wait to record a transaction until you've made or received payment. In other words, the date money changes hands is the date you record the transaction. This simple accounting method is the most common for small businesses.

- **Accrual-based.** If you use accrual-based accounting, you record income on its due date and expenses on the date you incur them, no matter when the money actually changes hands. Accrual-based accounting tells you what you've earned, not what you've collected. It can help you to get a stronger sense of overall cash flow than cash-based accounting. The downside is that it's more complicated and that you can end up paying taxes on money you've earned but not yet received.

Note: If you maintain an inventory for your business, the IRS says you must use the accrual-based accounting method.

Whichever accounting method you use, you should create a *balance sheet* to give an overall snapshot of your business's financial picture at a given moment in time. Here's what you need to include in a balance sheet:

- **Assets** are what your business owns. There are two main kinds:

  - **Current assets** include cash and anything you could sell (and convert to cash) within one year, such as your inventory. If people owe you money (accounts receivable) and you're likely to collect it, this owed money also counts as a current asset.

  - **Long-term (or fixed) assets** include anything whose useful life lasts beyond a year. Property, office equipment, and office furniture are examples of long-term assets. In figuring the value of long-term assets, you also figure out their depreciation: how much does it cost to use the asset over the course of its useful life? To figure depreciation, estimate how many years you're likely to use an asset, like your computer, and then divide its original cost by the number of years you think you'll use it. For example, if your computer cost $1,800 and you plan to use it for six years before replacing it, divide 1800 by 6 to get a depreciation of $300 per year.

- **Liabilities** are the bills your business owes. Like assets, these come in two main flavors:

  - **Current liabilities** are anything you have to pay within the next year, including accounts payable and taxes.

  - **Long-term liabilities** are debts due over a period of years. If you've taken out long-term loans to support your eBay business, like a mortgage on a warehouse, include this loan in your balance sheet as a long-term debt.

- **Equity** is your initial investment in the business plus any earnings that you've reinvested in the business.

The balance sheet got its name for a reason: it should balance assets against liabilities and equity. After you've made all your entries, your business's balance sheet should reflect this equation: Assets = Liabilities + Equity. Another way to work the equation is: *What you have* (assets) – *what you owe* (liabilities) = *what you're left with* (equity).

Note: If your balance sheet is unbalanced, you haven't recorded everything correctly. Go back and check for missing entries and typos.

Preparing a balance sheet lets you take a peek at your business's *liquidity*, which basically means its ability to pay the bills. A balance sheet can let you know whether you have enough money to pay upcoming bills, so when you're getting started, it's a good idea to prepare and review a balance sheet regularly, perhaps once a quarter. It takes some time to get familiar and comfortable with reading financial statements like balance sheets, so if you're doing your own accounting, go over your statements with an accountant or tax professional the first few times you prepare them.

Keep It Legal

eBay can seem like a free-for-all, a giant swap meet where anyone can join in and no one's keeping tabs. Uncle Sam and your state government see things a little differently. If you're making money by selling things on eBay, you need to be aware of the laws and tax obligations governing e-commerce.

License to sell

Although nobody's likely to come around spying to see whether you're selling stuff out of your garage, if you don't file the necessary paperwork to do business in your city, county, or state, skipping that little detail could come back to haunt you. Do you need a license to do business in your town? What about zoning—is it OK to work out of your home in your neighborhood? Does the warehouse you're planning to use have a certificate of occupancy that lets you move in and do business there? Take the time to find out what government offices you need to contact, and then make the calls. It could save you fines and penalties in the future. A good place to start is with your local chamber of commerce, which is a great source of information for starting a local business.

Here's a list of licenses, permits, and other legal issues to consider:

- **Business license.** Call your town, city, or county clerk to learn about whether you need a business license and, if so, how to apply for one.

- **Zoning issues.** Most of the time, you can do business out of your home without worrying about whether you're breaking zoning laws. But strictness in enforcing these laws varies from place to place. If you regularly have big trucks pulling up to your house in support of your business—or even if a nosy neighbor complains—you might have to choose whether your home business is going to be out of your home or just plain out of business. Call your local zoning department to find out what zoning laws permit.

- **Fire department permit.** If your business is open to the public—for example, if people come in to drop off items you sell for them on consignment—you might need a permit from the fire department. If your business uses flammable materials, you should also check with the fire department to see whether you need a permit.

- **Health department permit.** eBay restricts the kinds of food you can sell, but if you do sell food, be aware that you have to pay attention to federal, state, and local laws regarding its preparation and sale. Call your local health department to schedule an inspection and apply for a permit.

- **Reseller certificate or sales tax license.** The name of the permit varies, but if you're selling things you didn't manufacture yourself, you may need this certificate. Check with your state tax office. On the plus side, having a reseller's certificate exempts you from paying sales tax on items you buy in order to turn around and sell them.

Note: In some states, it's a criminal offense to sell things without a sales tax license.

- **DBA certificate.** If your business is a sole proprietorship or partnership (page 249) and you want to do business under a name that's not your own legal name, you probably need to register the name and obtain a DBA ("doing business as") certificate. For example, if you want to sell used clothes under the business name Retro Threads, you probably need to register that name. Call your town, city, or county clerk for more information. In some places, you'll have to advertise the DBA name in the local newspaper for a certain period of time.

FREQUENTLY ASKED QUESTION

Insurance

Do I need to insure my eBay business?

Neglecting to buy insurance is a common—and unfortunate—mistake made by a lot of small business owners. Too many home-based businesspeople assume that their homeowner's insurance policy also covers any business they operate from home. But as some have found out the hard way, this isn't necessarily true.

Check with your insurance agent to see whether your homeowner's policy covers at-home businesses. If it doesn't (and most don't), or if your coverage is insufficient, it's time to shop around. This can take some time and research.

Rates can vary widely from one insurer to another. Get several bids. Enlist the help of your insurance agent and look on the Internet. Even if your homeowner's policy doesn't cover your home-based business, the insurer who holds that policy

might offer you a multiple-policy discount on business insurance, so be sure to ask. You might be able to save more money by consolidating your auto, home, and business insurance with one company.

Look for coverage that protects your inventory and business equipment (go for full replacement cost), protects you against personal liability, and also protects your business against general liability. General liability policies tend to have a lot of exclusions—such as shoddy workmanship—so know exactly what the policy you buy does and doesn't cover. If you have employees, you'll need workers' compensation insurance. Also, consider business-interruption insurance. Sometimes an unexpected catastrophe can put your business on hold for days or even months. Business-interruption insurance will help you meet costs until you can resume normal business operations.

CHAPTER 7: GOING FROM HOBBY TO BUSINESS

- **Certificate of occupancy.** Depending on local regulations, you might need a certificate of occupancy for a building or space you plan to use for offices or storage. A certificate of occupancy is proof, issued by your city or town, that the building is fit to use or inhabit. Call the building inspector's office to find out.

- **Sign permit.** If you hang out a shingle—or any kind of sign—to show the world you're in business, you don't want to have to haul it back in because it's too big. Drop-off consignment stores (page 273) or proprietors of brick-and-mortar stores are likely to need a sign permit. Many towns restrict the size, location, lighting, or style of signs that can hang in the community. Find out whether that's the case in your area.

The preceding list isn't comprehensive, by any means; it just shows the kind of regulations and laws you might need to consider. Do your homework to find out any and all local regulations that apply to you before you take your eBay business online.

FREQUENTLY ASKED QUESTION

State Regulations

Does my state regulate online auction sellers?

It was bound to happen sooner or later. Online auctions are such big business that states are looking for ways to get their piece of the eBay pie. More than half a dozen states, including Ohio, Tennessee, California, Illinois, Florida, Maine, Missouri, and Texas, have passed or are considering bills that will mandate state regulation of some online sellers.

Some states, like Tennessee and Ohio, are taking the approach that online sellers are auctioneers and therefore need to get an auctioneer's license, a process that may include shelling out money for classes, passing tests, and paying the actual licensing fee. Other states, like California, are trying to classify some online sellers as pawnbrokers.

Because this is a whole new area of regulation for states, the new and proposed laws can be confusing, and it's not always clear which eBay sellers must comply. Most of the laws seem to target Trading Assistants (page 273) or consignment sellers (sellers who list and sell goods for other people), but the laws may affect other sellers too. Besides the cost, the regulations threaten to consume sellers' valuable time with additional paperwork.

More confusion arises from fixed-price Buy It Now sales, which technically speaking aren't auctions. Many sellers combine BIN listings (for example, in their eBay Stores) with listings in the traditional auction format. Will state regulations apply to all these sales or just some of them?

To find out whether your state has laws regulating online auctions, contact your state's business-licensing entity; you can probably find a link from your state government's home page (often located at *www.yourstate.gov*; for example, *www.minnesota.gov*).

eBay has set up a Government Relations page at *http://pages.ebay.com/governmentrelations*. Here you can find eBay's official position on regulatory issues like auction regulation and government-imposed barriers to e-commerce. You can also click links to find out the names and contact information for your U.S. Senator and Representative, so you can contact them with your concerns. eBay has drafted a letter you can use or adapt to let your state legislators know your concerns. You can find the letter at this URL: *http://pages.ebay.com/sellercentral/governmentrelations/write-rep.html*.

Taxing issues

eBay emphasizes that it's a venue, not a party to the sales that take place within its marketplace. That's a polite way of saying that tracking and reporting taxes is *your* business, not eBay's. And *that* means you want to keep good records, know which tax laws apply to you, and follow those laws to the letter.

Below are some general tax guidelines you need to be aware of. For more specific information, the Internal Revenue Service's Small Business/Self-Employed Web site (Figure 7-6) is a good place to start.

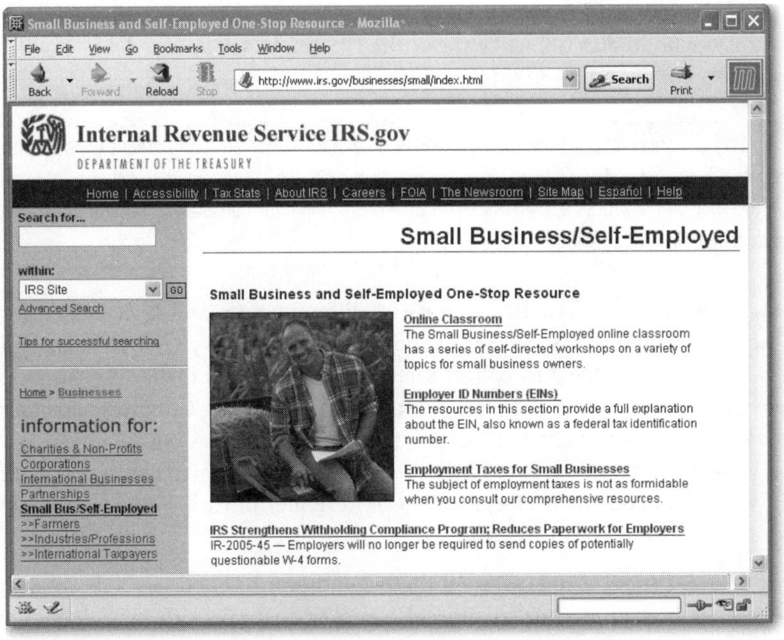

Figure 7-6:
The IRS resource page for small businesses (www. irs.gov/businesses) features articles answering common questions and explaining various tax-related issues; you can also search for specific information. The Online Classroom offers self-directed classes on tax issues.

- **Income taxes.** The IRS requires that you report any income over $600—and that includes money you make on eBay. In addition, unless you're an employee of someone else's eBay business, your eBay income comes from self-employment. That means in April you must file IRS Form 1040 Schedule C, Profit or Loss from Business. Be prepared to pay self-employment taxes and file estimated payments each quarter.

Note: There are a lot of crazy rumors flying around about eBay and income taxes. Don't believe hearsay. Check with your accountant or tax professional, or look for information on the official IRS Web site (*www.irs.gov*).

- **Employees.** If you hire other people to work for you, you have to handle your employees' withholding and payroll taxes. To ease the workload and make sure you do this right, hire an accountant. One way to avoid the hassle of payroll taxes is to work with *independent contractors*—self-employed workers who work with your business on a contract or freelance basis, but don't work for you as employees.

For example, you might pay a shipping service to pack and ship your items; the shipping service is an independent contractor, not your employee. But be warned: the IRS has strict guidelines to define who's an independent contractor and who's an employee. Is the person working for you free to work for others, as well? Can the worker decide when, where, and how to perform the work? If you answer *no* to questions like these, the IRS might say you're dealing with an employee, not an independent contractor.

Note: To find out more about how the IRS defines an employee vs. an independent contractor, visit *www.irs.gov*. You can even download a form to submit to the IRS, who'll determine whether or not someone is your employee: Form SS-8, Determination of Worker Status for Purposes of Federal Employment Taxes and Income Tax Withholding.

- **Sales taxes.** Sales tax law is a morass of different state and local regulations. Some states collect sales tax; others don't. In general, if your business is in a sales-tax state, you have to collect sales tax on sales you make to residents of that state. This issue is in flux, however; states are lobbying Congress to ask for a federal law that will make it easier for them to collect sales tax on online sales, and regulations could change quickly. Keep an eye on any changes by visiting the Web site of your state's Department of Revenue, and ask your accountant or tax professional to keep you informed.

The good news about paying taxes—if there could ever be good news about such a thing—is that reporting your income also means that you can take deductions against it. Here are some common deductions you might be able to take:

- **Startup costs.** Costs related to researching products and markets and startup advertising expenses may qualify as a deduction.

- **Home office.** If you use part of your home regularly and exclusively for business, you may be able to take this deduction.

- **Business equipment.** It's possible to deduct the equipment you use in your business, such as your postage meter and your computer (if you use it exclusively for the business).

- **Business expenses.** You rack up a lot of expenses running an eBay business, including eBay and PayPal fees, items you purchase to sell, advertising, ISP and telephone fees, legal and professional expenses (like that accountant you keep consulting), payments to independent contractors for shipping and such, subscriptions to services or publications, software, insurance, and more. All of these are legitimate, deductible business expenses. If you have employees, you can deduct their wages and benefits packages, too.

- **Vehicle expenses.** If you use a vehicle in connection with the business (think about all those trips to the post office), you can deduct mileage and fuel costs for business-related trips.

- **Travel expenses.** You might travel to auctions or estate sales, trade shows, or conventions. If you do, you can deduct reasonable travel-related expenses.

Again, your mileage may vary. Be sure to work with your accountant or tax professional to learn exactly what—and how much—you can deduct.

Setting Up Shop with an eBay Store

Imagine a marketplace lined with tables, each stall piled high with carpets for sale. Somewhere in the midst is your table—also piled high with carpets. As a shopper strolls down the street, the merchants all cry, "Carpets for sale!" "Beautiful carpets!" "Buy my carpets!" "No, buy mine!" With all that shouting, it's hard to make your voice heard above the din.

Now imagine you sell your carpets from your very own shop. When someone walks in, you don't have to clamor for her attention. As she looks around, she's examining your merchandise, and if she buys, she buys from you.

eBay is like the marketplace; when a shopper searches or browses for an item, your auction is crowded among many others in the search results list, each vying for attention. But if you open an *eBay Store,* a page on eBay that contains your listings, and only yours, you have a virtual shop where buyers can look around, search your inventory, compare your products—and buy from you.

eBay stores feature all your listings: both regular auctions and fixed-price BIN listings. In addition, you can create long-term and even nonexpiring listings for your store. A store costs $15.95 to $499.99 a month, depending on the level of service and prominence on eBay you want. But after you've been selling for a while, there's a bunch of good reasons to open your own eBay Store:

- **You get your own e-commerce Web site, right within eBay.** Your eBay store has a name and a Web address of its own—*http://stores.ebay.com/name-of-store*—so you can promote your store within eBay and across the Internet.

- **When a buyer checks out one of your regular auctions, you can advertise your store right from the auction page.** That way, an interested buyer can easily find your goods.

- **An eBay store makes it easier for buyers to make multiple purchases from you.** Rather than watching and waiting for several auctions to end, they can buy as much as they want all at one time.

- **eBay helps store owners with their marketing.** The program advertises items from your store on the Bid Confirmation and Purchase Confirmation pages (Figure 7-7), giving buyers an extra chance to see your goods.

- **If you specialize in a particular kind of merchandise, a store is a great way to attract interested buyers.** When you change the merchandise often, you keep 'em coming back.

- **A store can save you time.** Auctions run out of time after ten days at most, at which point you have to go through all the work of relisting the item (if it didn't sell). Your store listings can last for 30, 60, 90, or 120 days—or until you cancel the listing (called a Good 'Til Canceled, or GTC, listing). No more time wasted relisting the same items after a slow week.

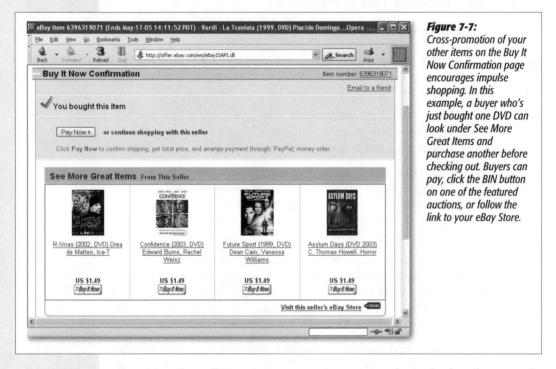

Figure 7-7:
Cross-promotion of your other items on the Buy It Now Confirmation page encourages impulse shopping. In this example, a buyer who's just bought one DVD can look under See More Great Items and purchase another before checking out. Buyers can pay, click the BIN button on one of the featured auctions, or follow the link to your eBay Store.

eBay claims that sellers see a 25 percent increase in sales in the first three months after opening a store—that's the good news. The bad news is that those buyers have to work pretty hard to find your merchandise. Items sold in eBay Stores don't always come up in the list of results when a buyer conducts a search. (When they do appear, they're at the very bottom of the search results page.) Instead, there's a link at the bottom of the results list that says, "See additional Buy It Now items from eBay Store sellers." Most buyers won't even notice that link; they'll just start going through the items on the results list.

Still, a store can be worthwhile if you have a good-sized inventory of related products, like if you typically have several dozen listings going at one time for, say, baby clothes (or for all kinds of baby-related products: clothes, baby blankets, bibs, toys, and so on). Buyers shopping for baby booties who find one of your auctions are likely to venture into your store to see what else you have to offer.

Tip: The best way to get buyers into your store is to feature it prominently in your regular auction listings. Mention your store's great deals in the item description (page 157) and cross-promote your store listings in your auctions (page 211).

Creating Your Store

Before you can open an eBay Store, you must be a registered seller on eBay and meet at least *one* of these criteria:

- You have a feedback score of 20 or higher *or*
- You've gone through the ID verification process (page 155) *or*
- You have a PayPal account in good standing.

You don't have to meet any requirements about volume or how long you've been selling, but the most successful eBay Store owners are those who have a steady volume of sales and enough experience to have refined their listing and customer service skills. You'll get better results from your store if you've already got some selling experience under your belt.

Tip: If you sell mass media items—books, music, movies, video games, and game systems—take a look at Half.com (page 284) before you open an eBay store. Half.com is a separate site owned by eBay that specializes in mass media. Half.com doesn't charge you to list items (it only charges a commission when you sell something), so listing your items there might save you some fees.

Before you go create your store, think of a good name for it. Your store name doesn't have to be the same as—or even related to—your eBay ID. Make it easy for buyers to remember your store with a catchy name that relates to the merchandise you sell, like Turkey Calls Unlimited or Mini-Maison Dollhouse Furnishings. (The box on page 264 lists eBay's naming rules.)

Tip: The best names clue shoppers in about what you sell. For example, a store named *Fall Creek* doesn't offer much information; *Fall Creek Fishing Gear* or *Fall Creek Furniture* is a lot more likely to catch the eye of potential customers.

If you want to check out stores others have set up, type *http://stores.ebay.com* into your browser's address bar or, from the eBay home page, select Buy → eBay Stores. Either will take you to the Stores home page, shown in Figure 7-8. From there, you can browse the directory of existing stores or click the Open a Store button to create your own.

Figure 7-8:
The Stores home page displays links to featured stores and a directory of stores by category. If you're looking for a particular store or kind of merchandise, the upper-left-hand "Find a Store" search box will help you find it. When you're ready to create your own eBay Store, the right-hand "Open a Store" button will get you started.

When you click "Open a Store," eBay prompts you for your password, and then explains what you need to get your store up and running: a name, a short description of the store (up to 300 characters), a design for the store (you can choose one of eBay's designs or create your own), and a subscription level (page 264). Click Open Your eBay Store to continue to the first step of the Open Your Store form, where you choose a theme to give your store a consistent look and feel. Here's how the process works:

1. **Choose a theme.**

   After you've decided on a name, you can begin the process of opening an eBay Store. Go to Services → eBay Stores, and then click the big blue "Open an eBay Store Now!" button. On the next page, click Open Your eBay Store. The first page of the Open Your Store form, shown in Figure 7-9, asks you to select a *theme*, which gives a unified look to your store. eBay shows you popular predesigned themes, or you can design your own theme by clicking the Easily Customizable link. Select the theme you want and click Continue. On the next page, you name and describe your store.

2. **Fill in the blanks.**

   On the next page, Open Your Store: Provide Basic Information, you tell eBay what your store's all about, as shown in Figure 7-10. In addition to the name and description, you can select a logo. You can choose one of eBay's cartoonish-looking logos, which relate to merchandise categories, or you can use your own logo. If you have a logo stored on your computer, you can upload it to your eBay Store or, if your logo appears on a Web page, you can type in the Web address where eBay can find the logo. Or, if logos aren't your thing, you don't have to have one at all.

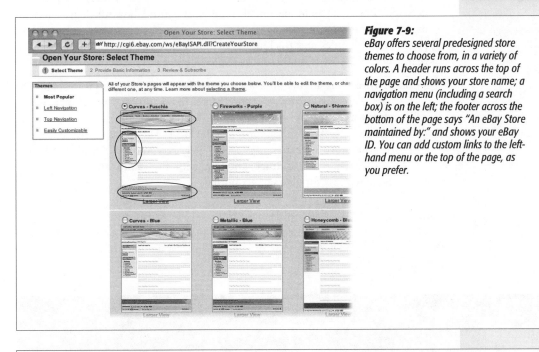

Figure 7-9:
eBay offers several predesigned store themes to choose from, in a variety of colors. A header runs across the top of the page and shows your store name; a navigation menu (including a search box) is on the left; the footer across the bottom of the page says "An eBay Store maintained by:" and shows your eBay ID. You can add custom links to the left-hand menu or the top of the page, as you prefer.

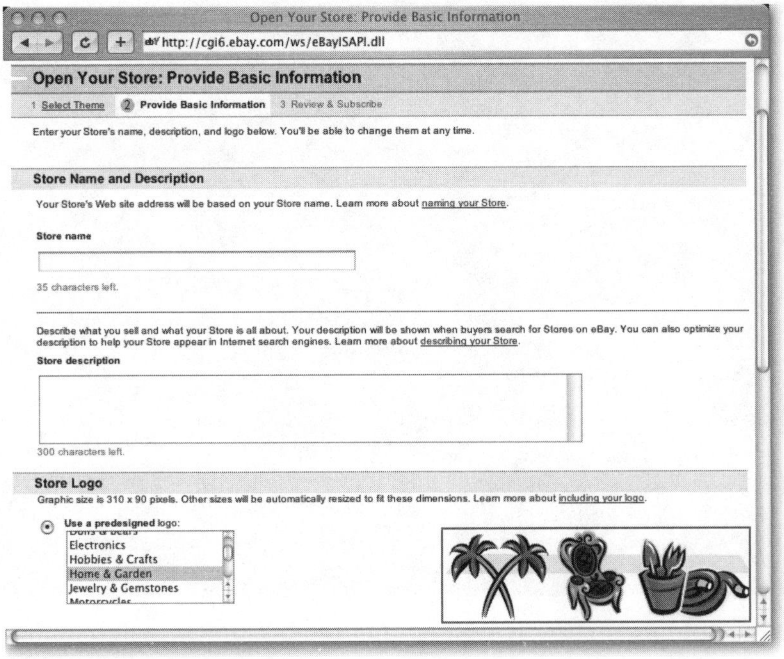

Figure 7-10:
This form asks for the name of your store, a short description, and whether or not you want to include a logo. If you already have a logo (perhaps from your own Web page), you can upload it to eBay's Picture Manager or link to it from a location on the Internet.

3. **Choose a subscription level.**

On the final page of the Open Your Store form, Review & Subscribe, the last decision eBay asks you to make is also the most painful: how much are you willing to pay each month to operate your store? All stores offer customizable pages, monthly sales and tracking reports, and cross-promotion tools. Beyond that, you can choose from three subscription levels:

- **Basic store.** This level is the cheapest and most popular, and is probably the best place to start. The basic store offers five additional pages beyond the storefront and free use of eBay Selling Manager, eBay's sales-management tool (page 332). Basic stores appear in the Stores Directory, organized by category; your store appears under every category you have items listed under. The Stores Directory is huge, though, with thousands and thousands of stores, so it's easy for yours to get buried.

Note: In February, 2005, eBay increased the monthly fee it charges for Basic stores by more than 50 percent: from $9.95 per month to $15.95 per month. This big price jump motivated many sellers to close their stores and shift their merchandise to regular auctions—or to find another online marketplace to sell their wares.

The Naming Rules

The name of your eBay Store has to be unique; you wouldn't want to deal with the confusion of two stores with identical names, anyway. Also, if it's someone else's ID, it can't be the name of your store. (You know in your heart you're not the first person to come up with *elvis4ever,* even if your store will be jam-packed with memorabilia honoring the King.)

In addition, eBay imposes these additional rules about naming:

- The name of your store must contain no more than 35 characters.

- Your store name must begin with a letter or a number.

- You've seen it in the Yellow Pages, but you can't do it on eBay: you can't have four or more consecutive *A*s at the start of the name. So *Aardvark Gifts* is OK, but *AAAA-1 Gifts* isn't.

- The name can't confuse shoppers by containing *eBay, Half.com,* or *PayPal*. Neither can you start the name with the letter *E* followed by a number, so *e8ay Electronics* or *e3Bay Toys* are out.

- You can't use the consecutive letters *www* or the characters <, >, or @ anywhere in the name. Along the same lines, your store name can't end with a top-level domain name (the last part of a Web address), like *.edu, .net, .com, .biz,* and so on. In other words, you can't use your Web site address or your e-mail address as the name of your eBay store.

- Even though you can't use another eBayer's ID for the name of your store, you can use your own.

If eBay doesn't like the store name you've chosen (or if someone else has already taken it), eBay will prompt you to change it after you've clicked Continue. Keep trying until you find a name both you and eBay like.

- **Featured store.** This level leaps forward in terms of both benefits and price; you'll have to decide whether the monthly fee of $49.99 is worth it. You get 10 pages, an upgrade to eBay Selling Manager Pro (page 333), more detailed sales reports (page 343), and a featured spot on the Stores home page. To decide whether or not a featured spot is worth the extra money, think like a buyer. How often do *you* shop eBay by starting on the Stores page and browsing the stores featured there?

- **Anchor store.** For $499.99 a month, you get all the benefits of a Featured store plus 15 pages for your merchandise, advertising on both the Stores home page and eBay itself, and 24-hour dedicated tech support (a big deal on eBay). Obviously, this option makes sense only if you're a high-volume seller with a very active store.

Managing Your Store

You've got a memorable name and a sharp-looking storefront. Now it's time to fill your digital shelves and bring on the buyers.

All your eBay listings appear in your store, so any regular auctions you have running will appear in your store automatically. However, the items you specifically list in your store appear only there. Buyers have to go to your store to find them.

Tip: If you have an eBay Store, run some regular auctions, too, to get broader exposure and cross-promote your store.

You list your store items using Store Inventory format: when you create a new listing (page 154), select "Sell your items in your own eBay Store." This format offers the lowest listing fees on eBay: just two cents per item per month. If you want the Gallery feature to show off your photos, it costs just an extra penny per item. And your listings last longer: you can choose 30, 60, 90, or 120 days for a listing, or you can make a listing good 'til canceled (GTC), which means that eBay automatically renews your listing every 30 days until the item sells or you pull the listing.

FREQUENTLY ASKED QUESTION

Good 'Til Canceled

How do fees work on a GTC listing?

A GTC listing sounds like it ought to be not just good 'til canceled but *great* 'til canceled—just one listing fee until the item sells? Well, it's not quite that great.

Even though there are no surcharges to list a GTC item, eBay does charge what it calls a Store Inventory Listing fee, currently two cents for every 30 days. That means for as long as you list an item among your store inventory, you'll pay two cents per month until the item sells or you cancel the listing.

Not a bad price, but it's still a recurring charge to keep in mind—and it can add up if your store has lots of items that aren't selling from one month to the next. In addition, if you've chosen any optional bells or whistles for an extra charge, you pay for those every 30 days, as well.

Tip: eBay Stores let you list multiple examples of a single item. So if you have a lot of dessert spoons to sell, list them only once; don't create a separate listing for each spoon. If you list the spoon once, allowing buyers to choose how many spoons they want to buy in a transaction, you'll save on listing fees *and* save yourself the inconvenience of having to relist a new spoon each time you sell one.

I-need-a-vacation mode

It sounds convenient to be able to list many items that automatically renew themselves, but what if you go on vacation? Do you have to cancel every single item in your Store until you come back—or else risk angry customers? eBay offers Store owners Vacation Hold, which lets you put your store on hold in various ways when you're not around to pack and ship items.

Here's how to do it: on your My eBay page (page 32), find My Subscriptions and then click Manage Your Store → "Change vacation settings." Choose the settings you want:

- **Hide all your Store listings.** This option hides your Store inventory, but it doesn't work for regular auctions, so be sure to cancel those if necessary, or else plan ahead so all your current auctions end before you plan to leave.

- **Place an "on vacation" message in your Store.** eBay has a prewritten message you must use, which includes the date you'll be back.

- **Place an "on vacation" message in individual listings.** This option applies to all active listings, not just Store inventory.

After you've selected the option you want, click "Turn vacation settings On," and then click Save Settings. Now you're ready to head for the beach, the city lights, or that cabin in the mountains.

Bulk editing

One great time-saving feature of eBay Stores is that you can edit multiple items at once. If your waffle makers are selling like hotcakes and you want to raise the Buy It Now price, you can do it for all the waffle makers in your store.

To edit a bunch of items at once, go to My eBay → Items I'm Selling, click the Format drop-down menu, and select Store Inventory. Click Go. Turn on the checkbox next to each item you want to edit. When you've selected all the items you want to change, click Edit Item. The Edit Item page opens; make the changes you want, and then click Submit. You've edited a whole list of items with just a few mouse clicks!

Cross-promotions

The Cross-Promotions tool, available only to sellers with eBay Stores, lets you get the right item in front of a potential buyer at just the right time—when they're already looking at what you have to sell. With the Cross-Promotions tool, you can display items from your store on your auction page. So, buyers who are about to bid can keep shopping, heading straight to your store. Figure 7-11 shows what a cross-promotion looks like.

Figure 7-11:
Cross-promotions appear at the bottom of an auction page, just above your shipping and payment details. Clicking any ad takes the buyer to the relevant auction.

When you open a Store, eBay has already set things up to cross-promote items in the same or similar categories when buyers browse your auctions. If a shopper bids or buys, four cross-promoted items appear on the confirmation page.

But if you don't like eBay's choices, you can modify the cross-promotion to feature the items you really want to sell. Try featuring slow-moving items (you know people would buy the product if only they thought to look for it!) or high-value items that mean more profit for you. To change cross-promotion rules, head to the auction page of the listing you want (find it in My eBay's Selling view under Items I'm Selling). Click "Change cross-promotions" and swap in the items you want to display.

Selling Internationally

eBay is a worldwide marketplace—with eBayers in more than 150 countries—and you can expand your sales reach dramatically if you're willing to sell beyond the borders of the U.S. And theoretically, the more bidders you attract to your auctions, wherever they happen to live, the higher your selling price. That said, if you're thinking of selling internationally, you need to consider the hassles and extra expenses involved, including how you'll communicate with buyers, how you'll get paid, and how you'll deal with shipping and customs issues. Knowing both the advantages and the difficulties of international selling lets you make an informed decision about whether to expand your business overseas.

Parlez-Vous eBay?

One of the first difficulties in selling internationally is communicating with your potential buyer. Their English might be hard to understand, and your ability to speak French or Portuguese or German or Italian or Spanish or Dutch—to name just a few possibilities—might be nonexistent in a transaction already made more complex by customs, tariffs, and other restrictions. The result? More misunderstandings and, possibly, negative feedback for you.

Tip: When you're communicating with a buyer whose native language isn't English, try not to use slang or abbreviations. Avoid words the reader can't look up in a dictionary.

If you've received an email in a language you don't understand, visit AltaVista's free translator, Babel Fish (the name's an homage to Douglas Adams's *Hitchhiker's Guide to the Galaxy*), at *http://babelfish.altavista.com*. You can copy and paste in the text of the email and get a rough translation. (You can only paste in up to 150 words—about half a page of text—at a time. If your email is longer, just break it up into a couple of segments.) The translator is far from perfect, but Babel Fish should give you the gist of what your buyer wants to tell you. Similarly, if you want to communicate in the buyer's language, you can type your message in English into the "Translate a block of text" text box, and then have Babel Fish translate it into the language you want. Currently, Babel Fish can translate between English and the following languages: Chinese, Dutch, French, German, Greek, Italian, Japanese, Korean, Portuguese, Russian, and Spanish.

You can also get translation help without leaving eBay, thanks to multilingual eBayers willing to share their expertise. On the navigation bar, click Community → Discussion Boards → International Trading. Post the text of the non-English email and give the post a title that indicates you're looking for help with a translation.

Money Makes the World Go 'Round

Whatever the language, getting paid is sweet. But before you list international auctions, give some thought to how you'll get your money. Different currencies can make things complicated. How much is a euro or a Canadian dollar worth today in U.S. dollars? How much will it be worth two weeks from now? Even if you know how much your selling price is in the buyer's local currency, you've got to receive payment in a form you can use. There are several ways to do this.

- **Let the buyer worry about currency conversion.** In the "Shipping, payment details, and return policy" section of your auction page, spell out that you accept payment only in your local currency. Buyers will have to pay any conversion fee; you just wait for the money to arrive. This is the easiest option. Be aware, though, that if the buyer sends you a check drawn on a foreign bank, it might take a whole month for that check to clear, no matter what currency it's in.

Tip: To get up-to-the-minute currency values, use an online currency converter, like the one at *www.xe.com/ucc*.

- **Accept PayPal.** A more flexible strategy is to accept international payments through PayPal. More than 45 countries have access to PayPal (Figure 7-12). Buyers can pay using yen, euros, British pounds, or Canadian, Australian, or U.S. dollars. You receive payment in the currency of your choice. Better yet, there's no currency charge for currency exchange when you withdraw funds to your local bank account. Be aware, though, that PayPal's Seller Protection (page 170) does not cover most international sales.

Note: To see which currencies work with PayPal, visit PayPal's Multiple Currencies Center. On Paypal.com, go to Merchant Tools → View Directory of Tools. Scroll down the list to Currency Manager and then click Learn More.

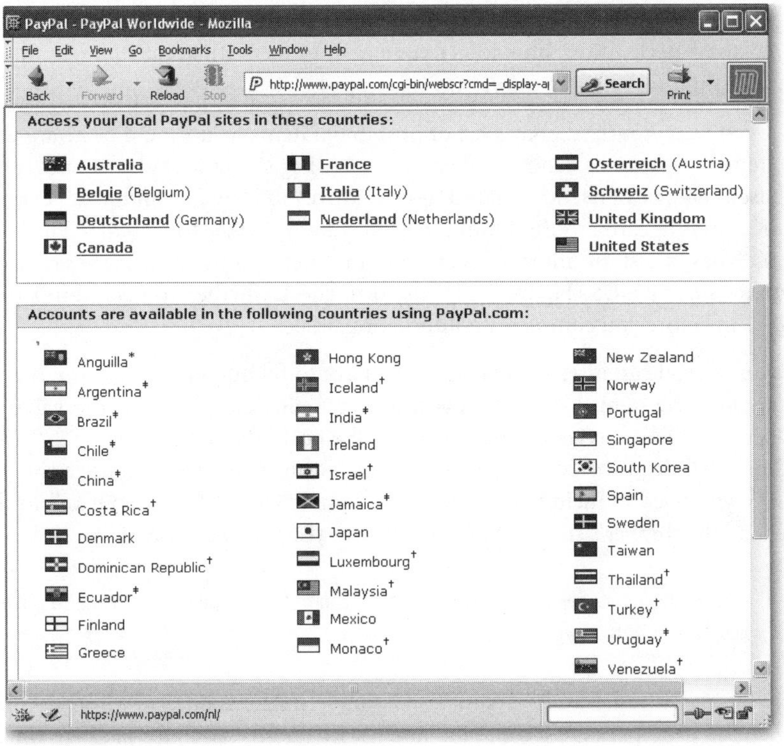

Figure 7-12:
To see the current list of countries whose residents can use PayPal, go to www.paypal.com/cgi-bin/ webscr?cmd=_display-approved-signup-countries-outside. Countries at the top of the page have local PayPal sites; residents of countries in the bottom part of the page can open an account on www.paypal.com.

- **Use BidPay.** Another option is BidPay, Western Union's money-order service designed for online auction payments (page 56). For sellers, the cool thing about BidPay is that the buyer pays the fee (just like when you purchase a money order at the post office, a store, or a bank). For U.S. sellers, BidPay will send you a money order or deposit funds directly into your U.S. checking account—your choice. Go to *www.bidpay.com* and click "Sign in/Register" to set up a BidPay account.

- **Consider bank wire transfers.** Bank wire transfers are a popular payment method in Europe. A bank wire transfer is different from an instant wire transfer (the kind Chapter 4 warns you about), because the money is wired directly into your checking account, rather than picked up at a Western Union office. It's a safe, secure way to receive money; just make sure that the buyer sends payment in your local currency so you don't have to pay exchange fees. Some sellers don't like to give out their checking account information (even though that's exactly what you do every time you write a check); if you're uncomfortable making that information known, be sure that potential buyers understand that you don't accept bank wire transfers.

Worldwide Shipping

International shipping is about more than just calculating rates. You need to know what you can't ship out of your country (or into a particular country), how to fill out a customs declaration, how to get your item to its destination in a reasonable amount of time, and how to prove you've shipped.

Even if you've memorized eBay's list of prohibited items, you should be aware that some items are illegal to send to other countries. For example, did you know that U.S.-based sellers can't send certain kinds of knives to New Zealand, beef jerky to the U.K., playing cards to the Philippines, or a baby walker to Canada? The UPS Web site has a list of international shipping regulations at *www.ups.com/ga/CountryRegs?loc=en_US* (Figure 7-13). Use it to check whether you can ship a particular item before you complete an international sale.

After you've made an international sale, you have to fill out a customs form before you can ship the item, listing the package's contents and declaring the value of those contents. You can get customs forms at the post office or go to *www.usps.com* and choose All Products & Services → Customs Forms Online. If you use a shipper like UPS, you need to include three copies of your invoice (that is, your bill to the buyer) and the shipper's shipping document with your customs form.

Note: The U.S. Postal Service has three different types of customs forms. Find out which one you should use, and when, at *www.usps.com/global/customs.htm*.

When your package gets to its destination country, customs officers will review the form, check your package's contents, and—with luck—send the package on its way. Sometimes, however, the Customs Office will hold on to the package for a while. If a customs duty is due, the buyer may have to make a trip to the customs office to pay the duty and pick up the package.

Some international buyers will ask you to declare that the item is a gift or write in a value that's less than the item's cost so that the buyer can save on customs duties.

This is a bad idea. Not only is lying on a customs form against the law, you can't claim insurance on the full amount if the package is lost or damaged. To avoid being put in a sticky situation by an insistent buyer, state clearly in your terms of sale that international buyers are responsible for all taxes and duties associated with the purchase. Then fill out the customs form to reflect the actual price of the item. Don't include shipping and handling in the price you specify; the buyer shouldn't have to pay tax on those.

Tip: To make sure that an international buyer isn't overcharged on customs duties, remove any original price tags from the item before you ship—especially if those price tags reflect a higher price than the buyer paid you. If the package is opened by Customs, officials may charge a duty based on the price tags, not on what you say the buyer paid.

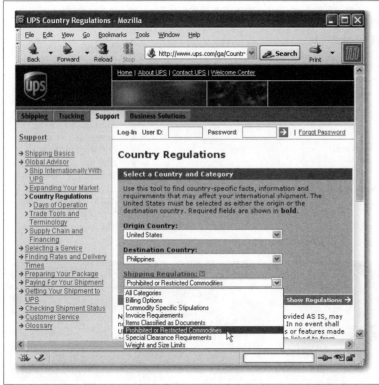

Figure 7-13:
Know what you can't ship before you try to sell contraband on eBay. Choose the destination country, and then select Prohibited or Restricted Commodities from the drop-down list. Click Show Regulations to find out what's taboo.

What's the cheapest way to ship internationally? "Cheap" may not be the best word to use here. It's expensive to send items overseas. The U.S. Postal Service is probably the least expensive way to go; to get an idea of how much shipping will be to a particular country or region, use the calculator at *http://ircalc.usps.gov* (Figure 7-14).

For some countries, such as Canada, the U.S. Postal Service is the only shipper that does not charge the buyer hefty "brokerage" (in addition to the customs duties the buyer must pay). Before you select a private shipper, like UPS or FedEx, be sure to check out brokerage fees that shipper charges. If your buyer refuses to pay the brokerage fee, you could get stuck with the bill.

Private shippers like UPS and FedEx offer tracking (so you can prove an item arrived at its destination) and fast delivery, but these shippers tend to be pricey. To compare prices, go to the Web site of your favorite shipper (*www.ups.com*, *www.fedex.com*, *www.dhl-usa.com*, and so on) and use their shipping calculator to get an estimate.

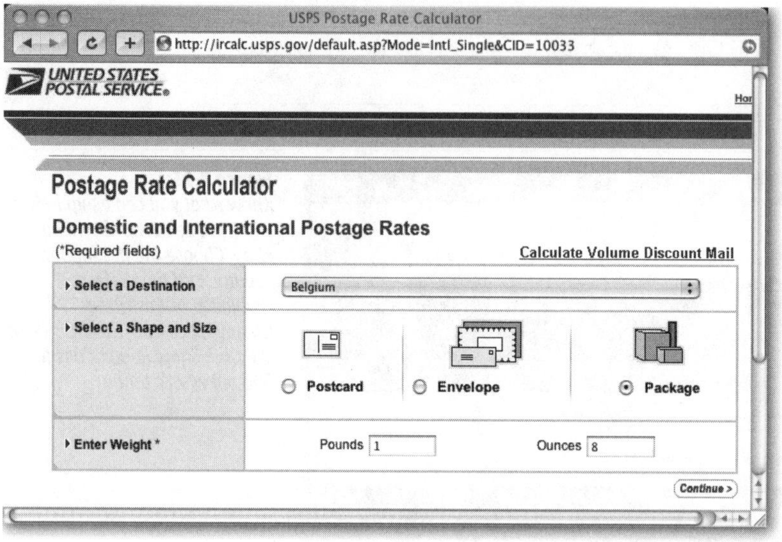

Figure 7-14:
Calculating international shipping costs is easy using the U.S. Postal Service's Postage Rate Calculator. All you have to do is select your package's destination country and size, type in its weight, and then click Continue. The next pages let you select the shipping type and speed (Global Express Mail, Airmail Parcel Post, and so on) and any extra services you want, like a Certificate of Mailing. After you click Add Extra Services, the calculator displays the total it will cost to mail the package to your destination country.

FREQUENTLY ASKED QUESTION

Global Warning

I've heard lots of stories of international scams. Is it safe to sell outside the U.S.?

There's nothing inherently dangerous about international transactions. You just have to use a little common sense when dealing with people you don't know, whether they live across town or on the other side of the globe.

That's not to say that international sellers don't have problems. Many of the credit card and cashier's check scams that plague eBayers originate beyond the U.S. Don't get greedy; scammers prey on greed. If a buyer is offering you a deal that seems too good to be true, it probably is. Don't

use any international escrow service other than those approved by eBay (go to *http://pages.ebay.com/help/sell/escrow.html#escrow* to see the list of international escrow sites). As long as you're aware of the scams (page 232) and use common sense in your trading, you'll avoid the handful of international scammers and have the pleasure of doing business with the many honest eBayers who live outside the U.S.

If you decide to restrict your auctions to certain countries, you can block bidders from countries you don't ship to (page 227).

Sell for Others

You know how to move items on eBay—how to write good auction descriptions, set a price, and take enticing photos. There are plenty of people out there who'd love to pay you for those skills.

A 2004 Nielsen survey found that the average American household has more than $2,200 worth of unused stuff lying around: computers, cell phones, cameras, jewelry, and more. (That was the purchase price; the secondhand items in decent condition are probably worth about a thousand bucks.) Multiply that by the number of households in your area, and each street becomes a hidden gold mine.

You can build your eBay business by selling items on consignment for people who are either unfamiliar with eBay or who don't have time to list and manage auctions on their own. Instead of hunting down suppliers, you can have suppliers come to you. You run the auction and claim a commission when the item sells. You can choose from several different selling-for-others options.

Become a Trading Assistant

eBay has a program for consignment sellers, called *Trading Assistants* (TAs). It doesn't cost anything to join, and it's easy to qualify for the program; once you do, eBay includes you in its directory of trading assistants so that other eBayers can find you. You also get a logo to include in your listings, which gives you some marketing reach; eBayers who buy from you might also ask about your TA services.

To become a TA, you must be a registered seller and meet these criteria:

- You must have sold four or more items in the past 30 days.

- Your feedback score must be 50 or higher. (That's *total* feedback, not feedback as a seller.)

- Your positive feedback rating must be 97 percent or better.

- Your eBay account must be in good standing.

It's possible to become a TA by buying enough items to get your feedback score up to 50, then selling four items and signing up, but it's a good idea to have some real selling experience before you take the TA plunge. You'll be offering your services as a seller to other people; to get repeat customers, be sure that you're an effective seller before you start.

To sign up, from the eBay home page, click Services → Trading Assistants → Create/Edit TA Profile. Your profile includes your phone number and location (folks looking for a TA search the directory by Zip code); items you specialize in selling; a short description of the services you offer; and your fees, terms, and conditions.

Note: You don't have to be a registered TA to sell consignment items on eBay. You can sell items on behalf of other people at any time. Registering as a TA just makes your consignment business more visible by listing it in the TA Directory.

Setting up shop as a trading assistant

You can become a TA the moment you meet eBay's criteria. Before you set up shop, however, you need to make a number of decisions:

- **Drop off, pick up, or both?** How will your clients get their items to you? Some TAs have a storefront where clients can drop off items. Others let clients bring items to their homes. Still others prefer to go to the client's house to pick up items. Each has its problems: renting a storefront is expensive and may not be cost-effective when you're starting out. Letting clients bring items to your home is convenient, but many TAs aren't comfortable giving out their home address—especially when their home is full of valuable items to sell. Picking up items means the hassle of driving all over the map to meet with prospective clients. (And most clients will want your contact information before you drive off with their stuff, so print up a batch of business cards with a physical address on them.)

- **To specialize or not to specialize?** If you've got expertise in a certain field or you've developed a successful selling presence on eBay for a particular kind of item, consider specializing in your consignment sales, as well. You've already got the buyers; offer them more of what they love to buy.

- **How much will you charge?** Many TAs charge around 20 to 25 percent of the winning bid, plus eBay and PayPal fees. Others base their fees on a sliding scale, much like eBay's FVFs. For example, a TA might charge 40 percent of the winning bid for items that sell for less than $50; 30 percent for items that sell for $50 to $150; and 20 percent for items that sell for more than $150. Research other TAs in your area to see what's competitive.

- **Minimum value?** It's not worth your time to sell a lot of cheap items for a few cents' profit. eBay recommends that TAs set a minimum value of $50 on items they'll agree to sell. Some TAs have raised the bar, setting a minimum of $75 or $100.

- **What if the item doesn't sell?** If you list an item on consignment and it doesn't sell, the item's owner should pay the listing fees. But you've spent time creating and managing an auction; consider charging a flat fee for your services if the item doesn't sell. Many TAs charge an up-front fee of $10–$15, which counts toward their commission if the item sells. Also, don't let clients dump their junk on you. If an item doesn't sell, reserve the right to dispose of it if the owner hasn't picked it up after a few weeks.

Think about these issues ahead of time. Check out other TAs' policies by looking them up in the TA Directory (click Services → Trading Assistants → Find a Trading Assistant). When you've done your research and planned ahead, you can write a good service description and set policies that will attract clients to your consignment business.

When you become a member of eBay's TA club, you get a "badge" to prove it. You can add the Registered Trading Assistant logo to your auction listings. Here's how:

1. **Find your TA number.**

   After you've registered as a TA (page 273), find your listing in the Trading Assistant Directory: from the eBay home page, click Services → Trading Assistants, type your Zip code into the text box, and then click the Search button. When you find your own listing, click it. Your TA number is at the very end of the Web address for your directory listing, after this text: *profile&profileId=*. So, if the address for your eBay listing is *contact.ebay.com/ws/eBayISAPI.dll?TradingAssistant&page=profile&profileId=123*, your TA number is 123. (In reality, the numbers are several digits longer than that.)

2. **When you create a new auction, add the logo to your listing.**

   eBay provides HTML code to put the TA logo on your auctions. To add it, type the following code into your item description with one change; replace *XXXXX* with your TA number:

   ```
   <center>
   <a href="http://contact.ebay.com/ws/eBayISAPI.
   dll?TradingAssistant&page=profile&profileId=XXXXX">
   <b>I am a Trading Assistant - I can sell items for you!</b>
   <br>
   <img scr="http://pics.ebaystatic.com/aw/pics/tradingAssistant/imgTA_88x33.
   gif" vspace="5"
   border="0" height="33" width="88"> </a>
   <br>
   </center>
   ```

Tip: To get a version of this code that you can cut and paste into your form (and then edit), head to MissingManuals.com, click the link for Missing CD-ROMs, and then click the link for this book. There you'll find a downloadable copy of this code.

This code displays the words *I am a Trading Assistant – I can sell items for you!* and the TA logo on your auction pages. Anyone who clicks the logo is taken to your listing in the TA directory.

Tips for TAs

When you sell for others, you're putting your reputation on the line. Think ahead to minimize problems and keep your feedback rating high. Here's a list of best practices for selling consigned items:

- **Have items in hand.** Before you list any item, make sure you have physical possession of it. Inspect it to make sure that it works and has all its parts. Not only does having the item in front of you prevent you from creating inaccurate listings, it also prevents the seller from misplacing it (or selling it or giving it away) between the time you list the auction and the time someone wins it.

- **Know your consignor.** Don't become an unwitting fence. To discourage crooks from bringing you stolen items to sell, authenticate each consignor's identity. Ask to see a driver's license, and write down the license number.

- **Get it in writing.** Don't assume that the consignor understands and agrees to all your terms. Draw up a contract to spell things out, and get it signed. Your contract should include information about the consignor (name and contact information), the item (age, condition, known problems), the auction (format, length of listing, starting/reserve price, number of photos, any listing features), and your terms as a consignment seller (fee schedule, any flat rate, terms of payment, what to do if the item doesn't sell).

- **Get advice.** Not sure what to put into your contract? Uncertain about what to charge? Go to the Trading Assistant Discussion Board (Community → Discussion Boards → Trading Assistant) and ask.

Some generous souls there will share their contract boilerplate and answer your questions.

- **Do your homework.** Research items to determine their likely value, just as you would if they were your own. Check eBay's recent sales and other Web sites. Consider having jewelry appraised. Get as much information as you can from the seller about the item's history, so that you can write an appealing item description.

- **Manage expectations.** Many clients have heard about eBay but don't understand what's realistic in terms of actually selling on the site. They might think a family heirloom is worth far more than buyers searching for a bargain are willing to pay. Or they might not understand that a "gently worn" designer suit is worth considerably less than they paid for it. Your research skills will help your clients come up with reasonable expectations about how much they can get for their goods. If a client insists that you list a $50 teapot with a $100 reserve, it's probably better to turn down the consignment than to deal with a disappointed consignor. After the auction, continue to keep the client informed: show her the bid history and final price at the auction's close.

- **Pay promptly.** You expect it of buyers, and you owe it to your client. As soon as the transaction is finished, send your client the money you owe her (minus, of course, your fees). Some TAs pay as soon as they receive the buyer's money. Others wait to make sure the buyer is happy and doesn't want to return the item. Either way, explain your terms and pay your client as soon as possible.

Find Business Beyond eBay

Your trading assistant logo can help you find clients already on eBay, but consignment sellers should look further afield to drum up business. There are many people out there who've heard about eBay but who, for one reason or another, will never even look around the site, let alone register or try their hand at selling. These people are perfect clients for consignment sellers.

Here are some ideas for bringing clients to you:

- **Advertise your services in local publications.** Try running a small display ad or classified ad in your local newspaper. Trade papers, like a regional newsletter for antiques dealers, are also a good place to find clients with an interest in what you can sell for them. Weekly papers and regional publications can offer good rates.

Note: If you're a Trading Assistant who's also a PowerSeller, eBay will help you pay for advertising, reimbursing you for 25 percent of insertion fees through its Co-op Advertising Program (page 280).

- **Create flyers and put them up around town.** Make sure you do this legally; many communities don't allow flyers to be stapled to trees, telephone poles, fences, and so on. You probably don't want to get the kind of free publicity that comes with a court appearance. Many bookstores, coffee shops, and convenience stores have bulletin boards you can use, but always remember to ask first.

- **Hand out business cards.** Carry a good supply of business cards and be ready to pass them around. You never know when you'll meet a prospective client, from the line at the grocery store to your spouse's office party to the tag sales and auctions you attend looking for merchandise.

- **Offer a local seminar about online auctions.** Contact your local community college to see if they'll host a course about buying and selling on eBay. You might have several class meetings or just one. Let your students know about your services as a Trading Assistant. You don't need any special certification to teach about eBay—just your own experience and business smarts. If you want the official eBay stamp of approval, though, you can take an online course to become an "Education Specialist Trained by eBay." To sign up, go to *www.poweru.net/ebay*, as shown in Figure 7-15.

Tip: For more marketing ideas, see page 214.

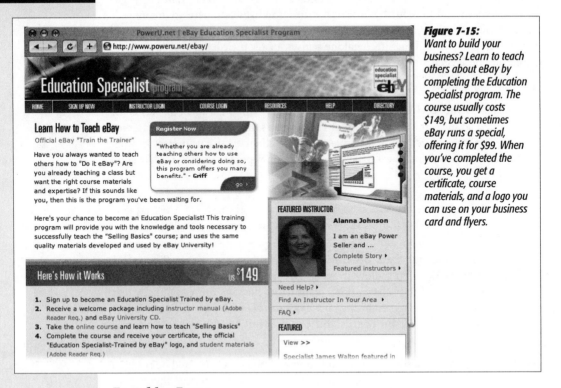

Figure 7-15:
Want to build your business? Learn to teach others about eBay by completing the Education Specialist program. The course usually costs $149, but sometimes eBay runs a special, offering it for $99. When you've completed the course, you get a certificate, course materials, and a logo you can use on your business card and flyers.

Franchise Fever

One of the fastest-growing trends in online sales is the *drop-off franchise*. When you buy a franchise, a central company gives you permission to sell its goods or services in a particular location. Many fast-food restaurants operate as franchises; they're owned and operated locally but sell the brand of a national company. A drop-off franchise lets you run a consignment business.

When you open a franchise, you tap into a network of similar stores. The franchiser supplies you with a professional logo, software, marketing materials, and a store design, so you don't have to do any of that from scratch. Franchisers offer training and ongoing support. And as franchises multiply, your store will have nationwide recognition.

The catch is that it can cost a lot of money to buy a franchise: you'll have to pay a franchise fee as well as startup costs, which can easily add up to $80,000 or more just to open your doors. And you have to do things by the book, buying supplies through the franchiser and following their prescribed business practices, cutting into your profits and cramping your style.

That said, drop-off franchises are booming across the country. In time, one or more franchise operations might develop the same brand recognition as the giants of franchising, like McDonald's or Subway. The following list shows some of the drop-off franchises now leaping out of the starting gate. All of them have information about franchise opportunities on their Web sites:

- QuikDrop (*www.quikdropfranchise.com*)
- iSold It (*www.i-soldit.com*)
- Snappy Auctions (*www.snappyauctions.com*)
- NuMarkets (*www.numarkets.com/franchise*)
- Orbit Drop (*www.orbitdrop.com*)

Become a PowerSeller

PowerSeller is the designation eBay gives its best sellers—the superheroes of the eBay universe. As you ramp up your eBay sales, you might be able to join their elite ranks.

This section describes how to qualify for PowerSeller status, what the program offers, and a couple of surprising reasons why some sellers choose not to participate in this popular program.

Join the Big Leagues

There's no charge to become a PowerSeller, but you do have to measure up in terms of sales, feedback, and customer satisfaction. Here's what you need to become a PowerSeller:

- An eBay registration at least 90 days old.
- Average sales of at least $1,000 per month for three months in a row.
- A total of 100 or more feedbacks with a 98 percent positive rating.
- An account in good standing.

When your account satisfies these criteria, eBay invites you to become a Power-Seller; you don't have to do anything. You get a nifty PowerSeller logo to stick next to your eBay ID and add to your auction pages, along with some other benefits (page 280).

Warning: One kind of scam making the rounds is a fake invitation to become a PowerSeller, providing a link you click to "accept" the invitation. In fact, the link leads to a phony Web site that tries to collect details about you and your eBay account. Don't become a victim. Forward any suspicious emails to *spoof@ebay.com*. If you think the invitation is genuine, log in to eBay, go to your My eBay page, and check your messages. Official eBay communications appear there.

Once you've become a PowerSeller, you must maintain the high standards that got you into the program. If your sales volume or your feedback rating dips, you could lose your PowerSeller status.

Membership Has Its Privileges (and Problems)

Besides the cool logo, what does becoming a PowerSeller have to offer? Some benefits are open to all PowerSellers; others depend on the level. There are five levels of PowerSeller, as shown in Table 7-1, and the more you sell, the higher you climb.

Table 7-1. PowerSeller Levels

Level	Minimum Monthly Sales Volume
Bronze	$1,000
Silver	$3,000
Gold	$10,000
Platinum	$25,000
Titanium	$150,000

eBay makes the following benefits available to all PowerSellers (some are free, others aren't):

• Personalized sales and feedback information.

• A discussion board open only to PowerSellers.

• A monthly email newsletter and a quarterly print newsletter.

• Co-op advertising (eBay helps pay your advertising costs) for PowerSellers who are also Trading Assistants or own an eBay Store.

• Health insurance for PowerSellers and their employees.

• Free banner ads in eBay's Keyword Ads program (page 197), up to $200 per quarter.

• PowerSeller logo merchandise and stationery templates.

Some benefits—like improved customer support—become available as you climb the PowerSeller ladder. (To get the details, go to Services → PowerSeller Program → Program Benefits.) All levels of PowerSeller receive priority customer support via email. Silver and above get toll-free telephone support. And gold and above also get a real, live account manager. Of course, as some eBayers have pointed out, if you've got eBay figured out well enough to make PowerSeller status, you probably won't need to call that coveted phone number for help too often.

Other benefits are less tangible. Some eBay buyers seek out the PowerSeller logo for assurance that they're dealing with a professional seller. All other things being equal (price, shipping cost, feedback rating), many buyers will choose a PowerSeller over a lower-volume seller. So joining the program can boost your sales.

On the other hand, some sellers who are qualified for the PowerSeller program choose not to become PowerSellers (or choose not to display the PowerSeller logo on their auctions). Why? They cite a number of reasons:

- Some eBayers have high expectations of PowerSellers—they want super-fast shipping and personalized service, and believe PowerSellers are just the ones who'll give them these things. But it can be hard to meet inflated expectations when you're dealing with many sales each day, so buyers end up disappointed—and leave the feedback to say so—even when you've shipped their items as quickly as you could.

- Many eBay newbies are attracted to PowerSellers; they feel safer buying from someone with this recognition from eBay. While this is a great way to attract new customers, it can also be a hassle to deal with buyers who don't yet understand how eBay works.

- Other eBayers who've been around for a while feel, fairly or unfairly, that PowerSellers are the wrong people to rely on for customer service. They figure that PowerSellers do enough business that they don't care about whether or not a particular buyer is happy.

If you want to avoid these hassles, you can choose not to display the PowerSeller logo next to your eBay ID. From your My eBay page, go to Preferences → Seller Preferences to hide the logo.

UP TO SPEED

Different Strokes for PowerSelling Folks

You might occasionally notice an eBayer whose feedback rating is below 98 percent but who still has the PowerSeller logo next to his ID. What gives?

eBay uses a different, behind-the-scenes method to calculate PowerSellers' feedback scores. To get the feedback rating displayed on a Member Profile page, eBay counts feedback from individual eBayers. So if you buy five items from the same seller and leave positive feedback for each one, that seller's feedback rating goes up by just one. The feedback score is the result of adding up all the unique positive feedbacks and dividing them by the total number of positive and negative feedbacks. That percentage is the number you see when you check someone's Member Profile.

Somewhere in the depths of its operations, eBay looks at PowerSeller feedback differently. The feedback score used for the PowerSeller program counts each and every feedback separately. So if you buy five items from a PowerSeller and leave five positive feedbacks, in eBay's eyes that increases the feedback score by five. You won't see that number on the Member Profile page, but it's how eBay keeps score—for PowerSellers only.

eBay says that high-volume sales and repeat customers mean that PowerSellers deserve to have their feedback rating calculated differently. Happy repeat buyers are a good thing, and the eBay community should know about that by seeing who's earned PowerSeller status. On the other hand, some eBayers question why eBay should treat PowerSellers differently. Aren't happy repeat buyers a good thing no matter what your sales volume is?

CHAPTER 8

Specialty Selling

In recent years, eBay has worked to grow beyond its early reputation as the World's Biggest Flea Market. Now, the company also wants you to think of it as the World's Largest Big-ticket and Specialty-item Market. Less catchy, but potentially more lucrative.

eBay blazed trails into online car and house buying—items that were once thought off-limits for online sales. It took a little over four years, from April 2000 to June 2004, to reach one million car sales on eBay; now eBay Motors accounts for nearly one-third of eBay sales volume—and is still growing fast. Real estate listings have increased more than 35 times over since 1999, and real estate is one of the most popular categories for browsing.

In addition, eBay's other specialty categories, including Half.com, Giving Works, and Live Auctions, are all doing robust business. (In Half.com's case, business kept booming despite eBay's efforts to shut down the site.)

This chapter shows you how to get in on the action and create a sales niche within eBay's specialty auctions:

- **Half.com:** books, CDs, video games, and more.
- **eBay Motors:** cars, motorcycles, and just about anything else with a motor.
- **Real estate auctions:** houses, land, and time-shares.
- **Live auctions:** bringing eBay into your brick-and-mortar auctions.
- **Giving Works:** auctions to benefit nonprofit groups.
- **B2B auctions:** from one business to another.
- **Elance:** sell your services.

Half.com: Mass Media Mania

You buy a video game and play it until you've mastered it. Then what do you do with it? You can let it lie around and collect dust, or you can sell it on Half.com and put the money toward a new, more challenging game. The same thing goes for books you've read, movies you've watched, and CDs that have worked their way to the back of your collection.

Half.com specializes in fixed-price books (including audio books and textbooks), movies, music, video games, and video game systems. People who shop the site go there for good deals on used or remaindered mass media items.

Registering on Half.com

If you have an eBay account, you also have an account on Half.com, but the two sites require separate seller registrations if you want to sell on both. Moreover, some people like to use separate IDs for selling on the two sites; for example, you might have one account on eBay to sell estate jewelry and another on Half.com to get rid of books you've read and movies you've watched.

Note: One way that eBay has limited Half.com's growth is by restricting who can trade there. Only people who live in the U.S. can sell on Half.com. (The U.S. includes military personnel who are stationed overseas and have an APO or FPO mailing address.) Canadians can buy on Half.com but cannot sell on the site. Others who live outside the U.S. can neither buy nor sell on Half.com. If you don't live in the U.S., Half.com directs you to eBay.

To create a Half.com account, go to *www.half.com*, look in the upper-right corner of the page, and click the "sign in" link. On the page that opens, click Register. The registration process is the same as for eBay (page 4).

When you list your first item on Half.com, the site asks you to register as a seller, even if you have a seller's account on eBay. There are two steps to creating a Half.com seller's account:

1. **Provide credit card information, a billing address, and contact information.**

   Half.com collects this information to verify your identity. Unlike eBay, where you can avoid giving your credit card information by getting ID-verified (page 155), you must submit a credit card number to sell on Half.com.

2. **Provide your bank account number and choose shipping options.**

   Half.com makes payments directly into your checking account, so you must supply the name of your bank, its routing number, and the account number you want deposits to go to. (The numbers appear at the bottom of your checks.) Half.com sellers must agree to ship via U.S. Media Mail. You can also give buyers the option of choosing faster shipping at a higher price.

Tip: Offering expedited shipping is a good idea. It might make all the difference to a buyer who needs an item fast, like a student who needs a textbook at the start of a new term.

When you've completed these two steps, click Register. Half.com adds you to the ranks of its sellers and takes you back to the process of listing your item.

Half.com: Mass
Media Mania

UP TO SPEED

A Little Half.com History

Half.com, launched by entrepreneur Joshua Kopelman in July 1999, began as a place where people could sell their used mass media: books, CDs, video games, movies, software, and so on. Sellers set a fixed price for their items, but that price had to be at least 50 percent lower than the retail price. Hence the name.

By offering a central location where sellers could easily weed out their CD or video collections and make a little money, Half.com quickly developed a following. Students, for example, could resell their textbooks at prices that offered buyers a bargain and sellers a leg up on college bookstores' buyback prices. Within months of its launch, Half.com started to appear on top-10 lists ranking online retail sites. In December 2000, one out of every eight online shoppers visited the site, situating it just behind Amazon.com and eBay in popularity.

One difference between Half.com and eBay was the fixed price sellers set for each item on Half.com. Another was the way the site made its money. Rather than charging listing fees and following up with Final Value Fees, Half.com collected buyers' payments, then, twice a month, sent that money to sellers minus a 15 percent commission. Half.com handled the credit card transactions; sellers didn't have to set up a merchant account, and buyers felt safe knowing that the company—not an individual seller—was processing their credit card numbers.

On its meteoric rise to popularity, Half.com developed a reputation for some newsworthy marketing gimmicks. In 1999, it paid $100,000 to the town of Halfway, Oregon, and installed a couple dozen computers in schools there. In exchange, the tiny town of 345 residents agreed to change its name to Half.com. (You can check out the town's Web site at *http://town.half.com*.) Half.com also printed ads on peanut bags—about "buying for peanuts," natch—and offered tiny $5 coupons inside millions of fortune cookies.

In the summer of 2000, when Half.com had barely reached the ripe old age of one year, eBay snapped up the company in a $300 million stock deal. About the same time, eBay instituted a fixed-price option on its own site: Buy It Now. eBay integrated the two sites' feedback and registration systems (causing major migraines for some Half.com sellers when their inventories and selling histories disappeared) and for a while toyed with the idea of renaming Half.com "eBay Express Buys." For the next few years, it seemed like eBay didn't really know what to do with a fixed-price subsidiary—not many shoppers even realized that Half.com was part of eBay—and in March 2003 eBay announced plans to phase out Half.com and "migrate" its items to a section of eBay called, lamely, "The Half Zone."

Half.com sellers rebelled. They preferred Half.com's fee structure, which charged a seller only when an item sold (no up-front listing fees like on eBay). And they worried that the projected closing date for Half.com—July 13, 2004—would ruin their prime selling season: the back-to-school market. Sellers lobbied eBay vigorously to save Half.com, or at least delay its demise until after students had bought their textbooks. eBay agreed to postpone the closing until October 14, 2004.

But then two things happened: many sellers didn't budge, refusing to transfer their inventories to eBay, and traffic on the site didn't slow down. New buyers and sellers kept right on registering and using the site. And some Half.com sellers defected to other e-commerce sites, like Amazon, rather than list their items on eBay, complaining that owning an eBay Store for low-cost items like used books and CDs was just too expensive.

In September, 2004, eBay relented and announced that Half.com would operate indefinitely as an independent site: Half.com by eBay.

CHAPTER 8: SPECIALTY SELLING   **285**

Listing an Item

Selling on Half.com is easy. To get started, go to the home page, *http://half.ebay.com*, shown in Figure 8-1. At the top of the home page, under the tabs, click Sell Your Stuff to get to the page shown in Figure 8-2. From the "Sell your items" page, click the category link—Books, Music, Movies/DVDs, and so on—that matches what you have to sell.

FREQUENTLY ASKED QUESTION

eBay vs. Half.com

Is it better to list an item on eBay or on Half.com?

All the Half.com categories are also categories on eBay. So when you're selling books, CDs, movies, or video games, how do you decide which site to use? Half.com charges no listing fees but takes a 15 percent bite out of your selling price. eBay's Final Value Fees are lower, but you have to pay just to list an item, whether or not it sells, and (unless you have an eBay Store) you have to be pretty sure your item will sell in about a week.

Choose Half.com if:

- **You have a large inventory of individual items that you think will take a while to sell.** On Half.com, you can list items for as long as it takes to sell them without paying for that privilege; you pay when you've made a sale.

- **You want to list items indefinitely.** An eBay Store costs $15.95 (plus a two-cent listing fee per item) each month, and you pay those fees whether or not you sell a single thing. If you're selling the stuff that buyers look for on Half.com—mass media items—Half.com offers increased exposure to the right kinds of buyers and no up-front fees.

- **Your inventory includes a lot of college textbooks.** The start of a new semester brings students flocking to the site in search of used books in

good condition. Since Half.com is an established market for textbooks, use it to reach those student buyers. August, September, January, and February are the hot months for textbook buying.

Go with eBay if:

- **You're selling a particularly rare or valuable book, like a first edition that will get collectors salivating.** Take advantage of the auction format to get the best price. You never know how much collectors are willing to pay until they start bidding against each other, so an auction makes better sense than a fixed price.

- **You're clearing out your inventory and want to get rid of items in lots.** On eBay, you can sell groups of slow-moving items together, rather than piecemeal. And eBay buyers tend to get more excited about a lot of video games or books rather than those listed separately.

- **You want to set your own shipping and handling fees.** Half.com uses set shipping prices; eBay lets you set your own. You can add a little for handling to the sale price on Half.com, but if setting your own shipping and handling fee is important to you, list on eBay.

Tip: Or use Half.com's Quick Sell to skip a page and jump to Half.com's listing form. Just type the ISBN (for books) or UPC number (for other products) into the box and then click Continue. (Don't include the dashes when you type either of these numbers into a Half.com sales form.)

Figure 8-1:
You can point your Web browser to www. half.com or half.ebay.com; either gets you to this page. The tabs across the top of the page take you to the various categories. In the bar directly below that, links let you buy gift certificates, start or view a wish list of items you'd like, preorder items not currently available on the site, sign up for recommendations in the different categories, or list items you have for sale. Click the upper-right sign-in link to register; the home link takes you to eBay's home page.

Figure 8-2:
The first step in selling items on Half.com is choosing a category. Click the appropriate link to go to the listing form for that category. If you know your item's ISBN or UPC (see the box on page 289), type it into the Half.com Quick Sell text box to skip a step. If you've got a number of items you want to list, speed up the process by clicking Multiple Item Listing.

When you choose a category, like Music, Half.com asks you for the UPC number—or the ISBN for books (see the box on page 289 to learn what these numbers
are and how to find them). If you type in the number (leave out the dashes) and
then click Continue, you land at step 1 of Half.com's two-step listing form.

1. **Describe Your Item.**

On this page, a stock photo of the book or game or disc you're selling magically
appears on the left-hand side of the page, along with some basic information
like publisher/company and release date. Check to make sure this matches your
item, and then select the condition of your item—from "brand new" to
"acceptable." Table 8-1 shows how Half.com defines each condition.

Table 8-1. *Item Conditions According to Half.com*

Condition	Description
Brand new	Never used. Still in original, shrink-wrapped packaging (if applicable). The item is precisely the same condition as one bought in a department store.
Like new	Could easily be mistaken for brand new. No damage whatsoever to cover, packaging, or item itself. Nothing missing or marked in any way.
Very good	Not quite brand new, but little or no noticeable wear and tear. For books, this means minimal or no writing inside and no damage to any pages. For music, movies, and video games, the undamaged case or box comes with the item; no missing instructions or liner notes. CDs/DVDs don't skip; VHS tapes have good picture quality (no snow). An item listed as "very good" is one that you wouldn't be embarrassed to give as a gift.
Good	Minimal wear and tear (such as light creases or scuff marks) to cover or case. For books, there might be some creased pages or light underlining, but no colored highlighting. The condition should be such that you'd be willing to use the product yourself but hesitant to give it to someone else as a gift.
Acceptable	A little beaten up but still worth using. For books, this might mean that there are some tears or holes in the cover, heavy creases in the spine, and highlighting or extensive marking on the pages. For movies, music, and games, there might be a hole in the cardboard box or minor damage to the case; cover art, liner notes, or instructions might be missing.
Unacceptable	Damaged in a way that impairs someone's ability to use the items. You can't sell unacceptable items on Half.com.

Next, on the Describe Your Item page, type a short description of the item into
the Comments box. You've got up to 1,000 characters (including spaces) to use
when writing your description, but only the first 40 characters appear on the
search results page when a buyer searches for the item, as you can see in
Figure 8-3. When a buyer clicks the "More info…" link to check out an item,
the full comment appears. So use those first 40 characters wisely: make them
your sales pitch so your item stands out from all the others like it.

Note: Half.com says that you can use a comment *only* to describe the item up for sale. So you can't
advertise your Web page here.

After you've written an item description, click Continue to go to the second step of the listing form.

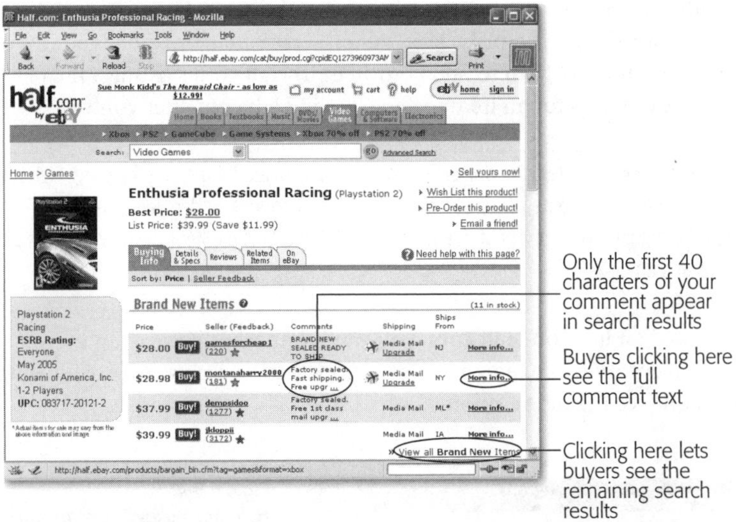

Figure 8-3:
When a buyer searches for an item, Half.com sorts results by condition (Brand New, Like New, Very Good, and so on), showing the four lowest-priced items in each category. If your item isn't among the four cheapest listed, the buyer won't see it on this page. Buyers must click the "View all…Items" link for that category to get the whole list. eBay also pushes the eBay site pretty hard in Half.com searches; search results include Buy It Now listings and auctions for the same item on eBay.

Only the first 40 characters of your comment appear in search results

Buyers clicking here see the full comment text

Clicking here lets buyers see the remaining search results

UP TO SPEED

ISBN and UPC

ISBN? UPC? Knowing what these are and where to find them is the key to listing items on Half.com.

ISBN stands for *international standard book number*, and UPC stands for *universal product code*. Each is an identifier that uniquely labels a particular kind of product. Just as retail stores use these numbers to keep track of their inventory, you can use them to list and manage your inventory on Half.com.

Every published book has its own ISBN. Look on the back of your book, CD or DVD case, or VHS or video game box. An ISBN has ten digits (and sometimes ends in X, which is part of the number), and it often (but not always) appears near a bar code.

UPCs began as a way for grocery stores to keep better track of their inventory, but soon spread to all kinds of retail products. The UPC number is the 12-digit number beneath the familiar bar code scanned at the checkout when you buy something in a retail store. A UPC has 12 digits; sometimes the first and last digits look like they're separate from the rest of the number, but don't forget to include them or Half.com won't be able to find your item.

When you type an ISBN or UPC into a Half.com sales form (page 286), Half.com searches its massive database for the book or product the number represents. It brings up a stock photo of the item—a book cover or CD cover art, for example—so you don't have to scan or photograph the mass media items you sell. Other information, such as publication or release date, edition number, and publisher or studio, also magically appears in your listing. You don't have to find or type any of that stuff.

What if your item doesn't have one of these numbers? Use the Search box at the top of each page to search for the item you want to sell. Select the one like yours from the results list. In the upper-right corner of the item page, click the "Sell yours now!" link. This takes you to the Sell Your Item form, with the stock picture (if Half.com has one) and item title already supplied.

2. **Set Price & List Item.**

Before Half.com shows you the Set Price & List Item page, it does some lightning-fast market research to help you pick a selling price, based on your item's condition and the competition's prices, as shown in Figure 8-4. Half.com even suggests a price in the price box; either accept that price or type in your own, and then click List Item to add your item to Half.com's listings. It can take up to a couple of hours for an item to show up on Half.com after you've listed it.

Tip: If you're listing a bunch of items in one sitting, you can streamline the process by using Half.com's multiple listing form. From the home page, click Sell Your Stuff, then look under Half.com Quick Sell for the Multiple Item Listing link (you can see it in Figure 8-2). Click the Multiple Item Listing link to list up to 10 separate items at a time.

After you've listed an item on Half.com, you can list another item, shop the site, or manage your inventory by changing a description, setting a new price, canceling a listing, and so on (see the next section).

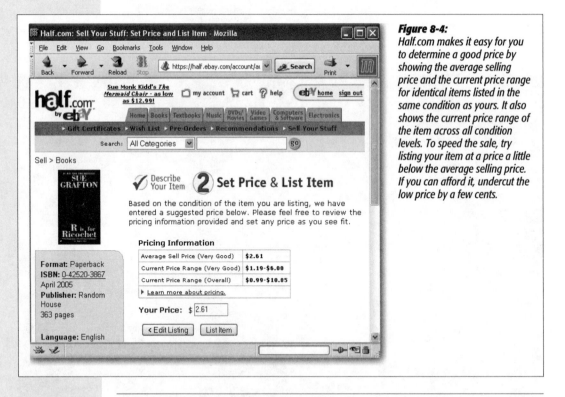

Figure 8-4:
Half.com makes it easy for you to determine a good price by showing the average selling price and the current price range for identical items listed in the same condition as yours. It also shows the current price range of the item across all condition levels. To speed the sale, try listing your item at a price a little below the average selling price. If you can afford it, undercut the low price by a few cents.

Note: Half.com shoppers must pay for their purchases with a credit card. Half.com doesn't accept PayPal.

Managing Your Inventory

If you need to make changes to items you've listed, go to Half.com's home page and click Manage My Inventory. Sign in (if you haven't already), and then select the inventory category you want to manage (Books, Music, Games, and so on). A page like the one in Figure 8-5 opens.

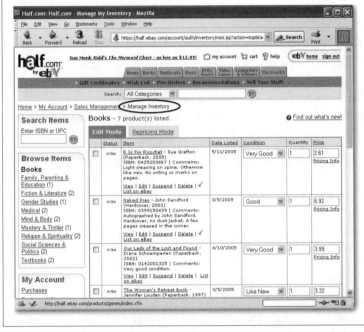

Figure 8-5:
To make changes to your Half.com listings, use the Manage Inventory page. You can edit your description, or you can change the description, quantity available, or price. To delete or suspend a listing, turn on the checkbox next to the item, go to the bottom of the list, and then click the appropriate button. Suspend is a convenient option if you'll be away from your computer for a few days. This view shows Edit Mode. Click the Repricing Mode tab to get current sales data.

The Manage Inventory page offers two different modes (look for the Edit Mode and Repricing Mode tabs in Figure 8-5). Each mode shows you different information and lets you make changes to your listings:

- **Edit Mode.** Shows your item and its description, its status (active or suspended), the date you listed the item, its condition and quantity, and the price. You can sort your inventory by status, item (in alphabetical order), date, condition, or price. Use Edit Mode to change an item's status, description, condition, quantity, or price.

- **Repricing Mode.** Like Edit Mode, Repricing Mode shows the item, description, status, and price—but it also offers current information about how this kind of item is selling: the last sold date and price, average selling price, and current price range. Repricing Mode lets you see whether you've priced your item too low or too high, in comparison with what's on Half.com right now; you can change the price right in Repricing Mode.

Tip: If your item might sell better on eBay, Half.com's Manage Inventory page lets you know with a check mark between the Delete and "List on eBay" links. Click the "List on eBay" link to suspend the Half.com listing and transfer the item to eBay. If your eBay listing ends without a buyer, you can reactivate the item on Half.com.

Making a Sale

When someone buys an item you've listed on Half.com, you get an email from Half.com asking you to confirm that you have the item and can ship it within 24 hours of your confirmation. Don't ignore this email! If you don't confirm within two business days, Half.com cancels the order.

Confirm the sale by replying to Half.com's email or by signing in to Half.com and going to your My Account page (click the "my account" link at the top of any page). From My Account, click Sales to see a list of orders that await confirmation or that you confirmed within the last week. Click the Confirm/Cancel link next to the appropriate order. The next page gives you more information about the order, including the buyer's shipping address and preferred shipping method (media mail or expedited). Click Confirm to proceed with the order or Cancel if you reject it.

Tip: If you know you can't ship within 24 hours, buy yourself some time to get to the post office by waiting a day before you confirm.

After you've confirmed an order, ship the item within one business day. Half.com frowns on slower shipping. Besides, buyers expect quick shipping, so if you drag your feet they might complain or leave negative feedback.

If you want to let the buyer know that you've shipped the item, go to your My Account page and click the Sales link to see a list of recent sales, each with a unique transaction number. Find the sale you want, click its transaction number, and then click the Contact Buyer button. A form appears that lets you email the buyer.

Tip: As with eBay sales, it's a good idea to get delivery confirmation from the shipper when you ship. Then, if any problems arise, you have proof that you sent the item.

GEM IN THE ROUGH

Use Half.com to Drive Buyers to Your eBay Auctions

As on eBay, you can't use your Half.com listing to direct shoppers to your own offsite Web page. You can, however, point shoppers to a Web page that contains more information about your eBay auctions. If you regularly sell items on eBay that may be of interest to Half.com shoppers, include a link to your eBay auctions in your Half.com item description.

Also, remember that Half.com searches turn up the same items for sale on eBay. So when you list items on eBay that Half.com shoppers are searching for, your eBay auctions will appear in their search results—and you don't have to do a thing to make them show up there. Even better for eBay sellers, Half.com searches display only the four lowest-priced items in each condition category, but there's no such limit on the "Related Items on eBay" category.

Since eBay integrated registrations on eBay and Half.com, feedback left for Half.com sales appears in your Member Profile on eBay. Half.com feedback follows the same rules as feedback on eBay (page 40).

Selling on eBay Motors

When you list a car in the local classifieds, your marketing reach is only as wide as the paper's subscriptions. When you list a car on eBay, you have the potential to reach *10 million* buyers who are browsing the site looking for a deal. eBay may thus be able to help you get a faster sale, a better price—or both.

Note: eBay Motors isn't just for cars. There are categories for motorcycles, boats, RVs, scooters, airplanes—just about any transportation with a motor. You can also list vehicle parts and accessories on eBay Motors.

Revving Up

Before you can sell on eBay Motors, you have to be a registered seller on eBay (page 154). Beyond that, there's no separate registration needed to sell a car.

Tip: Don't make selling a car the first thing you ever do on eBay. Buyers are wary of zero- or low-feedback sellers offering high-priced items. Spend some time on the site and build up your feedback (page 40) before you try to sell a car or other big-ticket item.

You do, however, have to do some research before you list. To make this easy, eBay has created a Sell Your Vehicle Checklist. Print it out and fill it in offline to save time and frustration during the listing process. You'll find the checklist, shown in Figure 8-6, at *http://pages.motors.ebay.com/sell/Sell_Your_Vehicle_Checklist.pdf*.

Here's what the checklist covers:

- **Vehicle information.** This section includes your car's unique vehicle identification number (VIN); year, make, and model; engine size; transmission type; any warranty or special equipment; and a checklist of photos buyers want to see.

- **Vehicle description.** This section asks a bunch of questions that will help you write a good vehicle description. The main categories are the car's history and current condition, and the terms of the sale.

- **Vehicle price.** This section explains your pricing options: starting price, reserve price, and Buy It Now.

After you've gathered information about your vehicle and done your research, you've got one more thing to do before you create your listing: take photos. As you probably noticed when checking out other auctions, car sales tend to include lots and lots of photos. And that's a great a strategy. When a buyer can't inspect a car in person, multiple photos are the next-best thing.

---

eBay recommends that you take exterior photos of the car's front, back, and both sides; the front and back seats; the dashboard (including a close-up of the odometer); the trunk; the engine bay; any special features; and any damage. Try to take photos so that the subject fills the frame as much as possible. Buyers are going to be looking closely at the car; they don't want to see your garage door or the neighbor's kids playing across the street. Avoid shadows or harsh lighting that make the details difficult to see. For general photography tips, see page 198.

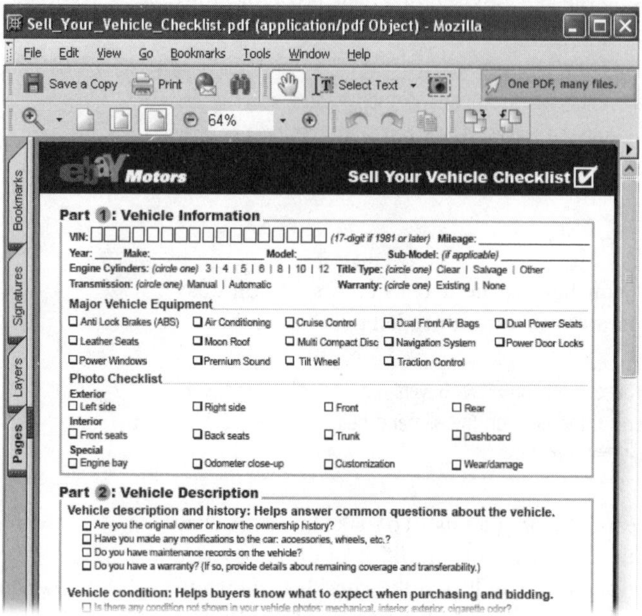

Figure 8-6:
The Sell Your Vehicle Checklist makes sure you gather all the information you'll need to list a vehicle before you start the Sell Your Item process. The checklist is comprehensive, so it takes some time to fill out, but if you check off everything on the list, you'll whiz through the process of listing your vehicle.

Creating Your Listing

Listing an item on eBay Motors is similar to the Sell Your Item process on eBay: you choose a category, write a title and description, add photos, set payment and shipping, then review your listing and submit it. When you're ready to create a listing for your vehicle, go to eBay Motors (*http://motors.ebay.com*) → Sell → Sell Your Item. The Sell Your Item: Choose a Selling Format page appears. eBay Motors offers regular auction and fixed-price listing formats. Choose one, and then click Continue to go to the five-step Sell Your Item form. This form looks a lot like the Sell Your Item form you use for auctions on the main eBay site (page 156), but it's specialized for motor vehicle sales.

Note: You have to have at least 10 feedbacks or be ID-verified (page 155) to run a fixed-price auction.

1. **Choose a category.**

   On the Sell Your Item: Select Category page, choose the general category that matches your vehicle, as shown in Figure 8-7, then select the appropriate subcategories from the choices that automatically appear. Click Continue to move on to step 2, the Sell Your Item: Describe Your Item page.

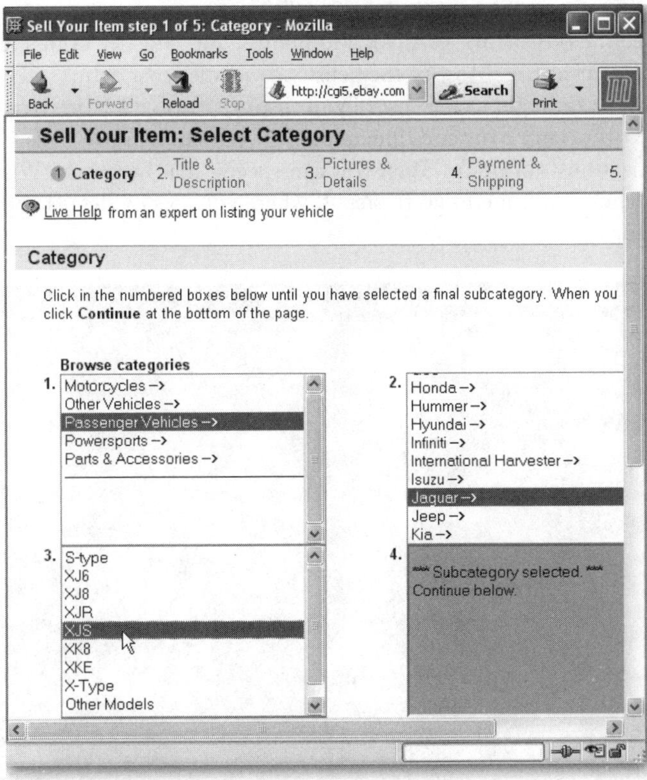

Figure 8-7:
Selecting a category for your listing on eBay Motors is the same as on eBay's main site. Choose a general category, and then keep choosing subcategories until you run out. If you have any questions, you can ask an eBay Motors staff person: just zip to the top of the page and click the Live Help link.

2. **Write a title and describe your vehicle.**

   On this page, start by writing a title for your listing. As on eBay's main site, titles can be no more than 55 characters long. (For tips on writing a good title, see page 194.)

   The "Item specifics" section of the Sell Your Item: Describe Yor Item page asks for all the details of the vehicle, from year and mileage to safety features (like airbags and anti-lock brakes) and luxury options (like leather seats and sunroofs). "Item specifics" is where you type in your vehicle's VIN (vehicle identification number). eBay requires a VIN for all cars whose model year is 1981 (the year VINs began) or later. If you're having trouble locating your vehicle's VIN, check out the box on page 298.

Below "Item specifics" is the box where you write your item description. It's just like the "Item description" box in the Sell Your Item form of eBay's main site (page 157). Click the links to spell check and preview your description. When everything's all set, click Continue to go to step 3, where you add photos and other details.

3. **Provide photos and details.**

The Sell Your Item: Enter Pictures & Item Details page is where you set your starting price (see the box below for tips), add photos, and choose various features to enhance your listing. Most of the bells and whistles cost extra, so keep an eye on how much they add to the cost of your listing. If you'd like to participate in Giving Works (page 310) and donate part of your auction proceeds to a nonprofit organization (minimum $10), you can specify that here, too. When you've finished, click Continue to go to step 4, where you specify details about payment and shipping.

FREQUENTLY ASKED QUESTION

Setting a Price

How do I determine a good price for the car I want to sell?

If you were selling a car locally, you'd probably check out the classified ads, used car dealerships, and maybe a guide like the Kelley Blue Book before you set your asking price. When you sell on eBay, you can use the same strategies.

Start with an online pricing guide: Kelley Blue Book (*www.kbb.com*), NADA Appraisal guides (*www.nadaguides.com*), or Edmunds (*www.edmunds.com*). Each of these sites lets you search by year, make, and model to get an idea of what your car is worth. You can be sure that potential bidders will be checking out these price guides, too.

Next, search eBay for cars similar to yours. Don't think in terms of just make and model; look at mileage, condition, features, and so on to find the best matches. Make a note of the starting price and whether there's a reserve (page 161). Then use Advanced Search to search completed listings (page 19). Notice which cars sold for a good price and which failed to meet the reserve or generate any bids. Study the successful auctions for tips about how to set up

your own auction. (Don't, of course, violate eBay policies by actually copying text or pictures.)

Use your research—the books plus the current and recent auctions on eBay—to determine a price range. What's the lowest price you'd be willing to settle for? What's a price you might want to pay if you were buying this car? What price (within reason) would make you happy with the sale?

Once you've determined a target price, think about your strategy for getting that price. Setting a relatively low starting price will attract interest and get the bidding going—and once you've got a few bids, more are likely to follow. If there's a threshold price you can't sell below, set a reserve price. (There's a fee to set a reserve price, but eBay refunds that fee if the item sells.) If the bidding doesn't reach the reserve, you have no obligation to complete the sale. Another option to get the price you want is to make your auction a Buy It Now auction. As soon as someone clicks the Buy It Now button, you've sold your car. Just don't set the BIN price unreasonably high; you'll be wasting your listing fees if you do.

Tip: Car auctions feature a lot of photos, and eBay typically charges 15 cents for each photo beyond the first one. To save money, choose the Vehicle Picture Pack: for $2.00, you can display up to 24 photos. You also get the Supersize option (buyers can click a small photo to enlarge it) and a slideshow of your photos at the top of the auction page as part of the deal. Or you can host your photos on another site (page 203).

4. **Set payment and shipping terms.**

This page, Sell Your Item: Enter Payment & Shipping, is where you tell buyers how they'll pay you and whether you'll ship the car or allow local pickup only. Common practice on eBay Motors is for the buyer to pay a deposit within three days of the auction's close. Most sellers accept a deposit through PayPal and the balance in the form of cash (forked over in person) or a cashier's check. If you want to accept a personal check, you can. (For your own sake, don't hand over the keys and title until after the check has cleared.) In most cases, buyers are responsible for traveling to your location to pick up the car, but if you want to offer a different shipping method, you can. After you've explained your payment and shipping policies, click Continue to go to the last step, the Sell Your Item: Review & Submit Listing.

Note: eBay now offers financing to buyers who want to purchase a vehicle on eBay Motors. Buyers can prequalify for a loan, which means that buyers know they can afford your car before they bid—and you end up with more dependable bidders and faster payment at the auction's end. If you want to accept eBay financing as a means of payment, look under "I accept the following payment methods" and turn on "Loan check."

UP TO SPEED

eBay Motors Listing Fees

If you've been selling for a while on the main eBay site, you might turn a bit green imagining the fees when you see cars selling for tens of thousands of dollars on eBay Motors. Fortunately, eBay Motors has its own fee schedule.

You pay a fixed insertion fee when you list a vehicle and a fixed transaction service fee when you sell one—no graduated FVFs. As on the main eBay site, if your vehicle gets zero bids (or if you've set a reserve price and bidding fails to meet it), you pay only the insertion fees.

Here's how eBay Motors fees work:

- **Passenger vehicles.** $40 when you list the vehicle and $40 when you sell it.

- **Motorcycles and powersports.** $30 when you list the vehicle and $30 when you sell it.

- **Pocket bikes (mini–racing motorcycles).** $3 when you list the vehicle and $3 when you sell it.

- **Other vehicles.** $40 when you list the vehicle and $40 when you sell it.

- **Parts and accessories.** These items are subject to eBay's regular listing policies (from the bottom of eBay's main page, select Policies → Listing Policies to stay up to date on eBay's listing policies).

Of course, any listing features you select when you create your listing—extra photos, gallery-featured, listing designer, reserve price, and so on (page 163)—cost extra. And because they're associated with the listing, not the auction, you have to pay for these features whether or not your car sells.

5. **Review and submit your listing.**

Take your time before you hit that Submit button. Check everything over carefully; use the Sell Your Vehicle Checklist you put together (see page 293) to make sure you've included everything buyers might possibly want to know about your car.

UP TO SPEED

Help! I Can't Find My Car's VIN

What, you don't know your car's VIN like you know your phone number?

Actually, nobody does. Here's how to find it.

Check the driver's side dashboard and door jamb for a small tag with a combination of 17 letters and numbers. If you can't find the number in either of those places, check your auto insurance card or vehicle registration.

If your car was built before 1981, it may not have a VIN. You can still sell it on eBay. On the right half of the page that asks for the VIN, there's a section for older cars. Click Continue in this section to fill out specific details about the car and proceed with your listing.

During the Auction

Stay involved in your auction while it's running. You're likely to get questions from potential buyers; answer those questions promptly and accurately. You might also see bidders who make you nervous moving in on your auction, like a bidder who registered yesterday and is already bidding on three cars. Check the auction often to see who's bidding. If you have a question about a low-feedback buyer, contact that person to make sure they're serious about following through. If you're not convinced, cancel their bid (page 230).

Tip: Avoid troublesome bidders during the auction. Before you auction a vehicle, block bidders you know you don't want messing with your auction (page 227), such as bidders with negative feedback, recent Unpaid Item strikes, or no PayPal account.

What if nobody bids? You can edit your listing to add information or photos, but chances are that you set your starting price too high; try lowering it. You can also lower your reserve price (page 161), even if potential buyers have already made bids on your auction.

Note: When you lower a reserve price, eBay sends an email to all bidders notifying them of the price change, but still keeping the reserve a secret. If you lower the reserve price to meet the high bidder's current bid, eBay automatically lowers the high bid to $1 below the new reserve price, giving the high bidder a chance to confirm that he or she still wants the vehicle. In other words, you can't force the high bidder to buy your car simply by dropping your reserve to meet her bid.

Crossing the Finish Line

The transaction is complete when you've received your money and turned over the car, the keys, and the title to the buyer. You specified payment and shipping terms in the auction listing, and the buyer should go by these; you're under no obligation to change your terms if the buyer finds them inconvenient. When the buyer arrives to pick up the car, have a receipt ready for both of you to sign. You also have to transfer the vehicle's title to the buyer. Different states have different rules governing title transfers, so check with your state's Department of Motor Vehicles to find out what you need to do. Don't transfer the title until you've got the payment in hand—cash nestled in your wallet or a personal check safely cleared in your bank account.

What if there's no sale?

Buyer's remorse is widespread on eBay Motors. That hot-looking car a buyer can't live without can look a lot colder when the time comes to fork over the cash. If the winning bidder backs out, or if the auction didn't meet your reserve price, you have two options:

- **Relist the vehicle.** After the auction has ended, go to the auction page and click the Relist link. eBay takes you through the listing process again, with most of the fields filled in and choices made. Change anything you want to change; click through each of the Sell Your Item form's five steps to list the item again.

Note: If you're relisting because the winning bidder backed out, you have to file an Unpaid Item (UPI) dispute (page 184) to recoup your original listing fees. If you're relisting because there were no bids or because the bids didn't reach your reserve price, the item must sell the second time around for you to get the insertion-fee credit.

- **Make a Second Chance Offer (SCO).** You can contact any of your bidders and offer to sell them the vehicle at a lower price than the auction's reserve price. You can send a nonwinning bidder an SCO from your My eBay page: look under Items I've Sold, find the vehicle, then use the drop-down menu to select Send a Second Chance Offer. Or you can click the Second Chance Offer link on the auction page itself. Either lets you send an underbidder a Second Chance Offer.

Warning: Bogus SCOs are one of the biggest scams on eBay, so most buyers are wary when they get one for a big-ticket item. Whatever you do, don't try to contact bidders and offer to sell them the vehicle off eBay. At best, they'll ignore you. At worst, they'll report you to eBay as a possible scammer—and you could lose your account by offering to sell off eBay. If you want to offer a bidder a second crack at buying your car, use eBay's Second Chance Offer form.

Tips for a Successful Sale

Car sales are hot, hot, hot. Vehicles zoom off the eBay Motors site at an astonishing rate. To attract buyers to your auction and get the bidding off to a good start, follow these tips.

Build up your feedback score

You know you're honest, but there's only one measure eBayers rely on to confirm that: your feedback rating (page 40). If you try to sell a car with a brand-new account and a low feedback rating, your auction might get some bids, but it won't generate the excitement it would if you had a nice, high feedback score and a 100-percent positive rating. If you want to get a good price for your car, don't rush it into an auction. Spend some time on eBay, get to know the site, and prove that you're someone worth doing business with.

Make your vehicle look great

Before you start snapping photos, make sure your car looks its best. On the outside, give it a wash and a wax, shine up that chrome, clean the windows, and polish the hubcaps and tires until they gleam. Inside, wipe off the dashboard, clean out any junk from the back seat and the trunk, vacuum the rugs and the seats, and take those fuzzy dice off the rearview mirror. The car should look ready for its new owner to hop in and drive it away.

Perform needed maintenance

Spring for routine servicing or an oil change if it's time, and take care of any minor maintenance issues you've been putting off. Dig out maintenance records and include information about what was done and when in your item description. Buyers are impressed by someone who takes good care of his vehicle.

Think like a buyer

If you were buying a car online, what would you want to know about it before you bid? Play up any extras, like an enhanced sound system or headrest DVD screens for the kids. But *don't* downplay the problems. If the rugs are stained or the upholstery is torn, say so. If you've driven the car for five years, smoking cigars with the windows rolled up while transporting a couple of carsick German shepherds, buyers will want to know. (If you're a nonsmoker who doesn't own a pet, they'll want to know that, too.) An honest description makes you more trustworthy as a seller.

Advertise locally

Even while you're running an auction on eBay, put a For Sale sign in the car and tack up some flyers around town. For a minimal cost, you might be able to sell to a local buyer. Just remember to cancel your eBay auction before it ends—and don't forget eBay's 12-hour rule (page 176)! If you do advertise locally, say in your auction terms that you reserve the right to end the auction early if you make a local sale. Before you end an auction early, cancel all active bids. And be aware that if you cancel a running auction, you forfeit your insertion fees.

Have the vehicle inspected

Buyers may be more confident bidding on a car that's been inspected by a third party. You can let buyers pay for an independent inspection (page 128), or you can have one done yourself and share the results with bidders in your item description.

Spiff up your listing with CARad

CARad, shown in Figure 8-8, is an eBay subsidiary that helps you create an attractive, complete, professional-looking listing. CARad lets you choose and even customize a listing template and select your preferred photo layout. It offers some cool photo-display options, like an impressive zoom feature, and hosts up to 35 photos for your listing—as opposed to eBay's max of 24. During and after the auction, CARad offers a variety of management tools, like an email manager and listing reports. CARad costs $9.95 for a listing (that's in addition to the eBay Motors insertion fee) or, if you have a lot of cars to sell, $299 a month for unlimited use. Check it out at *www.carad.com*.

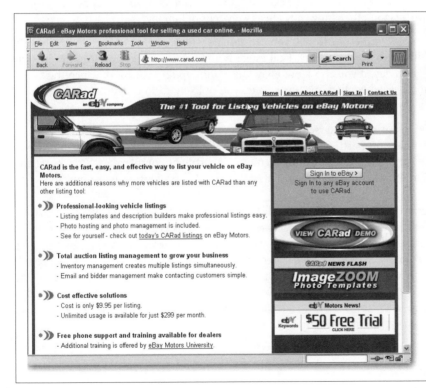

Figure 8-8:
CARad.com helps you create and manage listings for eBay Motors. Its Web site offers a free demo so you can see what CARad can do for you. Click the "today's CARad listings" link to see live auctions created by CARad. Then compare these auctions to current auctions for similar cars to see whether they get more bids and higher prices.

Get help

It's always true: the only question you really regret is the one you didn't ask. So if you have questions about what you should do before, during, or after an eBay Motors sale, ask. At the top of every auction page on the eBay Motors site is a Live Help link. Click it if you want to chat online with an eBay staffer. (Be sure that you follow a link from eBay Motors—not the main eBay site—to chat with a vehicle specialist.)

To get advice from other eBayers who've been there, jump into one of the discussions going on in an eBay Motors–related discussion board. From the eBay home page, go to Community → Discussion Boards and, under Category Specific Discussion Boards, select either eBay Motors or Motorcycle Boulevard.

Selling Real Estate Online

It might sound crazy to buy real estate over the Internet, but more and more people are doing just that. According to a 2005 survey by the California Association of Realtors, nearly two-thirds of first-time home buyers used the Internet to find their new home. In addition, Internet home buyers had higher incomes and made the decision to purchase faster than traditional home buyers: while traditional home buyers averaged seven weeks to find the home they ultimately bought, Internet buyers took the plunge after just two weeks of looking.

If you have real estate to sell, you can reach a wide audience of eager home buyers and investors through eBay. Real estate is a fast-growing category on the site. On any given day, if you check out eBay Pulse (*http://pulse.ebay.com*), which tracks the 10 most-watched auctions on the site, you're likely to find that a couple of those top auctions are for real estate.

All kinds of real estate sell on eBay, from time-shares to single-family homes to investment properties. People have used eBay to sell castles, former schools, converted churches, vacation homes, motels, apartment complexes, RV parks, factories, hunting camps, B&Bs—just about any kind of property you can imagine.

Note: In late 2004, eBay bought Rent.com. Rent.com's Web site (*www.rent.com*) matches up landlords and tenants. People looking for an apartment can use the site for free. (In fact, Rent.com has offered a promotion giving tenants a $100 gift card when they sign a lease through the site.) It costs nothing for landlords or property managers to list on Rent.com; when a property owner or manager signs a lease with someone who found an apartment through the site, the owner/manager pays Rent.com a "success" fee, usually $375. If you've got an apartment to rent and you want prospective tenants around the world to know, go to Rent.com and register. (Registration on Rent.com is separate from eBay registration.) Click "List a Property on Rent.com," then fill out the form.

Two Ways to Sell

eBay offers real estate sellers two options: you can sell your property in an auction format, or you can advertise a fixed-price deal on eBay.

Auction it off

You can run a real estate sale like any other auction on eBay: set a starting price (and perhaps a reserve price), determine how long the auction will run (from one to 30 days), and sell to the highest bidder. (For the skinny on regular auctions, check out Chapter 5.) The fees are different, as the following list shows, but the auction format is the same as a regular eBay auction:

- Insertion fee for land, a time-share, or a manufactured home:

  — 1-, 3-, 5-, 7-, or 10-day auction listing: $35.

  — 30-day auction listing: $50.

- Insertion fee for residential, commercial, or other real estate:

  — 1-, 3-, 5-, 7-, or 10-day auction listing: $100.

  — 30-day auction listing: $150.

- Final value fee (FVF) for land, a time-share, or a manufactured home: $35.

- Final value fee (FVF) for residential, commercial, or other real estate: None.

eBay states that this kind of auction is binding, but that's not really true. A high bid in an eBay real estate auction is *not* a legally binding commitment to purchase the property. Because of the bewildering variety of state laws governing real estate transactions—not to mention everything that could go wrong in a given sale, from deed and title problems to undisclosed defects to a buyer's inability to get a mortgage—a "binding" auction means only that buyer and seller both promise to follow through in good faith. This means that a so-called binding sale can easily bite the dust after the auction ends.

Tip: To protect yourself against all the pitfalls that could scuttle your real estate sale, require a nonrefundable deposit of at least $1,000, payable within the first couple of days after the auction ends. This deposit is called *earnest money,* and it shows the buyer's good faith in completing the sale. If the buyer backs out of the deal, you get to keep the earnest money. Be sure to list your requirement in your terms of sale.

To list a piece of property in an auction format, follow the same steps you'd take in creating any auction (page 155). You do have to provide some information specific to a real estate sale on the Sell Your Item: Describe Your Item page, such as the property's address, as shown in Figure 8-9.

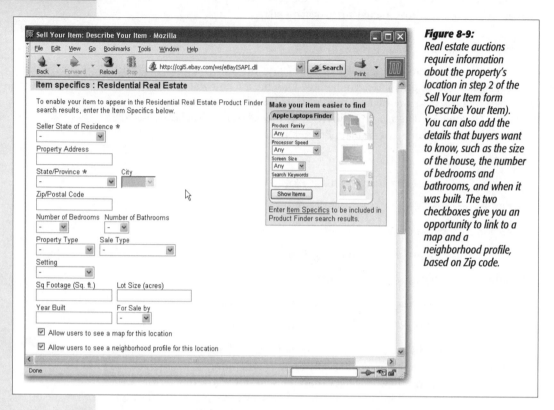

Figure 8-9:
Real estate auctions require information about the property's location in step 2 of the Sell Your Item form (Describe Your Item). You can also add the details that buyers want to know, such as the size of the house, the number of bedrooms and bathrooms, and when it was built. The two checkboxes give you an opportunity to link to a map and a neighborhood profile, based on Zip code.

Advertise on eBay

The other format eBay offers isn't an auction at all—it's really just an online ad. You can advertise your property on eBay for 30 or 90 days. Your ad will appear in search results lists and categories browsed by shoppers. But instead of a Place Bid button, there's a "Contact seller/agent" form. Interested buyers fill in their name, email address, other contact information, and any questions about the property, and then click Submit to send you that information in an email, so you can get back to them with more information or to set up a viewing.

Because ads have no bidders and no final bid, there are no Final Value Fees. Whatever type of property you're listing, the insertion fees are the same: $150 for a 30-day ad and $300 for a 90-day ad. This offers a cost-effective way to get your ad in front of millions of potential buyers.

To advertise your property on eBay, from the navigation bar click Sell → Sell Your Item, and then select "Advertise your Real Estate," as shown in Figure 8-10.

The Sell Your Item: Select Category page asks you to select a category: commercial, land, manufactured homes, residential, time-shares for sale, or other real estate. After you've chosen a category, the Sell Your Item: Describe Your Item page asks for your listing title and description and shows the same form shown in Figure 8-9. In step 3, Sell Your Item: Enter Pictures & Item Details, you type in the property's asking price, choose the ad's duration (30 or 90 days), upload photos, and select any special features you want for the ad, such as featuring it in Gallery view (page 16) or on eBay's home page.

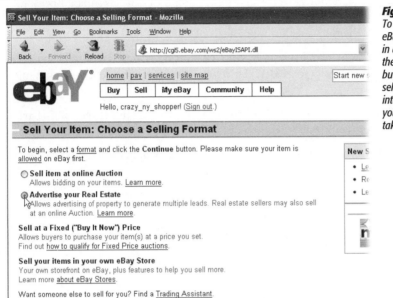

Figure 8-10:
To advertise your property on eBay (as opposed to selling it in an auction format), turn on the "Advertise your Real Estate" button when you choose a selling format. Ads simply allow interested buyers to contact you through eBay; no bidding takes place.

What's It Worth?

Unless you're a real estate professional, it can be hard to decide on a good asking price for your property. You don't want to sell it for less that it's worth, and you don't want to price it so high that you scare off buyers. Many homeowners have overly optimistic expectations of how much they can get for their home. Take the time to find out what's reasonable before you list your property.

There are a number of ways you can get a ballpark figure. Invite a couple of realtors to take a look and suggest a price, comparing your property with recent sales in your area. You might even end up listing the property with one of these realtors; many real estate agents are open to advertising on eBay.

You could also do the research yourself. Many county assessor's offices have online databases of properties with information about assessments, prior sales, and taxes. Check the newspaper for asking prices of properties similar to yours. Go to *www.realtor.com*, type in your Zip code, and search their database for property that's currently on the market.

Of course, asking prices aren't selling prices. You can buy a simple report of recent comparable sales or a detailed appraisal of your property at Electronic Appraiser (*www. electronicappraiser.com*). For Sale by Owner offers free price reports but doesn't cover all areas. At *www. forsalebyowner.com*, choose Home Sale Prices to see if your neighborhood is in their database.

Tips for Selling Property on eBay

The average real estate listing on eBay attracts about 1,000 views. That means that a lot of people are already out there looking for properties like yours. Follow these tips to get them to look twice.

Spell it out

Real estate transactions involve a lot more complexity and fees than other kinds of eBay sales. Make sure you spell out your terms clearly. Think about these issues—and address them in your terms of sale (TOS):

- Do you want to require a deposit? (Requiring a deposit—also called earnest money—is a really good idea.) How long after the auction ends do you want the buyer to pay it?

- Do you want to require bidders to have a PayPal account (page 227)? (PayPal is how many real estate sellers accept the deposit.)

- Should buyers be prequalified or have the money in hand? (It can take weeks to apply for a mortgage.)

- Can the buyer inspect the property in person during or after the auction?

- When will the closing take place?

- Who pays closing costs?

Include the neighborhood profile

When you list a piece of real estate, eBay gives you the option during step 2 (Describe Your Item) to automatically include a map and a neighborhood profile. The neighborhood profile gives demographics, housing facts, and a crime index for the area, as shown in Figure 8-11. If you don't include a neighborhood profile, buyers are likely to wonder what you're trying to hide. Is your asking price much higher than the local median home value? Is the property located in a high-crime or low-employment area? It's better to let buyers know the facts about the area up front.

Be careful about down-payment-only auctions

Many real estate auctions look like a great deal—but when you read the fine print, you realize that bids are not for the purchase price but for the *down payment* only. The seller is offering the property for a fixed price that's much higher than the bids.

There's nothing wrong with setting up your auction this way, as long as you make it clear how much the property really costs. In their excitement, many buyers don't read the whole ad. Yes, it's their responsibility to read before bidding, but if they've got an itchy bidding finger, it can become your problem as much as theirs. A buyer who doesn't understand your terms is likely to default on the sale. Even though you can file a UPI dispute and get some fees back, you've wasted your time.

To avoid this problem, put the words *down payment* in your auction title and feature the actual purchase price prominently in your item description.

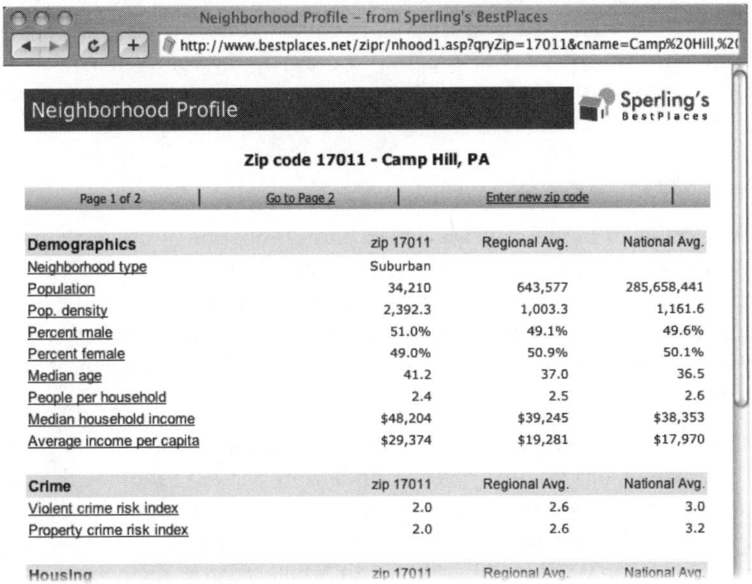

Figure 8-11:
The neighborhood profile, supplied by Sperling's Best Places, offers demographics and other statistics based on the property's Zip code. Investors and other buyers get a snapshot of the area they're considering buying into, so including a Neighborhood Profile broadens your sales reach by providing information to far-off buyers who can't visit the area in person.

Court investors

Real estate investing is hot. A 2005 *Money* magazine survey showed that more Americans think of real estate as a sure path to wealth than any other investment strategy. You can tap into this trend. When you list your home on eBay, don't just think of it as a place to live; think of it as a potential investment. Put a phrase like *investment opportunity* in your auction title. If home prices have been going up in your area, say so, and show investors how much the average price has increased in the last five years. Research the local rental market to find average rents on a property like yours, and feature this info in your description. If your area is a strong rental market, like a college town or popular vacation spot, let potential buyers know why the property will be easy to rent. You can even get the names of some local property managers to share with those who ask—and they will ask.

Consider owner financing

Owner financing—where you hold the mortgage instead of a bank—is popular with buyers. They save money in mortgage application and other bank fees. You get a monthly payment, and you can set a nice, high annual percentage rate. Offering owner financing can increase the number of bidders you get on your property.

Note: Owner financing isn't feasible if you're still paying a mortgage on your property—unless you happen to have a wad of cash lying around. You have to pay off your mortgage before you can sell your house to someone else.

Be careful, though. You don't want the buyer to default on the mortgage, putting you through the legal hassles of foreclosing and leaving you with the same house on your hands that you'd tried to sell. If you're going to offer owner financing, get a good real estate lawyer to advise you and to draw up the contract. You should also check the credit history of any bidders, stating in your terms that you offer financing only to qualified bidders.

Use photos to show curb appeal

When you're selling a home, you want it to have what realtors call *curb appeal;* your house looks so great on the outside that potential buyers driving by will want to see the inside. On eBay, you can give your home curb appeal by using lots of pictures, inside and out, that show off the property and give far-away buyers a feel for the neighborhood. The more pictures, the better. You can host them on a site outside of eBay to save listing fees (page 203).

Before you take a single photo, mow the lawn, trim the bushes, hide the trash cans, and pick up any junk or kids' toys lying around. Move the car out of the driveway (or else viewers tend to look at the car, not the house.) To avoid deep shadows that make the house hard to see, take the photos with the sun behind you. Inside, clear away clutter, and don't try to take photos of whole rooms; focus on features instead. Is there a fireplace, an attractive staircase, a gorgeous view out of the family room picture window? Photograph these things and feature them in your listing.

Market (or rent) your time-share

Time-shares are a tough sell online. When you bought your time-share, some salesperson probably fed you, entertained you, promised you a great prize—and subjected you to high-pressure sales tactics. You don't have that advantage on eBay.

People who are looking for a time-share are as interested in the area it's in as they are in the property itself. You're selling a relaxing or exciting vacation experience, so play up the area as a vacation spot that will appeal to buyers. Think about what made you want to vacation in the area, then use those thoughts to convince the buyer that it's a great place to spend a week. Is the time-share on the beach or tucked away in the mountains? Is it on a quiet lake or near the entertainment district of a lively city? You also want to list the number of bedrooms, the week, the type of ownership, annual fees, and whether time-share owners can exchange or bank weeks. Don't forget to include any closing costs that the buyer must pay.

Note: If you want to rent your time-share rather than sell it, list it in eBay's Travel category under Vacation Rentals. Normal listing fees apply (as opposed to real estate listing fees), so listing in this category can be a lot cheaper than listing a time-share for sale.

eBay offers special tools for time-share sellers, including a value estimator and closing service, as well as lots of advice. (The first two cost money; the third is free.) To find them, from eBay's home page go to Sell → Seller Central → Category Tips → Timeshare Seller Guide → Timeshare Seller Information Guide.

Warning: A lot of Web sites offer to sell time-shares for you. If you're thinking of going with one of these, check out the company carefully. *Don't* agree to pay an up-front fee to an agent who promises to sell your time-share. It's probably a scam.

Live Auctions

Anyone can bid at eBay Live Auctions, but not just anyone can sell. You have to be a licensed auctioneer (or someone who's paying a licensed auctioneer to control the bidding at your real-time auction). If that's you, you can apply to sell on eBay Live Auctions by going to *www.ebayliveauctions.com* and choosing "Sign up as a seller" → "eBay Live Auctions application form." When you do, the eBay Live Auctions form shown in Figure 8-12 appears.

Tip: To find an auctioneer, or if you're interested in becoming one, check out the info at the National Auctioneers Association at *www.auctioneers.org/aboutNAA/index.php*.

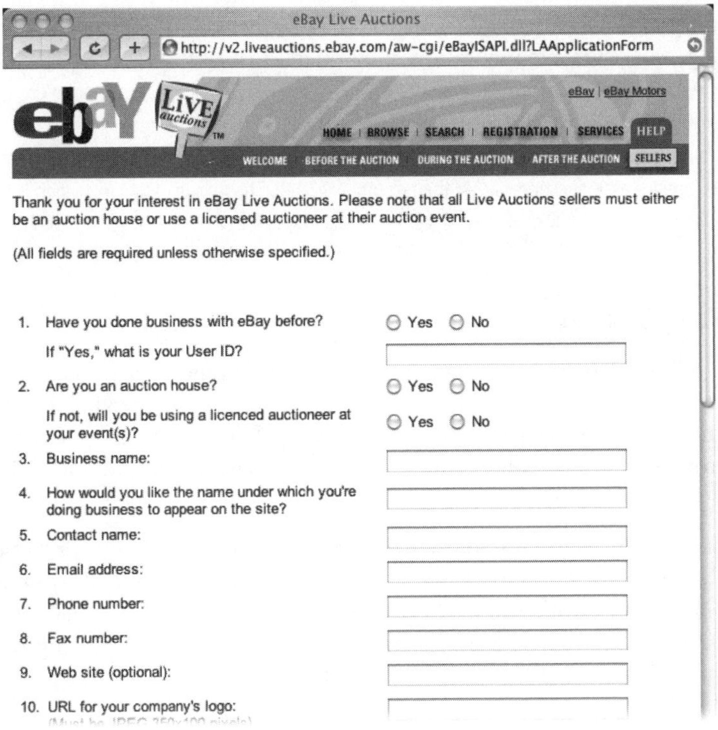

Figure 8-12:
The application form for becoming a Live Auctions seller is straightforward. You need to supply your business name and logo, contact information, and the categories you want to sell in. Only licensed auction houses (or those using their services) can sell through Live Auctions.

Once you've registered, eBay lets you post your auction catalog on the site, but it's pricey: $1,500 to list up to 10,000 lots. Live auctions are subject to a Final Value Fee of 5 percent of the selling price, although this fee applies only if an Internet bidder wins the lot.

Note: Buyer's premiums, an additional fee that buyers pay on top of their final bid, are standard at most auction houses. Similarly, most Live Auction sellers charge a buyer's premium of 15 percent to 20 percent. If you charge a premium, let buyers know in the catalog how much extra they'll have to pay.

Besides opening up your real-time auction to millions of bidders who'd never fit into your auction house, eBay Live Auctions offers auctioneers these benefits:

- Bulk upload tools make it easy for you put your catalog on the Internet.

- Buyers must sign up for an eBay Live Auction before they can bid in it. You can set your own registration requirements for your auction; you can require that bidders have a credit card registered with eBay or are ID verified. If you prefer, you can even approve all bidders yourself before letting them bid.

- eBay collects absentee bids in advance and delivers them to you at the start of the sale.

During the auction, you need a computer with a high-speed Internet connection in the sales room and a worker to input bids as they're made from the floor (so eBay bidders can see who's bidding how much on the auction floor) and to call out bids that come in from eBayers (so bidders at your sale know what the eBay competition is bidding). After the auction, eBay sends you a list of all the winning Internet buyers, so you can contact them and get paid.

Note: Several states are attempting to pass laws requiring online consignment sellers (like eBay Trading Assistants) to become licensed auctioneers (see the box on page 256). The upside of this regulation is that TAs who have to get this license may qualify as a "licensed auction house" and be able to sell on eBay Live.

eBay Giving Works

Most people sell on eBay for one simple reason: to make money. But you can give some (or all) of the profit to causes you support through eBay Giving Works, shown in Figure 8-13. The program lets sellers select and donate to nonprofit organizations through their eBay sales. Since 2000, eBayers have raised more than $40 million for good causes.

You can donate to the charity of your choice anywhere from 10 to 100 percent of the final selling price of an item. There's a $10 minimum donation, though, so inexpensive items don't work well in charity auctions. There are about 5,000 registered nonprofits to choose from, so it's not hard to find a cause you can support.

Nonprofit interests range from the arts and humanities to animals and the environment to civic and religious groups, as shown in Figure 8-14.

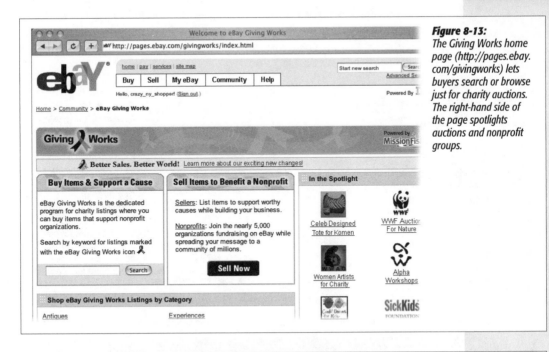

Figure 8-13:
The Giving Works home page (http://pages.ebay.com/givingworks) lets buyers search or browse just for charity auctions. The right-hand side of the page spotlights auctions and nonprofit groups.

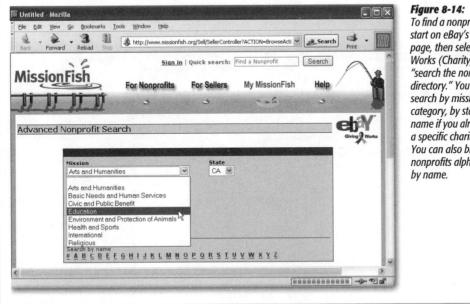

Figure 8-14:
To find a nonprofit group, start on eBay's home page, then select Giving Works (Charity) → "search the nonprofit directory." You can search by mission category, by state, or by name if you already have a specific charity in mind. You can also browse nonprofits alphabetically by name.

Signing Up to Contribute

By teaming up with Mission Fish, a clearing house for nonprofits, shown in Figure 8-15, eBay has made running a Giving Works auction easy. Whenever you list an item (page 154), the Sell Your Item: Enter Pictures & Item Details page (page 160) gives you the chance to choose a nonprofit and a donation amount, as shown in Figure 8-16.

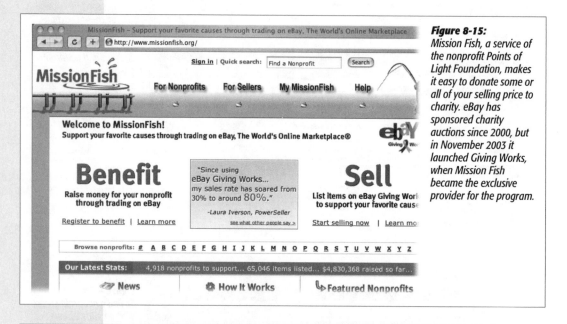

Figure 8-15:
Mission Fish, a service of the nonprofit Points of Light Foundation, makes it easy to donate some or all of your selling price to charity. eBay has sponsored charity auctions since 2000, but in November 2003 it launched Giving Works, when Mission Fish became the exclusive provider for the program.

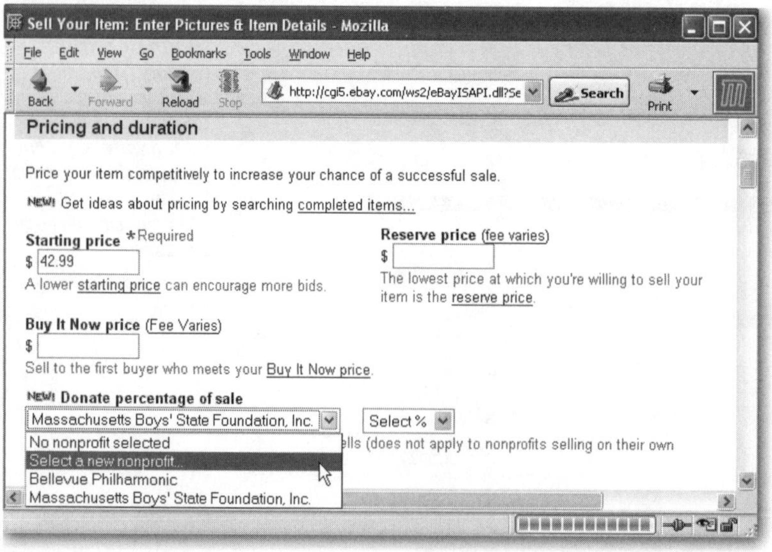

Figure 8-16:
After you determine a starting price, you can select a nonprofit to benefit from the proceeds of your auction. To find a group, choose "Select a new nonprofit…" from the drop-down list, which takes you to the nonprofit directory. If you find a group and click Select, the group will appear in the drop-down list whenever you list an item. You can opt to donate as little as 10 percent or as much as 100 percent of your selling price (minimum donation $10); the "Select %" drop-down shows your options in five-percent increments.

When you select a nonprofit for the first time, eBay asks your permission to share information with Mission Fish. Then Mission Fish asks you to register with a credit card number and contact information. (Mission Fish uses your credit card as insurance that you'll pay; the system is described on page 314.) You can opt to receive emails (or not) from Mission Fish and the nonprofits on your list.

How Can Buyers Tell It's for Charity?

Giving Works auctions look a little different from other eBay auctions, as shown in Figure 8-17.

Figure 8-17:
In a Giving Works auction, the item description (just below the photo and auction details, not shown here) starts off with the logo and mission statement of the charity the seller has chosen. All Giving Works auctions also display the two-colored ribbon symbol you can see in the upper left corner. Buyers can see what percentage of the selling price the seller has pledged to the charity.

How Donations Work

How much of the percentage I donate actually goes to the nonprofit I choose?

When you run a charity auction, eBay and Mission Fish still want their share; the only exception is if you give 100 percent of the selling price to charity. (More on that in a minute.) So how much of the proceeds does the nonprofit collect?

For auctions where you donate between 10 percent and 95 percent of the selling price, regular eBay fees apply; that comes out of *your* profit. Mission Fish deducts its fee from the donation itself: $3 plus 2.9 percent of the final price. Here's an example to show how it works. You list a stained-glass art panel, pledging half of the selling price to the I Have a Dream Foundation. If the winning bid is $76, your donation is $38.

From that $38, Mission Fish deducts $3 plus 2.9 percent (in this case $1.10), like so: 38 – 3 – 1.1 = 33.9. The I Have a Dream Foundation makes $33.90 from your sale.

Don't forget eBay and PayPal fees, because those come out of your share, and they're based on the whole final selling price, as with any other auction. So with a $78 auction, you'd pay insertion fees based on your starting price and listing options, plus $2.77 in Final Value Fees. (To see how to calculate eBay FVFs, see page 153.) If the buyer pays with PayPal, PayPal standard fees also apply to the full amount the buyer deposits into your PayPal account.

Things work differently if you donate 100 percent of the selling price. When you donate the full selling price, Mission Fish still charges its fees, but eBay donates both the insertion fee and the FVF to the nonprofit you've chosen.

Buyers can find charity auctions in several ways: they can search from the Giving Works home page by starting from eBay's home page and clicking Giving Works (Charity), then filling in the Search box or browsing categories—the results show Giving Works auctions only. Or, when doing an Advanced Search, buyers can restrict their search results to Giving Works auctions by checking "eBay Giving Works Items for Charity."

ALTERATE REALITY

eBay for Nonprofit Groups

If you work for a nonprofit organization, you don't have to wait around for sellers to find and select your group from among thousands of others. You can raise money through eBay by becoming a nonprofit direct seller yourself and listing auctions whose proceeds benefit your organization.

Of course, you can just sign up and sell on eBay the regular way (page 154), but registering with Mission Fish offers some perks worth having. Other sellers who want to donate to a nonprofit can choose your group as their beneficiary, and your auctions will turn up in the search results of buyers who are looking specifically for charity auctions. eBay's Giving Works ribbon, your logo, and your mission statement appear on the auction, along with a statement that 100 percent of the selling price will support your group. And because Mission Fish screens the nonprofits it lists, buyers have confidence that your group is legit.

First things first: you must sign up with eBay and register as a seller (page 154). Next, register for a Mission Fish account. Go to *www.missionfish.org* and click the "Register to benefit" link. Any nonprofit group can register; to do so, you'll need:

- An email address.

- A copy of your group's logo (as a .gif or .jpg file).

- A brief mission statement about 40 words long.

- Proof of nonprofit status, such as your 501(c)(3) letter.

- A voided check from your group's bank account. (Mission Fish needs this to deposit donations into your account.)

After Mission Fish has activated your account (it does screen nonprofits, so this might take a few days), go to the Mission Fish Web site (*www.missionfish.org*) and sign in. Click the My Direct Seller tab, then type your eBay ID into the "Add a Direct Seller" box. Click Add, and your accounts are linked.

Then, whenever you list an item on eBay, you have the opportunity in step 3 of the Sell Your Item form (Pictures & Details) to donate a percentage of the sale price. Always select your organization as the beneficiary, and 100 percent as the donation amount.

When you've connected your eBay and Mission Fish accounts, you get some pretty good benefits:

- You don't have to commit to the minimum donation of $10, so you can sell a range of items, big and small.

- Mission Fish doesn't deduct any fees, and eBay donates its fees to your charity, so your group gets 100 percent of the selling price.

After the Auction

When someone wins your Giving Works auction, the buyer pays you in the usual way, according to the payment options you specified in the auction listing. Soon after, Mission Fish emails you with payment instructions and how much you owe. You can pay Mission Fish by credit card, wire transfer, or certified check. Mission Fish deducts its fees and passes on what's left to your chosen nonprofit. You get a receipt for your donation via email; you can also view your receipts in your Mission Fish account. To do so, from the Mission Fish home page (*www.missionfish. org*), click My Mission Fish, sign in, and then click My Donations.

Note: Be sure to print out your donation receipts from Mission Fish and save them for tax time; most donations to Giving Works charities are tax deductible. In general, your deduction will be the percentage of the selling price you indicated when you listed the item. (Go to *www.irs.gov* to check current rules.)

If you don't follow through on the donation you promised by the second Monday after your auction ended, Mission Fish charges your credit card for the amount you owe. This is to ensure that sellers can't defraud eBayers into thinking an auction is for charity when it's not. If you find yourself stuck with a nonpaying bidder, though, you're not also stuck making a donation based on an item you didn't sell. File a UPI dispute with eBay (page 184). If the bidder still doesn't pay up, file with eBay for an FVF credit (page 185). When you've done that, you can file for a nonpaying bidder refund from *www.missionfish.org*. Sign in to your Mission Fish account, and then select My Mission Fish → Pay A Donation → "File a refund request." When Mission Fish confirms that eBay refunded your FVF, they'll issue you a refund.

eBay B2B

Most of eBay is people selling to people, or small businesses selling to individuals. The Business Marketplace, shown in Figure 8-18, is where businesses trade directly with other businesses, called *business-to-business* (or B2B) trading.

In fact, the Business Marketplace is still a concept in search of its identity. For a while, its name was the Business Exchange, but perhaps that sounded a little *too* B2B. Nothing restricts the Business Marketplace to businesses; you don't have to register or prove that you're a business to buy or sell there. The Business Marketplace page merely brings together categories that might be of interest to businesses: office products and equipment, industrial and agricultural equipment, wholesale lots, businesses for sale, and so on.

In practice, the Business Marketplace (Figure 8-18) isn't all that different from eBay's Business & Industrial category (Figure 8-19). You'll find the same subcategories on the two pages; they're just arranged a little differently.

Figure 8-18:
eBay's Business Marketplace (www. ebaybusiness.com) is a showcase for categories and sellers of interest to business buyers. You can browse business-related categories or search within the Business & Industrial main category. Right-hand links (Under Services & Resources) provide information about what technical specifications mean and how to offer financing for buyers of your equipment, as well as general eBay info.

Figure 8-19:
eBay's Business & Industrial category main page lists categories and their subcategories, making browsing a little more targeted than if you start in the Business Marketplace.

You can find the Business Marketplace—sometimes—through a link on eBay's home page. Because eBay is always tinkering with the site and moving things around, you might have to type the Business Marketplace's address into your Web browser to find your way there: *www.ebaybusiness.com*. You don't have to do anything special to list your items here; if your items are in any of the categories shown on the Business Marketplace home page (Construction, Desktop PCs, Office Products, and so on), shoppers can find them by browsing the categories from this page.

If you've got a brick-and-mortar business in addition to eBay, consider eBay as a place to sell your business's surplus equipment, goods, and office furniture. In this case, you probably don't want to mess around with shipping, especially if you're selling bulky items like desks or construction equipment. You can let buyers know you won't ship the item in step 4: Payment & Shipping of the Sell Your Item form, shown in Figure 8-20.

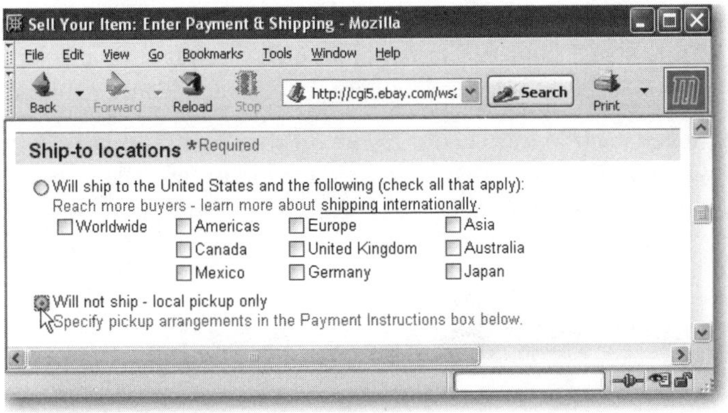

Figure 8-20:
If you don't want to waste employee time shipping a bulky item, select "Will not ship – local pickup only" in the Payment & Shipping step of listing the item. Giving further information in the Payment Instructions text box is a good idea—for example, telling the buyer to pick up the item between 9:00 a.m. and 5:00 p.m., Monday through Friday.

If eBay *is* your business, use the Business Marketplace to unload stock or equipment as your business grows and changes. There are always other dealers out there looking for stock, so if someone can resell something, it's business-related. When you buy new equipment for your business—whether it's computers, phones, postage scales—try listing the stuff you're replacing if it's in usable condition. Other businesses are probably looking for just those items, so you can make a few bucks instead of paying someone to haul away the things your business no longer needs. And selling on eBay can be quicker (and cheaper) than selling through classified ads or trade journals.

Tip: If you're selling pricey business equipment, offer your buyers financing through eBay. You'll attract more bidders, get higher bids, and—the biggest incentive—if your buyer buys an item using eBay Financing, eBay waives your Final Value Fees. To become eligible to offer eBay financing, go to *http://financingcenter.ebay.com/ebaybusiness* and click "enroll now."

Sell Your Services on Elance

eBay has a category called Specialty Services, where you can auction off your skills; subcategories include Web & Computer Services, Lessons & Tutoring, Music Composition & Poetry, Custom Clothing & Jewelry, Appraisal & Authentication, Packing & Shipping, and Logo Design, to name just a few. You can offer personalized items (from business cards to T-shirts to mugs), jewelry or antique restoration/repair, video editing, shopping assistance, interior design, personal training, and more. Although legitimate services do appear in this category, a lot of what you'll find here is junk, like eBooks and CDs touting get-rich-quick schemes or effortless weight loss. And if you browse the categories, you'll see that most of the auctions here end with no bids.

If you have a skill or service you'd like to market, there's a better place to do it: Elance (the name comes from "electronic freelance"). Elance is a separate site that helps people and businesses looking for professional help find freelancers with a service or skill to sell. Elance is not a part of eBay—though there's a loose affiliation between the two sites. In fact, the affiliation seems to be getting looser. It's hard to find a mention of Elance anywhere on eBay. Rumors have surfaced and faded that eBay is creating a Professional Services category on its own site, but so far that hasn't happened. When it does, expect the last strings between eBay and Elance to break.

In the meantime, if you want to learn about Elance on eBay itself, you have to type in this Web address: *http://pages.ebay.com/business_services* to find eBay's mystery Professional Service page, shown in Figure 8-21. Once there, you can follow a link to Elance.

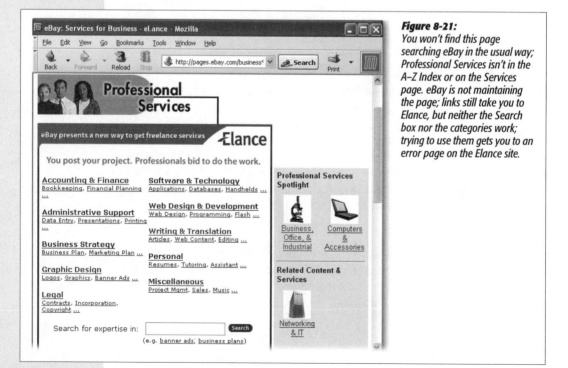

Figure 8-21:
You won't find this page searching eBay in the usual way; Professional Services isn't in the A–Z Index or on the Services page. eBay is not maintaining the page; links still take you to Elance, but neither the Search box nor the categories work; trying to use them gets you to an error page on the Elance site.

Of course, it's easier to go straight to Elance itself: point your Web browser to *www.elance.com*, shown in Figure 8-22. Elance has three divisions; you want Elance Online. Click the "Go to Elance Online" button, then click the Sell Services tab to go to the page shown in Figure 8-23. That's where you get started as a service provider.

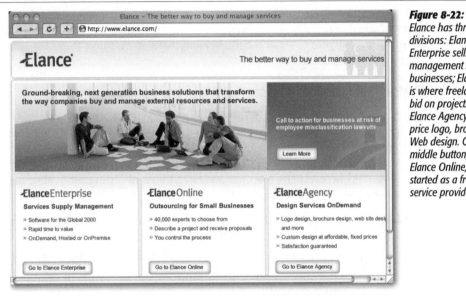

Figure 8-22:
Elance has three main divisions: Elance Enterprise sells management software to businesses; Elance Online is where freelancers can bid on projects; and Elance Agency sells fixed-price logo, brochure, and Web design. Click the middle button, Go to Elance Online, to get started as a freelance service provider.

Figure 8-23:
The Sell Services page provides general info about Elance and displays categories that have open projects. Click Start Here or Subscribe Now if you want to register and subscribe to one of Elance's service packages, which start at $12 a month. There's no charge if you want to post a project and hire a freelancer. If that's what you're looking for, click Buy Services and follow the instructions on that page.

How Elance Works

You could say that Elance is the opposite of eBay. At Elance, if you have a service to sell, *you're* the bidder. Sounds backwards, but it makes sense. A business or individual has a project they need help with. Instead of locating and approaching a range of freelancers and explaining that project over and over again, they post the project on Elance and let qualified freelancers find them. From your point of view as a service provider, this process eliminates cold calling. When you contact a potential client, you know there's a need for your services. Your job is to convince the prospect that your skills fit the project and that you can meet the client's time and budget requirements.

Elance Professional Services

Today, many businesses outsource projects to save money on employee benefits or to cope with busy times in their business cycle. Certain kinds of professional services lend themselves better to outsourcing than others. Elance is always keeping an eye on which categories generate a lot of business and which languish, and it updates the site accordingly, creating new categories and getting rid of slow ones. Here's a sampling of recent Elance categories and subcategories:

- **Administrative support.** Bulk mailing and mailing-list development, data entry, research and fact checking, travel planning, word processing.

- **Architecture and engineering.** Computer-aided design (CAD), contract manufacturing, interior and industrial design, and the various flavors of engineering (electrical, civil, mechanical).

- **Audio, visual, and multimedia.** Animation, music and radio jungles, film and video, new media, voice talent, streaming audio/media.

- **Graphic design and art.** Brochures, letterheads, logos, book illustration, direct mail campaigns, 3-D graphics, photography, book layout, print ads, press kits.

- **Legal.** There are categories for just about all legal specialties.

- **Management and finance.** Accounting, bookkeeping, collections, financial planning and reporting, management consulting, human resource policies and plans.

- **Sales and marketing.** Advertising and branding, business plans, lead generation, market research/surveys, promotions, public relations, telemarketing.

- **Software and technology.** Application and database development, system administration, scripts and utilities, security, technical support.

- **Training and development.** Business and corporate training, policies and manuals, media and sales training, programming languages and technical training.

- **Web site development.** Flash, HTML email design, Internet marketing, search engine optimization, Web hosting and design.

- **Writing and translation.** Copywriting, editing, proofreading, grant writing, test materials, proposals, resumes, speeches, newsletters, translation, creative writing.

To look at specific projects, you can browse by category or search by keyword; Elance has a Search box on every page.

Tip: People with projects don't always post them in the obvious category. And sometimes, the category isn't so obvious in the first place; for example, does writing a technical manual belong under software and technology, training and development, or writing and translation? To find the most projects, don't browse by category. Choose a keyword like *writing* or *sales* and search the whole site.

Signing Up and Bidding

Before you can bid on Elance projects, you need to register on the site. On the Sell Services page (the one in Figure 8-23), there's a Subscribe Now button. Don't click it unless you want to buy one of Elance's subscription packages, which cost you a monthly, quarterly, or annual fee. Until you've had a chance to explore the site and decide whether it's worth the money to subscribe, you just want to register, which is free (but hard to find).

To register, first find a project listing: either do a search or browse a category and click any project. Figure 8-24 shows a typical project description page. On the right-hand side is a box where you can register for Elance.

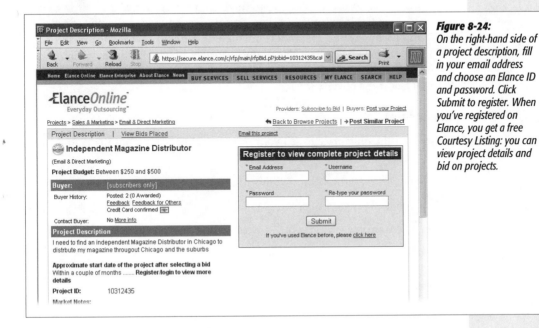

Figure 8-24:
On the right-hand side of a project description, fill in your email address and choose an Elance ID and password. Click Submit to register. When you've registered on Elance, you get a free Courtesy Listing: you can view project details and bid on projects.

Registration lets you view projects and bid on them, but your competition probably has more presence on the site than that. Elance offers several subscription levels, starting at $12–$30 a month and going as high as $75–$245 a month, depending on the category of professional service and the level of subscription. (That's not all using Elance will cost you; the company also charges an 8.75 percent fee on your invoice, and the minimum service charge per project is $10. Note that you're responsible for paying that fee, not the client.) Elance offers three subscription levels:

- **Enhanced listing.** This level lets you view and bid on projects and create a custom business profile with a portfolio showcasing up to 20 items. You can also get email notification of new projects and the ability to receive feedback for completed projects. At this level, you get up to three "leads" per month—which means that you can bid on three projects for no extra charge.

- **Professional package.** You get all the benefits of an enhanced listing but with a bigger portfolio (up to 200 items) and more leads: up to 80 per month.

- **Select professional package.** With this level, you get up to 120 leads per month. You also get featured listings to make you stand out from the hundreds of other freelancers, access to "select" projects (which tend to pay better than regular projects), and the ability to offer instant purchase packages to buyers (like eBay's Best Offer option).

The Drawback

As with most online freelance project sites, Elance is a buyer's market. There are far more registered professionals than there are projects available. This is great if you're looking to hire a freelancer, but it's not so great if you're hoping to sell your services. You might find that others are bidding far below what's reasonable for a given project. When you consider all the lowball bidding, plus the monthly fee and the per-transaction service charge, you've got to be careful that you're not bidding yourself below the poverty level.

Other Sites

Elance isn't the only place to sell your services online. Check out these other sites, too:

- Sologig (*www.sologig.com*)

- Guru.com (*www.guru.com*)

- Get a Freelancer (*www.getafreelancer.com*)

- Contracted Work (*www.contractedwork.com*)

Warning: Watch out for work-from-home scam sites, especially those promising big bucks for easy work, like stuffing envelopes. It's also a bad sign if you have to pay a fee before you can browse current listings. Check out a site with the Better Business Bureau (*www.bbb.org*) before you pay.

Cool Tools for Sellers

If you're a small-volume or even a medium-volume seller—you auction off a handful of items a week, say—you can get by with doing everything by hand: listing your auctions with the Sell Your Item form (page 155), following up with buyers after the sale (page 177), leaving feedback (page 182), and all the other niggling little details.

On the other hand, if you sell by the truckload, you're going to want software that helps you automate the selling process. And you have a lot of options to choose from, as you'll discover in this chapter. eBay is so popular, it's spawned a cottage industry just for automation software—everything from freebie programs that help you create listings in batches to high-dollar analysis tools that graph your sales so you can figure out what's selling best and why.

Not everyone needs a bulk listing tool, but most sellers will find something here that they can use to make selling on eBay easier and more fun. This chapter describes software you can use for:

- Automating the listing process.
- Managing your auctions once they're running.
- Linking your eBay sales directly to your accounting software.
- Analyzing your sales (and others') to spot trends and problems.
- Automating post-auction tasks, such as leaving feedback and tracking disputes.

eBay Tools

When you're looking around for tools to help you automate selling, see what eBay has to offer. One advantage of using eBay's tools is that when eBay makes changes to the site, it updates the tools. Third-party software and services can take some time to catch up to eBay's changes. (Of course, sometimes it takes eBay a little time to get its own changes working, too.)

Note: Even though thousands and thousands of listings for Apple computers appear on eBay every day, eBay seems to forget about all the Mac fans who use the site. eBay's downloadable software for sellers works only with Windows. But all eBayers can use Selling Manager (page 332), Selling Manager Pro (page 333), and Sales Reports (page 343), which are Web-based.

To see the latest eBay tools for sellers, use the navigation bar to go to Sell → Seller Tools, shown in Figure 9-1.

Tip: eBay is always making changes and improvements to its tools for sellers. To stay in the loop, subscribe to the Seller Tools newsletter. From the navigation bar you find on any eBay page, go to Community → Groups → News & Events → Announcements → eBay Seller Tools News Group. Click Join Group to subscribe.

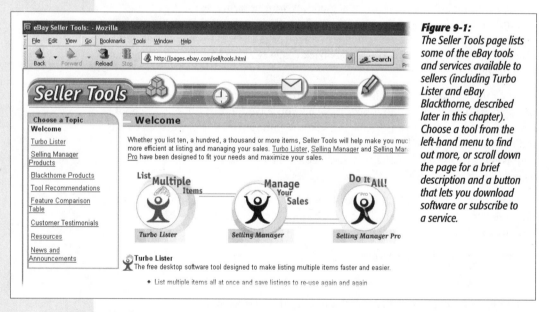

Figure 9-1:
The Seller Tools page lists some of the eBay tools and services available to sellers (including Turbo Lister and eBay Blackthorne, described later in this chapter). Choose a tool from the left-hand menu to find out more, or scroll down the page for a brief description and a button that lets you download software or subscribe to a service.

Turbo Lister

eBay's Sell Your Item form (page 155) works OK when you're listing just a few items at a time. But if you're ramping up your sales and listing a bunch of things at once, the Sell Your Item form doesn't cut it. You need a *bulk listing tool,* a program that lets you create a large number of auctions and list them all on eBay quickly and easily. Even if your sales volume doesn't qualify as turbocharged, you might find Turbo Lister a more convenient way to get your auctions online.

To download Turbo Lister (it's free), go to *http://pages.ebay.com/turbo_lister*. Before you click the Download Now! button, make sure you have these things:

- A PC (Windows 98 or later) with a 100 MHz processor or better.

- At least 50 MB of free space (100 MB for high-volume sellers).

- 64 MB of RAM for Windows 98 or Windows ME, although 128 MB is better.

- 128 MB of RAM for Windows 2000, Windows NT, or Windows XP, although 256 MB is better.

- Internet Explorer 5.5 or above.

Tip: If you have trouble installing Turbo Lister, it may be the fault of your virus scanner. Try turning off your virus-scanning program during the installation—but don't forget to turn it on again when you've finished!

Specifying settings

After you've downloaded and installed Turbo Lister, you can save yourself the time and effort of typing in the same information every time you list an item by heading to the main menu and selecting Tools → Options. Then choose one or more Auction Defaults categories (Ship-To Locations is shown in Figure 9-2) and type in any information you want to apply to more than one auction. The more blanks you fill in, the less time you'll spend at the keyboard when you start listing items.

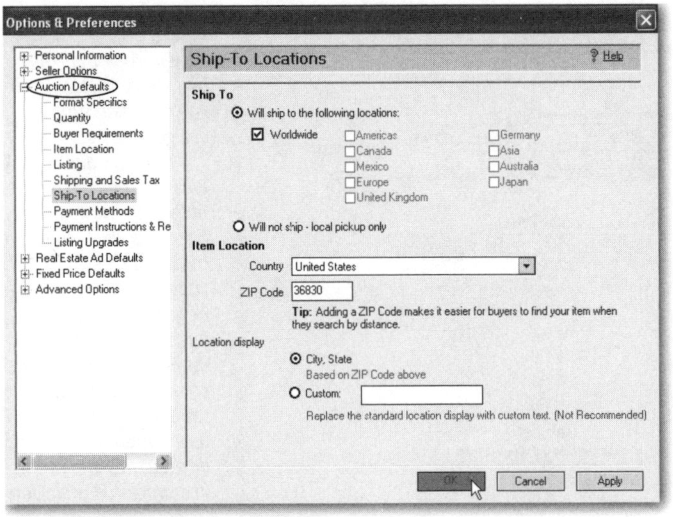

Figure 9-2:
Turbo Lister lets you set various options and use them every time you list an item. On this screen, specify your standard shipping options. You can also type in or change your Personal Information (eBay ID, mailing addresses, PayPal account), Seller Options (eBay site, auction format, eBay Store), and Auction Defaults (see left-hand menu for options). Advanced Options lets you set your preferences for receiving Turbo Lister updates, getting reminders, and displaying and storing photos.

Tip: eBay is always adding new categories and features. To make sure that your version of Turbo Lister keeps up, open Turbo Lister, select Tools → Options → Advanced Options, and then turn on the "Automatically download updates when I start the program" checkbox.

Creating new listings

When you're ready to create a new listing, go to Turbo Lister's main page and select Create New → Create New Item, as shown in Figure 9-3. Turbo Lister walks you through the listing process. You fill out a series of screens like the one shown in Figure 9-4, which aren't really all that different from eBay's Sell Your Item form (page 155).

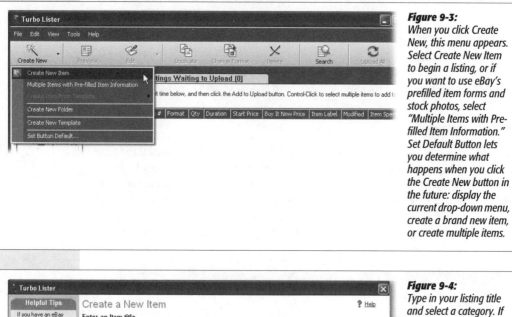

Figure 9-3:
When you click Create New, this menu appears. Select Create New Item to begin a listing, or if you want to use eBay's prefilled item forms and stock photos, select "Multiple Items with Pre-filled Item Information." Set Default Button lets you determine what happens when you click the Create New button in the future: display the current drop-down menu, create a brand new item, or create multiple items.

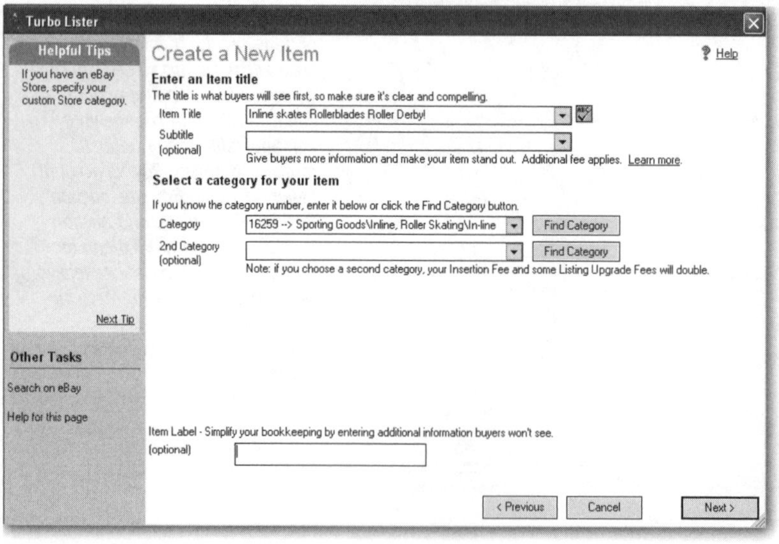

Figure 9-4:
Type in your listing title and select a category. If you don't know the category number (and you probably don't), click the Find Category button. At the bottom, you can label your item, adding a comment (like how much you paid for it) that will be invisible to your buyers when your auction is running. In the screens that follow, you write a description, insert one or more photos, and add features and options in a process very similar to the Sell Your Item form.

When you're done with the last screen, click Save. Your listing appears in something called an inventory list, shown in Figure 9-5.

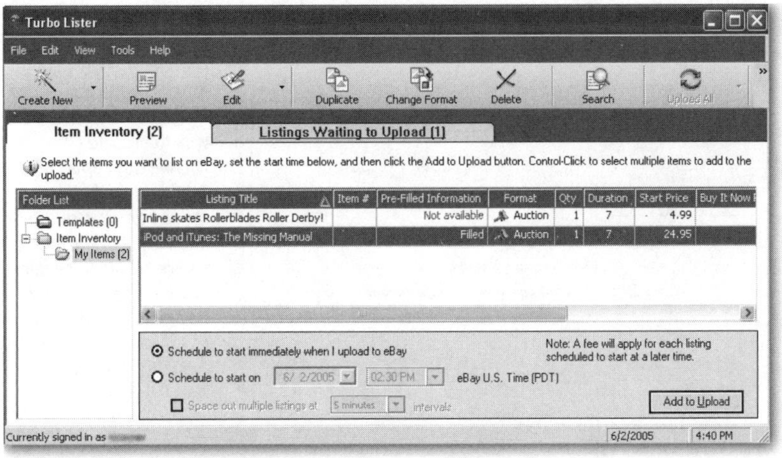

Figure 9-5:
On the Item Inventory tab, Turbo Lister shows you a chart of the auction listings you've created. At the bottom of the window, you can schedule auctions to start as soon as Turbo Lister puts them on eBay, or you can schedule a start time. When you're finished with a listing, select it and then click "Add to Upload."

The cool thing about Turbo Lister comes *after* you've created an auction. If you sell the same item in multiple auctions—say you bought a wholesale lot of shiny yellow rain boots and you're selling them pair by pair—simply click the toolbar's Duplicate button. Turbo Lister asks you how many duplicates you want to list; type in the number and then click OK. With just a couple of clicks, you can create as many duplicate listings as you need—whether it's just one or a couple hundred. It would take you dozens of tedious hours to do that through the Sell Your Item form.

The Duplicate feature speeds up your listing creation time even when the items you're selling aren't identical. If those rain boots come in different sizes, for example, you can duplicate one listing and then edit the duplicates to make sure that each auction advertises the right size. It's easy to edit a listing: just select the listing you want and then click the toolbar's Edit button to go to the Edit Item screen shown in Figure 9-6. Make your changes and click Save.

Uploading your listings

All the listings you create in Turbo Lister stay right on your machine until you upload them to eBay, at which point your auctions go live (unless you've scheduled a start time, as shown in Figure 9-5). When you're ready, start up Turbo Lister and make sure you're on the Item Inventory tab. Select the listings you want to transfer to eBay and then click "Add to Upload." (You can select multiple listings at one time: click the first item you want, then hold down the Shift key and click the last item you want: Turbo Lister selects those two items and everything in between. To pick and choose items rather than select them in a block, hold down the Ctrl key as you click the items you want.) Turbo Lister puts the listings you've selected on the "Listings Waiting to Upload" tab, shown in Figure 9-7.

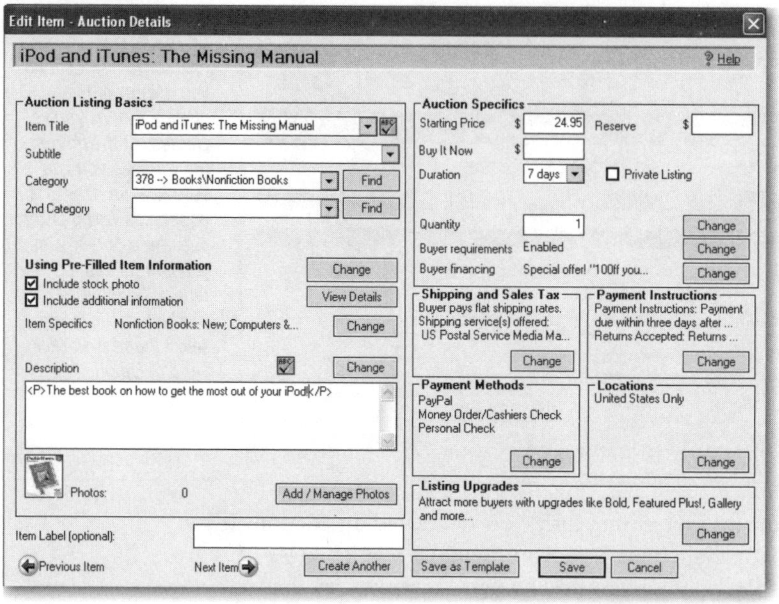

Figure 9-6:
If you need to make changes to individual listings you've duplicated, the Edit Item screen is the way to go. You can change any aspect of the listing. At the bottom of the screen, Previous Item and Next Item arrows let you go through the items in your inventory list to edit them; you don't have to keep going back to the main list. The Create Another button duplicates the listing. Clicking Save as Template saves the listing in your Templates folder, which is handy the next time you want to create a listing for an identical or similar item.

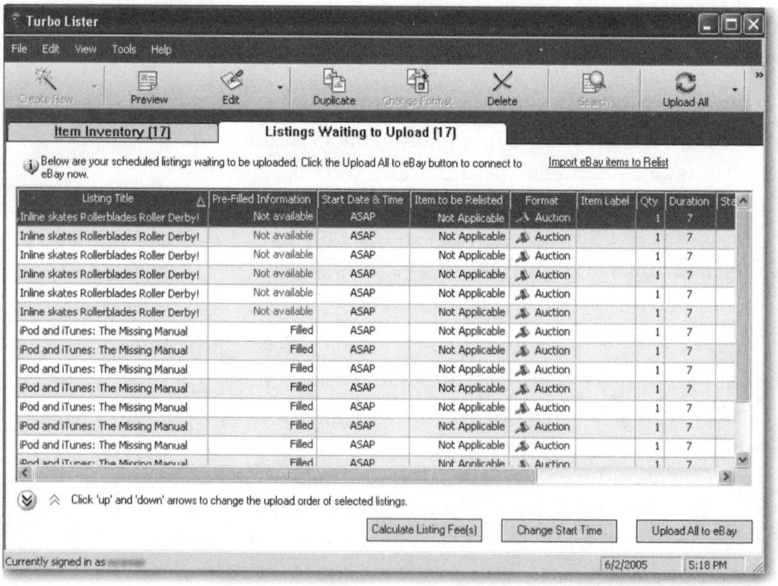

Figure 9-7:
You can upload all the listings in the "Listings Waiting to Upload" tab with one click of the "Upload All to eBay" button. If you want to see how much your listing fees will be before you start the auctions, click Calculate Listing Fee(s); clicking this button also lets you check for eBay updates to Turbo Lister. The Change Start Time button lets you change an immediate-start auction to a scheduled one (for eBay's usual scheduled-start-time fee) or the other way around; it affects whichever listings you've highlighted.

Tip: Before you click the Upload button, check your watch. If you happen to be using Turbo Lister at, say, two o'clock in the morning or some other low-traffic time, don't transfer your listings yet. Either schedule the auctions for better start and end times or, to save the scheduling fee, come back and upload the auctions at a time when you're likely to get more last-minute bidders (page 162).

If your items don't sell, you can relist them through Turbo Lister, if you subscribe to Selling Manager or Selling Manager Pro (page 332). If you qualify and you want to relist items, click the "Listings Waiting to Upload" tab's "Import eBay items to Relist" link.

WORKAROUND WORKSHOP

Turbo Fizzler

Some eBayers can install Turbo Lister and begin creating scads of auctions in mere minutes. Others aren't so lucky. If you're one of the cursed, you might encounter trouble downloading, installing, or using Turbo Lister. Here are some suggestions to help you get Turbo Lister working:

- **Update Windows.** Turbo Lister relies on various behind-the-scenes Microsoft components to do its thing. If your Windows software is out of date, you might run into problems installing Turbo Lister or reading and creating listings. The two components you probably need are the latest versions of MDAC (which stands for Microsoft Data Access Components, in case you were wondering) and Jet, Microsoft's database engine. You can get the latest versions of these programs from Microsoft's Download Center. Point your Web browser to *www.microsoft.com/downloads*, then search for *MDAC* and find the latest update. Make sure that the update you download works with your version of Windows. Then repeat the process, this time searching for the most recent update of *Jet*. Install the downloaded files on your computer, and then restart it.

- **Check your firewall settings.** Your computer's *firewall* is software that protects your computer from everything on the Internet that could cause damage or unauthorized access. But if your firewall is too fiercely protective, it will interfere with the information you try to transfer between your computer and eBay. Different firewall software needs different fixes. Go to eBay's Turbo Lister Troubleshooting page (*http://pages.ebay.com/help/sell/turbo-lister-troubleshooting.html*).

(You can also reach the page from Turbo Lister's menu bar by selecting Help → Online Troubleshooting.) Then, find your firewall program to get instructions on how to make it Turbo Lister–friendly.

- **Compact the database.** An unwieldy database can slow Turbo Lister to a crawl. Give it room to work by compacting its database from time to time. From the Turbo Lister menu bar, select Tools → Compact Database, and then click OK. It can take a couple of minutes for Turbo Lister to do the compaction.

- **Get help.** If you've done everything you can think of and Turbo Lister still refuses to list (in turbo fashion or otherwise), it's time to ask for some assistance. The place to start is eBay's Turbo Lister discussion board (Community → Discussion Boards → Tools → Turbo Lister). Post the problem you're having, and friendly fellow eBayers will try to help.

You'll probably need to show them a copy of your Turbo Lister log. Your computer stores this log in its hard drive. Open Windows Explorer, find *C:\Program Files\eBay\Turbo Lister*, and look for the most recent file ending in *.log*. Open the *.log* file in Notepad (not in Word), then copy it (highlight it and choose Edit → Copy) so you can paste it into your plea for help. The discussion board is probably the fastest way to get an answer to your question, but you can also contact eBay for support. To do so, from the Turbo Lister menu bar, select Help → Contact Customer Support. In the form that opens, explain your problem. Paste in the log file to help eBay help you. Click Send Email when you're done.

Turbo Lister archives every auction you create, so if you come across another collectible comic book just like the one you sold for a bundle a few months back, you can find the previous auction and duplicate it to save time creating the new listing. But it can get cumbersome keeping all your old listings in your inventory list. If you get tired of looking at them, get organized by creating and using your own folders. From the menu bar, select File → New → Folder. Name your new folder and then click OK. Now you can simply drag whatever listings you wish into the appropriate folder.

Turbo Lister tricks

To get the most out of Turbo Lister, use these tips and features:

- **Templates.** Any listing you create can serve as a template for similar listings. Just find the listing you want, click the Edit button, and make any changes that apply to the new auction. When you've created a listing that you know you'll want to use again, save it in the Templates folder by clicking the Save as Template button. That makes it easy to find your template later.

- **Insert.** If you have a logo or some favorite text (like *Don't forget to add me to your favorite sellers!*), you can save time by creating and storing these as *inserts*, the stuff that you like to add to most of your item descriptions.

  You create an insert during the step when you enter your item description (page 326). From the Inserts drop-down menu, select "Create an Insert." In the window that opens, name the insert and type in your text or logo-referencing HTML; you can use up to 1,000 characters. Click Save. Turbo Lister stores up to five inserts.

  Put an insert into your listing like this: on the Enter Your Description page, select the insert you want from a drop-down menu, as shown in Figure 9-8.

- **Backups.** Anyone who's ever spent more than about 10 minutes on a computer understands the importance of backing up his data. Imagine creating and storing hundreds or even thousands of listings, only to lose them in some computer catastrophe. Turbo Lister's backup feature creates a copy of each of your listings, including photos, descriptions, item specifics, and prefilled information. To back up your listings, from the menu bar select File → Backup Database to display the Backup Database window shown in Figure 9-9.

Tip: If you're the kind of person who'd benefit from someone occasionally looking over your shoulder to say, "Remember to back up that database," click Backup Reminder when you create a backup file. You can tell Turbo Lister how often you'd like it to remind you to save new data.

- **Importing/exporting.** When you need to move some of your listings from one computer to another—say you want to move them from your desktop machine to your laptop so you can work on your listings at the local coffee shop—use Turbo Lister's *import/export* feature. First you have to export the listings. Select the listings you want and then from the menu bar, select File → Export Selected Item → To CSV. (CSV stands for *comma-separated value;* it's the simplest method for storing data in a text file.) Turbo Lister prompts you for a file name and a location to save the file, and then creates a CSV file storing the selected listings. You can save that file to a storage medium, like a diskette or a flash drive.

To open the exported listings on another computer that has Turbo Lister installed, stick your export diskette (or flash drive, or whatever storage medium you chose) into the new computer. Open Turbo Lister and select Import Items → From CSV. Find the file you want and then click Open. Turbo Lister puts the listings into a new file called "Imported from CSV." From there, just work with the listings as you normally would.

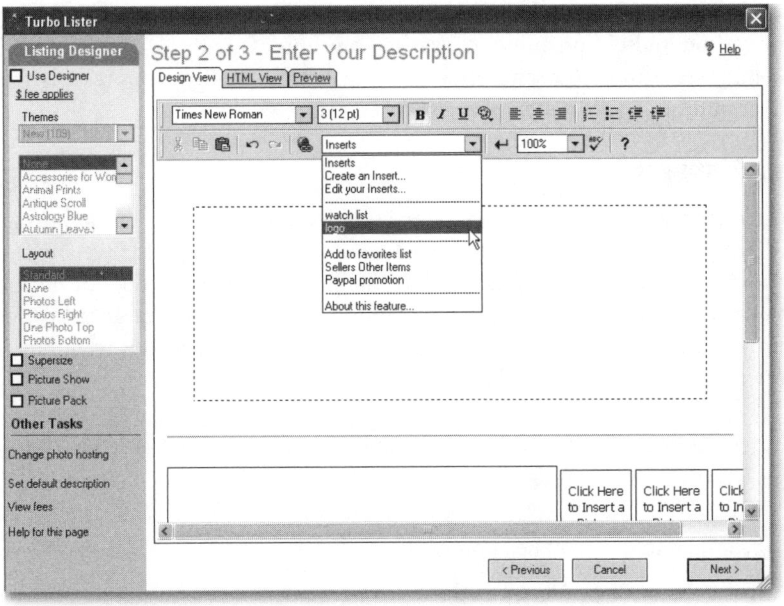

Figure 9-8:
After you've created an insert, it appears by name in the Inserts drop-down menu. Click the insert you want to put into your item description. You can also use this menu to create new inserts and edit or delete existing ones.

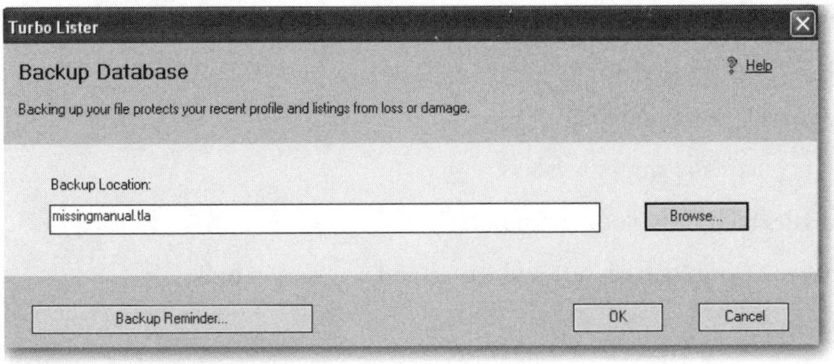

Figure 9-9:
Turbo Lister names your backup file based on your eBay ID. You can change the name if you like, but leave the extension (.tla) as it is. By default, Turbo Lister stores backup files under My Documents in the Turbo Lister backup file. If you want to store the backup file somewhere else, click Browse and find the folder you want.

Tip: Import/export is useful when you need to transfer selected listings, not the whole database. If you want to transfer everything, back up your data (page 330), then transfer the backup file.

- **Previews.** To get a sense of how your auction will look, click the Preview tab while you're typing description text and adding photos to a new item (page 326). This view puts everything together—your description, any Listing Designer frames you chose, your photos—exactly as it will appear in your auction. You don't have to guess whether you're getting your listing to look the way you want.

- **Uploading in batches.** If you're going to be running a number of auctions for the same or very similar items, consider transferring those auctions to eBay in batches, rather than all at once. If all your auctions end at the same time (or within seconds of each other), bidders who didn't win one auction don't have time to find and bid on another. Transfer a group of auctions, and then wait a few minutes before you send eBay the next batch. You'll get more bids from last-minute auction watchers and also-rans.

Selling Manager

Turbo Lister (page 324) gets your auctions online, but to track your auctions and do the paperwork *after* the sale, you need another tool. Enter Selling Manager, a Web-based program from the folks at eBay that helps you manage sales during and after your auctions. It's available by subscription (for a monthly fee after a 30-day free trial). Selling Manager is Web-based, so you can use it no matter what kind of computer you have.

Note: If you already subscribe to Blackthorne Basic (page 334) or own an eBay Store (page 259), subscribing to Selling Manager doesn't cost you a penny.

To use Selling Manager, you need one of the following:

- Internet Explorer 4.0 or later.

- Netscape 3.0 or later.

- AOL 3.0 or later.

Here are some of the things you can do with Selling Manager:

- Relist unsold items in bulk.

- Print invoices and shipping labels.

- Send sales records to your computer.

- Manage Unpaid Item reports and fee-refund requests in bulk.

- Leave feedback in bulk.

Selling Manager Pro, designed for high-volume sellers, adds the ability to list, so you don't have to use separate listing and sales-management tools (for example, Turbo Lister and regular Selling Manager). Selling Manager Pro offers everything that Selling Manager does and more:

- **Automated listings.** If you regularly sell the same items, you can schedule regular, automatic listings.

- **Automated relistings.** When an item doesn't sell, Selling Manager can relist it for you automatically.

- **Listing designer.** Use free templates to dress up your listings.

- **Inventory management.** Create templates for the products you sell most, update quantities, add notes, get restock alerts when inventory is low.

- **Listing statistics.** Keep track of the percentage of successful sales and average selling price.

- **Sales reports.** These monthly reports show all of your selling activity, including eBay fees.

- **Alerts.** You can receive alerts in My eBay when a buyer pays, when payment is overdue, or when you get negative feedback.

The basic version of Selling Manager works best for medium-volume sellers who run, say, a dozen or so auctions per week. Fewer than that, and it's not really worth the monthly fee; more than that, and you need a more powerful auction-management tool, like Selling Manager Pro or one of the many third-party options out there (page 344).

One useful feature of Selling Manager is that it helps you keep an eye on problematic auctions. Under Sold Items: Past Due, Selling Manager has these categories:

- Unpaid and eligible for an Unpaid Item reminder.

- Unpaid Item disputes awaiting your response.

- Unpaid and eligible for Final Value Fee credit.

Another useful feature is that you access Selling Manager from your My eBay page (page 32); it replaces the Sell page, as shown in Figure 9-10. This means that Selling Manager looks and feels familiar, so you can get up to speed fast.

To sign up for Selling Manager, go to your My eBay page and then click Manage Subscriptions. Find the version you want—Selling Manager or Selling Manager Pro—and click Subscribe.

Selling Manager updates your information every 10 minutes, so you don't have to worry that it's giving you yesterday's news. But if you need to check something from an old auction, the archive holds completed sales for up to four months. To see what's in your archives, look under My eBay Views and then click the Archived link.

Figure 9-10:
When you subscribe to Selling Manager, it replaces the Sell page in My eBay. Selling Manager continually updates your sales information, putting Scheduled and Active auctions into new sections ("today" and "within the next hour") as their time approaches, and moves listings through the post-auction process. In the left-hand menu, click any link under Selling Manager to get more detailed information.

eBay Blackthorne

Blackthorne, called Seller's Assistant before its mid-2005 redesign, is a downloadable software program that helps you automate and manage your auctions from start to finish. Here's a sample of what Blackthorne lets you do:

• List or relist items in bulk.

• Create listings quickly with templates and preset fields.

• Track sales status.

• Send after-auction emails in bulk.

• Leave bulk feedback.

Blackthorne comes in two flavors: Basic and Pro. Blackthorne Pro offers everything that the Basic version does, plus you can do the following (and more):

• Create multiple seller accounts if you sell, for example, CDs under one eBay ID and sporting goods under another.

• Print bulk invoices and shipping labels.

• Schedule listings.

• Manage inventory; know when you're getting low on widgets and need to order more.

- Get profit-and-loss and sales tax reports.

- Manage your suppliers and consignments.

Tip: To ask other eBayers about Turbo Lister, Selling Manager, and Blackthorne—how to use them, troubleshooting tips, which software they prefer—head over to the discussion boards. From the navigation bar, select Community → Discussion Boards. There's a Tools board for each program.

Here's what you need to run Blackthorne on your PC (sorry, Mac lovers—eBay has no immediate plans to make this tool available for Macs):

- Windows NT, 2000, or XP.

- 1 GHz of processing power.

- 256 RAM minimum (512 MB is better).

- 50 MB or more of free space on the hard drive.

Both versions of Blackthorne require you to download software and to subscribe to the service for a monthly fee. You can try either level of Blackthorne free for 30 days; go to *http://pages.ebay.com/blackthorne* and then click the Subscribe Now link for the version you want.

The first time you use Blackthorne, it asks a bunch of questions to help you set things up, such as your eBay ID, contact information, the email account Blackthorne will use, sales tax information, and so on. Then Blackthorne offers you the options of printing out a quick start guide, reading the user's manual, or getting started with Blackthorne.

UP TO SPEED

At Your Service

One of Blackthorne's improvements over Seller's Assistant is something called *the Servant,* a feature that runs in the background whenever you're online and have Blackthorne open.

With Seller's Assistant, eBay's previous sales-management tool, you had to instruct the program to contact eBay whenever you wanted to send information to eBay or retrieve information from it. In contrast, the Servant interacts with eBay automatically. You don't have to do a thing.

In fact, if you leave Blackthorne running and walk away from your computer, the Servant will periodically update your listings and sales information (as long as your computer is online). When you come back, your information in Blackthorne is up to date.

Listing items

To list items using Blackthorne, click the Create Items tab, shown in Figure 9-11, and then select New Item → Untitled to open the Item window, shown in Figure 9-12, where you create your listing. The great thing about the Item window is that you can do everything you need to list an item—write a title and

---

description, add photos, choose a category, determine price and shipping info—all in one window. No stepping through screen after screen before you're finally done.

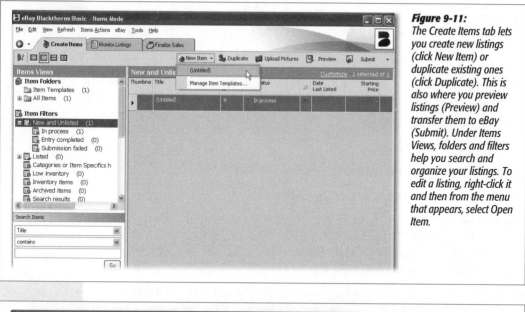

Figure 9-11:
The Create Items tab lets you create new listings (click New Item) or duplicate existing ones (click Duplicate). This is also where you preview listings (Preview) and transfer them to eBay (Submit). Under Items Views, folders and filters help you search and organize your listings. To edit a listing, right-click it and then from the menu that appears, select Open Item.

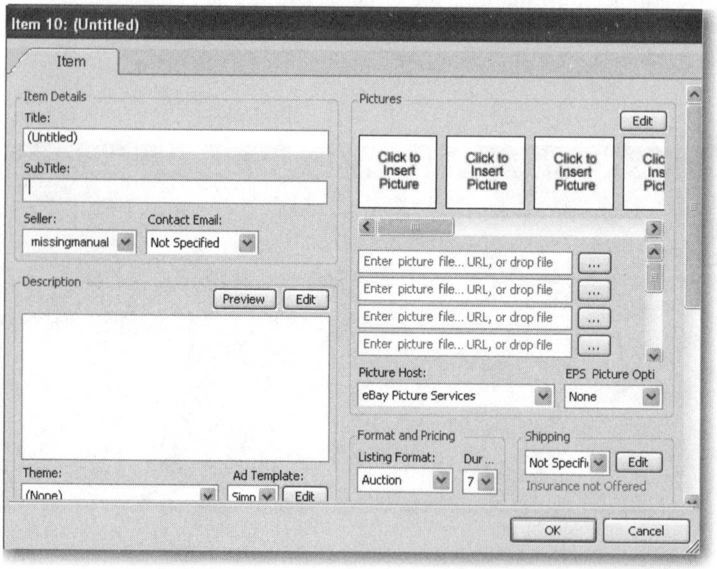

Figure 9-12:
Blackthorne's Item window, which you use to create a new item, is a little crowded; some of the fields are hard to read. You can spread things out by dragging the window's lower-right corner.

To speed up the data-entry process, Blackthorne uses *presets* for some parts of the listing, like shipping, return policy, picture host, and payment method. A preset is a group of preferences that you set once and then apply over and over again to your auctions. For example, if you sell clothing and charge a flat shipping rate for each item you sell, you can create a preset that includes your shipment method and the flat amount, and then name the preset *clothes*, as shown in Figure 9-13. To create a preset within the Item window, find the field you want to create a preset for, like Shipping, then click its arrow and choose Manage Presets. Follow the prompts to define your terms, name the preset, and then click OK.

Tip: Blackthorne offers Quick Tips in the lower left-hand pane (you can see it in Figure 9-11). To get an off-the-cuff explanation of a button, menu, or field, hover your cursor over the item you'd like to learn about. The Quick Tips pane displays a definition.

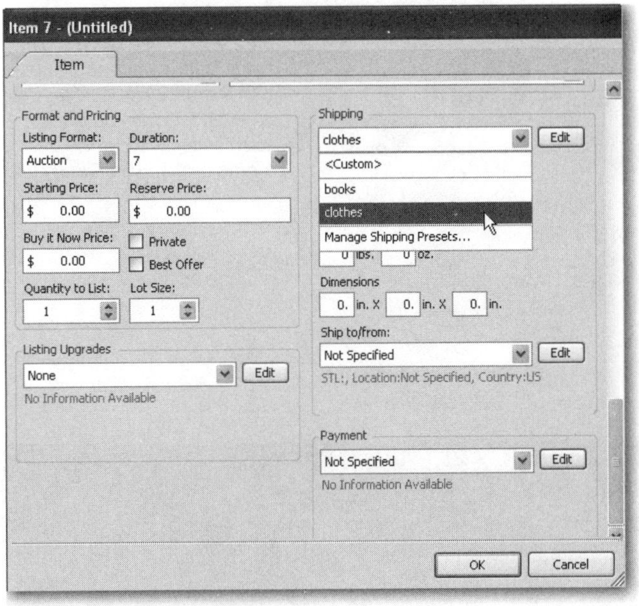

Figure 9-13:
Presets let you set your terms once and then reuse them as often as you like with just one mouse click. After you've created and named a preset, it appears in the drop-down list so you can select it easily. Selecting a preset automatically inserts your predefined terms into the listing.

When you've typed all the info that your auction needs into the Item window, click OK. Back on the Create Items tab, check your auction to make sure you've set it up correctly. Select Items Actions → Preview and Check Errors. You get a preview of the auction, shown in Figure 9-14. When Blackthorne checks for errors, it also calculates your eBay insertion fees, based on your starting price and any features you select. If you need to correct an error (or make any other changes), right-click the title and then, from the menu that appears, select Open Item. When you're good to go, click Submit.

When you click Submit, you can choose whether you want the auction to start immediately or, for a fee, start at a time you schedule. If you opt to schedule your auction's start (page 162), you can also select a time interval between listings to space out your auctions, giving last-minute bidders time to swoop in. Click OK to upload your listing to eBay.

After you've submitted the auction to eBay, Blackthorne changes the item's status from "In process" to "Entry completed" and creates a listing record. To take a look at the record, click the Monitor Listings tab. Look under Listings Views to find "Listings by Status," and then click the Running filter. Running (active) auctions appear in the main part of the window.

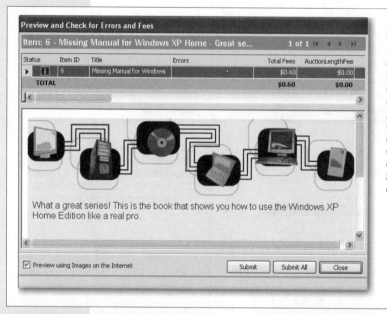

Figure 9-14:
Preview and Check Errors doesn't check for typos and misspellings, but it does make sure you've filled in everything you need to list your auction successfully. The bar above the preview shows your listing title, any errors, and the insertion fees. When you're ready to list the auction on eBay, click Submit. If Blackthorne finds an error, click Close, and then select Tools → Activity Log; the error is on the Listing History tab.

POWER USERS' CLINIC

The Magic of Filters

Blackthorne uses *filters,* which are akin to smart folders, to organize your search results. When you run a search, Blackthorne dumps the results in a filter called, not surprisingly, Search Results. It's a good idea to rename the filter to something more specific, indicating what's in it, like Bike Accessories or BIN Listings. (To rename a filter, simply right-click the filter name, choose Rename Filter, and type the new name.)

Unlike a folder, however, which merely holds a list of results from previous searches, a filter automatically runs the search again the next time you open it, so your results are always up-to-the-minute. As your Blackthorne content changes, so does the list of results in a given filter.

For example, say you specialize in selling vinyl LPs, and you've created listings for tons of Beatles records. To keep the listings together, you ran a search for *Beatles* a year ago and saved the results in a filter that you named "Beatles." Now, you want to create a listing for an import version

of The White Album—and if you already have such a listing, you want to duplicate it rather than start from scratch. But you can't remember whether you've listed that particular LP before. No need to run a search; all you have to do is open your Beatles filter. Every listing you've *ever* created with *Beatles* in the title is already in there, automatically.

Playing around with filters will give you a sense of how to organize your listings. You can create, name, duplicate, and delete as many filters as you like; just right-click the filter and select Rename Filter from the menu that pops up.

Blackthorne does have some built-in filters that you can't mess with; these are the filters that are already there the very first time you open Blackthorne, like "Inventory items," "Completed listings," "Sales by Status," and so on. You can't duplicate or delete these filters; the only changes you can make are to display options, such as which columns the filter shows.

During the auction

When your auctions are up and running, use Blackthorne's Monitor Listings tab to view listings, revise listings that haven't received any bids, add information to listings where bidding has started, or cancel an auction.

You can view running auctions by the following criteria:

• Auction format.

• Current auctions.

• Scheduled auctions.

• Recent bidding activity.

• Auctions that can be relisted.

• Seller account (for Blackthorne Pro).

You can also search for a particular listing by title, starting price, and almost any other criteria you can think of, as shown in Figure 9-15.

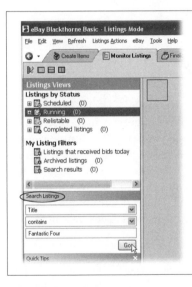

Figure 9-15:
You can search for specific listings from any of Blackthorne's main tabs. You don't have to search by title; you can look for almost any variable in an auction, from package weight to reserve price to bid count to starting price—and beyond. Choose whether you want the results to contain or not contain the words you type into the text box. Click Go to have Blackthorne display the results.

After the auction

If an item doesn't sell the first time around, you can relist it (page 177). Blackthorne makes relisting simple. First, find the items eligible for relisting. To do so, in the Monitor Auctions tab, under "Listings by Status," click Relistable to display the auctions you can list again. Highlight the auctions you want to relist and then select Listing Actions → Relist Items. Click Yes to bring up a window that lets you make the changes you want. (Was the starting price too high? Could your title or description be more appealing?) When you've finished, click either Relist (to relist the current item) or Relist All (to relist all the items you selected).

When you make a sale, Blackthorne automatically changes the status of the item to Sold and keeps track of its current place in the post-auction process—whether the buyer has paid, whether you need to ship or leave feedback, etc. You can find sold items on the Finalize Sales tab under "Sales by Status," as shown in Figure 9-16.

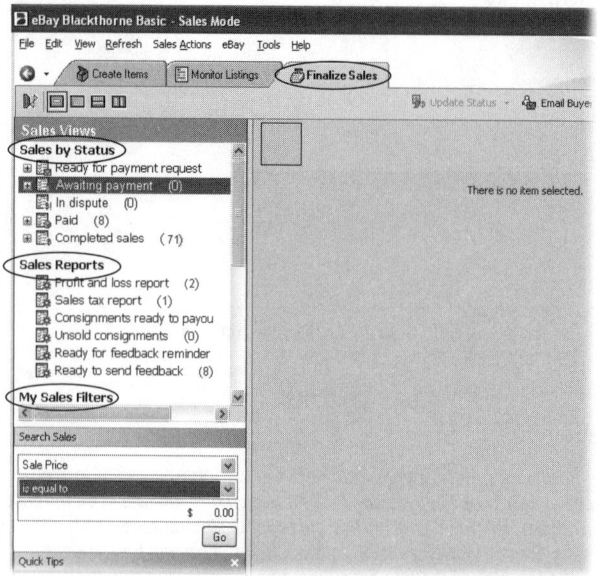

Figure 9-16:
The Finalize Sales tab shows the status of your sales, from awaiting payment to awaiting feedback. Search for any completed listing by final price, sales tax, shipping fee, buyer ID, and a bunch of other criteria. You can filter sales by archived sales or search results.

If you accept PayPal and all goes smoothly, the buyer might pay immediately after the auction. But if the buyer needs a nudge to send payment, Blackthorne lets you send a "first notification" email as a gentle reminder. To send this email, make sure you're on the Finalize Sales tab; from the menu bar, select Sales Actions → Email Buyer → "First Notification to High Bidder." You can also use the Email Buyer drop-down list. Blackthorne shows you the email, which is already filled in with the item number, titles, and the final amount the buyer owes. Click Submit to send the gentle reminder winging on its way.

Tip: If the high bidder ignores your requests for payment, you can file an Unpaid Item dispute right from Blackthorne. To do so, on the Finalize Sales tab, select Sales Actions → Report Unpaid Item Dispute.

Blackthorne comes with a variety of email templates that fit most of the emails you'll want to send. (To see them, just click Email Buyer.) Preloaded templates give you a quick and easy way to do the following:

• Request the high bidder's address.

• Send first, second, and third requests for payment.

• Notify the buyer that you've received payment.

- Notify the buyer you've shipped the item.

- Request feedback (shown in Figure 9-17).

Each of these templates is specific to whatever listing you've selected, prefilled with the information you need, like the item title and number. You can modify these templates or create your own, as shown in Figure 9-18.

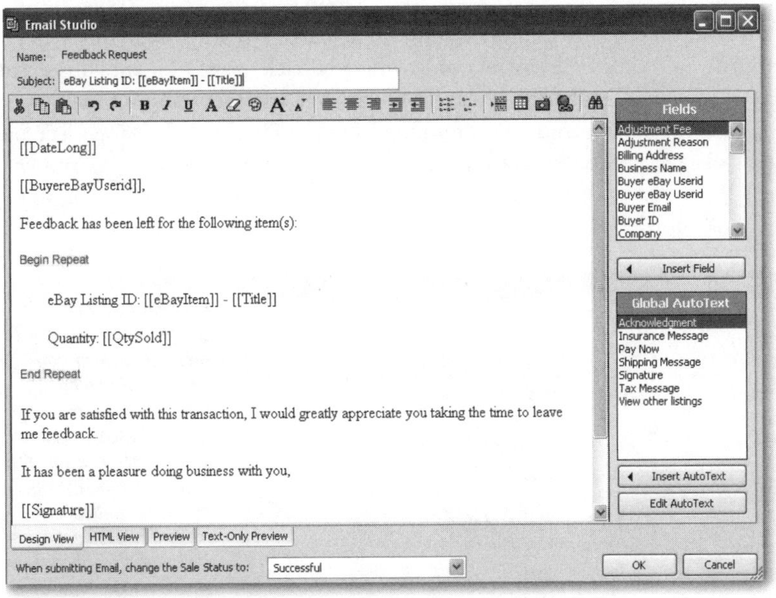

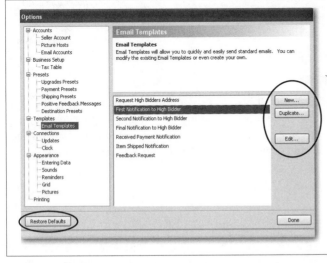

Figure 9-17:
Blackthorne's various email templates fill in the specifics of a particular auction automatically. Everything inside the double square brackets pertains to the specific auction you selected.

Figure 9-18:
To create your own email template, click New. The Duplicate button duplicates any existing template and saves it with a new name. You can also edit any template using the Edit button. If you fool around with a template and don't like the results, click Restore Defaults to put it back in its original, pristine state.

If the buyer pays with PayPal, Blackthorne automatically updates the auction's status to Paid. If the buyer pays by another method, you have to let Blackthorne know. From the menu bar, select Sales Actions → Update Sale Status To → Payment Received.

Note: When you update an item's payment status, it might seem to disappear. This is because Blackthorne has moved the listing to a different filter, from "Awaiting payment" to "Paid and ready to ship."

When the transaction is complete and (in a perfect world) everyone's happy, Blackthorne automates the process of leaving feedback (page 61), which is a great timesaver. (Leaving feedback the standard way, one transaction at a time through eBay, takes a lot of time and a lot of typing.) On the Finalize Sales tab, select Sales Actions → Leave Feedback and then choose the message you want, as shown in Figure 9-19.

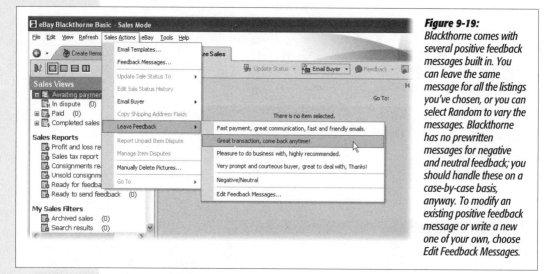

Figure 9-19:
Blackthorne comes with several positive feedback messages built in. You can leave the same message for all the listings you've chosen, or you can select Random to vary the messages. Blackthorne has no prewritten messages for negative and neutral feedback; you should handle these on a case-by-case basis, anyway. To modify an existing positive feedback message or write a new one of your own, choose Edit Feedback Messages.

Accounting Assistant

If you use QuickBooks, the small-business accounting program, to help you keep track of where your eBay-earned cash is coming from (and going to), Accounting Assistant can save you some time. With Accounting Assistant, you can transfer information about sales and payments from eBay to QuickBooks, including:

• eBay sales.

• eBay fees.

• PayPal fees.

It doesn't matter whether you use the Pro, Premier, or Enterprise edition of QuickBooks, but you must use a U.S. version of QuickBooks 2002 or later. (Other bookkeeping programs and international versions of QuickBooks won't work.) Accounting Assistant is available for free to all eBay Store owners and to those who subscribe to Selling Manager or Blackthorne. (If you don't fit one into one of those categories, you can't use Accounting Assistant.)

To download Accounting Assistant, go to *http://pages.ebay.com/accountingassistant* and then click Download Accounting Assistant Full Setup. After you've installed Accounting Assistant, it asks some preliminary questions about how you want your information entered into QuickBooks. Take the time to answer the questions carefully; this setup process saves you lots of time later. Another timesaver is Accounting Assistant's ability to match eBay sales transactions to existing customers and items in QuickBooks automatically. When you've been using Accounting Assistant for a while, it actually gets smarter about how to match sales, customers, and items, which means less time tapping the keyboard for you.

Note: For help with QuickBooks, check out *QuickBooks: The Missing Manual.*

---

eBay Sales Reports

If you want to see at a glance how your eBay business is doing from month to month, you can subscribe to eBay Sales Reports, a Web-based service shown in Figure 9-20. There are two levels: just plain Sales Reports, which are free, and Sales Reports Plus, which cost $4.99 per month (but you can try them out free for a month). Here's what they include:

- Sales.

- Ended listings.

- Successful listings (those that ended with a sale).

- Average selling price.

- eBay and PayPal fees.

Sales Reports Plus tacks on some diagnostic tools you can use to analyze your auctions:

- Metrics to measure success by category, auction format (like regular or BIN), day/time of auction end.

- Buyer counts.

- A detailed breakdown of your eBay fees.

- Unpaid Item credits you've requested.

To sign up, from the eBay home page go to My eBay → Manage Subscriptions, find the level of sales reports you want, and then click the Subscribe link. You can view your Sales Reports from your My eBay page. In the left-hand menu, look under My Subscriptions, and then click Sales Reports.

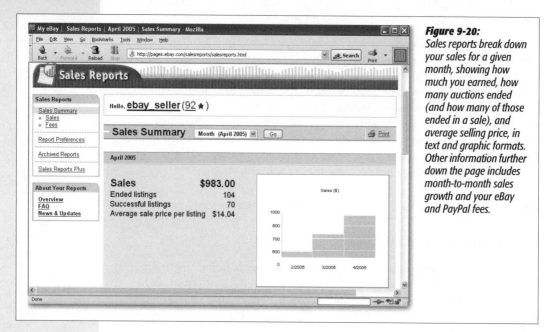

Figure 9-20:
Sales reports break down your sales for a given month, showing how much you earned, how many auctions ended (and how many of those ended in a sale), and average selling price, in text and graphic formats. Other information further down the page includes month-to-month sales growth and your eBay and PayPal fees.

Third-Party Software

eBay has spawned an entire industry of companies whose business is making it easier for you to sell. Some, like Andale and Terapeak, have official links to eBay as "certified providers"; others don't. (eBay screens certified providers before they can fly the eBay logo on their site; certified providers have to pass a certification exam, provide references, and prove extensive experience on eBay. You can see a list of certified providers and the products and services they offer at *http://developer.ebay.com/programs/certifiedprovider/catalog.*) There are about as many software programs as there are tasks to organize and automate. A few are free, and most of those that aren't offer a free trial. Shop around and try several, until you find the program that best fits your business needs and work style.

If you want to see what others have to say about these programs before you commit, check out the software-review resources on page 405.

Note: The main disadvantage of using tools and services provided by companies not affiliated with eBay is that when eBay makes a change, the tool can break. It can take a week, sometimes longer, for the company to catch up and get the tool working again.

Market Analysis

Researching the market—in other words, the stuff everybody else is selling on eBay and who's buying it—helps you decide what products to sell and what to charge for them (page 240). Do prices drop on 3- or 4-megapixel cameras when a snazzy 7-megapixel model comes out? Could Cabbage Patch dolls be making a comeback as a collectors' craze? If you're a serious seller, market analysis lets you stay on top of the trends, positioning you to keep your sales in high gear.

Web-based market analysis

An advantage to using Web-based market-analysis software is that its information stays up-to-the-minute. Of course, you have to be online to use these services, although most offer reports that you can print out or download and study at your leisure.

Note: Downloadable market-analysis software for Macs is about as rare as hens' teeth. If you use a Mac, your best bet is one of the online services in this section.

Vrane. Amherst Robots/Vrane (*www.vrane.com*), shown in Figure 9-21, updates its statistics daily. The site offers a variety of free and fee-based services, including these:

- **Sale Analysis.** Provides daily or monthly sale figures, fees, and success rates, including charts. Register on the site and import your sales data from eBay to use this free service.

- **Sale Reporter.** Creates a comprehensive report, including graphs of daily and monthly transactions and an itemized summary of all your transactions. Fee-based.

- **Free stats.** In the Stats category, click Sale, Hits, or Categories to compare your sales data with an eBay-wide snapshot. These statistics record data for sellers using Vrane products, but they offer a quick overview, updated daily, of typical eBay activity.

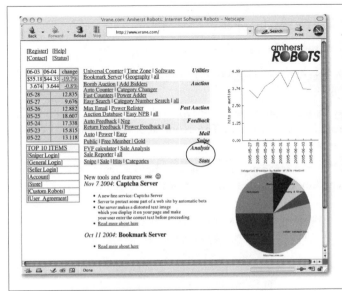

Figure 9-21:
Amherst Robots' Web page (www.vrane.com) tracks daily sales data. The left-hand table shows successful snipes in the top row and average hits per auction in the second row, including the percentage change from one day to the next; track these to find the best days to end your auctions. The table below shows the average successful sale price (per day) of sellers using Vrane products. The middle of the page lists Vrane services. The top-right graph charts average hits per auction by the month, and the pie chart below it displays the most popular categories.

For its fee-based services, Vrane charges by what it calls *universal credits*. You buy a number of credits for a specified price, and then pay with those credits as you use the company's services. You can share credits with your friends and use them for a variety of services—that's why they call them universal.

Tip: Credits expire, so start with the cheapest package and see how long it takes to use up the credits while you're learning the site.

Andale Market Research. Andale, known for its popular auction-page hit counters (page 208), sells a Market Research Pack for a monthly fee. Go to *www.andale.com* to subscribe. The Market Research Pack includes these reports:

- **What's Hot.** Best-selling products in different categories.

- **Price Finder.** Average selling price, price range, and success rate.

- **How to Sell.** Selling strategies based on actual market data.

- **Sales Analyzer.** Detailed analysis of your sales—and suggestions on how to do better.

- **Counters.** A record of how many shoppers look at your auction.

Terapeak. Terapeak (*www.terapeak.com*) offers subscription-based market analysis at two levels: Research Lite ($9.95/month) and Research Complete ($16.95/month). Both levels cover this info:

- Analysis of three months' worth of completed listings to help you set the right price.

- Category analysis of the best time, day, and season to sell. Also covers auction length.

- Hot list that predicts the next big thing.

Research Complete throws in these goodies:

- **Competition analysis by category.** Does your category have room for more sellers, or is it too tight?

- **Analysis of eBay listing promotions.** Is it worth the extra money to boldface your title or spring for Featured Plus? This report tells you which extras might actually help your sales.

- **Saved research.** You can save your Terapeak searches and email them to yourself, then use them offline, like when you're creating listings with Turbo Lister.

Tip: For a free monthly report on which categories are on the way up and which are sliding down the slippery slope, check out eBay's own Hot List (page 208). It's free and available at *http://pages.ebay.com/ sellercentral/hotitems.pdf.*

Downloadable market-analysis software (for Windows)

If you use Windows, this section describes a couple of good choices.

AuctionIntelligence. AuctionIntelligence (*www.certes.net*) includes software and a subscription service; upgrades to the software are free for as long as you subscribe. AuctionIntelligence searches eBay, including eBay Motors and the British and Australian sites, to find the information you need to scope out the competition and improve your auctions. Features include the following:

- Search by title, seller, category (or a combination of these).

- Run searches in the background while you're viewing a report.

- Acquire detailed information about every auction in your search, including complete Bid History.

- Generate a variety of reports to analyze the raw data you gather. For example, you can get reports on the most profitable categories, the most effective keywords, changes in a product's price over time, and even the sell-through rates of other sellers.

HammerTap's Deep Analysis. Deep Analysis, shown in Figure 9-22, analyzes eBay data to uncover market trends and help you develop your sales strategy.

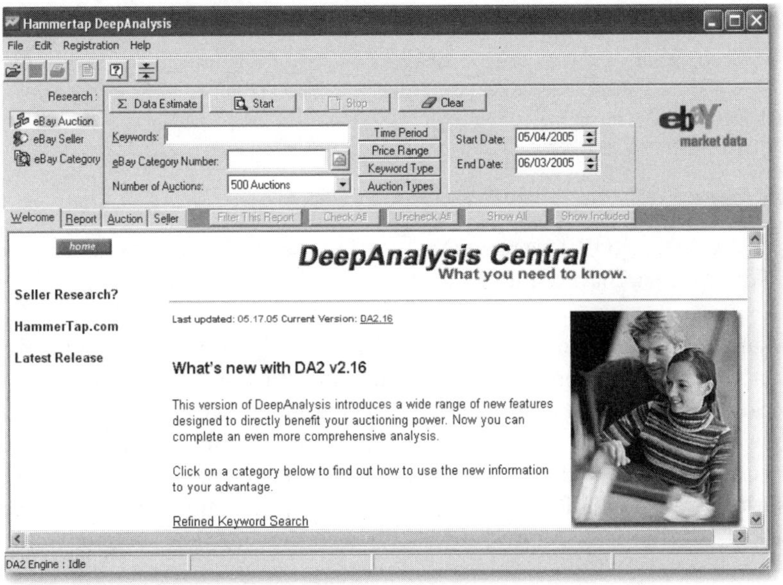

Figure 9-22:
On the Deep Analysis Welcome page (www.hammertap.com), type in your search criteria and then click the Start button to launch your search. You can search from 500 to an amazing 100,000 auctions. In the upper left, use the Research categories to analyze Auction, Seller, or Category data. Use the tabs above the main window to view results in report form, by individual auction, or by seller.

You can search by keyword or category within a time period or price range you specify, by keyword type, or by auction type. View the results by seller or auction, or in a report that tells you the number of auctions, average price, overall success rate, and success rate by seller. The report also breaks down data by the following:

- Auction type (regular, BIN, Dutch).

- Feature analysis (bold, highlighting, gallery, and so on).

- Starting and ending days.

- Auction length.

- Top sellers.

Deep Analysis is available at *www.hammertap.com*. The first year costs $179 and the annual renewal fee is $49.95, but you can try it free for two weeks.

Listing and Auction Management

Listing tools streamline the process of creating and starting auctions. Auction-management tools make it easier to run, keep track of, and follow up on those listings. A complete auction-management tool includes everything you do from start to finish in the course of an auction: listing, auction watching, relisting, after-auction emails, printing shipping labels and invoices, and following up with feedback. Not all the auction management tools discussed here include all these functions; decide what's important to you and see which one best meets your needs.

Note: Some of these products and services are free; others will cost you (but many offer a free trial). Check individual Web sites for pricing.

For Mac fans

It wasn't that long ago that there were no auction listers or managers designed for Macs. Now, Mac fans have a number of choices.

eLister and Auction Monitor. Just as eBay has created Turbo Lister and Selling Manager to work together to create and monitor auctions in Windows, Black Magik Software (*www.blackmagik.com*) has paired up eLister and Auction Monitor, shown in Figure 9-23, to give Mac users the same capabilities. ELister lets you create auction listings offline and transfer them to eBay at your convenience. It comes with a variety of built-in templates. You can preview your listings and get an estimate of insertion fees before your auctions go live. Auction Monitor notifies you when an auction gets a new bid, when negative-feedback bidders try to jump in on your auctions, when you receive feedback, and when an auction ends.

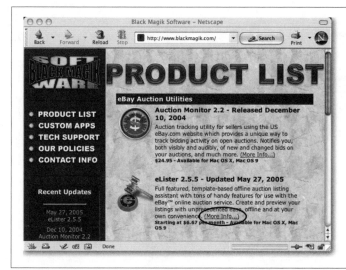

Figure 9-23:
Black Magik Software's listing and monitoring tools are available for OS 9 and OS X. ELister works with auctions using U.S. dollars only, and it doesn't work with eBay Motors. Click More Info to read about and download the software.

CALC for OS X. Cycline3, a company that offers graphic design and software services, developed CALC (Cycline Auction Listing Creator) to help sellers create professional-looking listings without knowing a single HTML tag. CALC lets you choose a background and colors, insert tables and photos, make your text look great, and preview your listing, all by pointing and clicking. CALC works with OS 8.5 through OS X. Get it at *www.cycline3.com/calc.*

GarageSale. GarageSale is available at *www.iwascoding.com/GarageSale*, or you can get it from the Mac OS X Downloads page, shown in Figure 9-24. (Go to *www.apple.com/downloads/macosx*, click Productivity Tools, and search for *garagesale.*) GarageSale is a listing tool with everything you'd expect: templates, support for multiple accounts, easy access to photos, and the ability to create and preview listings when you're offline. In addition, GarageSale lets you use the iSight Webcam as a digital camera for auction photos and access your iPhoto library from right inside GarageSale. There's even an active GarageSale group on Yahoo! (*http://groups.yahoo.com/group/GarageSale_Users*): get help, share tips and templates, or just chat with other GarageSale aficionados.

iSale. iSale (*www.equinux.com*) integrates with iLife, Apple's suite of media programs, to simplify auction creation and tracking, online or offline. Use iSight to take digital photos, upload those photos to the iDisk storage area of your .Mac account (saving money on photo hosting), get buyer details with a single click, and track the status of completed auctions. iSale's Smart Groups feature lets you create categories, such as *Last Week's Sales,* and automatically sorts your listings into them.

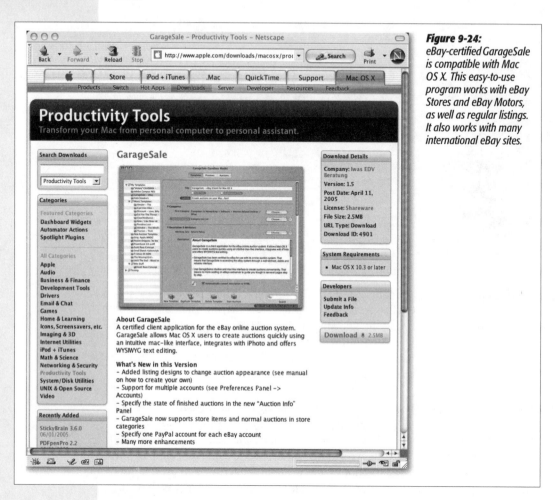

Figure 9-24:
eBay-certified GarageSale is compatible with Mac OS X. This easy-to-use program works with eBay Stores and eBay Motors, as well as regular listings. It also works with many international eBay sites.

For Windows

There are tons of third-party programs out there for sellers who use Windows. Most of them offer the same core tools: for listing, monitoring auctions, and following up sales. When considering different auction managers, focus on cost and ease of use; when it comes to bells and whistles, make sure the extras offer something you actually need.

Lister Pro. Andale's Lister Pro (*www.andale.com*) is an offline listing tool, shown in Figure 9-25. Lister Pro is free, but to use it you need to subscribe to one of Andale's listing plans, which start at $2 a month to list 10 auctions. Here are some of the features Lister Pro offers:

- A Design Center with more than 100 ready-made themes and layouts.

- Recommendations for the best title, category, and pricing strategy for your item, based on Andale's extensive eBay research.

- In-auction price comparisons for BIN auctions; convince shoppers your auction is a great deal by displaying similar items that sold for a higher price.

- Listing archives and templates.

- Bulk listings and immediate automatic relistings.

- Inventory management.

- Auction tracking and monitoring.

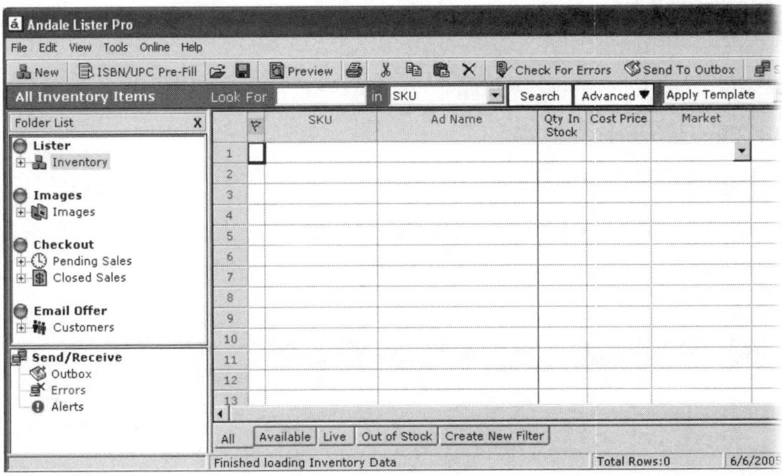

Figure 9-25:
Most of the buttons in the toolbar are self-explanatory; there are also buttons (not shown) for bulk editing and restocking. To create a new listing, click New to open Andale's One-Step Lister. The left-hand menu holds folders to organize your auctions.

Auction Wizard 2000. The folks who developed Auction Wizard 2000 realized how hard auction management could be back in the late '90s, when they found themselves faced with the prospect of selling off a 3,000-piece collection of Hollywood memorabilia. Swamped by all the responsibilities of high-volume selling, from creating listings to inventory management to answering emails to following through on sales, they realized automation was the key to maintaining efficiency—and sanity. Auction Wizard 2000, shown in Figure 9-26, was the result.

When you've downloaded Auction Wizard 2000 from its Web site (*www.auctionwizard2000.com*), start by creating an *Auction Profile*, which collects the settings you'll use, including auction site (eBay, Yahoo! Auctions, and so forth); your ID, password, and email account for that site; email and feedback templates for bulk responses; tax profile; and optional settings for auction length, listing template, consignor, store category, and so on. You may eventually want to have several Auction Profiles; you need at least one to create your first listing.

Auction Wizard 2000 is easy to learn. When you get up to speed, here's a sampling of what you can do with it:

- Create listings from your inventory database.
- Edit photos with a built-in image editor.
- Categorize inventory and track stock you've listed or sold.
- Send and receive email automatically using email templates.
- Create an email address book.
- Identify repeat buyers.
- Print invoices.
- Create combined invoices for multiple-item buyers.
- Track and report sales tax.
- Track income and expenses with a built-in ledger.
- Print shipping labels.
- Generate and print sales reports.

Auction Wizard 2000 offers a generous, nothing-held-back free trial for 60 days. After that, you pay an annual subscription fee to keep using the software.

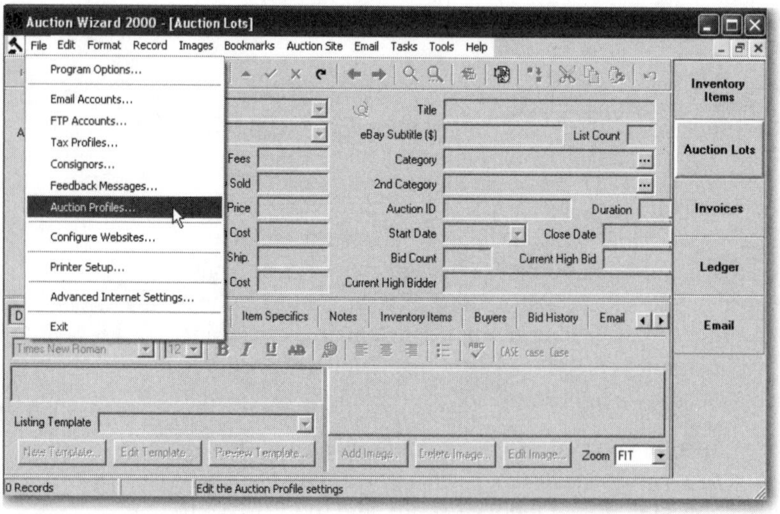

Figure 9-26:
The first step in using Auction Wizard 2000 is creating an Auction Profile to store information you'll use again and again when creating listings. To make a new listing (Auction Wizard 2000 calls each listing a lot), make sure you're on the Auction Lots page (if not, click the far-right Auction Lots button), then click the toolbar's plus sign and start filling in your information.

HammerTap. Besides Deep Analysis market-research software (page 347), HammerTap (*www.hammertap.com*) offers a number of tools of interest to sellers:

- **Auction Informant.** When one of your auctions receives a bid (or someone retracts a bid), Auction Informant sends you an email to let you know.

- **BayCheckPro.** With one click, you can get any eBayer's selling, bidding, and feedback histories. Useful when you're unsure about a bidder who's been sniffing around your auction.

- **BayMailPro.** You can send email to eBayers by their ID, without knowing their email address. BayMailPro also lets you send bulk email (but watch out for eBay's no-spam policy; you can't send unsolicited commercial email), create an address book, and save mailing lists and email templates.

- **Fee Finder.** This tool is useful in keeping track of *all* your fees—eBay insertion fees, eBay FVFs, PayPal, shipping—helping you make sure that your expenses aren't eating up your profits.

Note: You can get these tools individually, but HammerTap offers a package called HammerTap Value Pack, which bundles together the tools listed here for $54–a 20 percent savings. If you want market research, too, HammerTap Studio throws in Deep Analysis (page 347), but the price skyrockets to $209.

Other Windows-based listing and management tools. There are dozens of software companies out there that would love to help you set up and manage your auctions (as long as you're running Windows). Here's a selection you might want to check out:

- All my Auctions for Sellers (*www.rajeware.com*).

- Auction Sage (*www.auctionsagesoftware.com*).

- CALC (*www.cycline3.com/calc*)—see page 349 for a description.

- Spoon Feeder (*www.spoonfeeder.com*).

- Shooting Star (*www.foodogsoftware.com*).

Web-based (Windows or Mac)

If you're uncomfortable typing your eBay ID and password into a non-eBay Web site, you won't be able to use an online service; they need this info to sign in to eBay and act on your behalf. On the other hand, there are several advantages to using online auction-management services: it doesn't matter what kind of computer you use, you can still manage your auctions when you're on the road and away from your computer, and you don't have to worry about how downloading and configuring strange software might mess up your computer. You do have to be online to use them, but even the offline listing and management programs need to jump online once in a while to interact with eBay.

If an online management service sounds good to you, take a look at the services listed in this section. Many work by subscription; some charge a percentage of your sales and others a per-transaction fee. Trial periods and fees vary.

Andale One-Step Lister. Two minutes after they start using eBay, a lot of sellers are already sick of the time it takes to slog through all five steps of the Sell Your Item form (page 155). Andale (*www.andale.com*) solves that problem with One-Step Lister, shown in Figure 9-27. Do everything you need to create your listing all on one page, then click Preview to see the results, save to come back later, or Launch to start your auction.

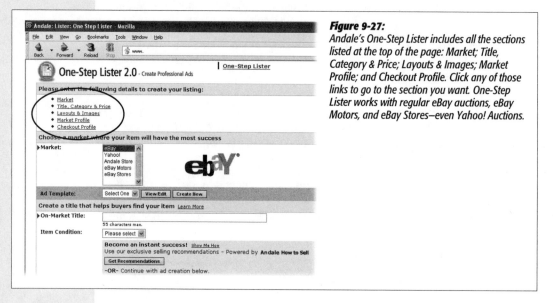

Figure 9-27:
Andale's One-Step Lister includes all the sections listed at the top of the page: Market; Title, Category & Price; Layouts & Images; Market Profile; and Checkout Profile. Click any of those links to go to the section you want. One-Step Lister works with regular eBay auctions, eBay Motors, and eBay Stores—even Yahoo! Auctions.

Auction Hawk. For a flat fee that allows a certain number of listings per month—from $12.99 a month for 110 listings all the way up to $89.99 a month for unlimited listings—Auction Hawk (*www.auctionhawk.com*) offers a one-page lister, picture hosting, easy checkout, automated after-sale tasks and emails, plus a few extras:

• Auction Hawk imports all your eBay listings when you sign up, so you don't have to figure out how to get your pre–Auction Hawk auctions onto the site.

• Auction Hawk takes hourly hit counts and produces bid-to-hit ratio reports.

• BuyScraper checks your bidders' histories for negative feedback and sends you a report to help you avoid potentially troublesome bidders.

• Email Ping notifies you when a buyer reads email you sent.

Meridian. If you're an official Trading Assistant (page 273) or if friends and family are always asking you to sell stuff for them, see what Meridian (*www.noblespirit. com*) has to offer. In addition to the usual auction-management features, Meridian lets you manage your consignors (the folks whose stuff you're selling). Each consignor account you create contains contact information, commission plan, and room for notes. You can view a list of all consignors or of the items you're selling for a particular consignor and filter by item status. Especially useful is the ability to create a variety of commission plans, so you don't have to charge your little brother the same fee for selling his skateboard that you charge the fancy antique dealer across town.

Vendio. Vendio (*www.vendio.com*) gears its Sales Manager editions (not to be confused with eBay's Selling Manager, described on page 332) to two distinct kinds of sellers:

- **Inventory Edition.** This tool works best for sellers who sell many items in multiple quantities: computers and consumer electronics, clothes and jewelry, sports gear, car parts, books, CDs, movies—any seller who makes money by moving multiple items quickly. Vendio designed Sales Manager Inventory Edition to let high-volume sellers create and edit multiple listings fast, save time with automated auction launches, and keep close track of their inventory.

- **Merchandising Edition.** If your specialty is one-of-a-kind items, such as antiques, coins, collectibles, handmade items, and so on, Sales Manager Merchandising Edition can help you create listings that attract the buyers you want, with free custom templates and photo hosting.

The Merchandising Edition is simpler and easier to learn; the Inventory Edition offers more automation. You'll invest some up-front time learning it, but if you're a high-volume seller, you'll more than make up the time. Rates vary depending on the level of service you want; check the Vendio site for details.

Other online auction-management services. New auction-management services spring up just about every week. Here are some that have been around for a while:

- AAA Seller (*www.aaaseller.com*). Offers extra-large "SuperZoom" photos.

- AuctionHelper (*www.auctionhelper.com*).

- AuctionTamer (*www.auctiontamer.com*).

- ChannelAdvisor (*www.channeladvisor.com*).

- HammerTap Manager (*www.hammertap.com*). Most of HammerTap's products are Windows-based, but not this online service.

- InkFrog (*www.inkfrog.com*). InkFrog's i-Tools include i-Showcase (a clickable gallery of your other listings) and i-Checkout (page 356).

• ManageAuctions (*www.manageauctions.com*). If you like this service, you can make a few bucks referring your friends.

• Marketworks (*www.marketworks.com*).

• SpareDollar (*www.sparedollar.com*).

• Zoovy (*www.zoovy.com*).

Email and Feedback Automation

Most auction-management programs have some kind of email and feedback automation. But maybe you're not looking for a full-blown auction-management program. Maybe you just want some help staying caught up with email or feedback duty. If so, these tools might help (prices, of course, vary):

• **Amherst Robots** (*www.vrane.com*). Offers a variety of Web-based options for automating both email and feedback. Auto Mailer checks for completed auctions once a day and sends notification emails to the winners; Power Mailer can helps you deal with Dutch auction winners and combined shipping when one buyer wins two or more of your auctions. Feedback tools include Power Feedback Gold, which sends a "thank you" email to your buyers at the same time you leave them positive feedback.

• **Customer Manager** (*www.vendio.com*). Imports buyer info from eBay to build a searchable database of your customers, making it easy to find emails relating to a particular transaction. Filters help keep out spam and organize incoming email. Web-based.

• **InstantFeedback** (*www.pctechzone.com*). Automatically responds in kind to positive feedback and lets you know when you get hit with a negative or a neutral. For Windows.

Other Tools

A few seller's tools fit into the "miscellaneous" category. They're not essential, but if your selling process could improve and you've got a few minutes to kill, check them out—they might be useful.

Auction checkout

Some sellers dislike eBay's checkout process; either they want to accept credit cards directly, without using PayPal, or they want access to their payments faster than PayPal allows. Others want a checkout tool that makes it easy to search and find information about past sales. If any of these sellers sounds like you, consider one of the following software programs:

• Andale Checkout (*www.andale.com*)

• Auction Checkout (*www.usaepay.com*)

• InkFrog i-Checkout (*www.inkfrog.com*)

Warning: eBay buyers like PayPal. If you're looking for an alternative checkout merely to avoid using PayPal, think again. You'll lose potential buyers. Other checkouts work best when they include PayPal as an option but also let buyers pay directly with a credit card.

ALTERNATE REALITY

Get Creative with Unusual Tools

Most sellers' tools and services perform the same basic functions, but Ethical Technologies (*www.ethicaltools.com*) has some innovative ideas that just might shake up your auctions. The company does offer the standard seller tools (image hosting, a customizable listing tool, an auction scheduler, and a relister), but here are some tools you won't find in any run-of-the-mill selling solution:

- **Price Dropper.** If you're sick of items sitting there day after day without a bid, Price Dropper will hold an automated sale on your behalf. Set the lowest price you're willing to accept, the increment by which you want Price Dropper to lower the starting price, and the time intervals between price drops (from 12 hours to six days).

- **Sell It Now.** Ethical pitches this tool as a way to speed up your auctions and go straight to the sale. When you activate Sell It Now, it checks all your auctions and ends any that have bids, making the current high bidder the buyer. Be warned that Sell It Now checks *all* your auctions when you set it loose, so don't use it if you think one or two of your auctions are heading into a bidding war. You should also give this tool a pass if your auctions have a lot of watchers—who might turn into snipers in the final seconds.

- **Category Rotator.** Get your auction more exposure and do a little market research at the same time by trying out a listing in different categories. With this tool, you select up to five categories for listing your item and specify a rotation time (from six hours to two days). After the amount of time you choose has passed, Category Rotator automatically revises your listing, placing it in the next category. (Once your auction has a bid, you can't revise categories, so it'll stay in the category where the bidder found it.

You also can't revise a category during the last 12 hours of an auction.) Find out which categories attract bidders and which don't.

- **Title Rotator.** This basic idea of this tool is the same as for Category Rotator, but instead of changing categories, you try out up to five different titles for your auction, letting you experiment to find the most effective keywords. As with categories, you can't revise an auction's title after someone's made a bid or in the auction's last 12 hours.

- **Item Rating System (IRS).** If you ever wonder what shoppers and bidders *really* think of your auctions, here's an easy, free way to find out. The IRS tool puts a rating system in your listings; anyone who visits one of your auctions can rate it on a scale of one to 10. You get a report that shows the average rating for each of your listings that received votes.

- **Thank You Tool.** This one has generated a lot of buzz. It establishes early contact with bidders, with the idea that the personal touch turns bidders into buyers—repeat buyers, if you're lucky. When someone places a bid in one of your auctions, the Thank You Tool does just what it promises; it sends an email thanking the bidder for his or her bid. You get three prewritten emails to choose from. Just saying "thank you" can make your auctions stand out.

Even if you decide not to use any of these tools, it's worth going to *www.ethicaltools.com/Toys* to play some auction-related games. In Shipper, boxes roll down conveyor belts, and you have to catch them and load them into the right truck. And when you need to let off some steam after filing an Unpaid Item dispute, there's nothing better than a quick game of Whack a Nonpaying Bidder.

Seriously miscellaneous: FVF calculation and bombing

Sometimes you don't want to go to all the bother of opening a big program to get a little information or perform a simple task, like calculating FVF fees or ending your auctions early. In these cases, go to *www.vrane.com* for a quick FVF calculator, shown in Figure 9-28, or to *bomb* your auctions. Bombing your auctions means that you cancel all bids and end your auctions early with just one click—a quick way to protect your feedback rating if an emergency arises or you take off on a spur-of-the-moment vacation.

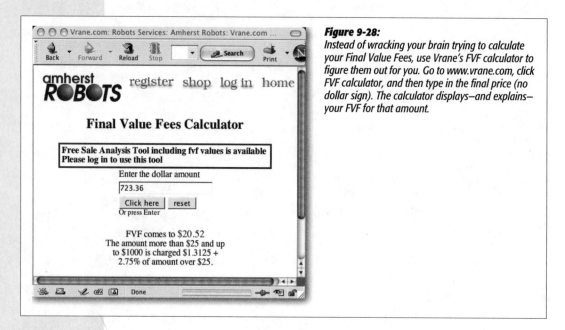

Figure 9-28:
Instead of wracking your brain trying to calculate your Final Value Fees, use Vrane's FVF calculator to figure them out for you. Go to www.vrane.com, click FVF calculator, and then type in the final price (no dollar sign). The calculator displays—and explains—your FVF for that amount.

3

Part Three:
Finding Other eBayers and Getting Help

Connecting with Other eBayers

Before they started spending all their time checking email and surfing the Web for celebrity gossip, people used to go their local marketplace to meet up with friends and flirt with the cute merchants. In the Internet age, eBay provides the same function.

More than just a place to buy and sell, eBay is also a place to network and socialize. People have started long-term partnerships and friendships on eBay. One couple even met on eBay and married at eBay's annual convention (he bought her engagement ring in a last-second snipe).

Even if you're not looking for new buddies, you can maximize your buying and selling power on eBay by building relationships with other eBayers. You can trade tips and tricks, find others with similar interests, and ask for advice. This chapter presents general and specialized discussion groups, both on and off eBay, that will help you make satisfying connections. Here are some of the topics it covers:

- eBay discussion boards.

- Live chats.

- Workshops and classes with other eBayers.

- The eBay Affiliates program.

- Offsite eBay discussions.

- eBay's annual in-person convention, eBay Live!

Connect with the Community

eBay's Community page, shown in Figure 10-1, offers a host of different ways to make connections with other eBayers: through discussion boards, chat rooms, workshops, and more.

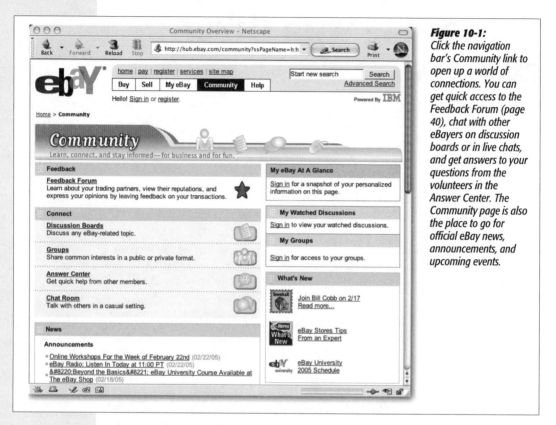

Figure 10-1:
Click the navigation bar's Community link to open up a world of connections. You can get quick access to the Feedback Forum (page 40), chat with other eBayers on discussion boards or in live chats, and get answers to your questions from the volunteers in the Answer Center. The Community page is also the place to go for official eBay news, announcements, and upcoming events.

Discussion Boards

A *discussion board* is a Web page where people can "talk" to each other by posting messages and posting replies to others' messages. (In Web parlance, discussion boards are sometimes called *bulletin boards*.) eBay's discussion boards are *threaded*, which means that whenever someone starts a topic (called a *thread*), all responses to that topic show up under the original post. If you want to change the topic, you can start a new thread. When you look at a discussion board, as in Figure 10-2, you're looking at the titles of various threads. To read messages posted in response to a particular topic, click the thread's title.

eBay has five kinds of discussion boards:

- **Community Help Boards.** Ask questions and get answers from other eBayers about all things eBay: how to use your My eBay page, how to buy items, and how to list and sell them. This is a good place to start if you have a question about eBay in general or one of its features, from About Me pages to feedback to using eBay's sellers' tools (page 324).

- **General Discussion Boards.** These boards are for general topics that may or may not relate to eBay. They have cutesy names like The Front Porch, The Homestead, The Soapbox, and Night Owl's Nest. Each board has its own personality. A good one to check out when you're getting started is the "New to eBay" board.

- **Category-Specific Discussion Boards.** These discussions are great for collectors, hobbyists, and sellers who specialize in a certain kind of item, like Disneyana or books. Share tips and talk with like-minded people.

- **Workshops.** Workshops, described in detail on page 406, are a scheduled, hourlong discussion between a leader and any eBayer who wants to attend.

- **eBay Giving Works.** This board discusses the fund-raising auctions held through eBay Giving Works to benefit nonprofit organizations and other causes (page 310). If you're interested in learning how to support your favorite cause through eBay or want to meet others who support the same cause, check out this board.

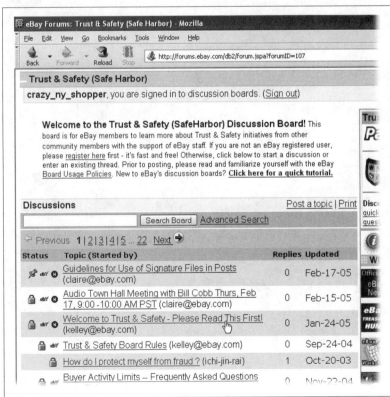

Figure 10-2:
To read a discussion, from the navigation bar choose Community → Discussion Boards. Click the name of a board that interests you. The page that opens contains all the current threads in that board. The pictures in the left-hand column indicate various things: the tack means that the thread will always appear at the top of the list; the lock means you can read a thread but not reply to it; the eBay logo means that the thread contains a post from an eBay employee; and the N means that you haven't read that thread yet.

You can read a discussion board's threads simply by going to the navigation bar and clicking Community → Discussion Boards, and then clicking any board's name (like Book Readers, Outdoor Sports, or Seller Central). A list of threads appears. Click any thread to read its messages.

Tip: Discussions can get messy as many people chime in. You can cut through the clutter by searching the discussion boards for words or phrases that relate to your topic. Just click the Search button at the bottom of any thread page. You can specify search terms, a date range, a particular eBay ID, and the number of results you want per page.

When you're reading a discussion and you want to chime in with your two cents, click "Post a reply" in the thread you want to answer; the link is at the top of the list of messages. To post, you have to sign in to the discussion boards (a separate process from signing in to eBay). After you've signed in, you see a box similar to the one shown in Figure 10-3.

UP TO SPEED

Keeping Discussions Above Board

Any get-together can turn rowdy, and eBay's discussion boards are no exception. To maintain a level of decorum, eBay has set some basic rules that apply to everyone who takes part in eBay's discussion forums. You can read the rules in full by heading to the bottom of the eBay home page and then clicking Policies → Boards, but here they are in a nutshell:

- Don't publish anything personal about someone else on the boards, including contact information, real name, or email content.

- Be yourself. Don't pretend you work for eBay or impersonate another eBayer.

- Keep it clean. Don't post anything pornographic or obscene.

- Don't post Web addresses or item numbers in a thread title.

- Don't advertise auctions or commercial Web sites. This rule includes want ads; post these to Want It Now (page 86) instead.

- Watch the flames. Comments that include threats, hate speech, vulgarity, or profanity are subject to removal.

- Color inside the lines. Make sure that your post fits a discussion board's purpose. For example, don't complain about eBay's fees in the Feedback Help board. Also, don't discuss posts that have been pulled by eBay. And don't encourage other eBayers to violate eBay's policies.

You have to be 18 or older to participate in discussions, and if your feedback score (page 40) is below 10, you can post only 10 messages a day.

If you want to report a post that violates these terms, click the Report button at the top of any message, and eBay will look into removing the post.

Anyone who violates eBay's discussion-board policy gets a warning. Anyone who ignores that warning may get a *sanction*, which means they can't post to any eBay board, or a *suspension*, which means they're kicked off the site entirely. Sanctions and suspensions can be temporary, lasting one day or longer, or they can be permanent; the final say is eBay's.

To post a new thread on a discussion board, go to Community → Discussion Boards and click the name of the discussion board you want. Sign in to the discussion boards (if you haven't already). Look above the threads, on the right side of the page, and then click "Post a topic" to get to the box shown in Figure 10-3.

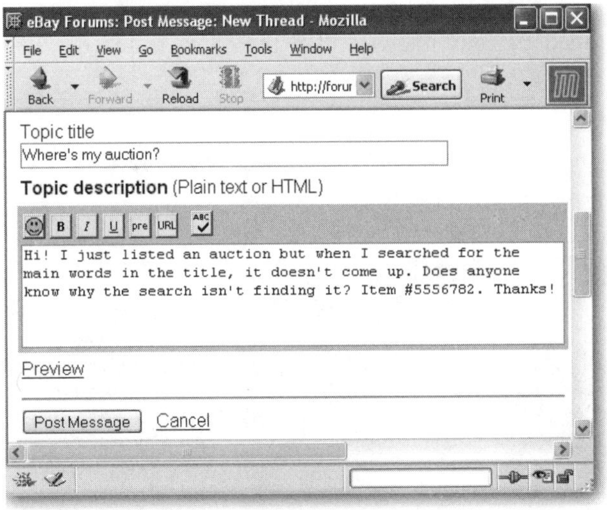

Figure 10-3:
When you start a new thread or reply to a current post, type your message in the text box. You can add smiley faces, formatting, and check your spelling. (To use all these features, you must have JavaScript enabled on your browser; on most browsers, you can control this setting from the Tools menu.) Click Preview to see what your post will look like. If you're happy with what you've written, click Post Message to put it up on the discussion board.

Note: On the discussion boards, eBay staffers are called *Pinks* because the ID/timestamp bar on each message they post is (you guessed it) pink. For regular eBayers, these bars are gray. And if a staffer reprimands an eBayer (usually because the eBayer posted something inappropriate), it's called being "pink-slapped."

UP TO SPEED

Community Values

eBay operates by five principles that it calls *community values*, a set of beliefs that support all activities on eBay. Here is how eBay defines those values (to see them online, on the navigation bar, click Community, and look on the right-hand side of the Community page):

- People are basically good.

- Everyone has something to contribute.

- An honest, open environment brings out the best in people.

- Each person deserves recognition and respect.

- eBayers should treat other people the way they want to be treated.

Trust, openness, and honesty are what make eBay work; without them, you wouldn't even think of buying from a stranger. And because a group can't really call itself a community if its members don't talk to each other, eBay provides a place for discussions.

As with all activity on the site, eBay expects eBayers to remember and uphold its community values when they interact with each other in the Community area. (But just in case you forget, there are plenty of rules in place to govern board use. See the box on page 364 .)

Groups

eBay *groups* are online clubs created and administered by eBayers. Besides chiming in on discussions, group members can receive newsletters, answer polls, and look at and post photo albums. To find eBay groups, from the navigation bar select Community → Groups. When you do, the main Groups page shown in Figure 10-4 appears. Because groups are defined, set up, and maintained by eBayers, you might find them more fine-tuned to your interests than the eBay-created discussion boards.

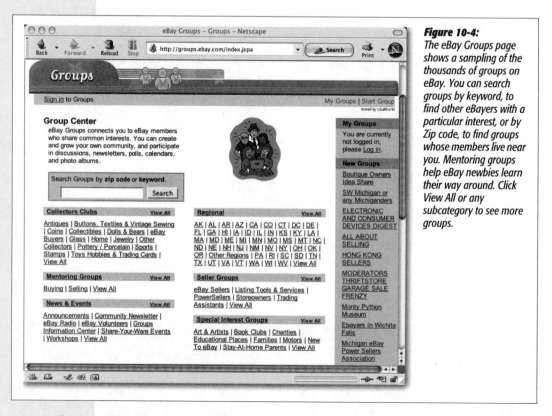

Figure 10-4:
The eBay Groups page shows a sampling of the thousands of groups on eBay. You can search groups by keyword, to find other eBayers with a particular interest, or by Zip code, to find groups whose members live near you. Mentoring groups help eBay newbies learn their way around. Click View All or any subcategory to see more groups.

To join a group, click its title. You see the group's Welcome page, like the example shown in Figure 10-5. This gives you the scoop on when the group was formed, who leads it, and whether there's been recent activity. *Public groups*, like the group in Figure 10-5, are open to everyone; just click the Join Group button to join. If you want to join a *private group*, you have to get approval. Click the Join Now button, explain in the text box that appears why you'd like to join, and then click the Send Request button to email your request to the Group Leader. When the leader has approved your application, you'll get an email. Then you can read messages, post, and do everything else you can do on a public group.

After you've joined a group, you can set preferences to customize the way you interact with the group. You can specify how many messages you want to see at a time, how you want to receive email from the group, and more, as shown in Figure 10-6.

Figure 10-5:
Before you join an eBay Group, you can look at its Welcome page but not participate in discussions or polls, or look at events and photo albums. Once you've become a member, the left-hand menu links become active. When looking for a group to join, look for one with lots of members and a recent Last Update; this one, with more than 1,800 members, is likely to be an active group.

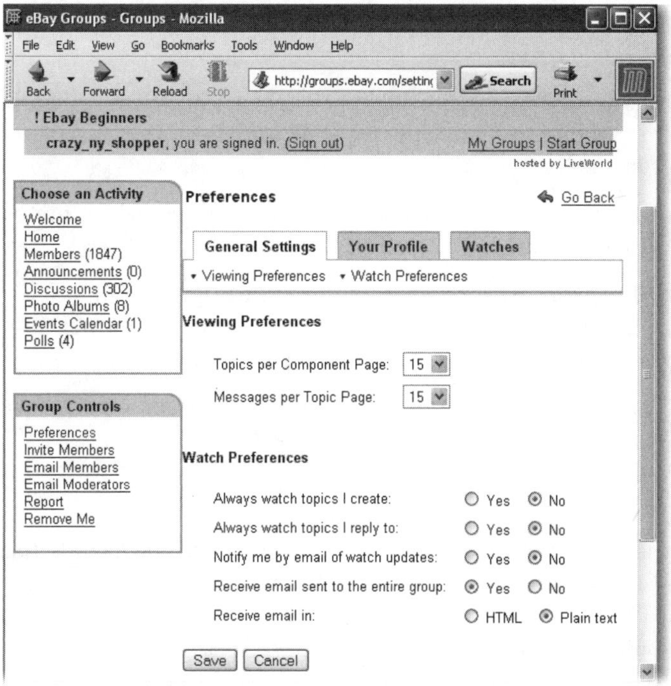

Figure 10-6:
Set the number of items you want to display when you're looking at group discussions. You can also watch certain discussion threads, which means you receive email notification when someone posts a new message in that thread.

But if you can't find a group that's right for you, no problem. Just start your own. To do so, from the navigation bar click Community → Groups and sign in to Groups (like the discussion boards, Groups require a separate sign-in). Then, in the Groups main page (back in Figure 10-4), click the Start Group link and then fill out the form that appears.

Note: You have to have a Feedback Score of 50 or better and have been a registered eBayer for at least 90 days to start a group.

Answer Center

Imagine you had a mentor, an eBayer with lots of transactions under her belt, ready and willing to listen to your questions and give you the straight scoop in reply. Now imagine that you had a few dozen such mentors.

You do—they hang out at the Answer Center. The Answer Center (AC) is where you can go to ask questions—and get smart answers from knowledgeable, experienced eBayers.

You can get to the AC from the navigation bar: select either Community → Answer Center or Help → Community Answer Center. Either choice takes you to the AC's main page, shown in Figure 10-7, where you can click a topic (Bidding, Feedback, Technical Issues, Trust & Safety, and so on) to read posts on the board related to that topic. You can search for a topic (use the Search box shown in Figure 10-7) or read any thread without signing in, but you have to sign in to the AC to post. To sign in, click any topic; on the page that opens, look under the board's name for the "Sign in" link. Click it, sign in, and you can post your question.

Like eBay's other discussion boards, the AC lets eBayers ask questions and answer them. But eBay does a few things differently in the AC, making it your best place to get focused help from other eBayers:

- Each question can have no more than 10 follow-up answers, which prevents threads from getting too long or going off topic.

- Any registered eBayer can ask a question (you must be signed in to the AC to ask), but only eBayers with a feedback score of ten or more can answer. In the AC, you know the people answering your question have experience.

- To keep the Q&As from getting cluttered up with cute cartoons and pet photos, you can't use HTML in AC posts; eBay has disabled HTML in the AC. (The exception is the Photos/HTML board, where using HTML is relevant to the questions.)

- The AC's format is a little different from the eBay Discussion Boards (page 362). In the AC, when you look at the list of threads for a topic (like Auction Listings or PayPal), the entire question (not just a subject line) appears. So you can read the whole question before you look at its answers.

- You can set up a *watch* on threads that interest you. eBay will send you an email when a new post appears in a thread you are watching. To watch a thread, look at the top of any discussion thread to find the binoculars icon, which you can see in Figure 10-8. Right next to the binoculars, if you click Watch this Question, you'll get email with a link to the discussion when someone posts a new answer.

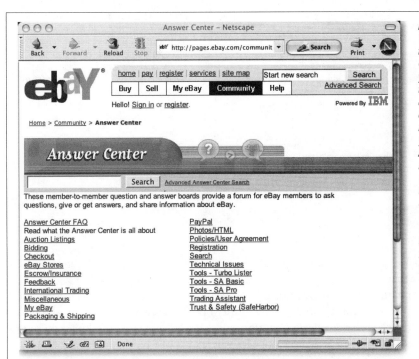

Figure 10-7:
The best place to start in the AC is the Answer Center FAQ, which gets you up to speed on what the AC is all about. Click any topic to read questions and answers related to that topic. If you want to search the AC, type a keyword that relates to your question (like shill or escrow) into the Search box and then click the Search button. The Advanced Answer Center Search link opens a page where you can narrow your search, as explained on page 370.

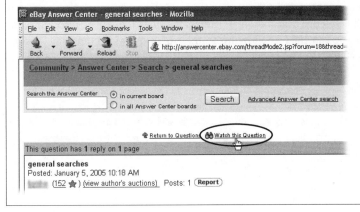

Figure 10-8:
To watch a thread in the Answer Center, click the Watch this Question link next to the binoculars. You can receive notifications by email when someone posts a new answer—immediately, daily, weekly, or not at all.

Before you ask a question in the AC, spend a little time searching through its threads for your topic (Figure 10-9). You'll find that a lot of other eBayers have had the same questions you do, and you can get a real education from the answers.

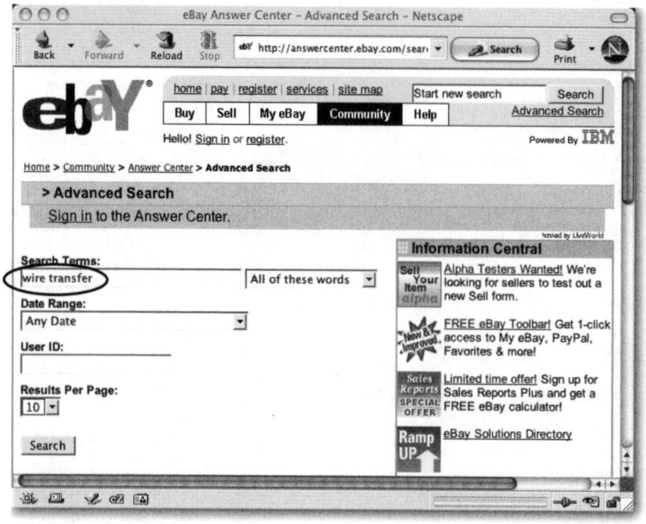

Figure 10-9:
To search the AC archives, type your search term in the text box and then click Search. An Advanced AC Search lets you choose a date range (so you're not looking at last year's answers), search for posts from a particular eBayer (in case you've noticed someone whose advice really hits home), and specify from 10 to 30 results per page.

To ask a question, make sure you're signed in to the AC (page 368), then go to the topic that best fits your question: Packaging & Shipping if you want advice on getting a hard-to-pack item ready to go, International Trading if you have a question about customs forms, and so on. On the topic's main page, just above the list of threads, click the Ask New Question link. (If you don't see the link, you're not signed in to the AC.) A page appears where you can type in a subject and your question; click Post Message when you're done.

To answer a question, click the Answer link at the bottom of any thread; a page opens where you can type and submit your reply. You won't see an Answer link if you have a feedback score of less than 10 (unless the question you're responding to was yours—anyone can post a follow-up to their own question), and the Answer link disappears when a thread is full (when it has 10 posts).

Tip: Remember that the folks who answer questions in the AC are regular eBayers volunteering their time and eBay wisdom. So when you post a question, show a little respect. Any AC regular will tell you that the attitude you exhibit when you ask a question directly affects the attitude with which AC gurus answer it. As long you're polite, they'll explain something like the UPI process for the umpteenth time.

Chat Rooms

Discussion-board threads can span days, weeks—some of them keep going for years. If you're looking for something a bit more I-want-to-talk-to-someone-right-this-second, you might be interested in chat rooms.

A chat room is kind of like an online living room, where people hang out and chat with each other in real time. You type in a message like, "How's the weather?" and others immediately respond with messages of their own: "Two feet of snow here in Bangor, Maine"; "It's raining in Atlanta"; "Snow? What's snow? I live in Hawaii"; and so on. Whenever you refresh your screen by clicking your browser's Refresh/Reload button, you see the new messages posted since the last time you refreshed it.

With eBay Chat Rooms, while you're searching or managing auctions in one browser window, you can open another and join in the conversation with other eBayers. Many chatters like to post pictures, too, from cartoon characters to photos of pets and their local area. Chat rooms feel a little disorganized until you get used to following the flow of the conversation. Messages don't appear in nice, orderly threads; instead, they show up in chronological order, and several conversations are always going on at once. And messages don't stick around for more than a day, so you can't search the chat rooms the way you can search Discussion Boards. Even so, chat rooms are fun and worth a look (or a lurk).

Tip: Chat rooms can be, well, chatty. Their discussions contain a lot of off-topic posts, as well as hellos and goodbyes as people enter and leave. If you're the kind of person who starts biting his fingernails when things get off-topic, choose a discussion board instead. (The Answer Center is your best bet for on-topic posts.) But if you need a quick answer to a specific question and Live Help is too busy, the member chat rooms can help. There are always some eBayers hanging out in them.

To start chatting, from the navigation bar go to Community → Chat Rooms, and then click the name of the room you'd like to enter. To follow the conversation, you have to refresh the screen every minute or so. Or scroll down the page and type a message in the box shown in Figure 10-10 and click the "Save my Message!" button to join in. (You must be registered and signed in to Groups in order to chat.)

There are two kinds of chat rooms: general and category-specific. In the general chat rooms, you can talk about pretty much anything at all; but technically speaking, each general chat room does have an official focus:

- **The eBay Café.** The café goes way back; it was eBay's first discussion area. A lot of the regulars have known each other for years. Discussions range from eBay gossip to thoughts on current events to what's going on in the chatters' lives. The AOL Café is a similar room for people who use AOL.

- **Holiday Board.** Although people do talk about holidays here, they also talk about their families, the weather, and whatever they've been up to.

- **Giving Board.** This room is for big-hearted eBayers who help others. People post their stories and request help, cards, and prayers; others post fundraising ideas and resources where people can get help.

- **Discuss eBay's Newest Features.** This is a lively chat room where participants don't hesitate to speak their minds. Chatters do discuss eBay's newest features, and a lot of other topics besides—and they're never shy about the aspects of eBay they don't like.

- **Images/HTML Board.** This is a good place to get advice if you need to spruce up your auctions with photos and formatting gewgaws. Some very computer-savvy people hang out here.

- **eBay Q&A.** If you've got questions, the eBayers here have answers. Ask about anything related to eBay—buying, selling, services, how to report a problem—and you'll get a quick and knowledgeable answer.

- **eBay International Boards.** If you buy or sell internationally, you'll be interested in the other global thinkers here. Try the international chat rooms to meet eBayers from all over the world. Besides the general International Board, there are chat rooms for the U.K., Australia, Canada, and Germany (auf Deutsch, natürlich!).

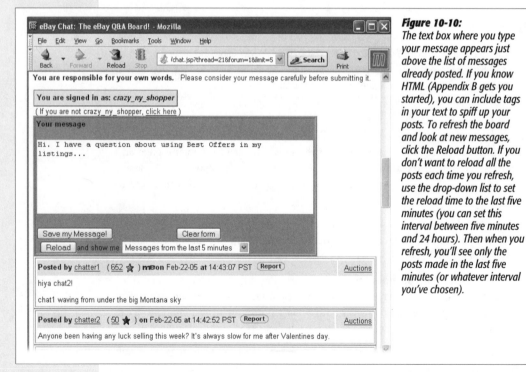

Figure 10-10:
The text box where you type your message appears just above the list of messages already posted. If you know HTML (Appendix B gets you started), you can include tags in your text to spiff up your posts. To refresh the board and look at new messages, click the Reload button. If you don't want to reload all the posts each time you refresh, use the drop-down list to set the reload time to the last five minutes (you can set this interval between five minutes and 24 hours). Then when you refresh, you'll see only the posts made in the last five minutes (or whatever interval you've chosen).

- **Emergency Contact.** The volunteers here provide a truly useful service. If your computer crashes, an accident or illness puts you temporarily out of commission, or you have another emergency that interferes with your eBay activity, they will get in touch with your trading partners and explain what's happened. Or, if you can't get in touch with another eBayer, the volunteers will try to help you track that person down.

Note: The Emergency Contact chat room is for help with contacting people. It's not for just any situation you consider urgent, although the regulars here show great patience in directing people with questions about fraud, eBay features, listing problems, and so on, to the right place.

UP TO SPEED

Netiquette

If you've never participated in a discussion board or live chat, be aware that certain rules and expectations are in play when you're interacting with others. The quickest way to make enemies of people you've never met is to treat these forums like some sort of free-for-all.

Netiquette (short for Internet etiquette) dictates that before you post, you take a few minutes to peruse eBay's board usage policy (page 364). Next, spend a little time reading the board or observing the chat room that interests you. You'll get a feel for the culture and tone of the place, and you may even find the answer to your question before you have to ask it.

When posting, use conventional capitalization, punctuation, and spelling. Be sure your Caps Lock key isn't on; using all capital letters IS AKIN TO SHOUTING AND SO ARE MULTIPLE EXCLAMATION MARKS!!!!! Read over your question with the same scrutiny you'd give a business letter. Use "magic words" like *please* and *thank you*. Don't use profanity or indulge in name-calling.

Because of the limited number of answers allowed for any question posted in the Answer Center (10 tops), people using this board frown upon *piggybacking*. Piggybacking is when you change the topic of a thread without starting a new thread yourself. For example, if you're on the Answer Center's Packaging & Shipping board reading someone's question about how to pack a clown-shaped piggy bank, and one of the answers mentions plastic peanuts and you get to thinking, "Hmm...I wonder if anyone here knows a good source of packing peanuts," *don't* hit the Answer link to post your question.

Instead, click the Return to Questions link above the posts, and then look above the list of questions for the Ask New Question link. Click that to start a new thread, and ask away. If you don't start a new thread, your question may get overlooked—*and* you're burning up the original thread's precious 10 posts.

Cross-posting, which is posting identical threads on more than one board, and *clones*, which are exact repetitions of an earlier question posted as a new thread, are also bad ideas. (Rude!) Choose one board that seems to fit your question best, post once, and have a little patience as you wait for an answer. Someone will help you out before long.

Keep in mind that it's not just you who can report posts that violate eBay's policies; other eBayers can, too. (Each message has a Report button right next to the posting time.) Play nice.

---

eBay Affiliates

You love eBay. If you're not bragging to your friends, relatives, and colleagues about the great deals you got on eBay (from your vintage '70s necktie to your hula-girl bedside lamp), then you're bragging about the money you made selling off the junk in your garage. If only you had a nickel for every time you told someone how great eBay is....

If you have a Web site or email newsletter, you can get a lot more than a nickel for putting out the good word. When you become an *eBay Affiliate*, eBay pays you when visitors to your Web site click a link, register with eBay, and buy or bid on at least one item within 30 days. These referrals earn you from $20 to $45 each, depending on how many people you've referred. In addition, you get paid 10 to 25 cents every time someone coming to eBay through your link makes a bid or uses Buy It Now. Figure 10-11 shows the payment structure.

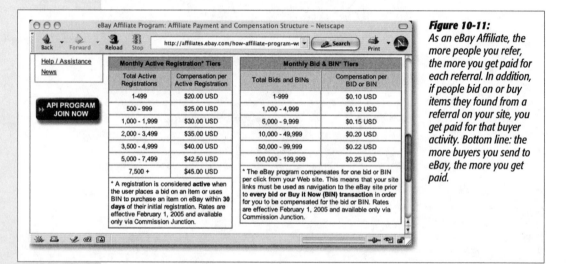

Figure 10-11:
As an eBay Affiliate, the more people you refer, the more you get paid for each referral. In addition, if people bid on or buy items they found from a referral on your site, you get paid for that buyer activity. Bottom line: the more buyers you send to eBay, the more you get paid.

The eBay Affiliate Program is free to join. On the navigation bar, click Services. Under Tools, click the eBay Affiliate Program link. The Join Now link gets you started. After you've read the Affiliate agreement, and given information about your Web site and how to contact you, you get an email with your password and instructions on how to sign in to eBay's affiliates-only site. When you sign in, you'll find banners, links, and search boxes to put on your Web site and direct visitors to eBay.

Note: There are also Affiliate programs for eBay Stores (page 259) and Half.com (page 284). Look for them at the bottom of the Join the Program page (*http://affiliates.ebay.com/join-program*).

As an eBay Affiliate, you can use several different strategies to refer your site visitors to eBay:

- **Content sites.** If you have a Web site, put up eBay links, banners, buttons, and even links to currently running auctions. For best results, display auctions related to your site's content, like auctions for DVDs if you have a movie review site. If you have a merchant site where you sell any kind of product, eBay gives you the tools you need to link to your own eBay auctions.

- **Newsletters.** Editors of email newsletters can include links and banners promoting eBay. Make sure the newsletter is by subscription, though; eBay doesn't let its Affiliates send spam.

- **Natural search.** When Web surfers use a search engine like Google, Yahoo!, AltaVista, and so on, they look first, naturally enough, at the results that appear at the top of their search list. Some eBay affiliates build their Web sites with the specific intention of coming out on top of the search pile. When Web surfers check out one of these sites, they find prominent, tempting links to eBay and eBay auctions.

- **Paid search.** If you've ever used a search engine, you've seen the Sponsored Links set off in a colored box at the top and sometimes to one side of the results list. Those links are ads, and they're there because people have bid on search keywords, paying the search-engine company every time someone clicks their Sponsored Link. You can bid on keywords to direct searchers to your Web site; and then, when thousands of surfers show up at your site, you can pass them off to eBay. Even if you don't have a Web site of your own, you can still pay for an ad to send searchers directly to eBay (and get paid Affiliate bucks for your trouble).

Tip: To learn more about Sponsored Links on Google, or to help boost your Web site in the search engine's rankings, or even to get a full-blown tutorial on Google Groups (next section), check out *Google: The Missing Manual*.

Other Places to Talk About eBay

You can stick around eBay to discuss it with other eBayers, but if you want a no-holds-barred discussion, look beyond eBay itself. All eBay-sponsored discussions and chats have a Report button or link at the top, and eBay will remove posts that violate its policies (page 364) and sometimes suspend eBayers from posting.

So if you want to get down and dirty, check out one of the other places online you can go to discuss eBay. You can find eBay-related groups on sites like Google and Yahoo! and forums on a number of sites.

Google Groups

Usenet is a network of discussion groups, called *newsgroups*, that began in 1979 with a couple of computers linked by a single network and grew into a huge, complex system that links millions of people and computers to more than 20,000 active newsgroups. Topics include everything you can imagine—and probably more. There are dozens of groups devoted to eBay and online auctions.

The easiest way to check out Usenet is through Google, which has hosted the groups since 2001. Point your Web browser to *www.google.com* and then click the Groups link (or just go to *http://groups.google.com*). Type *ebay* or *"online auctions"* into the text box and then click Search Groups. The page that opens looks like the one in Figure 10-12.

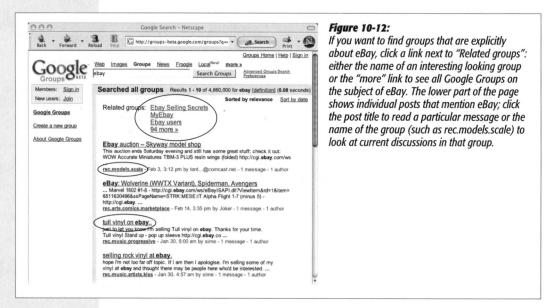

Figure 10-12:
If you want to find groups that are explicitly about eBay, click a link next to "Related groups": either the name of an interesting looking group or the "more" link to see all Google Groups on the subject of eBay. The lower part of the page shows individual posts that mention eBay; click the post title to read a particular message or the name of the group (such as rec.models.scale) to look at current discussions in that group.

Google's Group Directory page (which you get to by clicking the "more" link in Figure 10-12) shows you a list of groups and lets you sort them to find a good match. When you search Google Groups for a keyword like eBay, the page that appears (the Group Directory) lets you sort the results by region (like Canada, Europe, or the U.S.), language, activity level (high, medium, or low), and number of members (from fewer than 10 to more than 1,000). Figure 10-13 shows the Group Directory.

You can read Google Groups just by surfing around. If you register with Google, you can sign in to reply to posts, or you can subscribe to a group and get messages in your email inbox. (All you need to register is an email address; head to the Groups home page, *http://groups.google.com,* and then click the Join link to open short form you fill in to become part of the club.)

Note: Google Groups include both Usenet newsgroups and Google-sponsored groups and email lists. To create your own Google group, look on the Google Groups main page for the "Create new groups" link.

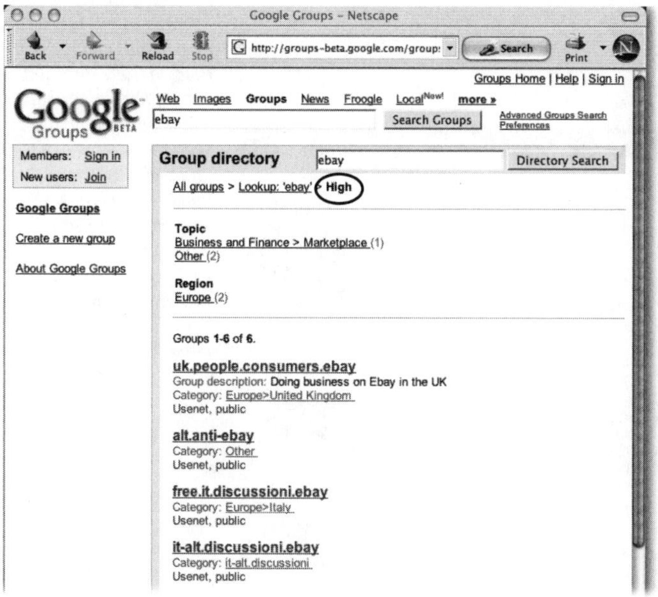

Figure 10-13:
This page shows the eBay groups that have an activity level of "high," meaning there are lots of discussion threads but possibly also lots of spam.

Yahoo! Groups

Yahoo! offers a number of groups that discuss all things eBay. Go to *www.yahoo. com*, click Groups (or just point your Web browser to *http://groups.yahoo.com*), and then type *ebay* into the text box and click Search. Figure 10-14 shows what the results page looks like. Yahoo! hosts *thousands* of eBay-related groups. Some are large, some small. Some have dozens of posts every day; others haven't had a post since the Clinton administration.

When you find a group that looks interesting, click its title to go to that group's main page. On a group's page, you can read the group's rules and see how many posts have appeared on that group in the last seven days, as well as a calendar that tracks the number of monthly posts. Look for an active—but not overwhelming— group that states on its page that it doesn't allow spam posts.

Here are some popular Yahoo! groups related to eBay:

- eBay-sellers (*http://groups.yahoo.com/group/eBay-Sellers*)
- ebay_spamfree_dealers (*http://groups.yahoo.com/group/ebay_spamfree_dealers*)
- selling_on_ebay (*http://groups.yahoo.com/group/selling_on_ebay*)

- eBay (*http://groups.yahoo.com/group/eBay*)

- eBay_For_Newbies (*http://groups.yahoo.com/group/Ebay_For_Newbies*)

Figure 10-14:
Searching Yahoo! Groups for ebay brings up more than 3,000 groups, ranging from fewer than 5 members to more than 1,000. In addition to a short description of each group, the list shows the number of members, whether a group archives (saves) its posts, and whether you have to be a member to read posts. Click the title of any group to join.

When you find a group you want to join, go to its main page and click the Join This Group button. You must have a Yahoo! ID to join a Yahoo! group. (If you don't have a Yahoo! ID, you can sign up for one as part of the process of joining a group.) The registration process asks you to make a few choices. You can receive messages via email, either individually or in daily digests, or you can choose not to get group-related email at all, reading messages on the group's Web site instead. Digest or Web-only subscriptions are good for highly active groups that threaten to overwhelm your inbox with a constant bombardment of email. Click the Join button when you're done to start reading and posting.

If you want to change your settings later—for example, if you signed up for email messages but would rather read posts on the Groups page, you can. Go to *http://groups.yahoo.com* and then sign in. Signing in takes you to My Groups, a page that lists all the Yahoo! groups you're a member of. Above the list of groups is a link that says Edit My Groups. If you click it, you can change your settings or leave a group.

Forums on Other Sites

Sites related to Internet auctions and commerce often have places for visitors and members to chat. At these sites, anyone can read the discussions, but you have to register with the site if you want to participate.

FatWallet

FatWallet, shown in Figure 10-15, is a bargain hunter's resource that posts deals, coupons, and cash-back offers from various retailers. Some eBay sellers use Fat-Wallet to find bargains to resell at a profit on eBay.

Figure 10-15:
FatWallet hosts a number of forums related to getting a good buy; its discussion boards have names like Hot Deals, Travel Deals, and Free Stuff. eBay discussions take place in the Online Auctions forum. To find it, go to www.fatwallet.com, click the Forums tab, then look in the left-hand menu and click Online Auctions.

Online Traders Web Alliance

The Online Traders Web Alliance (OTWA) has been around since 1999 and bills itself as "the largest Independent Auction Community on the Internet." OTWA's forums (*www.otwa.com/community*) include the following:

- **@OTWA.** General discussion boards, including new member orientation, a forum specifically for eBay, and another for non-eBay auctions.

- **OTWA Marketplace.** A section for classifieds, where you can advertise your auctions or describe what you're shopping for.

- **eBusiness.** Discussion boards related to doing business online, including security, Web design, and marketing/advertising.

- **Antiques and Collectibles Arena.** Buying, selling, and collecting items from breweriana to sports memorabilia to period furniture and vintage jewelry.

- **Member SIGs.** SIGs are special interest groups run by OTWA members on a range of topics, including disability issues, freebies, and graphic arts.

If you register with OTWA, you can post, take polls, or send a private message to an OTWA member. On the OTWA home page, click the "join our community today!" link to sign up.

AuctionBytes

AuctionBytes (*www.auctionbytes.com*) has a massive collection of resources for online auctions, including news stories, interviews, selling tips, and two free email newsletters reporting up-to-the-minute auction news (page 403). Look in the left-hand menu of any page on the site for the Forums link to peruse these discussion areas:

- **Announcements.** Includes announcements about the boards themselves and a place to talk about auction news.

- **Online Auction Sites & Services.** Includes discussions of issues related to safe trading, marketing, packing and shipping, and copyright issues.

- **Collector's Forums.** Includes discussions of all types of collectibles.

- **Fixed-Price Store Fronts.** Includes classified ads for buyers and for sellers.

eBay Live!

Just about every line of work has its annual convention, where professionals gather to talk shop, network, learn about recent developments, and have a good time. eBay calls its annual convention eBay Live! For three days in June, more than 10,000 eBayers from all over come together in one big, face-to-face celebration of all things eBay. The conference is in a different location each year, and the fees are relatively inexpensive: in 2005, they ranged from $30 to $70 (for all three days), depending on when you registered and how many events you wanted to attend.

Some of the highlights of previous eBay Live! get-togethers have included:

- Classes geared toward beginner, intermediate, and experienced eBayers to improve success on eBay.

- One-on-one meetings with eBay selling experts to boost your sales.

- Special classes and events just for PowerSellers.

- A keynote address by eBay CEO Meg Whitman.

- Networking breakfasts and dinners for informal conversation. If you want to meet others with a special interest, organizers can put together a group for you and make dinner reservations.

- An exhibition area where you can buy official eBay T-shirts, mugs, keychains, and other cool eBay gear, and look at vendors' eBay-related products.

- A Buddy Matching program to help new eBayers make friends.

- A big party, the Saturday Night Gala, which includes dinner and entertainment.

- Email stations and WiFi hotspots (where you can use your wireless laptop to go online) so you can stay in touch with home—and with your eBay business— while you're at the convention.

- Child care for kids and teens. (No one under 18 is allowed at the convention itself.)

To find out more about eBay Live!, type *http://pages.ebay.com/ebaylive* into your Web browser and visit its Web page, as shown in Figure 10-16.

Note: You can keep an eye out for late-breaking news about eBay Live! by clicking Community → "See all Announcements."

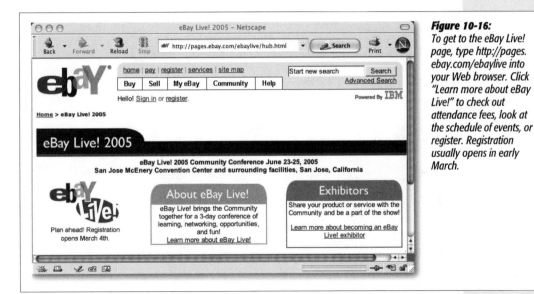

Figure 10-16:
To get to the eBay Live! page, type http://pages. ebay.com/ebaylive into your Web browser. Click "Learn more about eBay Live!" to check out attendance fees, look at the schedule of events, or register. Registration usually opens in early March.

Finding Help

It's 2:00 a.m. You want to bid on a pair of rare, pricey Bart Simpson flip flops in an auction that ends in four hours. But the seller has a feedback score of 96 percent and not many comments. Where do you go to ask whether this seller is worth a risk?

eBay offers help in several different formats, including a Learning Center just for newbies, a Help page, interactive help via live chat or email, a centralized Services page, a site map, discussion boards, and more. This chapter covers them all.

Note: What eBay doesn't have, to the disappointment of many, is a number for telephone support. Top-level PowerSellers and owners of eBay Stores get a phone support number, but that's it. From time to time, you can find "eBay phone numbers" posted on discussion boards and around the Internet, but these numbers are usually bogus.

Learning Center

When you're new to eBay, the site can feel overwhelming. Instead of jumping in at the deep end, you can test the waters before you take the plunge, thanks to eBay's Learning Center.

The Learning Center offers tutorials designed expressly for eBay newbies. You can take an audio tour to get an overview of eBay as a whole, or to learn how to register and start buying. You can sign up for courses at eBay University (page 410) and read tips on eBay basics, like leaving feedback, trading safely, and getting started as a seller. The Learning Center brings together in one place the topics new eBayers need to know about *now*.

Get there from the navigation bar (Help → Learning Center) or by going to *http://pages.ebay.com/education.*

Help Page

If you're looking for answers, eBay's Help page—which you find by going to the navigation bar and clicking the Help link you find there—is the best place to start.

As you can see in Figure 11-1, eBay's Help page contains a search box, a list of frequently asked questions, and a breakdown of other questions by topic, such as getting started, how to find an item, eBay policies, how to pay, and so on. Each link you click narrows down the topics until you get to the information you want. It might take some drilling down, but there's a wealth of information in these pages.

Tip: The A–Z Index is a quick way to find a specific topic, from About Me to Want It Now. (OK, so it's an A–W Index; it's still the fastest way to get to the info you need when you know what you're looking for.)

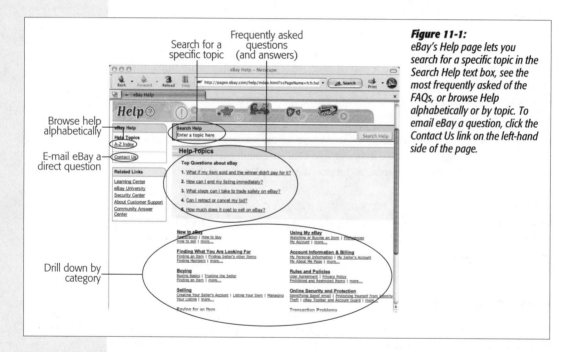

Figure 11-1:
eBay's Help page lets you search for a specific topic in the Search Help text box, see the most frequently asked of the FAQs, or browse Help alphabetically or by topic. To email eBay a question, click the Contact Us link on the left-hand side of the page.

Help via Email

If you can't find an answer in the Help topics or the A–Z Index, you can shoot off an email to eBay. It might take a little while, but sooner or later a staffer will get back to you. Often the answers are canned responses cut and pasted straight from the Help files, but sometimes you get an answer that zeroes right in on your problem. It's worth asking.

Note: If you can't wait around for an email, or if you need a little give-and-take to get to the bottom of your problem, see "Live Help" on this page or "Chat" on page 389.

To send an email to eBay, start on the Help page (click Help on the navigation bar). Look on the left-hand side of the Help page for the Contact Us link; click it to email a question to eBay's support staff. A page opens where you choose a category and two subcategories that best describe your question. Putting your question into a category helps eBay to route your question, but it also means that eBay controls the kinds of questions you can ask. Take a look at Figure 11-2 to see an example.

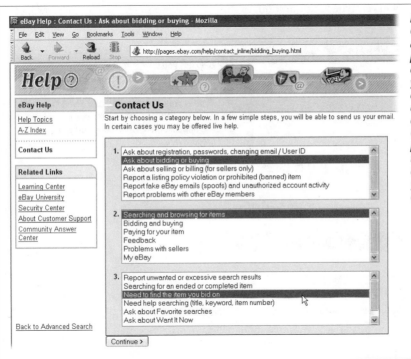

Figure 11-2:
Contact Us lets you ask a question or report problems with auctions or other eBayers. When you've selected the topic and subtopics that describe your communication, click Continue. On the next page, eBay suggests Help topics you might check out and provides a link you can click to type your email.

After you specify a category and click the Continue button, as shown in Figure 11-2, a page appears giving you Instant Help (links to topics eBay thinks will answer your question). If none of these topics offers the information you're looking for, click the Email link to send off your question—and be prepared to wait a day or two for your answer.

Live Help

For the truly frustrated, Live Help lets you chat instant-messenger-style with a living, breathing eBay customer support person.

Note: Live Help uses pop-up windows. If you have a pop-up blocker installed on your Web browser, you need to turn it off to use Live Help.

From eBay's home page, zip to the right-hand side of the page and click the Live Help link. The chat window that pops up shows links to popular topics in the Help database.

If your question doesn't relate to one of these topics (or if you've been through those topics a hundred times already and couldn't find an answer, which is why you're trying to reach a human in the first place), type in your email address or eBay ID, select a category, and then click the Send button.

Then you can type your question, as shown in Figure 11-3.

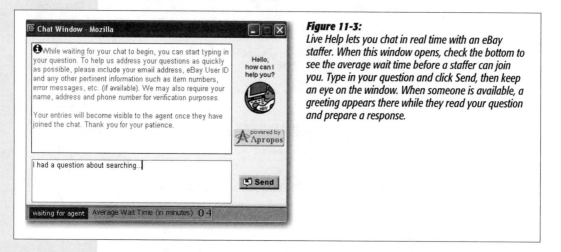

Figure 11-3:
Live Help lets you chat in real time with an eBay staffer. When this window opens, check the bottom to see the average wait time before a staffer can join you. Type in your question and click Send, then keep an eye on the window. When someone is available, a greeting appears there while they read your question and prepare a response.

Tip: Live Help can get extremely busy at times, so you might answer your own question more quickly by searching the Help database or the Answer Center (page 387).

Site Map

Click the Site Map link at the top of the navigation bar to get a bird's-eye view of the entire eBay Web site. The site map can take you into interesting corners of eBay or provide a quick overview of a broad topic, such as buying or selling. It's handy for seeing all of eBay at a glance or finding your way back to an area of the site you just *know* you saw a day or two ago.

eBay Services

If you're looking for a centralized place that links to the different services that eBay offers buyers and sellers, check out the Services page at *http://pages.ebay.com/services.*

This page gathers together all the different things eBay can do for you. From Services, you can resolve a dispute, retract a bid, find an expert to authenticate items from Beanie Babies and comic books to jewelry and sports autographs, buy a warranty for an eBay purchase, and more. The Services page is divided into three main areas:

- **General Services.** This section covers services of interest to both buyers and sellers. There are links to pages for safe trading (including conflict resolution), money-related stuff (PayPal, escrow information, and financing), the Feedback Forum (page 40), and pages where you can download the eBay Toolbar (page 89) or learn about eBay Anywhere Wireless (page 93). You can also get to the main pages for Giving Works (page 310), eBay's charity auctions, and the eBay Affiliate program, which lets you earn money by directing people to eBay from your Web site (page 374).

- **Bidding and Buying Services.** From this section, you can file a report if you didn't receive an item you bought. You can also buy a warranty for eligible eBay items (including most new, used, or refurbished electronic items), learn about buyer-protection programs (page 72), or follow a link to retract a bid (page 68).

- **Selling Services.** If you're a seller, links in this section will help you create listings (page 154), find an expert to authenticate your items, find a Trading Assistant (page 189) to sell on eBay for you, promote your listings, learn about becoming a PowerSeller (page 279), download tools for sellers (page 324), let eBay foot the bill for some of your advertising costs with Co-op Advertising (for PowerSellers only, page 280), and more.

Help from Other eBayers

Sometimes, the best (and fastest) way to get a good answer is not from the powers that be, but from other people who actually use the site. eBay makes member-to-member help possible in three ways: the Answer Center, Discussion Boards, and Chat. You can find all three through the eBay navigation bar's Community link. Chapter 10 gives you the details about how to talk with other eBayers (page 362); this section highlights the places where you can get help fast.

Note: You must be a registered eBayer (page 4) to participate in any of eBay's community discussions. You also have to sign in to the discussion boards and chat rooms to post in them (you can read posts without signing in). Look for the sign-in link at the top of any discussion board or chat page.

Answer Center

When you need a frank answer from expert eBayers, the Answer Center (AC in eBay lingo, page 368) is the place to start. You find the AC by going to the navigation bar and then clicking Community → Answer Center.

The Answer Center page lists topics on everything eBay—bidding, searching, listing an item, how to get the most out of your My eBay page, safe trading issues, and more. Click any topic to read eBayers' questions and the AC experts' answers. (You have to have a feedback score of 10 or higher to answer questions in the AC, so questioneers know they're dealing with experienced eBayers.)

The AC limits each discussion to 10 posts, max. This restriction keeps discussions on topic instead of wandering off into conversations about someone's new puppy or Florida vacation.

Tip: You can search the AC for a specific topic or watch a particular question to see when a new answer appears. See pages 368-370 to find out how.

To ask the AC experts a question, make sure you're signed in to the AC (page 368). Click any topic on the main Answer Center page, and then look above the list of threads for the Ask New Question link. Click it to type and submit your question.

Discussion Boards

eBayers don't just love to buy and sell on the site; they love to talk about eBay, too. The conversation's always going full steam on eBay's *discussion boards*, bulletin-board-style Web pages where one person posts a topic and then others jump in with their views (page 362). Whatever the hour, somebody's hanging out on the discussion boards, reading posts, answering questions, and chiming in with their two cents. If you've got a question, post it on a discussion board for a fast answer.

To see all of eBay's discussion boards, go to the navigation bar and click Community → Discussion Boards.

Discussion boards fall into five main categories (page 362), but if you're looking for help, head for one of these:

- **The Community Help boards.** These boards, which you find on the left-hand side of the Discussion Boards page, are arranged by topic (Live Auctions, PayPal, and so on).

- **The New to eBay board.** Scroll down to the General Discussion Boards section and click the New to eBay link to see answers to eBay newbies' questions.

- **Category Specific boards.** On the right-hand side of the Discussion Boards page you find category-specific boards: everything from Animals to Vintage Clothing. If you have a question about an unusual item—for instance, if you need help identifying the maker's mark on a piece of pottery—ask the knowledgeable folks who hang out on these boards.

Note: Some of eBay's discussion boards can get pretty raucous, and each thread can go on and on (and on). If you're looking for quick, accurate answers, head for the AC. Discussion boards, on the other hand, are good for lengthy or philosophical discussions, like "Who leaves feedback first?" or "Is sniping unethical?"

Chat

Questions posted to the Answer Center (page 368) or a discussion board (page 362) usually get answered pretty fast—often within an hour or so. But if your question is super-urgent, you might try asking it in one of the live chat rooms (page 371). (To get to the live chat rooms: from the navigation bar, click Community → Chat Rooms.)

The eBay Q&A chat room is your best bet for posting eBay-related questions and getting an immediate response from other eBayers. Refresh the page frequently to see the latest posts.

Note: Keep in mind that several discussions are running at once in each chat room, so a lot of the posts will have nothing to do with what you asked.

Part Four:
Appendixes

4

Where to Learn More

eBay evolves almost daily. One day you find a new checkbox in Advanced Search; the next day you find a category change when you're listing an item; the day after that, there's a new feature in your My eBay page. With workshops, one-day listing sales, promotions and contests, tweaks of familiar features like Search and Sell Your Item, and more, there's always something new to learn.

This chapter shows you where to go to stay current and learn the latest strategies for making the most of your time on eBay. Here's what it covers:

- eBay updates

- Newsletters

- eBay Radio (and other radio programs of interest)

- Offsite auction news

- Auction software reviews

- Further education

eBay Updates

In its ongoing quest to become the perfect online marketplace, eBay is constantly tweaking the site: adding new categories, putting mysterious checkboxes on the Sell Your Item form, creating search options that you didn't even know you wanted. Just when you think you've learned your way around, something changes—and you want to know why. To help eBayers keep up with what's going on, eBay posts frequent announcement bulletins to keep eBayers informed of changes, new features, and problems.

The three most recent announcement bulletins appear on your My eBay page. (To bring up your My eBay page: on the navigation bar, click My eBay and then sign in, if necessary.) But if you need to get caught up on announcements, or if you just *know* you read something in an announcement but you can't find it in My eBay, go to the Announcements page. You can access the Announcements page (shown in Figure A-1) from anywhere on the site by clicking Community → "See all Announcements." You can also find an Announcements link at the bottom of any eBay page.

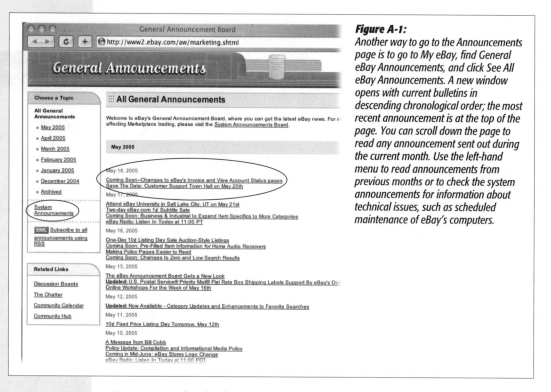

Figure A-1:
Another way to go to the Announcements page is to go to My eBay, find General eBay Announcements, and click See All eBay Announcements. A new window opens with current bulletins in descending chronological order; the most recent announcement is at the top of the page. You can scroll down the page to read any announcement sent out during the current month. Use the left-hand menu to read announcements from previous months or to check the system announcements for information about technical issues, such as scheduled maintenance of eBay's computers.

eBay posts two kinds of announcements:

- **General announcements.** Upcoming workshops (page 406), new features, category updates, and other changes to the site fall into this category. General announcements also contain some public relations stuff, like reminding you to listen to eBay Radio (page 399) or to check out a new issue of eBay's online newsletter, *The Chatter* (page 395).

Tip: For sellers, one of the best reasons to keep an eye on general announcements is that this is where eBay announces *listing sales* (promotions that offer reduced listing fees). Often these promotions are short and the announcement appears just one day before the listing sale starts. Check announcements regularly to save yourself some money on listing fees.

- **System announcements.** These bulletins have to do with the technical side of eBay. If a technical problem is interfering with your ability to use the site, eBay announces it here and puts up another announcement when they've fixed the problem. This is also where you can find notification of scheduled site maintenance; during the times eBay does this maintenance, the site can feel a little sluggish. Find out when maintenance is happening so you can avoid the frustrations of trying to list a couple dozen auctions when the system is slow.

POWER USERS' CLINIC

Testing, Testing

The fourth time you beat your head against the wall trying to get used to some unasked-for "improvement," you might wish eBay would just leave well enough alone already.

On the other hand, you might enjoy getting to play around with spanking-new features. And if that's the case, you might appreciate the fact that eBay takes its community into consideration before it overhauls the way things work. To participate, visit the General Announcements page (Community → "See all Announcements") and watch the General Announcements page for bulletins that begin with the

words "Input Wanted." You can sign up to test new site features, like changes to the Search engine or the site map.

Another way to get your voice heard is to sign up for surveys. From time to time, eBay sends out email surveys looking for feedback on new features and changes they're considering. To participate, click My eBay → eBay Preferences. Look for Notification Preferences and click View/Change. On the eBay Change Your Preferences page that appears, turn on the checkbox next to eBay Product Surveys. When you click Save Changes, you've signed up.

Start Spreading the News(letters)

eBay keeps its community informed about what's going on through a variety of newsletters delivered right to your email inbox. If you want to read feature stories about other eBayers, reminders about upcoming workshops (page 406) or the next eBay Radio broadcast (page 399), or to be among the first to hear about new eBay features and enhancements, there's a newsletter for you.

Specialized Newsletters

eBay uses eBay Groups (page 366) to send out email announcements on a bunch of different topics. To see what newsletters are currently available, go to Community → Groups → News & Events. The list of newsletters appears in Figure A-2.

The Chatter

The Chatter, shown in Figure A-3, is eBay's general community newsletter, published online monthly. It features news, behind-the-scenes stories about eBay and its staff, tips for buyers and sellers, a question-and-answer column, pointers on safe trading, and stories about other eBayers. To see what's in the latest issue, click the navigation bar's Community link; then, under News, click *The Chatter.*

Tip: Thousands of eBayers read *The Chatter* each month. If you're a seller, you can use this newsletter to expand your marketing reach. At the top right of *The Chatter's* front page is an email link you can use to suggest stories. Try pitching a story featuring yourself or your eBay business. Make it newsworthy instead of just trying to sell stuff. Aim for a story that will interest the community, like how you met your spouse collecting antique postcards on eBay or how you've turned your home into a museum showcasing your eBay-acquired collection of mechanical banks. Read through some of the stories in recent and back issues of the newsletter to get ideas about what *The Chatter* likes to publish.

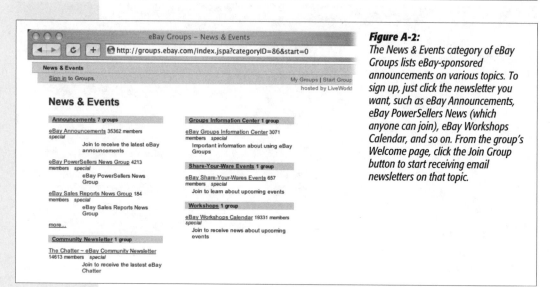

Figure A-2:
The News & Events category of eBay Groups lists eBay-sponsored announcements on various topics. To sign up, just click the newsletter you want, such as eBay Announcements, eBay PowerSellers News (which anyone can join), eBay Workshops Calendar, and so on. From the group's Welcome page, click the Join Group button to start receiving email newsletters on that topic.

Figure A-3:
To read one of The Chatter's featured articles, click the "Read more" link of the story you want, or look in the left-hand menu's Featured Articles section and click the article title. Look under Inside The Chatter for monthly columns. The Helpful Links section lets you look at previous issues of The Chatter (Chatter Archive) and sign up for email notification of new issues (Chatter Mailing List).

If you'd like to be notified by email when a new issue of *The Chatter* is out, you can sign up through eBay Groups (page 366). To do so, on *The Chatter*'s front page, click the Chatter Mailing List link. On the sign-up page that appears (Figure A-4) click the Join Group link.

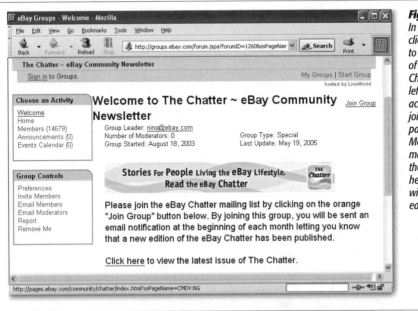

Seller Newsflash

From time to time, eBay sends out Seller Newsflash, an email newsletter for sellers, shown in Figure A-5. It contains articles of interest to sellers, but nothing that you can't find elsewhere on the site—by going to Seller Central, for example (Sell → Seller Central). It's worth getting if you like to read occasional selling tips.

You can find the latest online version of Seller Newsflash via a link on many of the category home pages; look under Category Community Links for a Newsletter link. To subscribe to this newsletter, go to My eBay → eBay Preferences, find Notification Preferences, and then click View/Change. On the Change Your Notifications Preferences page that appears, turn on the checkbox that says eBay Email. When there's a new newsflash, it'll arrive in your email inbox.

Newsletters for Buyers

eBay Store owners can send out up to five newsletters related to their stores (page 219). If you're a buyer with a favorite eBay Store or two, you can subscribe to these newsletters. Not every Store offers a newsletter, but those that do typically send out information you can really use: new items, sales and promotions, and special deals for subscribers.

To see whether your favorite eBay Store offers a newsletter:

1. **From eBay's home page, click eBay Stores.**

   The eBay Stores home page appears.

2. **In the Find a Store section, type the name of your favorite eBay Store into the text box and then hit Search Stores.**

   A page of search results appears.

3. **Click the link to the eBay Store you're looking for.**

   The Store's front page appears.

4. **On the Store's front page, click Add to My Favorite Stores.**

   The Add to My Favorite Sellers and Stores pages appears.

5. **If the store has a newsletter, the kind of newsletter it offers appears under Email Communication Preferences. Turn on the checkbox next to the newsletter you want, and then click the Add to Favorites button to save your preferences and begin receiving newsletters.**

Note: Store newsletters may be regular or few and far between, depending on how often a given Store owner can (or wants to) get them out.

Figure A-5:
eBay doesn't update Seller Newsflash very often. You might have tulips blooming outside while you're reading an issue that discusses winter holiday sales. Many categories (but not all) have their own version with a story or two targeting issues of special interest to sellers in that category; check a category's main page (click Buy on the navigation bar, then click a category name and look for a Newsletter link) to see whether your favorite category has a specialized version of Seller Newsflash.

eBay on the Air

eBay Radio is a weekly two-hour call-in program broadcast live over the Internet. The show's host is Jim Griffith, known around eBay as "Griff," eBay's first-ever customer service rep and currently in charge of eBay's education programs (page 410). You can listen to the live broadcast or recordings of archived shows right through your computer—just the thing when you're slaving over a hot auction.

Tip: Griff takes live calls during the eBay Radio broadcast. If you have a question to ask, call 888-327-0061. It's a rare opportunity to talk to a real live (former) eBay customer service rep by phone.

TROUBLESHOOTING MOMENT

Radio Daze

eBay Radio comes to your computer via *streaming audio,* a way Web sites can send data that lets you listen to live broadcasts over the Internet. To listen to streaming audio, your computer needs a sound card, speakers, and some kind of media player software for your computer; most computers come with these things already installed, and you don't need to do anything to get them working with eBay Radio. But if you try listening to an eBay Radio broadcast and it doesn't work, these tips can help.

Not all media players work with eBay Radio. For Windows, you need Windows Media Player or Real Player, which are probably already on your computer, although you may need to update your version. To get or to update Windows Media Player, go to *www.microsoft.com/windows/ windowsmedia;* for Real Player, go to *www.real.com/player* and look for the link to the free, basic RealPlayer—unless you want to pay for a fancier version. After you've downloaded the latest version of your media player, go back to the eBay Radio home page (*www.wsradio.com/ebayradio*) and click "listen live" or, if you want to listen to archived shows, click Audio Archives and then, from the eBay Audio Archives page that appears, choose the show you want and click the kind of media player you use.

For Mac fans, listening in is a little more complicated. First, you need to install Windows Media Player for Macs. You can download it free; go to *www.microsoft.com/windows/ windowsmedia,* look in the left-hand menu for Resources, then click Downloads and select the version of Windows Media Player for Macs that you want: 7.1 for Mac OS 8.1 and higher, or 9 for OS X.

You might encounter some problems trying to use Windows Media Player for Macs. One common problem is that you can't hear content—which is the whole point of getting the media player in the first place. If you have trouble hearing, try this: start Windows Media Player and then select File → Open URL. Type in the Web address of the program you want to listen to (or copy and paste it from your Web browser's address bar). That should force Windows Media Player to tell you what you want to hear. If not, head to wsRadio.com's special troubleshooting page for Macs: *www.wsradio.com/mac_help.htm.*

Occasionally, heavy Internet traffic can break the constant data stream. When this happens, the sound temporarily stops, and you'll see a *rebuffering* message on your media player. It means that your computer must pause and wait until it has collected enough data to keep playing.

Internet talk radio station wsRadio.com hosts the show. To start listening:

1. **Point your Web browser to** *www.wsradio.com/ebayradio.*

Figure A-6 shows you what the page looks like.

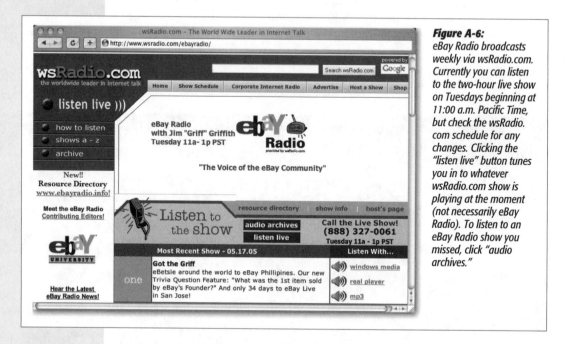

Figure A-6:
eBay Radio broadcasts weekly via wsRadio.com. Currently you can listen to the two-hour live show on Tuesdays beginning at 11:00 a.m. Pacific Time, but check the wsRadio.com schedule for any changes. Clicking the "listen live" button tunes you in to whatever wsRadio.com show is playing at the moment (not necessarily eBay Radio). To listen to an eBay Radio show you missed, click "audio archives."

Note: A million listeners from more than 180 countries visit wsRadio.com each month. eBay Radio is the site's most popular show.

2. **Click the "listen live" button to listen to a live broadcast of eBay Radio.**

The show currently airs on Tuesdays beginning at 11:00 a.m. Pacific Time. If that day and time doesn't happen to synch up with when you want to listen, you can always listen to a rerun. To do so, click "audio archives." Figure A-7 shows the archives for eBay Radio.

Tip: If you keep forgetting when the show is supposed to be on or if you want to know in advance what this week's show will cover, join the eBay Radio group and you'll get an email reminder before each show. From eBay, go to Community → Groups → News & Events → eBay Radio Broadcasts → Join Group to sign up.

More Radio Programs

In addition to eBay Radio, wsRadio.com offers an eBay Resource Directory filled with free (and fee) tips and workshops. On the main page (*www.wsradio.com/ ebayradio*), click the left-hand *www.ebayradio.info* link (or type that address into your Web browser's address box) to see what's in the eBay Resource Directory, shown in Figure A-8.

Tip: Want to add eBay Radio transcripts to your own Web page? Include this HTML code in your page:
```
<script language="javascript" type="text/javascript"
src="http://www.ebayradio.info/rssinclude.asp"></script>
```

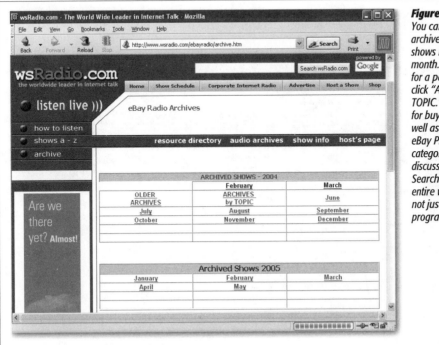

Figure A-7:
You can browse through archived eBay Radio shows by year and month. If you're looking for a particular topic, click "ARCHIVES by TOPIC." You'll find tips for buyers and sellers, as well as special topics like eBay Pioneers and category-specific discussions. The top-right Search box searches the entire wsRadio.com site, not just eBay Radio programs.

Figure A-8:
The buttons in the left-hand menu offer tips and resources to sharpen your eBay skills. If you'd rather skim through written transcripts than spend hours listening, there's a link that lets you do so. Some of the links are to free info; others are to products or services you can buy.

wsRadio.com has some other programming that eBayers might want to listen in on, including a couple of shows sponsored by *Entrepreneur* magazine: Making Money on eBay and the *Entrepreneur* E-Biz Show. Other shows in the Business category cover real estate, marketing, and best practices for business. Collectors of stamps, coins, or art will find shows about their passion in the Hobbies and Enthusiasts category. From the wsRadio.com main page (*www.wsradio.com/ebayradio*), click the left-hand "shows a–z" button to see the list of shows shown in Figure A-9.

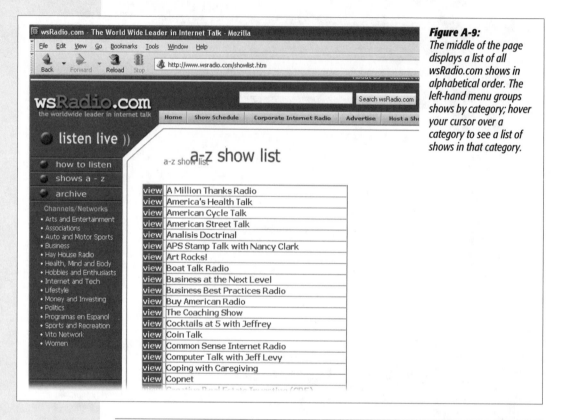

Figure A-9:
The middle of the page displays a list of all wsRadio.com shows in alphabetical order. The left-hand menu groups shows by category; hover your cursor over a category to see a list of shows in that category.

Tip: Get some publicity by hosting your own weekly or twice-a-month wsRadio.com show. If you have business or shopping tips to share or expert knowledge that relates to your eBay biz, let your inner talk show host out to play. Email your idea to *HostingaShow@wsRadio.com*.

The Unofficial Scoop

Sometimes you want info that goes beyond spouting the party line. There are plenty of places across the Internet where you can find news and views related to eBay. Read on to learn about some of these.

Auction News

Stories about eBay—especially the wackier auctions (see the box on page xxi for some real howlers)—appear in mainstream news outlets almost every week. But there's more going on in the auction world than the main news outlets report. If you want to stay up-to-the-minute on auction news, several Web sites can help you out. These sites watch the wires for auction news and post stories on their Web pages. Some also report their own stories and offer analysis of trends in online auctions.

Here are some of the best sources for auction news on the Web:

- **AuctionBytes.** AuctionBytes (*www.auctionbytes.com*), shown in Figure A-10, sends out a frequent email newsletter with news stories, tips, and original articles of interest to buyers and sellers. eBay is one focus, but you'll find news here about other online auction sites, as well. The newsletter lets you know when a new issue is up on the site and gives you a taste of what's in current articles.

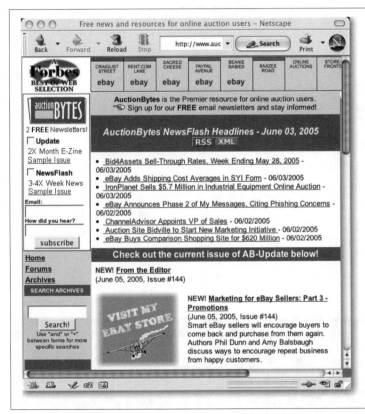

Figure A-10:
AuctionBytes provides some of the best, most comprehensive auction news on the Internet. The top of the page shows recent headlines; look below these for the current newsletter. The left-hand menu lets you sign up to have the AuctionBytes newsletter delivered to your inbox. Check the newsletter you want, type in your email address, and then click "subscribe." Below that, you can search previous issues by clicking the Archives link or typing a search term into the Search box and clicking the Search! button.

- **Auction Insights.** To get to the news area, go to the Auction Insights home page (*www.auctioninsights.com*), look in the left-hand menu for Auction News, and click that link. Doing so takes you to the Online Auction News page, shown in Figure A-11. Auction Insights collects news stories from all over the Internet and links to them from this page.

- **The Auction Board.** This site (*http://theauctionboard.tblog.com*) posts eBay announcements as they come out, as well as news stories about online auctions. The top of the page has a link to the site's discussion board, where you can read comments and opinions about eBay and other auction sites.

- **The Auction Software Review.** This site reviews third-party software for online auction buyers (pages 107 and 117) and sellers (page 344), but it also has a news page. Point your Web browser to *www.auctionsoftwarereview.com/news-auctions.asp* to read the latest headlines, with links to stories in the original publication.

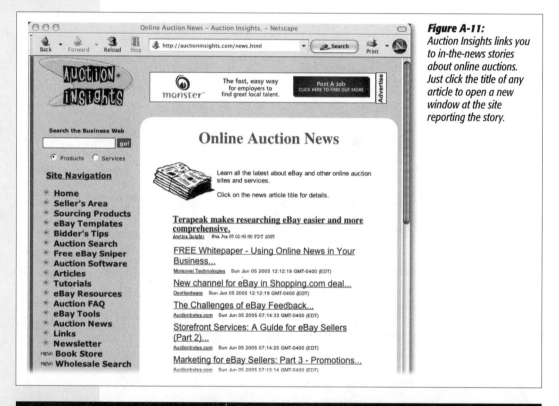

Figure A-11:
Auction Insights links you to in-the-news stories about online auctions. Just click the title of any article to open a new window at the site reporting the story.

Software Reviews

Whether you're a buyer or a seller, you want to keep up with the tools that help you do business faster, smarter, better. Buyers want the fastest and most flexible sniping tools (page 107), for example, and sellers want the most powerful and efficient auction managers (page 344). To learn about new software and find out whether a product lives up to its claims, visit these sites:

- **The Auction Software Review.** This site (*www.auctionsoftwarereview.com*) is available in full to subscribers only, but the price is cheap at $9.99 for a lifetime subscription. Find new products, read reviews by other subscribers, or write your own review. The site's organization makes it easy to find what you're looking for: categories include selling, buying, ads, and general; subcategories cover searching, monitoring, sniping, marketing, and so on. Each category lists products alphabetically; reviewed products get one star (don't bother) to five stars (great product).

- **Tucows.** Tucows (*www.tucows.com*) reviews and lets you download free and low-cost software. To find auction-related software, go to the Tucows home page and use the upper-right search box. Type in *auction* or *ebay*, use the drop-down menu to select your platform (Mac, Windows, Linux, or PDA), and then click Go. Figure A-12 shows a typical results page.

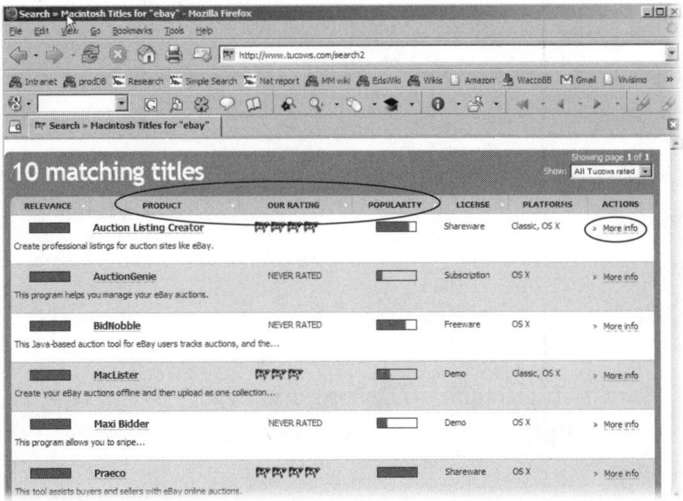

Figure A-12:
Tucows rates software according to four criteria: usability; help, documentation, and support; program enhancements; and overall evaluation. (The more cows, the higher the rating.) Products that don't make the grade don't make the site. Click the arrow next to Popularity to sort the software based on how many other folks are using it. To get more information or download a product, click either the product name or the "More info" link.

Tip: Another good way to get opinions about software is to go on your favorite discussion board (page 362), either on eBay or off, and ask what others use and why. Or, if you're considering a new product, ask what others' experience with it has been. These off-the-cuff software reviews are among the most valuable and candid you'll find.

Further Education

Most eBayers are self-taught. They might read some great books (like this one), go through the information in eBay's Help section (page 384), or ask questions in discussion groups (page 362). Mostly they just jump in and try the site: bid on an auction, pay for a purchase, go step by step through the Sell Your Item form (page 155). If you're someone who prefers instruction to trial-and-error, though (and since you're reading this book, you probably do), you might be interested in taking an eBay workshop or class.

Take a Workshop

Workshops are scheduled, Web-based hour-long chats on a particular topic. Each chat is a combination of lecture and Q&A. Someone leads every workshop: the leader could be an eBay staffer, an outside guest, or an everyday eBayer. Workshops cover just about every eBay-related topic you can think of. Here's a list of recent and popular workshop topics:

- Using keywords.
- Search strategies.
- Figuring out what to sell.
- Getting publicity for your auctions.
- Dealing with eBay changes (category, policy, procedures, new features, and so on).
- Protecting yourself from identity theft.
- Best practices for sellers.
- Shipping tips and tools.
- Cross-promotions.
- Digital photography.

Workshop schedules vary. Some months, eBay offers a dozen or more workshops; others, a mere handful.

To see a list of recent and upcoming workshops: from eBay's home page, click Community → Workshops. When you do, the Workshops page (Figure A-13) appears.

Note: The brown bag lunch is an informal workshop that's becoming increasingly popular. Staffers from an eBay department, such as eBay Stores or Shipping, go online for an hour to answer eBayers' questions. Check the Workshops calendar to see if one's scheduled.

Workshops function just like eBay chat rooms (page 371), except they open and close at specified times and have a leader to keep some semblance of order—they're not the free-for-all of a typical chat. Usually, an eBay staffer starts things off and introduces the workshop leader. The leader puts up a couple of posts that constitute his or her lecture. Workshop attendees read the posts and ask questions, which the leader answers until time runs out.

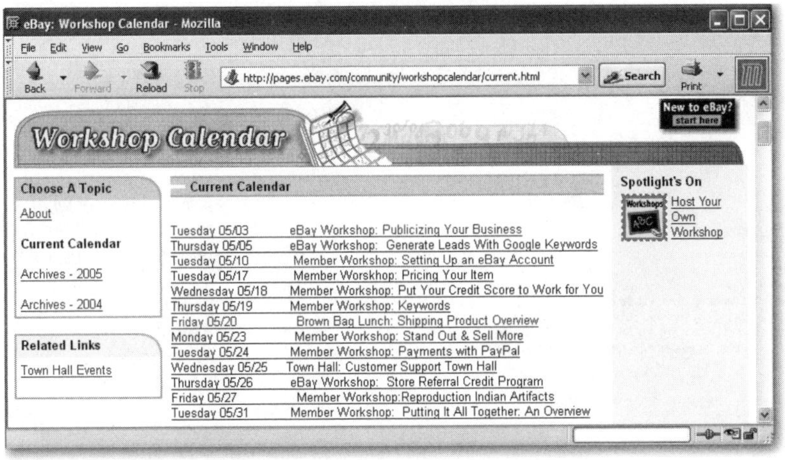

Figure A-13:
Choose Community → Workshops to get to the Workshops page. The list shows workshops scheduled for the current month. Click any workshop title to read its description. Left-hand menu links let you view archives of past months' workshops or check out Town Halls (see the box on page 409). If you have an idea for a workshop you'd like to lead, click the right-hand Host Your Own Workshop link.

Attending a workshop is easy. All you have to do is:

1. **Go to the Workshops page (from *www.ebay.com*, choose Community → Workshops) on the right date at the right time.**

   You can find out the date and time of upcoming workshops on the Workshops page.

2. **Click the workshop's title.**

   The workshop description appears, as shown in Figure A-14.

3. **Click the title again.**

   eBay asks you to sign in to the discussion boards (even if you're already signed in to eBay).

4. **Sign in.**

   The workshop page appears, and you're in.

5. **Keep hitting your browser's Refresh or Reload button to see new posts as they come in.**

   If you have a question or comment, click "Post a reply." Type whatever you have to say into the text box, and then click Post Message.

Note: Because of the chat-style format, workshops can be hard to read. Attendees might post several questions that show up all at once, and even an instructor with lightning-fast typing skills can take a few minutes to find and answer a question. That doesn't necessarily mean that the conversation slows down in the meantime, though, as more questions pour in and eBayers chat with each other.

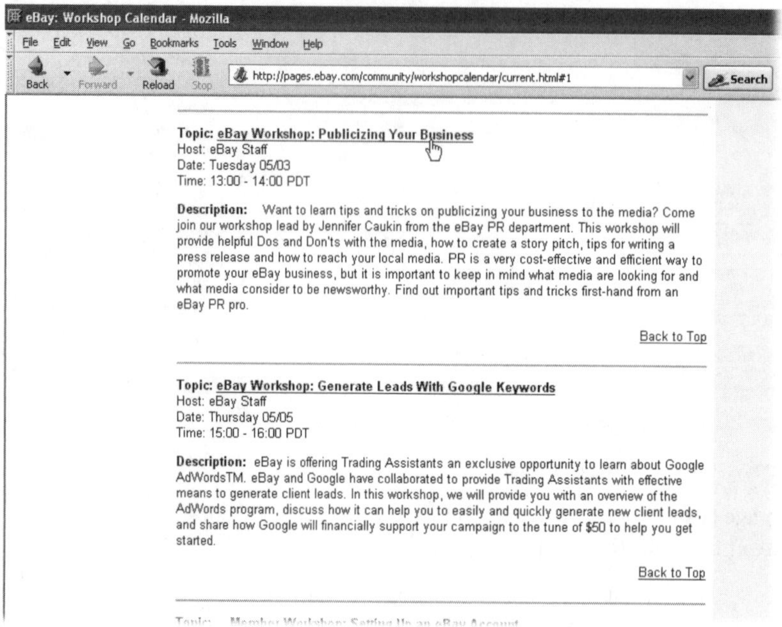

Figure A-14:
The workshop description tells you the time and date of a workshop, who's hosting it, and a brief overview of what the workshop covers. To attend a workshop, click its title and sign in. If a workshop you want has already happened, click its title to read a transcript.

If you can't attend a workshop, you can always read the transcript later. From the Workshops page (Community → Workshops), click the workshop's title (if it happened in the current month), or click one of the left-hand Archives links, then the workshop title. Archives go back through 2004, so there's lots of information to check out.

Tip: To network and get a little publicity, host your own workshop. eBayers can propose to lead a workshop at any time; just email your idea to *workshopevents@ebay.com*. It's a good idea to attend or study a few workshops before you lead one of your own. When you've got a workshop scheduled, write out your opening comments in advance, so you can save time by copying and pasting the "lecture" portion of your workshop into the text box (instead of typing it from scratch). You can even try to anticipate some of the questions you might get and type up your answers in advance, too, to keep things moving when the Q&A period starts.

Take a Live Class

Another way to learn more about eBay is to strap on a backpack and head back to school. Live classes let you put in some face time with the instructor and ask your questions as they come up. If you want to go to eBay school, you've got a couple of options:

- eBay University (page 410) takes its curriculum on the road, traveling around the country teaching day-long classes in how to sell: either how to get started or how to sell better. Go to Help → eBay University to see when they're coming to your neck of the woods.

- Many community colleges offer evening and weekend courses related to eBay: how to get started, how to buy, how to market your wares on the Internet. Call your local community college's Continuing Education office for a catalog.

Note: One of the biggest benefits you get from a live class doesn't happen in the classroom. If you take a course about eBay, use the opportunity to meet and network with other eBayers in your area.

FREQUENTLY ASKED QUESTION

Town Halls

I've seen announcements for Town Halls. Is that the same thing as a workshop?

Town Halls are a special kind of workshop that eBay offers from time to time. Town Halls give eBayers a chance to interact with some of the company's top brass in a question-and-answer format. Instead of an online chat, eBay broadcasts Town Halls live using streaming audio, so to listen, you need Windows Media Player or Real Player (see the box on page 399).

Recent speakers have included Bill Cobb, president of eBay North America, and vice presidents of Customer Support and Rules, Trust, and Safety.

When it's time for the Town Hall, go to the Town Hall page at *http://pages.ebay.com/townhall* to sign in and listen. You can ask questions in advance or during the broadcast. To submit a question: from the Town Hall page, click the

Town Hall Sign-in button. The page that opens has a text box where you can type in and submit a question. You can submit a question any time after eBay announces the Town Hall through the end of the broadcast; if a lot of questions come in, though, the speakers may not get to them all.

eBay often schedules Town Halls smack in the middle of a workday, so many eBayers can't listen in. For about a month after the broadcast, you can listen to the archived program from the Town Hall page. After that, you can read a written transcript; from the Town Hall page, find the discussion you want and then click the link that says "Click here for the transcript." Transcripts are in PDF format, so you need Adobe Reader or Adobe Acrobat to read them. If you don't have one of these products, download a free copy of Adobe Reader at *www.adobe.com* → Products → "Acrobat family" → Reader.

Get Your B.A. in eBay

eBay University doesn't give out any degrees. What it does, for a price, is teach you how to become a more effective seller. Type *http://pages.ebay.com/university* into your Web browser to get to the page shown in Figure A-15.

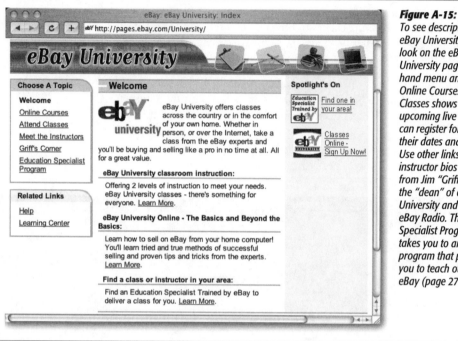

Figure A-15:
To see descriptions of eBay University classes, look on the eBay University page in the left-hand menu and then click Online Courses. Attend Classes shows you upcoming live courses you can register for, along with their dates and locations. Use other links to read instructor bios and tips from Jim "Griff" Griffith, the "dean" of eBay University and host of eBay Radio. The Education Specialist Program link takes you to an offsite program that prepares you to teach others about eBay (page 277).

Note: eBay offers a ton of free resources for sellers right on the site: how-to-sell tutorials in the Learning Center (page 383), workshops (page 406), seller tools like Turbo Lister (page 324). So is it worth shelling out the money to take an eBay University course? Ask other eBayers who've been there, done that. Click Community → Discussion Boards → Seller Central, and ask the folks there what they think.

---

eBay University offers two courses, both aimed at sellers:

- **Selling Basics.** Aimed at brand-new or inexperienced sellers, this course introduces you to selling on eBay, from opening a seller account and doing research to listing an item, using a PayPal account, and closing the sale.

- **Beyond the Basics.** This course targets sellers who want to ramp up their sales. Improve your listings, learn marketing basics, use eBay's listing tools, open an eBay Store.

If you want to take an eBay University course, you've got two options:

- **Computer classes.** These are self-paced courses that you take at home when you have the time. Both courses are available on CD; you can also take Beyond the Basics online (but only if your computer runs Windows 2000 or XP).

- **Live classes.** eBay University travels to large cities around the country, offering both courses as one-day workshops. Classes start at 9:00 a.m., break for lunch, and finish up mid-afternoon. To find out if there's a course near you, go to *http://pages.ebay.com/university* and then click Attend Classes. There's a drop-down menu under Register Now. Select a city and date; the next page has more information and a "register now" button you can click to sign up.

HTML for eBayers

HTML is one of those acronyms that rolls off the tongues of computer geeks while the rest of the world wonders what the heck they're talking about. For most people, knowing that the letters stand for *Hypertext Markup Language* probably doesn't help much. So here's what HTML does: it tells Web browsers (like Internet Explorer and Netscape) how to display Web pages. If, for example, you run across a Web page with text that's bold, italicized, blinking, or three inches high and bright green against an eye-splitting magenta background, you're witnessing HTML at work.

What all this means to you, if you sell on eBay, is greater control of how your auction listings look. HTML is easy to learn—you can master the basics in an afternoon—and with it, you can make your own templates and fine-tune your listings to create a look and feel that's all your own.

Note: HTML mostly comes into play in step 2 of the Sell Your Item form (Describe Your Item, page 157) to give your item description pizzazz with color, formatting, and extra photos (page 202). When you type or paste your item description into the "Item description" box, you can use HTML tags to create tables, center text, add colors and photos, and so on. When you've used some HTML, say you've created a table to display a digital camera's features at a glance, click the "Preview description" link (it's just below the "Item description" box). A new window opens, showing you how your table will look when a Web browser displays your item description.

This appendix introduces you to the basics of HTML. To hone your skills, you might want to check out one of the many fine HTML tutorials available online. A few to check out:

- **Auction Insights** (*http://auctioninsights.com/html.html*). This tutorial has a convenient pop-up practice window that lets you try out your skills as you learn them.

- **Ed O'Brien's Copy and Paste HTML Page for eBay** (*www.eobcards.com/tutorial3.htm*). Developed by an eBayer for other eBayers, this site lets you choose the effect you want, then copy the HTML and paste it into your item description.

- **Tozo's Sandbox** (*http://xample.net*). This site has a step-by-step tutorial geared to enhancing eBay listings by formatting text, using color, creating tables, and more. There's an HTML editor you can use to test out your code and see if it's doing what you want it to.

- **W3 Schools** (*www.w3schools.com*). Here you'll find a good general tutorial, complete with a quiz to test your knowledge when you're done (or think you're done).

Tip: This appendix only covers the most basic basics of getting started with HTML. To become an HTML hotshot, check out *Learning Web Design: A Beginner's Guide to HTML, Graphics, and Beyond* by Jennifer Niederst, from O'Reilly (*www.oreilly.com*).

Getting Started

To play around with HTML, you need a *text editor* to write the HTML code and a Web browser (such as Internet Explorer or Navigator) to read it. A text editor is a program that lets you create and edit text files. Three popular text editors are Text-Edit (on Macs) and Notepad and WordPad (on Windows). Fire up one of those programs to get started.

Note: Don't try to use a full-blown word processing program like Word or WordPerfect to write HTML. They use all kinds of behind-the-scenes formatting that will mess up your code.

HTML works using *tags,* which tell a Web browser how to format text. Tags appear inside angle brackets: < >. Most tags have a starting tag <tag> and a closing tag </tag> to show the Web browser where a particular kind of formatting begins and ends. You put your text in between the tags, like this:

```
<tag>text_text_text</tag>
```

HTML has lots of tags, but Table B-1 shows some simple tags you can use to juice up your eBay pages. (Note that some tags don't require a closing tag.)

Table B-1. *Basic HTML Tags*

HTML Tag	What It Does	How the Code Looks	How Browsers Displays It
`<h1></h1>` to `<h6></h6>`	Creates different heading sizes.	`<h2>`Big heading`</h2>` `<h4>`Small heading`</h4>`	**Big heading** Small heading
`<b></b>`	Boldfaces text.	`<b>`Bold text`</b>`	**Bold text**
`<i></i>`	Italicizes text.	`<i>`Italicized text`</i>`	*Italicized text*
`<big></big>`	Enlarges text.	`<big>`Big text`</big>`	Big text
` `	Inserts a line break.	Use` ` to force a line break.	Use to force a line break.
`<center></center>`	Centers text.	`<center>`Center` ` your text like this.`</center>`	Center your text like this.
`<p>`	Starts a new paragraph.	`<p>`Para 1 `<p>`Para 2	Para 1 Para 2
`<hr>`	Inserts a horizontal rule (line).	…horizontal rule tag,`<hr>` You don't need…	(See Figure B-1.)
`<sup></sup>`	Creates a super-script character.	E=mc`<sup>`2`</sup>`	$E=mc^2$
`<sub></sub>`	Creates a sub-script character.	H`<sub>`2`</sub>`O	H_2O
`<strike></strike>`	Strikes through text.	Oops. `<strike>`Never mind.`</strike>`	Oops. ~~Never mind.~~
`<!-- -->`	Inserts an invisible comment—you can read the comment in your HTML file, but it doesn't display in a browser.	Only $49.99`<!--`Don't forget to raise the price next week.`-->`	Only $49.99

Note: HTML tags are *nested*, which means if you use several on one piece of text, you have to close them in backward order from how you started them, like this: `<center><b><i>Hi There!</i></b></center>`.

Practice by typing some text into your text editor, marking it up with HTML tags. Here's a simple example (you see the results in Figure B-1):

```
<h1>My HTML Practice Page</h1>
<p><b>Bold</b> sentences and <i>italicized</i> words stand out. If<br> you're
running a sale, you can cross out the old price like this:
<p><center>Was <strike>$19.99</strike>, Now <b>$12.99!</b></center><!--
Compare sales at this new price with last month's figures.-->
<hr>Divide your description into sections with the horizontal rule tag.
<hr>You don't need to use the paragraph tag after a horizontal rule.
```

After you've typed your text, you need to name the document and save it as an HTML file before a Web browser can make any sense of it. Here's how:

- **In TextEdit,** *before* you save the file, select Format → Make Plain Text. When you save your file, type *filename.html* (with the name you want replacing *filename*) and when TextEdit asks you if you want it to add *.txt* for you, turn on Don't Append. After you've named and saved a new file, you don't have to do these steps again the next time you save that file.

- **In WordPad or Notepad,** select File → Save. Type *filename.html* (with the name you want replacing *filename*) into the "File name" box. From the "Save as type" drop-down list, select Text Document, then click Save. If you're using WordPad, you get a warning that you're about the save your document as text only, which strips out all formatting. Since this is exactly what you want to do, click Yes.

Tip: If you're using a text editor to create several different auction pages that you plan to list later, give each page a different name. You don't want to accidentally write over a page you want to save; if you do, you'll have to start from scratch.

When you've saved your HTML file, open your Web browser and use it to view the file. For example, in Internet Explorer, select File → Open and use the Browse button to locate your file. The results will look something like Figure B-1.

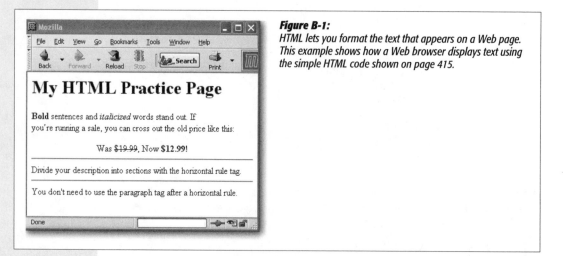

Figure B-1:
HTML lets you format the text that appears on a Web page. This example shows how a Web browser displays text using the simple HTML code shown on page 415.

As you experiment, make changes to your HTML in TextEdit or WordPad. Whenever you want to see how your work looks in a browser window, save the HTML file first, then go to the browser window and hit the Reload button. If you don't save the changes, the browser doesn't know they're there, and the browser window stays the same.

Note: You can make text slightly bigger and bolder with the `<big>` tag, but for more control, use the `<font size>` tag, like this: `<font size=7> I want this text to be really big!</font>`

Adding Colors and Backgrounds

The <body> tag lets you create a background for your auction description using a color or a photograph. Here's how to use it:

- **To specify a background color,** use bgcolor and one of these methods:

  — **A color name.** Specify a background color by name like this: <body bgcolor="yellow"> or <body bgcolor="blue">. There are 140 colors you can specify by name. To see a chart of them, go to *www.learningwebdesign.com/colornames.html.*

  — **A hexadecimal number.** These six-digit combinations of numbers and letters specify colors precisely: #000000 is black, and #FFFFFF is white. In between, you get combinations like #9900FF (violet), #9999FF (periwinkle), #FFFF00 (yellow), #999999 (gray), and so on. (The advantage of hexadecimal colors is that they give you more precise control over the shade.) So, if you want a yellow background, for example, your <body> tag looks like this: <body bgcolor="#FFFF00">.

Tip: If you don't habitually speak hexadecimal (and who does?), you can find a handy chart of colors and the codes that go with them at *http://auctioninsights.com/colors.html* or at *http://xample.net/htmlcolors.htm.*

- **To use a picture as your background,** type <body background="http://www.yourimagehost.com/picture.gif">, replacing *yourimagehost* with the name of the Web site that hosts your photos and *picture.gif* with the name of your picture (which could end with *.gif* or with *.jpg*). If your picture is smaller than the browser window, the picture repeats itself to fill the window, as shown in Figure B-2.

Figure B-2:
You can use a photograph or other image as the background for your auction listings. Be careful that the background doesn't overwhelm the foreground, though; this photo is too dark and "busy" to make a good background.

Tip: Don't go overboard with background colors and pictures. Either of these can make your listing harder to read. If there's not enough contrast between text color and background color, for example, the words don't show up. And a background picture can make your auction take too long to load—encouraging buyers to zoom off to other auctions rather than wait.

Coloring Text

If you want to change the color of your text, use the `<font color>` tag and the hexadecimal number for the color you want, like this:

```
<font color="#00ff00">I want this text to be green.</font>
```

Note: You can also choose a text color by using plain-English color names (red, green, blue, etc.), but doing so gives you less control of how the color will look. Using a color name, the example code looks like this: `<font color="green">I want this text to be green. </font>`.

Adding Pictures

To display an image as part of your item description (you do this in step 2 of the Sell Your Item Form, Describe Your Item, page 157), all you have to do is specify a *source* for the image tag, like so: `<img src="">`. The source is the Web address of the picture you want; put the address inside the quotation marks, like this:

```
<img src="http://www.myimagehost.com/myphoto.jpg">
```

Replace *www.myimagehost.com* with the Web address of your photo hosting site; replace *myphoto.jpg* with the actual file name of the photo you want to display.

Here's a neat trick if you want more control over the arrangement of your photos and text. Use `align` with the image tag to line up your words beside a picture, like this:

```
<img src="http://www.myimagehost.com/myphoto.jpg" align=left>
Line up your text to the right or the left of a picture. This makes your
auctions
look neater, with less blank space.
```

Typing *align=left* puts the image to the left of the words, as shown in Figure B-3, while *align=right* puts the image to the right of the words.

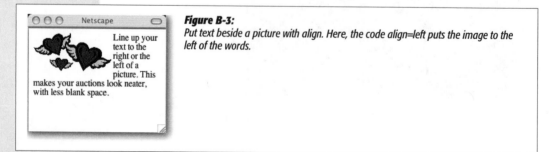

Figure B-3:
Put text beside a picture with align. Here, the code align=left puts the image to the left of the words.

Adding Links

eBay doesn't let you put links to outside commercial Web pages in your auctions, but you can link to an off-eBay page that gives more details about your items—specs, extra photos, and so on—as long as that page is for information only and doesn't sell anything. You can also link to other Web sites from your About Me page (page 191).

To add a link, use the `<a href=" ">` tag. In between the quotation marks, you type the Web address you want to link to; then you type a right-facing angle bracket (>) and the text that the visitor clicks to go to the Web address; and then the closing tag `</a>`. (Without text, visitors won't know there's a link there.) Here's an example, with the results in Figure B-4:

```
<p>Please visit my <a href="http://www.mygreatsite.com">Web page</a> to see
pictures of my dog!
```

Figure B-4:
When a visitor clicks the underlined text, her browser displays your Web page.

Creating Lists and Tables

Lists are both quick and easy. There are two kinds of lists: ordered (that is, numbered) and unordered (that is, bulleted). First, specify which kind of list you want:

• Ordered list: `<ol></ol>`

• Unordered list: `<ul></ul>`

Then, between the opening and closing list tags, introduce each new item on the list with a list item `<li>` tag. Here's an example; the results are in Figure B-5:

```
<ol>
<li>Here's
<li>a
<li>numbered
<li>list.
</ol>
<ul>
<li>Here's
<li>a
<li>bulleted
```

```
<li>list.
</ul>
```

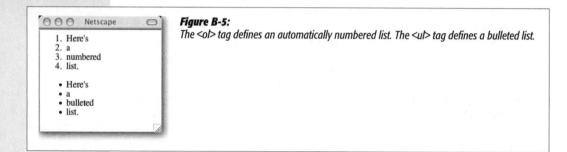

Figure B-5:
The <ol> tag defines an automatically numbered list. The <ul> tag defines a bulleted list.

By the way, you don't have to put each tag on its own line. You could just as easily write the HTML like this:

```
<ol><li>Here's<li>a<li>numbered<li>list.</ol><ul><li>Here's<li>a<li>
bulleted<li>list.</ul>
```

The code without line breaks is harder for humans to read, but browsers ignore line breaks in your HTML document (unless you type them in using the <br> or the <p> tag). So it doesn't matter how many times you hit Enter; the list appears the same as it does if you mushed everything together on one line. Because you're a human, though, when you're typing a list into an HTML document, it's easier to read your work if you put each list item on its own line.

Tables

Because HTML ignores spaces and line breaks, you need a special format if you want to control layout and positioning precisely. For example, if you want to create nice neat rows and columns, you have to use the <table> tag. No big surprise here: the tags for defining a table are <table> and </table>. When you're making a table, make the rows first (each row is marked with <tr> and </tr>), then add the text in each column using the table data tag: <td></td>.

Here's a simple example to create a three-row, three-column table of names; Figure B-6 shows you how it comes out:

```
<table>
<tr>
<td>Steve</td>
<td>Mbaki</td>
<td>Tamsen</td>
</tr>
<tr>
<td>Harold</td>
```

```
<td>Lois</td>
<td>Wolfgang</td>
</tr>
<tr>
<td>Fumiko</td>
<td>Sarah</td>
<td>Pavarti</td>
</tr>
</table>
```

Figure B-6:
This collection of names almost doesn't look like a table because nothing lines up.

Notice that the rows and columns, shown in Figure B-6, turned out a little crowded. To make your table look neater, add some cell padding and a border. To do so, change the first line of the table HTML from <table> to <table cellpadding="10" border="1">, keeping everything else the same. Just look at the difference (shown in Figure B-7).

Note: The border attribute sets the border width in *pixels*, a tiny width used to measure onscreen elements. Use 1 for a narrow border and 10 or 20 for a wide one. The cellpadding attribute sets the spacing *between* the cell walls and what's inside the cells; use a low number for a smaller, tighter table and a higher number for a roomy one.

Steve	Mbaki	Tamsen
Harold	Lois	Wolfgang
Fumiko	Sarah	Pavarti

Figure B-7:
Adding some padding and a border to each table cell results in a nicely formatted table. If you want to make the border invisible, set the border attribute to zero, like this: border="0".

Other Auction Sites

eBay may be the biggest game in town, but it's not the only one. Other auction sites let you use the same buying and selling strategies you'd use on eBay, but they also offer some different approaches: forums for buyer and seller to haggle over a price, auctions that keep snipers at bay by automatically extending an auction when a bid is placed during the final minutes, and lower fees—even no fees.

Hundreds of auction sites have tried to take on eBay, and hundreds have failed. It's not hard to attract sellers by promising lower fees or abolishing fees altogether. The problem is bringing in *buyers*—without them, the sellers simply have no one to sell to.

Buyers shop eBay because of the site's amazing selection and great deals. Until another auction site figures out a way to lure in more buyers, eBay will continue to dominate online auctions. Still, it's worth checking out a few of the other auctions described in this appendix; if you're a buyer, there's less competition for bargains, and if you're a seller, you might save yourself some fees.

By the way, this appendix lists other auction sites alphabetically.

Tip: This appendix barely scratches the surface of all the auction sites out there. For a longer list—including specialty sites for coin auctions, antique auctions, heavy equipment auctions, and so on—visit *www.nobidding.com*.

Amazon Auctions and Marketplace

Amazon (*www.amazon.com*) doesn't put a lot of effort into supporting the Auctions section of its site, but Amazon Marketplace, which lets you list items at a fixed price, is a great place to sell books, music, movies, and electronics (more on Amazon Marketplace in a moment). To find Amazon Auctions, you have to scroll way down the home page, keeping an eye on the left-hand menu, until you see the Bargains heading. The Auctions link is right beneath that heading. Or you can go to Amazon Auctions directly by pointing your Web browser to *http://auctions. amazon.com*.

On Amazon, listing fees are ten cents; when an item sells, sellers pay a sliding-scale closing fee similar to eBay's FVFs (page 153). You can relist once without paying another listing fee; after that, it costs you. Buyers pay for their purchases through Amazon's checkout, so you don't have to mess around with checks or pay PayPal fees.

But if you're really interested in finding good buys or in selling merchandise on the site, Amazon Marketplace—not Auctions—is probably the way to go. Shoppers browsing Amazon can find your item from the product page, as shown in Figure C-1. Amazon Marketplace doesn't charge a listing fee; when your item sells, you pay a 99-cent flat fee plus a commission of 6 to 15 percent, depending on what you're selling. If your item doesn't sell in 60 days, Amazon removes the listing and charges you nothing. (You can relist it if you like.) To list your items in Amazon Marketplace, go to *www.amazon.com*; then, in the navigation bar, click Sell Your Stuff.

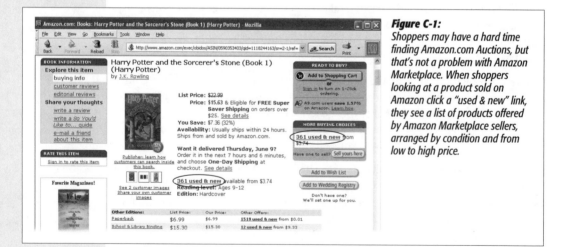

Figure C-1:
Shoppers may have a hard time finding Amazon.com Auctions, but that's not a problem with Amazon Marketplace. When shoppers looking at a product sold on Amazon click a "used & new" link, they see a list of products offered by Amazon Marketplace sellers, arranged by condition and from low to high price.

Note: For a monthly fee of $39.99, Amazon sellers can open a Pro Merchant account, which includes benefits like nonexpiring listings, waiving of the 99-cent flat fee, a bulk listing tool, and the ability to create an Amazon zShops storefront. (zShops are individual storefronts for people who sell on Amazon, a lot like eBay Stores (page 259).

AuctionAddict.com

AuctionAddict.com (whose Web address, oddly, is *www.auctionaddict.net*—not *.com*) charges no listing fees or commissions for sellers. If you decide to register with the site, you get a free Web-based email account.

AuctionAddict.com runs both fixed-price sales and ongoing auctions; ongoing listings have an automatic auction extension feature to discourage sniping. What that means is that if a new bid comes in within 24 hours before an auction's scheduled closing time, AuctionAddict.com automatically extends the auction by another 24 hours from the time of that bid. There's no limit on extensions; they keep going until no more bidding takes place.

Note: If 24 hours sounds like an awfully long time to extend an auction, it is. You could watch every single episode of *Friends* while waiting for an auction to end.

Bid4Assets

If you're looking for government auctions of seized property, Bid4Assets (*www. bid4assets.com*) is for you. The site hosts auctions run by the U.S. Marshals Service, various state and federal agencies, and county tax agencies, as well as private sellers. High-end items, including real estate, jewelry, artwork, and a variety of vehicles, change hands on the site. It's a great place to hunt for deals.

Bid4Assets offers three kinds of auctions: regular auctions, fixed-price sales, and *sealed bid auctions,* in which bidders submit secret bids that the seller can either accept or reject. To prevent sniping, Bid4Assets has an overtime period; if someone bids in the last five minutes, the auction continues for an extra five minutes until there are no more bids.

Bid4Assets charges a $5 listing fee per item as well as a commission (minimum $25). Sellers can avoid paying the commission, however, by making buyers pay it. Here's how: Bid4Assets lets sellers charge a *buyer's premium,* an amount from one to 10 percent on top of the selling price, to cover expenses associated with the sale. (Not surprisingly, if you browse the listings, every buyer's premium seems to be 10 percent.) A great deal for sellers, but kind of annoying to buyers.

Bidera

Bidera (*www.bidera.com*) listings are free; sellers pay a Final Value Fee of 2 to 2.9 percent. For $19.99 a month, sellers can become Premium Members and Bidera waives all their final value fees. Bidera has a referral program, paying registered members $5 for each new member they bring to the site.

BidMonkey

At BidMonkey (*www.bidmonkey.com*), there's no insertion fee for basic listings, but sellers can buy listing enhancements, like bold titles or an "attention grabber" picture, for various fees. BidMonkey does charge a Final Value Fee if an item sells. Monkey Bucks, similar to eBay's Anything Points (page 113), can buy things on the site.

Bidville

Bidville (*www.bidville.com*) doesn't charge insertion fees, but sellers can buy various listing enhancements, like highlighting or being featured on a category page. Final value fees (here called Final Success Fees or FSFs) begin at five percent and use a sliding scale.

Every day, Bidville's computers choose six sellers at random to list as Featured Sellers on the Bidville main page. To become a Featured Seller, you need to have at least 50 active auctions running (plus a little luck).

Bidders can't retract their bids on this site, so if you're shopping, think before you click.

Bidz

Bidz (*www.bidz.com*), shown in Figure C-2, does things a little differently. The site features a customer service telephone number right on the home page. They offer live three-minute auctions to encourage bidding frenzies. They let buyers view auctions in real time as the clock ticks down, or in a traditional view (where you have to refresh your browser window to update the info). And, to discourage fraud, they require that sellers have a business license to sell on the site.

Bidz doesn't have a feedback system the way eBay and some other auction sites do, but, as a sort of screening process, all sellers have to join its Certified Merchant Program, which means submitting reseller or tax certification, a valid ID, and a credit card number.

Note: Bidz itself sells the jewelry and watches that are up for auction on the site; jewelry is guaranteed by Bidz's own team of gemologists. Bidz does not accept applications from outside sellers to sell jewelry or watches or to list items in its three-minute auctions category.

Figure C-2:
Bidz features jewelry, but you can buy all kinds of items on the site. The Showcase auctions on the main page have a live ticker to count down the time left. Categories, listed on the left, include three-minute auctions, "extremely expensive" jewelry, items with free shipping, and live auctions.

Bidz is another snipe-free zone, although its extensions are pretty miniscule compared to some of its competitors: Bidz increments the auction time just 30 seconds when someone bids in the last 30 seconds.

Blujay

Blujay (*www.blujay.com*) isn't really an auction site; it's more like a giant classified ad section in a nationwide newspaper. Except unlike newspaper ads, Blujay is 100 percent free.

You don't have to register to shop on Blujay. When you view an ad, the listing price indicates whether the price is firm or the seller is willing to bargain. If you want to make an offer, click the Contact Seller button to start haggling via email. If there's a PayPal button in the ad, you can buy the item on the spot; click the button and a PayPal shopping cart opens. At that point, you can either keep shopping or sign in to your PayPal account to make your payment.

For sellers, Blujay offers free ads and free storefronts. You can include up to four pictures, and listings last for 180 days or until sold. And Blujay listings show up when buyers compare prices on Froogle (*http://froogle.google.com*), Google's comparison engine for shoppers. So buyers can find your ads even if they've never heard of Blujay.

iOffer

Another trading site that's based on the art of haggling rather than on traditional auctions, iOffer (*www.ioffer.com*) provides a venue for fixed-price and negotiable sales. The text of the each ad tells you whether the seller is willing to consider an offer. You can either buy the item outright for the asking price or make an offer. (Some ads don't even set a price, requesting offers only.)

There are no insertion fees; Final Value Fees function on a sliding scale. iOffer has stores for sellers and Want Ads for buyers, and both of these are free.

On eBay, only the transactions you've received feedback for appear on your Member Profile; if you sold a pogo stick and the buyer hasn't hopped over to the Feedback Forum to rate the transaction, no one who's reading your feedback knows that transaction ever took place. On iOffer, *all* of your transactions show up in your feedback profile. If the pogo-stick buyer hasn't given you feedback yet, the pogo-stick auction appears in your feedback profile, marked (appropriately enough) *Transaction Not Rated Yet*. Feedback includes the auction title, so anyone reading feedback can see what changed hands. Finally, the feedback profile also shows any official nonpayment marks a member has against them.

iOffer's way of doing feedback offers two advantages:

- Buyers can see everything a seller has sold. If you're thinking of buying a Power-Book laptop, you can see whether a seller has made other computer sales in the past or has mostly sold 99-cent refrigerator magnets.

- Sellers can see if a buyer has a history of nonpayment; nonpaying buyers (NPB) strikes (if any) are listed as part of the Member Profile. On eBay, such strikes are privileged information (page 73).

Tip: If you're a seller who wants to switch to iOffer, you can easily transfer all your eBay or Yahoo! auctions and feedback to iOffer with Mr. Grabber, a transfer tool. Go to *www.ioffer.com/mrgrabber* to download it.

Overstock Auctions

Overstock Auctions (*http://auctions.overstock.com*) is part of Overstock.com, an online discount outlet. It offers 10-minute auction extensions to prevent sniping, fixed-price sales (called *Make It Mine*), and charity auctions. Bidders can't retract a bid they've placed, so be careful when you're bidding. For sellers, Overstock.com offers O-Lister, a bulk listing tool, and Pay to Play, an optional feature that requires bidders to pay a deposit before they can place a bid that's higher than a certain amount (determined by the seller). Overstock.com charges both listing fees and FVFs (called *closing fees* here).

Overstock Auctions tries to build community through personal home pages (like eBay's About Me pages) and through Business and Personal Networks. Your Business Network consists of everyone you've done business with on the site, whether you were a buyer or a seller in the transaction. Each person in your Business Network can rate the transaction, precisely as in eBay's feedback system. On Overstock.com, this is called your *Business Rating*, shown in Figure C-3. Your Personal Network is made up of your Overstock.com buddies; you can invite anyone to join it (and kick them to the curb if they dare leave you negative feedback). Given this system, it's not surprising that just about everyone on Overstock.com has a five-star Personal Rating; it's the Business Ratings you have to keep an eye on.

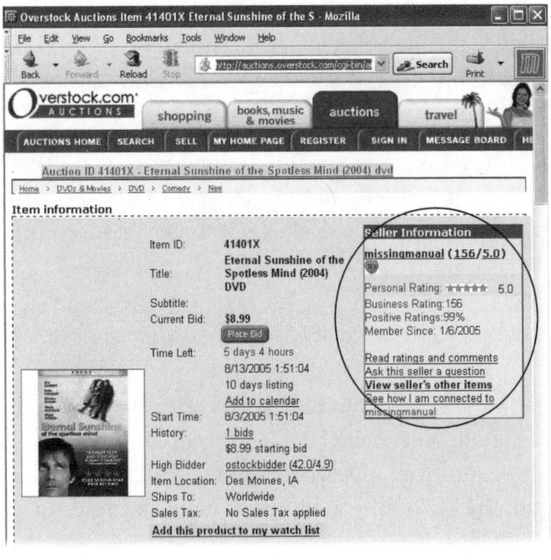

Figure C-3:
Overstock Auctions adds a new layer to feedback. The Business Rating is like eBay's feedback score, pertaining to transactions completed on the site. The Personal Rating—the one with the stars—is the rating given to an Overstock member by the "friends" in his or her personal network. Click "See how I am connected" for a reminder of whether you've done business with an Overstock member or joined his or her personal network in the past.

The Auction Man

The Auction Man (*www.theauctionman.net*) lists more than 3,500 categories and claims over 200,000 visitors per month. If you register on this site, you get a free Web-based email account. For sellers, The Auction Man offers free e-stores, free image hosting, and two levels of membership:

- **Basic.** Sellers don't pay for basic listings, although enhancements are available (for a fee). The Auction Man charges a commission of three percent of the final selling price.

- **Premium.** For $5 a month, you can sell as much as you want at no extra cost—free listing enhancements and not a single FVF.

The Auction Man makes it easy to move your eBay listings and feedback to their site. From The Auction Man home page, click eBay Feedback Migration and eBay Listing Migration.

uBid

Established in 1997, uBid (*www.ubid.com*) is a business-to-consumer auction site—which means that, like Bidz (page 426), uBid requires its sellers to prove that they're bona fide licensed businesses. UBid offers a few other advantages for buyers:

- **Express Auctions.** Every Monday through Friday, from 9:00 a.m. to 1:00 p.m. Pacific Time, bargain hunters can find great deals. Express Auctions always start at $1, and uBid posts new items every 20 minutes.

- **Mega-Auctions.** A Mega-Auction is like a giant Dutch auction (page 30). The seller has a large lot of identical items to sell, and bidders try to buy a quantity (or just one) for the lowest possible price. The trick is not to get knocked out of the bidding (for bidding strategies, see page 110).

Tip: If you're a seller, you can pick up some good deals in uBid's Mega-Auctions to resell on eBay.

- **Add-On Sales.** Some uBid auctions let you purchase accessories for the product up on the block: printer cables, a digital camera case, and so on. If an item is eligible for Add-On products, an order form appears right after you bid. Check any accessories you want; if you win the auction, you've also bought the accessories.

- **In-house Payment Processing.** When you win an auction, you pay for it with a credit card through uBid. You don't have to worry about scammers disappearing with your cash.

- **Overtime Policy.** If you hate sniping, you'll love this policy. Auctions don't end until there have been no bids for 10 continuous minutes. If someone makes a bid within 10 minutes of the auction's scheduled close, uBid automatically extends that auction for another 10 minutes.

Yahoo! Auctions

In June 2005, Yahoo! Auctions did away with all its fees. Since Yahoo! is the closest thing eBay has to a serious competitor, this was big news. Sellers gained access to a large, well-known site that doesn't take a bite out of their profits.

Unfortunately, the picture isn't all rosy. Yahoo! finances its auction site with annoying ads that clutter up the screen, as shown in Figure C-4. Some auction watchers worry that the lack of fees will invite tons of junk listings—auctions that look like they're for, say, an MP3 player but are really for outdated lists of wholesale suppliers or links to a multi-level marketing (MLM) site. Others worry that, if Yahoo! Auctions takes off, Yahoo! will go back to charging fees and sellers will either have to hand over a chunk of their profits or spend a ton of time reestablishing their businesses on another auction site.

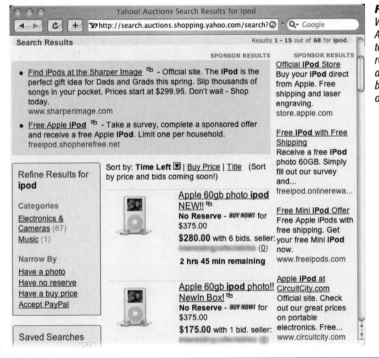

Figure C-4:
When you do a search in Yahoo! Auctions, ads appear along the top, bottom, and right side of the results page. And when you view a particular listing, there are a bunch of sponsored links tacked on to the bottom of it.

Still, it's worth giving Yahoo! Auctions a try. If you're a buyer, you can take advantage of the lower prices sellers can charge when they don't have to fork over fees. And if you're a seller, you've got nothing to lose besides the time it takes to set up a couple of test auctions.

Index

Colophon

Sanders Kleinfeld was the production editor and the proofreader for *eBay: The Missing Manual*. Marlowe Shaeffer and Claire Cloutier provided quality control. John Bickelhaupt wrote the index.

The cover of this book is based on a series design by David Freedman. Karen Montgomery produced the cover layout with Adobe InDesign CS using Adobe's Minion and Gill Sans fonts.

David Futato designed the interior layout, based on a series design by Phil Simpson. This book was converted by Keith Fahlgren from Microsoft Word to Adobe FrameMaker 5.5.6 with a format conversion tool created by Erik Ray, Jason McIntosh, Neil Walls, and Mike Sierra that uses Perl and XML technologies. The text font is Adobe Minion; the heading font is Adobe Formata Condensed; and the code font is LucasFont's TheSans Mono Condensed. The illustrations that appear in the book were produced by Robert Romano, Jessamyn Read, and Lesley Borash using Macromedia FreeHand MX and Adobe Photoshop CS.

Better than e-books

Buy *eBay: The Missing Manual* and access
the digital edition FREE on Safari for 45 days.

Go to www.oreilly.com/go/safarienabled
and type in coupon code ABKC-XN4J-CBTF-5WJZ-7V1L

Search
thousands of
top tech books

Download
whole chapters

Cut and Paste
code examples

Find
answers fast

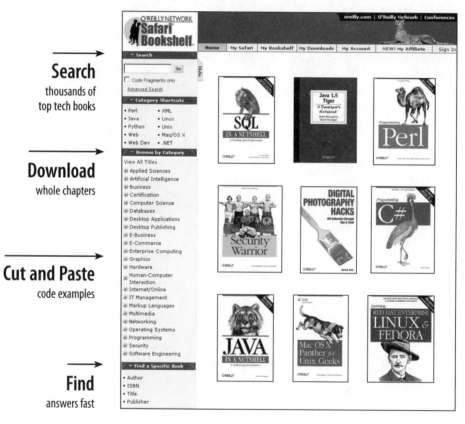

Search Safari! The premier electronic reference
library for programmers and IT professionals.